BASIC SOCIOLOGICAL PRINCIPLES

A Textbook for the First Course in Sociology

By

MARSHALL E. JONES, PH. D.

Associate Professor of Sociology
The University of Wyoming

GINN AND COMPANY

BOSTON · NEW YORK · CHICAGO · ATLANTA · DALLAS
COLUMBUS · SAN FRANCISCO · TORONTO · LONDON

72233

The Athenæum Press

GINN AND COMPANY · PRO-
PRIETORS · BOSTON · U.S.A.

SOCIOLOGY is becoming an increasingly important area of study in most college curricula. It is significant both as a major field of concentration for some students and also as part of "general education" programs through which it reaches many more students.

Those students who approach the subject for the first time often find it unnecessarily difficult, because most of the textbooks now available are either huge volumes which contain a mass of factual material with little integration at the student level, or they are specialized studies somewhat limited in scope and presupposing some acquaintance with the field. It is the writer's belief that a compact statement of elementary principles of sociology will help to clarify the material.

This present volume is an attempt to make such a statement of principles. It is not intended to be a comprehensive "system of sociology" or a final delineation of the field of sociology, or anything nearly so ambitious as those terms imply. It is intended primarily to be a teaching device, an instrument which will assist the teacher of beginning sociology classes in his task of introducing college students to sociology. In order to function as such an instrument, this book has been kept relatively simple and has been organized about a logical series of ideas, and developed in a systematic way.

The book is intended both for those students who wish a foundation of elementary sociology as the basis for further concentration in the field and also for those students who will meet with sociology only in a general-education program. It is the writer's belief that the same basic facts of sociology may be presented in the same way for both types of student. There seems little point in the current practice of presenting a few facts about social problems and social institutions to students in general education and then assuming that they know something about sociology as such. It is much more important to present to them the sociological approach and the sociological method illustrated by concrete examples. Such broad presentation will affect their attitudes towards their life in association with their fellows and towards social phenomena, one of the major goals of general education.

On the other hand, those students who intend to major in sociology also require an integrated framework in terms of which they may continue their studies. Surely the beginning course is not too early a point at which to start erecting such a framework.

A word about the term "principles": It is a word which has been much abused in discussions of sociology and especially, perhaps, in the titles of books on sociology. In this present work the writer has tried to make it meaningful in the sense of a statement of general tendency under given conditions of interaction, the accepted meaning in scientific usage.

Some ten years of teaching sociology for beginners indicates to the writer that the organization of sociological knowledge around relatively few principles does introduce a measure of understanding for the beginning student which is lacking when we approach sociology from the viewpoint of the average "introduction to sociology." If we begin, as the present book does, with statements of principle relating to the general factors of social interaction— man himself, his culture, and his environment—and then proceed to apply these general principles to specific aspects of interaction such as social institutions and social problems, we are able to see the "wholeness" of social phenomena and to begin to grasp some of the relationships involved in human association. It is this understanding of relationships which is most enlightening to the beginning student and which is most lacking in many of the current textbooks.

The assumption is, as it is in all scientific study, that the statements of principle given in this book are far from final. Obviously, as we learn more about the facts of human association we shall discover new tendencies which will modify our beliefs, precisely as scientists in other fields have modified their beliefs in the light of new discoveries. But it is the writer's hope that the principles here given present fairly the current state of sociological knowledge.

A textbook such as this must, of course, be used in connection with some type of supplementary readings. Lists of such readings given in the text are very brief, because most instructors have their own lists of "favorite" readings, because many libraries are limited, and because much of the most stimulating reading appears from day to day in current periodicals which should not be neglected in favor of rigidly established lists.

I find myself, as every writer doubtless does, indebted to many people for many things. First of all, I should like to acknowledge the help of the many sociologists who have studied and written in the field throughout the long past and in the dynamic present and whose ideas have become part of the current body of sociological thought with which we are all familiar. More specifically, I wish to thank Professor P. A. Sorokin, who "introduced" me to the higher branches of sociology, for the depth of his thought and for the brilliance of his insight; and Professor R. M. MacIver, who edited the book, for his patience and for his acute but gentle criticisms. I must also acknowledge my indebtedness to Professor J. F. Cuber for his stimulating paper "Are There Principles of Sociology?" first published in the *American Sociological Review*, which presents in vivid fashion the potentialities of a "principles" development in sociology.

I am also most happy to express my obligation to Professor Ralph E. Conwell for his encouragement and enthusiasm in connection with the book; to Professor Wilson O. Clough for his constant and ready help; and to Professor Paul Crissman, whose philosophical approach to the scientific method is most stimulating.

Other acknowledgments appear in the body of the text.

LARAMIE, WYOMING   MARSHALL E. JONES

CONTENTS

PART I

THE FIELD OF SOCIOLOGY

PART II

SOCIAL ORGANIZATION AND PROCESSES

PART III

SOCIAL PROBLEMS AND SOCIAL POLICIES

FOREWORD

Students of sociology often suffer the handicap that they have no systematic frame of reference within which to organize and integrate their studies. The various subjects they are taught, the various researches they pursue, are apt to fall apart in sprawling detachment. Textbooks are generally content to present a great variety of materials under a series of overlapping and loosely defined rubrics, such as "man and culture," "society and environment," "social institutions," "social disorganization," and so forth. Books on sociological theory are generally commentaries on the diverse positions taken by a series of sociological thinkers. The subject of sociology might thus seem to include somewhat indiscriminately all matters of human concern. Hence our students lack, more than the students of other sciences, a sense of the unity of their field. And there are those who encourage this tendency by approving the unhelpful response "sociology is what sociologists study."

Professor Jones offers in this book an admirable corrective. He enables the student to see the subject as a significant and demarcated area of knowledge. The student is given the opportunity to comprehend, and gradually to build up in his own thought, an articulated *system* of sociology. Unrelated bits of knowledge are at best information without insight. Detached researches lack depth and after a time are likely to degenerate into an exercise in the use of the techniques of investigation. As Professor Jones says, "Mere factual information changes with the changing times. Tables of statistics, charts, and similar materials are useful and interesting, but they soon become outdated. By contrast, an understanding of the methods of sociology, its approach to its field of study, and its insights into the facts of human life in association is of more permanent value." And also, let us add, this mode of approach retains a more enduring interest.

The serviceableness of his book is enhanced by the patient clarity that Professor Jones applies to the explanation of principles. He realizes that nothing should be taken for granted, that even the simplest-looking concepts contain the seeds of ambivalence and confusion. Consider, for example, the care and precision with which he explores the meaning of the term "organization" itself. He leads the student step by step to the understanding of society as "life in association." He distinguishes and interprets the complex interactions and patterns woven by the processes of association. And finally he proceeds with balanced judgment to examine the problems of social living that forever emerge out of the changing web of relations.

R. M. McIver

BASIC
SOCIOLOGICAL PRINCIPLES

PART ONE

GENERAL PRINCIPLES

CHAPTER I

THE FIELD OF SOCIOLOGY

"SOCIOLOGY is the study of the relationships between man and his human environment."[1] The chief interest of sociology is in the people, the ideas, the customs, and other distinctively human phenomena which surround man and influence him, and which are therefore part of his environment. Sociology also devotes some attention to certain aspects of the geographical environment and to some *natural*, as contrasted with *human*, phenomena, but this interest is secondary to its preoccupation with human beings and the products of human life in association. Our general field of study is man as he is related to other men and to the creations of other men which surround him. Let us add concrete content to these general statements.

THE BASIC PATTERN

Man's relationships to other men and to his surroundings fall into a basic pattern, the outlines of which we can trace from early times down to the present. Details of the pattern change from one era of man's development to another, but the fundamentals remain the same. In order to approach an understanding of those fundamentals, we move backward in time to the remote past.

Man one hundred and fifty thousand years ago was a biological organism much like other animals. He had developed few of the distinctively human characteristics with which we are acquainted today. His chief concern was the satisfaction of his bodily needs—the need for food, for shelter, for protection from his enemies.

He used the most readily available resources of his environment to satisfy his needs. He had no elaborate techniques for transform-

[1]H. P. Fairchild (Ed.), *Dictionary of Sociology*. Philosophical Library, New York. 1944. This and other quotations are used by specific permission of the author.

ing environmental resources from their existing state to something more suitable for his use. There was a time when he did not know even the uses of fire for cooking food. He could not travel long distances from one environment to another. He had to use what was available within his own limited area.

This process of early man's using the materials of his immediate environment to satisfy his basic needs is called the *interaction* between man and his environment. It is the earliest form of the basic pattern of human relationships, mentioned above, and it may be illustrated somewhat as follows:

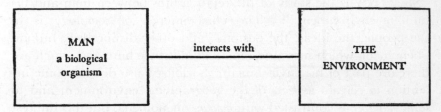

FIG. 1 · *Basic Interaction Pattern: Early Form*

With the passage of time, changes occurred in the details of this pattern. While at first man "naturally" used the most easily available resources of his environment to meet his needs, later he began to attach to certain ways of using environmental resources the idea that those were the "best" ways or the "right" ways to use them. It became the custom to satisfy his needs in one fashion and not in others. Gradually more customs developed and became generally accepted by the people living in a given area. Man became something more than an animal organism; he had begun to develop human ways of living. This collection of customs relating to man's ways of living is called his *culture*.

Culture arises from the continuing interaction of men with their environment as they come to follow certain accepted practices. This intermediate development in human history may be diagramed in Fig. 2 on page 5.

In the stage represented by Fig. 2, man is no longer simply an organism. He is "organism plus" because he has developed customary ways of living and of thinking. He has applied his learning abilities to the invention of simple tools and techniques and, in a rudimentary fashion, to his relationships with other men. He is not "human"

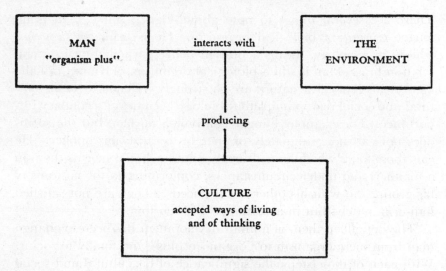

FIG. 2 · *Basic Interaction Pattern: Intermediate Form*

in the sense that contemporary man is human, but he is beyond the animal stage.

Again, as time passed, there were modifications in the details of man's pattern of relationships, very largely in the direction of the growth and elaboration of his culture. Tools and techniques were improved, human relationships became more complex, customs became more complicated. Culture assumed a place of growing importance in the interaction pattern. Man no longer reacted to the bare facts of a physical environment. He solved his problems of survival, including food-getting, provision of shelter, and protection from his enemies, not wholly naturally or haphazardly, but in terms of an integrated cultural system.

This advanced form of the basic interaction pattern of human association may be shown as follows:

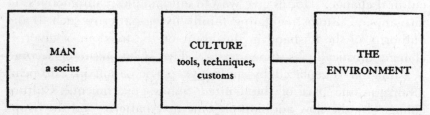

FIG. 3 · *Basic Interaction Pattern: Advanced Form*

There are several things to note about Fig. 3. First, man is no longer *primarily* a biological organism. He is primarily a *socius*, which, in sociology, means a human being participating in social relationships. Man is still a biological organism, of course, but the facts of his biological nature are so strongly influenced by his cultural and social relationships that biology becomes of secondary importance. For example, hunger is a biological fact, but the socius does not eat indiscriminately or merely to satisfy his hunger. He eats those foods which are culturally approved, and he eats them in a manner, and under circumstances, conforming to the customs of his group. So with his other bodily needs. They are not satisfied indiscriminately, but in accordance with custom.

The net effect, then, of human development has been to change man from mere organism to "organism plus" and finally to socius. With each of those steps, the significance of his cultural and social surroundings has increased.

Second, let us note that in Fig. 3 culture has risen from its position as a product of man's interactions to a position as an integral part of the interactions themselves. It stands between man and the physical environment because man no longer reacts directly to the facts of the physical environment: he acts through his culture, in terms of techniques, customs, and established ways of doing things.

Third, this fact should be clear: culture is not a static and unchanging thing. As man continues to develop, he discovers new ways of living and new ways of thinking. Some of these are only temporary and are soon forgotten. Others become accepted and, in time, are added to existing culture patterns. Similarly, some portions of existing culture patterns become outmoded. They may remain as unimportant and formal aspects of the culture, or they may be dropped entirely. Our own times are times of relatively rapid cultural change. Horses give way to automobiles; automobiles, to airplanes. Customs regulating family living-patterns, such as the authority of the husband in the home or the freedom of divorce, change drastically as time passes. The isolationism of George Washington is replaced by an active participation in European affairs on the part of the United States government. Culture changes by the slow addition of some new patterns and the dropping of some old patterns.

But these changes are slow, even in a period such as our own, which we have called a period of relatively rapid cultural change. They occur over periods of fifty or a hundred years. Because of the slowness of cultural change, there still remains, in the life of any one individual, a relatively stable culture standing between him and the physical environment.

These three factors—man, his culture, and his environment—are the components of the basic interaction pattern of human association which sociology studies. Let us examine them somewhat more in detail.

MAN

From the viewpoint of sociology, one of the most significant things about man is that he is impelled to act in certain ways by the varying conditions of his body. For example, human beings experience hunger periodically. Hunger causes feelings of discomfort, which may develop into feelings of pain. In order to remove the feelings of discomfort or of pain, we seek food. To use somewhat different language, we may say that we are "driven" by the discomfort of hunger to take certain steps which experience indicates will remove the discomfort. The same may be said of other bodily conditions, such as cold and sex tension. Because of the fact that such conditions *drive* us to take appropriate action, it is customary to refer to them as *drives*.

A drive is a form of impulse toward action, over which we have relatively little control. For example, we cannot very well control our impulse to get rid of the painful sensations that result from our being hungry or cold. Certain other kinds of impulses to action we can control. For example, such motives as greed, ambition, and hatred can be modified to the extent that they do not impel us to action. But we cannot prevent the operation of a drive.

We do not know exactly what the basis of our drives is. Presumably they are fundamentally a matter of physiology, operating through changes in body chemistry, with resulting effects on the nervous system. Thus, eating satisfies hunger partly because it fills the stomach, thereby preventing certain nervous reactions, and partly because, in the process of digestion, the body transforms much of the food into chemical products that it needs. Similar chemical reactions are involved in the operation of other drives.

Thus far we have been considering only *physiological* drives. There are, in addition, impulses to action which operate in the same way as physiological drives, but which we have not yet been able to connect fully with body chemistry. This second type of drive is referred to as a *psychological* drive.

Examples are the drive for security, the drive for response, the drive for adventure. *Security*, used in this sense, means a feeling of self-confidence and of certainty regarding our position in the world and in our social group. *Response* means desire to secure recognition from, and reaction by, other people with whom we come into contact. We often conduct ourselves in ways which we think will bring us security and response. These ways may, in fact, become very significant behavior patterns. Impulses arising from psychological drives may be just as powerful as those arising from physiological drives, especially in an advanced society, in which cultural techniques permit the ready satisfaction of physiological drives.

One interesting observation about all this is that the basic drives of all human beings are much the same—if we allow for some individual differences. One race differs very little, if at all, from any other race in this respect. One social group differs very little from any other social group. The basic physiology and psychology of all human beings are much the same.

Yet this also is true: observation of different races and social groupings indicates that their specific behaviors do differ a great deal. They wear different kinds of clothing; they eat different kinds of food; they have differing marital and sex customs; they exhibit different religious and other beliefs. If they all have much the same drives, how did these differences arise?

The answer to that question is, of course, that the differences we have mentioned are not differences in physiology, on which drives are based, but differences in means of reacting to drives. Any of the common human drives will give rise to feelings of discomfort or of pain in any human being, regardless of race or group relationships. But the means of removing those feelings may vary widely from group to group.

What is the source of that variation? To answer that question, we must approach the other two factors in our interaction pattern—environment and culture.

The Environment

Man must satisfy his basic needs with the resources available in his immediate environment, or with such modifications of those resources as he can devise. In simpler cultures the tendency is to use resources in a more or less unmodified form. Thus, the Eskimos do not build their houses of brick, stone, or wood; they use snow and ice, the most readily available product of their environment. They do not use iron and steel for nails, needles, and similar instruments; they use the bones of fish. On the other hand, people living in desert areas do not eat meat to any great extent, because grazing is scarce and the animals they have are worth more as means of transportation than as food. Again, some peoples eat insects and snakes because insects and snakes are plentiful in their environment and there is no easily available substitute for them as food.

We thus discover that many of the different patterns of human behavior are related to the simple fact of the availability of certain environmental resources. We must, however, exercise caution here, for it is true also that peoples living in very similar environments develop very different behavior patterns. For example, though the Eskimos build their houses of snow, the Buriats, who live in Siberia under much the same conditions of weather, build theirs of skin. Again, one grouping of people in India has developed a "pottery" civilization, which includes the making of pots and other containers as an important factor. A neighboring grouping has developed a "dairy" civilization, dependent on the herding of animals. The two are close enough together so that the dairy group gets its pots from the pottery group, but their ways of life differ. Much the same situation existed in the case of neighboring tribes of American Indians.

Obviously, then, the environment, though it is one important factor in the development of differing ways of life, is not always a determining factor. Similarity of environment does not always and inevitably produce similarity of behavior. Suppose, for example, that there are several possible ways of satisfying human needs in a given environment. What factors cause the use of one resource rather than another? We are not able to answer that question definitely. The probabilities are that, in many instances, it is a matter of chance—the chance that a certain plant is discovered first to be useful for food or a certain material to be useful for shelter.

In other instances, it is a matter of chance plus some elementary reasoning. If any unfortunate occurrence takes place in connection with the use of a particular plant for food, the tendency is to connect the misfortune with the use of the plant, though no connection may exist. Storms, eclipses, and other natural phenomena were not, of course, understood by early man, and they were frightening experiences. If some such natural event took place after the use of a certain food, or after some other behavior, it was not difficult for primitive man to draw the mistaken, but none the less effective, conclusion that the behavior in question *caused* the terrifying natural occurrence. Consequently it was avoided.

There are two sources of information which indicate that the explanation we have suggested above is accurate. One of those sources of information is the observation of our "primitive contemporaries," that is, peoples now living in various areas of the world under simple culture patterns. Their reactions do not differ markedly from those described above.

The second source of information is the observation, in our own culture, of remnants of the attitudes that we have suggested as characterizing early man. Thus, a student passing in the hall says, "Whenever I wear this coat, I have bad luck." He is not referring to any defect in the coat; it is not too big or too short or poorly adapted to the weather. He has simply (half jokingly) made a connection between his wearing that coat and certain incidents in his life. We are strongly inclined to doubt that any such connection exists, except in his own mind.

Similarly, some people carry rabbit's feet to bring good luck; others fear the number thirteen, with the result that sometimes we "omit" the thirteenth floor in hotels and other buildings by skipping from twelve to fourteen in numbering the floors. There is no real connection between what happens to us and any such thing as rabbits' feet or the number thirteen, but the imagined connection, which is at the basis of the superstition, remains significant. For early man this imagined connection was much more potent.

The environment, then, is a significant factor in the basic interaction pattern of human association because it offers us resources which we can use for the satisfaction of our needs; and we choose (on one basis or another) among those resources. It does not compel us to adopt one specific way of life, but it does limit the possible ways of life. Within the limits that it imposes we can make a number of adjustments.

There is another important point to be made here: granted that our ways of life do differ, and that some groups have developed more adequate and efficient techniques for utilizing environmental resources, why does not one group learn from another? Why, for example, do not the dairy and the pottery people learn from each other and combine dairying and pottery-making? Why do not modern nations take over one another's patterns of living?

The answer to those questions is, of course, that in modern times groupings do learn from one another, and perhaps they always have learned from one another to a certain extent. But the learning is apt to be selective. We learn some things from other groups and not other things. At the basis of this matter of selective learning is the third factor in our interaction pattern—culture.

CULTURE

Culture has a twofold nature: it is the product of the interaction between a grouping and its total environment, and it has an existence independent of the members of the group living at any one time. By virtue of its independent existence it very strongly influences the group members in their ways of living and in their ways of thinking.

Thus, as a group develops certain ways of reacting to the environment, those ways come to be established as the "best" ways or the "right" ways or the "only" ways of living. In addition to the utilization of the material resources of the environment for food, shelter, clothing, and defense, groups gradually develop attitudes toward the environment and beliefs about themselves. The *immaterial* attitudes, beliefs, and customs are just as significant a part of their culture as are the material factors. They influence the relationships of one group to other groups in very significant ways.

Thus, the dairy people undoubtedly need pots, but they do not learn the manufacture of pots, because that is not part of their culture. Probably they regard the people who make pots as inferior. The potmakers, on the other hand, agree among themselves that the making of pots is a special skill of much higher caliber than herding cattle. To them it is obvious that those who make pots are superior to herders. They will use the products of cattlemen, but they will not lower themselves by handling the cattle! Similar attitudes on the part of one culture toward other cultures are almost as old as mankind itself, and they have by no means disappeared. We get echoes of them now in the attitude of the industrial East in the United States toward the agricultural West and Midwest, which, in turn, are antagonistic toward other sections of the country. In many of our present-day world relationships, frictions spring in part from similar cultural beliefs and prevent intergroup learning and co-operation in many areas of life.

The power of culture to influence human behavior is evident not only in such intergroup relationships as we have been discussing, but also within any one grouping. We react to the beliefs, practices, and customs of our culture in the sense that we do not readily transgress the customs of our grouping or act contrary to commonly accepted beliefs. Most of us are not comfortable when we dress differently or live differently or think differently from the customary modes. We avoid this discomfort usually in the simplest way possible, that is, by conforming, by ceasing to be different. Conformity is certainly not an absolute necessity; we may, as some individuals have done, change customs by influencing others to do as we do. But most of us choose the easiest way out of our difficulties by conforming.

SUMMARY

We have discussed here in some detail the three factors of the basic pattern of human association. We shall analyze each of them at some length in the chapters that follow. It is important at the outset, however, to have some clear understanding of them, since it is from human interaction in association that the material of sociology comes.

SOCIOLOGY AS MAN–IN–RELATIONSHIP–TO–MEN

Now, in more detail and more concretely, what is it that sociology is concerned with? With what specific situations does it deal?

Briefly, we study man's collective behavior as it is influenced by a number of factors in his surroundings and as he, in turn, influences those factors. This kind of mutual influencing is called a *relationship*. Sociology as the study of man-in-relationship-to-men investigates the reciprocal influences existing between human groupings and the cultural products which have resulted from human association.

Man is, of course, influenced by many aspects of his total surroundings. If sociology were to attempt to analyze all those influences, it would become equivalent to an analysis of the whole of human life, an analysis impossible for any one science. We therefore select certain aspects of man's relationships for study. Perhaps the simplest way to indicate the specific areas of sociological investigation is to refer to the chart below.

One of the most important influences on all of us springs from the fact that we live in association with other human beings. Our relationships to *other men* therefore become of great importance to

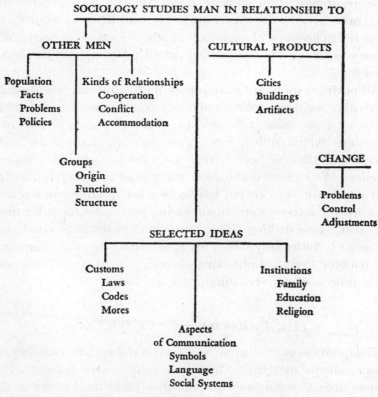

FIG 4 · *Chart of Areas of Sociological Study*

sociology, which deals with them in terms of population problems, of groups and their function, and of the kinds of relationships we establish, whether co-operative, antagonistic, or some variety of these.

Man is also influenced in a multitude of ways by the existence of *ideas* and of his ideational life. We study in sociology those aspects of his ideational life which become embodied in customs, institutions, and the whole area of the communication of ideas. So also with respect to man's relationship to *cultural products* such as buildings, cities, and artifacts. Some analysis of their influence on association is necessary to sociological understanding. In our own times, for example, we have developed an intricate industrial system devoted to the modification of environmental resources in many elaborate ways. How did this extreme pattern of modification arise, and what have been its effects on man-in-relationship?

Society also reacts to *change*, something which we cannot escape. Some groupings try to prevent change (which is one kind of reaction), others try to use it constructively (a different reaction), and others try to promote change (still another kind of reaction). What cultures do about change has important repercussions for associational life.

All of these, then, are examples of the kind of investigation that is typical of sociology. We do not, in modern times, exist as isolated individuals; we exist in the midst of a complex area of human relationships which influence our reactions in many ways. It is equally true that our society does not exist in isolation from other societies. We cannot realistically study man or society apart from their relationships. Current happenings are the result of a series of adjustments that we have made in the past, plus the adjustments that we are now making. This is true both of the individual and of the society. Obviously our study is not static and unchanging; it is a dynamic study, emphasizing change, growth, and development in the process of man reacting to life situations.

THE PURPOSE OF SOCIOLOGY

The question then arises why anyone should study sociology, and what results we may expect from sociological investigations. There is some disagreement among sociologists as to the answer to those questions. Let us suggest here that sociology has a twofold purpose:

(1) the *understanding* of society; and (2) the *co-operative control* of societal phenomena. Some further discussion of these two divisions of sociology is necessary.

UNDERSTANDING

The primary purpose of sociology is to acquire an understanding, as accurate and as complete as possible, of *what is happening* in our associational life and of *why* it is happening. Suppose we examine the area of population study as an example. We seek, first of all, facts about the birth rates, the death rates, and the increase or decrease of population in the United States at the present time. Then we examine the same facts relating to our past population, and we are able to indicate what the trends in population change have been over the given period of years. Next, we try to project these trends into the future, suggesting what the results will be for the coming population of the United States. Will it be a growing society, a declining society, a stronger society, a weaker society, one which will provide a larger or a smaller market for industrial goods, and so on? All these facts contribute to an understanding of what is happening in that particular area of our associational life.

We approach the study of institutions in a similar way. We seek facts about the family, for example, which will enable us to understand what is taking place in connection with marriage, divorce, child care, and other matters. We make comparative studies to discover what the trends have been; and we try to project those trends into the future. Similarly, we may study the attitudes we take toward change, or toward any other area of study indicated on the chart on page 13.

All that we have done thus far is to gather a number of facts which enable us to state clearly *what* is happening in associational life, and thus partially to fulfill our primary purpose of understanding society. In further fulfillment of that purpose, we also try to analyze the relationship between the facts we have gathered, in an attempt to discover *why* those facts exist. It is much more difficult to say, with any degree of accuracy, why situations exist than it is to demonstrate that they do exist. But, obviously, as we discover the reasons for their existence, we add to our store of societal understanding.

We may suggest in passing that, on the whole, sociologists in America have been very efficient at gathering facts relating to what is happening in society, and at stating trends which exist. They have not always been so gifted in discovering the reasons for many occurrences, but they are by no means completely ignorant of that area of sociology. Contemporary studies are daily increasing our store of factual knowledge.

So much for the primary purpose of sociology, which is to understand the facts of associational life. At this point disagreement arises. Is that the *only* purpose of sociology? Is the understanding of society (much as we may increase it in the future) enough, or may we go still further? What are we to do with all the facts about society and the understanding of society that we have? Is there a step beyond understanding?

There are two current answers to those questions. One group of sociologists answers by saying, in effect, "Do nothing more with the facts. There is no further step beyond understanding. It is the task of the sociologist to gather complete and accurate information about associational life. If some use is to be made of those facts by applying them to social policies and social programs, such application is the task of reformers or social workers or educators, rather than of sociologists." According to this viewpoint, sociology is wholly a *pure* science, as contrasted with the *applied* sciences which use the results of scientific investigation in practical ways.

There is another group of sociologists who take a different viewpoint. They hold somewhat the following position: "Obviously, we need a factual understanding of society; and it is the primary purpose of sociology to develop such a factual understanding, since, without it, we are unequipped to take any further steps. But it is also an important purpose of sociology to make some use of our understanding, either by ourselves working out social policies and social programs, or by actively assisting others in working out such policies and programs." This group believes that there is another step beyond understanding. They advocate the use in some practical way of the material they collect.

Obviously, there is a disagreement here between two important groups of sociologists. We can trace the origin of this disagreement with some degree of clarity. In the early days of sociology accurate knowledge about associational life was conspicuous by its absence;

and almost the entire emphasis of early sociologists was on "doing something about" existing conditions. The difficulty was that in a good many cases what they did about the conditions was largely haphazard, and in some cases unwise, precisely because they lacked a factual background for the understanding of associational life. Their programs were often based on general ideas of doubtful validity, on wishful thinking, and on moralistic judgments. It became evident to thoughtful people that they needed many more facts than they had before any intelligent programs could be set up. This situation led, in turn, to an emphasis on fact-gathering, on the scientific method, and on the avoidance of programs, policies, and evaluation in connection with sociological studies.

But the situation is somewhat different today. We now have an adequate collection of facts about societal life, and we have a growing understanding of society. In addition, we are very strongly impressed by the dangerous situations arising in connection with the Second World War and the years immediately following that war. Even the total destruction of all human society seems by no means impossible. As a result, the concept of "prevention" of problems is assuming greater importance. In view, then, of our factual knowledge and in view of our whole world outlook today, we are justified in saying that, while facts are undoubtedly important, they are not enough. We must try to make some constructive use of our knowledge. And so we set as the secondary purpose of sociology the co-operative control of societal phenomena.

Co-operative Control

Most Americans react unfavorably to the word *control* because it has not been part of our associational patterns during the major portion of our national existence. An additional reason for our dislike is that the word *control* carries with it the connotation of force, or coercion. We assume that in all conditions of control we must force an individual or group to do something it would rather not do, or prevent an individual or group from doing something it would like to do. Few people like that sort of thing.

It is true, of course, that a great deal of control is centered in coercion exerted on us by someone against our will. But there is another kind of control which may operate without force and which does not involve the complete domination of one individual by another. In the case of an individual, we call this second type of control *self-control*, that is, control practiced voluntarily and in accordance with our own better judgment. We control ourselves in our own interest and because we believe that such self-control will ultimately react to our own benefit. All of us, as individuals, practice some degree of self-control.

We are familiar with the individual aspects of self-control; we are not so well acquainted with its societal aspects. It is, however, perfectly possible for the collection of individuals who make up society to work out programs co-operatively for societal self-direction and then to carry out those programs. There are several reasons why we have not done so in the past to as great an extent as we might have. One reason is that, as we have indicated, we did not have a sufficient fund of facts about our associational life on which we might base intelligent programs. That is not true at the present time. Another reason for our unfavorable attitude toward co-operative control is the belief, common among many people, that such a device is necessarily contrary to our American way of life. This belief is, in turn, a reaction to the past circumstances under which the American people lived. In early pioneering times, and more recently as the West was developed, individuals were much more important than society. Individuals had to make their own adjustments to their surroundings because the society was not highly organized, and, in fact, in some areas was nonexistent. For many years of our national existence, then, there was a strong emphasis on complete individualism. And while most of us no longer live an individualistic existence, we still speak as though that were the ideal type of existence.

Actually, conditions of living have so changed that our associational life is as significant as our individual life. More and more we function co-operatively in business, industry, government, and other important areas of living. Sociological suggestions for co-operative self-control simply imply that the areas of co-operation should be extended to include societal self-direction and social planning. Those suggestions do not imply that control merely for the sake of control is an adequate social goal. Nor do they advocate the dominative control of society by a minority group. Instead, they advocate the common control of common problems by all of us, which is essentially democracy.

There is a further point to be made here: in spite of the continuing objection to societal self-control in some segments of our population, there are other segments which welcome the idea of control. That situation in itself makes it necessary for sociology to study and plan for co-operative control, since, as the attitude toward control becomes more favorable, a good many people will be moved to set up social programs and to make suggestions for social policies who are, to say the least, not precisely equipped to engage in that kind of activity. They will base their programs on ignorance, on prejudice and bias, and on a more or less complete lack of wisdom. Sociologists ought to be able to avoid most of those mistakes because their approach to the study of society is objective.

We are not implying that sociologists are the only ones qualified to develop social policies and programs. There are many others equally well qualified. But if sociologists persistently refuse to work in co-operation with those other people, a resource of value is removed from the whole mechanism of co-operative control.

We cannot, then, escape the obligation of including control as one of the purposes of sociology, secondary to understanding because effective co-operative control depends on understanding, but nonetheless an important purpose. Let us emphasize again the fact that what we have been saying does not imply primarily the control of people; it implies the control of societal phenomena.

SOME RESULTS OF SOCIOLOGY

Finally, what have been some of the results of sociological study thus far? What may we expect of it in the future?

In a complex culture such as ours is there are many different factors operative in the production of any social situation. We cannot accurately say that any one of those factors is the sole and only cause of the situation. This being the case, we cannot point to any contemporary aspect of associational living and insist that sociology, and sociology alone, produced it. Sociology may have had a part in producing it, but it was almost certainly not the only causal factor. What we can do is to examine the part which sociology played, along with other factors, in producing certain changes which we believe to be desirable changes.

Sociology has been significant, again as one of several factors, in changing certain of our attitudes toward human beings. In our culture we have come increasingly to emphasize the worth of people as human beings, quite apart from their wealth, their race, their social class, their color, or their nationality. Recent discussions of democracy have stressed the "dignity of man as man," quite apart from any externals of class or status. We are approaching the point at which we can say with Kant that human beings are ends in themselves and must not be used as instruments to further any other end. This emphasis, characteristic of democracy and of Christianity, is a basic necessity for world co-operative organization, since it insists on the unimportance of mere surface differences between groupings, and stresses the importance of human characteristics.

Sociology has contributed to the growth of this attitude toward human worth and dignity in a number of ways. One of its most important contributions has come through the sociological study of race, in the course of which the essential unimportance of race in relation to intelligence, personality development, morality, and ways of living in general, has been demonstrated. It is no longer possible seriously to believe that all individuals who are not members of the white race are therefore necessarily and inevitably inferior individuals. In a similar manner, sociological studies of social castes and social classes have indicated that they are unimportant externals as far as the individual human being is concerned. The fact that a given social caste or class exists at all, and that certain individuals belong in that class, is part of a total reaction pattern which may have been largely accidental in the first place, which may have outlived whatever usefulness it originally possessed, and which may be altered drastically in the future. Aristocracies rise and fall; the human being remains.

A second result of the increasing study of sociology lies in the changing attitude toward social problems and their treatment which characterizes our culture. The problem of crime and the criminal may stand as an example. Sociologists have analyzed the operation of the three factors of our basic interaction pattern in the production of criminal behavior and in the development of criminals. We know a great deal about how and why people become criminals. On the basis of that knowledge we no longer regard them as degenerate beasts to be locked away for the protection of society and left to degenerate still further. Instead, we are developing programs for the treatment of criminals which will lead to their rehabilitation in a realistic sense so that they become societal resources instead of societal liabilities. Much the same is true of other problem individuals such as the feeble-minded, the insane, and the chronically maladjusted. The whole development of modern social work and of modern social therapy is related to sociology.

Third, and as a result of the two developments we have just been discussing, the work of sociologists has also been a factor in the rise of the current realization that human resources are just as important as are natural resources. The older idea that we could measure the wealth of nations only in terms of money and goods is disappearing. A major part of the wealth of any nation is its people and their potentialities. A lack of people or failure to develop their potentialities is a major defect in any nation.

Finally, and most important, all the sociological studies of culture, its origins, its growth, and its function in producing differences of language, customs, and ways of living are of great importance in the solution of present-day world problems. If we understand how people have come to exhibit differing behavior, and what the significance of that difference is, we can make a more intelligent approach to the reconciliation of differences. Differences are not fixed and unalterable; they are products of human association. If we change the conditions of that association, differences become less significant than basic similarities.

These are four results of sociological study thus far. They may not sound very impressive at first reading. If they do not, it is perhaps because we do not grasp their implications, perhaps because we are not well enough acquainted with history to be familiar with the conditions and the attitudes of past cultures. We shall indicate at some length in coming chapters what their implications are, and contrast them with past situations. Their significance may then become clearer.

One final word: whatever the results of sociology thus far, we cannot remain satisfied with them. They are only partial and partially applied. There is much more to be done, both in the way of discovering facts and in the way of applying those facts to social policy. We can only see our way more clearly as the result of past studies; we cannot say that we have arrived at our goal.

READINGS

BERNARD, L. L. (Ed.). *The Fields and Methods of Sociology*. Farrar & Rinehart, Inc., New York, 1934. A general discussion of the fields of sociology and the methods applicable in each. Especially Part I, Chap. I, and Part II, Chap. I.

YOUNG, KIMBALL. *Sociology*. American Book Company, New York, 1942. An informative introduction to sociology. Especially pp. 1–14.

LUNDBERG, GEORGE A. *Foundations of Sociology*. The Macmillan Company, New York, 1939. An excellent, somewhat advanced, discussion of sociological principles in terms of a scientific approach. Especially pp. 89–100, "Frames of Reference in Sociology."

SOROKIN, P. A. *Society, Culture, and Personality*. Harper & Brothers, New York, 1947. A carefully developed and integrated system of sociology for advanced students. Especially the discussion of the superorganic world, pp. 3–6.

CUBER, J. F. *Sociology*. D. Appleton-Century Company, Inc., New York, 1947. A recent attempt to organize portions of sociological knowledge in the form of "principles." Especially Chap. I "Modern Sociology as a Field of Knowledge."

CHAPTER II

THE METHOD OF SOCIOLOGY

GRANTING that the primary purpose of sociology is to understand society as accurately and as completely as possible, and granting that such an understanding depends on the gathering of facts about society, our next problem is, "By what method shall we gather our facts?" Sociology shares with other sciences the belief that the scientific method is the only adequate device by which we can get the kind of facts we want to get about the areas of life we want to study. Other methods may be used in other situations, and the results may be satisfactory in those situations. But in the case of a science we can be content with nothing less than the scientific method.

ESSENTIALS OF THE SCIENTIFIC METHOD

Not only does sociology share with other sciences the belief in the validity of the scientific method; it also shares with them the belief that there are certain essential procedures which characterize that method and whose use is a primary requisite of the scientific approach. A discussion of those procedures follows.

OBSERVATION

Our first point is that *observation* is the basis of all scientific investigation. In summary form, we may say that the sociologist holds that

The observed facts of human experience constitute the only reliable basis
for scientific knowledge.

What we are saying here is, in effect, that if you want to learn about any aspect of life, the first thing you have to do is to look at it. That is what observation is: looking at the things you want to

23

study. All of us, of course, look at things. The point about scientific observation is that it must be done in a special way if its results are to be valid. We therefore refer to it as *controlled* observation.

There are several ways of controlling our observations. For example, physical sciences such as chemistry and physics can subject observation to a very rigid control by using the experimental method and procedures. An experiment is, in fact, only observation under conditions which the experimenter can set for himself. In physics he can set the temperature, the air pressure, and other circumstances related to his experiment at any point, within wide limits, at which he wishes them to be. In chemistry the concentration of solutions, the amounts of chemicals used, and other factors can be varied to suit the experimenter. Obviously, by thus setting the conditions under which experiments take place we not only control our own observation but make it possible for others to repeat our experiments under precisely the same conditions, and thereby check our results. Experiment is one effective way of controlling observation.

But experiment is not the only type of controlled observation. In sociology, for example, we find it very difficult to set or fix a framework of conditions that we want to study and then make people live within that framework while we observe them. This is what the physicist and the chemist do with their materials, but we can follow such a procedure in only a very few cases. For one thing, sociologists have some compunctions about the way they handle human material, and hesitate to experiment with people. For another thing, people, knowing that they are under observation and living under special conditions, may be so affected by that knowledge that they will not react as they would under ordinary conditions of living. Even in our everyday affairs the knowledge that someone is watching us tends to make us react in special ways.

We describe this whole situation by saying that human beings "react to the fact that they are made the subject of experiment" in a way that physical and chemical materials do not. A salt used in a laboratory experiment is not conscious of the fact that it is being observed, and hence does not alter its conduct when it is observed. Human beings, on the other hand, may be conscious of the fact and may alter their conduct because of it.

The control of observation in sociology, then, is usually in some other way than by experiment. There are several things we can do to secure control.

1. We may, for one thing, observe people as they live under ordinary conditions and note their behavior under those conditions, at the same time very carefully describing the conditions themselves. In other words, we do not set or fix the conditions, but we can say with a great degree of accuracy just what the conditions are and what the behavior patterns under those conditions are. This becomes a situation of controlled observation, because other investigators can observe people under the same conditions and thus check our results. Or they may note any differences between their conditions and ours, thus further controlling observation.

After making a sufficient number of such observations, carefully checked, we reach the point of suggesting that under a particular set of conditions people tend to react in a particular way. We have, in other words, established a relationship between certain aspects of human behavior and certain conditions of living. But that is exactly what the experimenter in the physical sciences can say about his material as the result of his experiments. Our different processes have led to the same general scientific result.

One danger in sociological procedure is that it may not be as precise and as accurate as that of the physical sciences, because we do not have instruments of observation comparable to the apparatus of the physicist and the chemist. That is a condition against which we must be on our guard. We offset it to the best of our ability by carefully checking our own results with those of other investigators and by demanding of ourselves the most scrupulous accuracy.

2. In some restricted areas of investigation we may approach the method of experiment somewhat more closely. Thus in observing the reactions of children, we may let them play together in a nursery which is equipped with a type of screen permitting an individual outside the room to see into it, but not permitting the occupants of the room to see out. They therefore do not know that they are under observation and so do not react to that fact. Using that or a similar method we can learn a great deal about the development of children and about the relationships of domination, antagonism, co-operation, conflict, and so on, which arise in group contacts. A very significant beginning has been made in this kind of child study.

But our observation both of people living under ordinary conditions and of children under the specialized conditions just described may suffer from a serious defect which arises, again, from
the fact that we are observing human beings instead of inert physical
materials. Our observations of human beings may tell us with a
great deal of accuracy *what* they are doing and what relationships
develop in human groupings. But how shall we discover *why* they
do what they do, and *why* the various kinds of relationships arise?
It is a matter of common knowledge that we often conceal our real
motives; we are not perfectly frank about ourselves. In addition,
sometimes we do not know what our real motives are, and so are
not able to analyze the reasons for our behavior, even if we want
to be frank about them.

We should, then, be very naïve if we simply asked people why
they behave as they do. In some cases they will not tell us, in other
cases they are willing to tell us but they do not know themselves,
and in still other cases they give us false motives by telling untruths,
either consciously or unconsciously. Of course the physical scientist
is not faced with this problem. He holds no communication with
his materials, and they are not interested in concealment.

3. In order to overcome this difficulty, some very interesting
procedures have been developed to reach the deeper layers of personality and to discover the motivations concealed there. Those
methods consist, in general, of devices through which we project
our feelings onto some object and a skilled person interprets the
meaning of our projections. For example, we may be shown pictures and asked to tell what they mean. The pictures selected are
neutral, in the sense that they do not have any obvious meaning:
we *read meanings into them*, and thereby give some indication of the
meanings life has for us. Thus, in the case of a young man pictured
standing before a table at which an older man is sitting, with a third
person standing behind the young man, one individual will tell us
that the picture "means" that the young man has been arrested
and is being brought before a judge. Another will tell us that the
picture "means" that the young man is entering college, his father
standing behind him and a college official interviewing both. A
third person will tell us that the situation represents the young man
being admitted to an insane asylum; a fourth, that it represents a
young man applying for a job of some kind.

What particular scene the picture represents is not as significant as the general kind of scene it represents. Obviously, two of the interpretations above connect the neutral picture with some unfortunate happening; two others connect it with pleasant happenings. If, using many different pictures, we get consistently unhappy interpretations, we are justified, or a skilled interpreter would be justified, in saying that the individual so interpreting neutral pictures is fearful or anxious about life in general. Tnis kind of fear or anxiety may be the dominating cause of that individual's behavior patterns. We might never reach that conclusion simply by observing the behavior of the individual concerned. We are enlightened as to the reason for his behavior when we use a projection test, one type of which we have just described. Obviously, then, a projection test becomes an instrument of observation analogous to a microscope or an electrical device in a physical-science laboratory.

Recent investigations at the University of Iowa made use of the projection device with a somewhat different technique.[1] Dolls were used instead of pictures, in the following way. Twelve delinquent children were each given a family of dolls representing father, mother, and two children. They were allowed to make the "people" represented by the dolls do anything and everything that came to their minds. It was expected that the children would project aggressive feelings against the father-doll, in accordance with a widely accepted theory that delinquent behavior often springs from a deep resentment against the father of the family who symbolizes the demands of authority. What actually happened, to the surprise of the investigators, was that the delinquent children were apparently less fearful of their fathers than nondelinquent children, since there was considerably less of the running-away-from-the-father theme in the manipulations of the delinquents than of the nondelinquents. In fact, the treatment accorded the father dolls indicated very little feeling of any kind toward him.

Naturally, this one investigation does not prove anything about the real motivations behind delinquent behavior. Much more use of this technique must be made before we are in a position to say positively that the older theory is incorrect. Our point in mentioning the incident here is to indicate that projection, used as an in-

[1] *Newsweek*, January 6, 1946, p. 49.

strument of controlled observation, has enabled investigators to go below the surface behavior of individuals and to get some idea of the motivations behind the behavior. The fact that the results were not what the investigators expected is all to the good, since what we are looking for in science is not confirmation of our own theories but the discovery of facts, regardless of whether the facts confirm our previous ideas.

In all these cases there is very possibly some reaction to the fact that we are being tested. But since most people do not know the details of the tests and are also unacquainted with the processes of projection, it is difficult to falsify the total result of a comprehensive series of tests. Many of the projection procedures are in a formative stage. They have not been used long enough to have full validity as observational instruments to reveal deeper motivations. But when they are standardized and further developed they will undoubtedly prove of great value.

The sociologist, then, is committed to the belief that observation is the basis of the scientific method. He cannot use the experimental method widely, but he has worked out substitute procedures by which he can control his observation. And he is developing techniques of specialized observation which approach the experimental method and which are useful in some situations. He is increasingly using projection devices and other instruments which will free him from the necessity of mere surface observation and which will permit him to reach a fuller understanding of human motivation as well as of human behavior patterns.

CLASSIFICATION

The second step in the scientific method is the whole group of procedures involved in classifying the facts that we gain through observation. In formal terms,

> *The observed facts of experience must be classified according to their interrelationships.*

We must classify our facts for two reasons. 1. Classification brings order into a collection of facts in the sense that it enables us to say what facts we have and gives us some quantitative information about our facts. Without this kind of order we have only a collection of haphazard information.

2. Much more important than that is the point that classification begins to suggest the *meaning* of our facts. Thus when we classify we group our facts according to certain characteristics which they possess. For example, suppose we choose two characteristics, say hair color and intelligence. We segregate blondes, brunettes, and redheads into three groupings, thereby beginning our process of classification. Then we choose some measure of intelligence and note the intelligence of each individual in those three classes. *IF* we discovered in this process of classification that all blondes were highly intelligent, all brunettes stupid, and all redheads of medium intelligence, we should be justified in suspecting that there was some relationship between hair color and intelligence. *IF* we found that there were all grades of intelligence in all our classes, we should be justified in suspecting that intelligence and hair color were not related characteristics. Of course classification in one instance only would not be sufficient; we should have to compare the results of many investigations before we could make any positive statement.

Our point here is that, in the process of classification according to the characteristics chosen, we have begun to bring to the surface the relationships that exist among our facts. It is only as we perceive those relationships that we can grasp the meaning of any collection of facts. Classification is not a minor phase of the scientific method; it is very important because it assists us in discovering relationships.

HYPOTHESIS

We noted above that, as a result of observation and classification, we may *suggest* or *suspect* that certain relationships exist among the data we have collected. This kind of tentative theory, or proposition, temporarily accepted as a possible explanation of what we observe, is called a *hypothesis*. The mark of a hypothesis is that it is *tentative:* it is a *possible* explanation. And yet it is something more than a mere guess or an unfounded opinion, because it springs from the observation and classification of material. We have some reason to believe that it may be a correct explanation, but we cannot demonstrate that it is correct without further observation and checking.

That, in fact, is one of the very useful aspects of a hypothesis. It gives us a basis on which we can organize our future investigations, a point about which further observations can be made. It directs

the future course of our work. Obviously, there is a certain amount
of danger involved in all this: the danger that we may become so
attached to a particular hypothesis that we shall lose our scientific
objectivity and try to *prove* that hypothesis, instead of honestly trying to discover whether or not it is true. That is a danger against
which we must be on our guard. We do not, in science, start out
with the assumption that a given idea *must* be true, and then try to
demonstrate its truth. We start with observation and classification.
From our work in those areas we may be able to form a hypothesis.
If we do form a hypothesis, we proceed to check with further observation and classification to discover whether we can continue to
accept it, whether we must modify it in some ways, or whether we
must reject it entirely and set up a new hypothesis.

For example, a popular opinion about the causes of delinquency
at the present time is that "delinquency is the fault of the parents
of the delinquent children." In the minds of most people, this is
merely an opinion, not a hypothesis; but some observation has perhaps been involved, so we may be generous and raise it from the
status of unfounded opinion to that of hypothesis. A sociologist, assuming this to be a hypothesis, would engage in studies of delinquent
children in an effort to discover whether or not it is true. Quite different is the behavior of some court and police officials who find that
"blaming the parents" relieves courts and police of responsibility
for delinquency, and who therefore are determined to *prove the truth*
of the hypothesis. They take no account of facts which contradict
it, they have lost their objectivity, and thus they become an example
of unscientific conduct which we should do well to avoid.

The testing of a hypothesis may be a difficult and time-consuming
process. We may, as we have already suggested, have to modify our
original hypothesis in a number of ways during the course of our
testing. We may have to drop it and formulate an entirely new
hypothesis. But if we are thoroughgoing and accurate in our continuing investigations, we have, at the end of our work, the basis
for a definite statement of the relationships that exist among the
factors of the social life we have been studying.

GENERALIZATION

Such a definite statement of relationships among facts is known
by several different names. One name often used for it is *generaliza-*

tion. This name arises from the fact that we *generalize* or *make general* the conclusions we draw from our observations by making those conclusions apply not only to cases within the scope of our limited observations but to *all cases involving similar conditions.* Our own observations are necessarily limited, since we cannot investigate every possible concrete situation in the realm of human relationships. Obviously, we cannot investigate future situations for the simple reason that they have not happened yet. But we can make our conclusions apply to future situations, and to all situations in general *which involve our specific conditions.*

Thus there is a very simple generalization in physics known as Ohm's law, which is a definite statement of the relationships existing between the amount of an electric current, the resistance present in the circuit, and the voltage applied to the circuit. In making use of that generalization, physicists say that *whenever* conditions of resistence and of voltage are of a particular pattern, then the amount of current flowing will be of a particular volume. Ohm's law is the product of many observations and many testings of observations in the past and present. Because it has been found accurate in all past instances, physicists *generalize* the law and say that it will also operate in the future *under given conditions.*

We do the same thing in sociology when, for example, we use so-called "tests" which analyze the "fitness" of a particular individual for marriage and "predict" whether or not that individual will be successful in marriage. The same may be said of tests of vocational aptitude, vocational interests, and similar inventories. All these are made up on the basis of studies of groups of individuals of certain types in the past. Classification of material gathered in the studies indicates what types of individual have been successful in certain social situations and what types have been unsuccessful. This experience is generalized and the statement is made that similar types *will* or *will not* be successful in those situations. This kind of generalization, then, is a statement of relationships between given social facts.

Another, and more familiar, name for the kind of definite statement we are discussing is *scientific law.* A scientific law is only a statement of the relationships we have observed to be consistently present in our data. We do not, however, stop at saying that that statement applies to relationships which we have already observed.

We say that it also applies to all data existing *under the same conditions* as the data we have observed. But that is exactly what we have been saying that a generalization is. Recall the fact that Ohm's law is simply a statement of relationships between voltage, resistance, and current. The law of gravity is a similar statement of relationships. It would be very difficult to prove that the law of gravity will operate a year from now. We assume, however, that it will because we believe that, given certain conditions, certain things will happen; and the law of gravity tells us what those things will be.

A third term which means exactly the same thing as generalization or scientific law is the term used in the title of this book, that is, *principle*. The *principles of sociology* are statements of what we may expect to happen under certain given conditions. Naturally, in stating principles of sociology we do not discuss voltage, current, and resistance; we discuss the three factors mentioned in Chapter I as components of our basic interaction pattern—man, the environment, and culture. When we have studied certain aspects of those factors sufficiently to go beyond hypothesis and to make a definite statement of relationships, we have established principles of sociology, or sociological laws, or sociological generalizations.

In formal terms we may put what we have been saying as follows:

> *Those interrelationships between facts which we find consistently present under given conditions we formulate into sociological principles.*

We prefer to use the word *principle* instead of the word *law* because it is easy for people to misunderstand the meaning of *law*. Sometimes it is confused with *statute law*, that is, the laws which are passed by legislatures. Because of that confusion our outlook on the world may be quite mistaken. Scientific laws have not been "passed" by a superior authority and explicitly stated for us. We have to discover for ourselves what the laws are in science. We have gradually, very gradually in some instances, come to perceive that things happen in an orderly way in nature, and we have tried to express that order in statements we call scientific laws. Very often our statements have been wrong; we have not actually understood the order of nature. But because we called our statement laws, people came to think of them as necessarily correct and necessarily unchangeable. Forgetting that the primary purpose of science is to understand nature, they fought for the preservation of some mistaken statement of a scientific law, with unfortunate results. Since *law* carries the connotation of rigidity and unchangeability to so many people, it is better to avoid the term.

We prefer the word *principle* to the word *generalization* because the latter may also be misunderstood. In ordinary speech, *generalization* often implies a loose sort of statement which may be true only in a very general way, and is inaccurate in detail. This is, of course, almost the opposite of the scientific meaning of the term.

PREDICTION

The last aspect of the scientific method that we shall discuss here is prediction. Prediction, in science, is not a matter of guesswork or of using crystal balls or some other means of prophecy. It is a matter of establishing definite and accurate principles so that we can say what will happen *under the conditions specified in our principles*. In scientific prediction we are not foretelling the future in the sense of telling what will undoubtedly happen a year from now or fifty years from now. We are limiting ourselves to the statement that, *given certain conditions*, we may expect certain relationships to exist. But we do not know whether those conditions will actually be present or not. If they are not, then our predictions will not come true.

We have to limit ourselves in this way because our principles result from observations made under given conditions. Thus to return to our former illustration, IF we discover a relationship between hair color and intelligence, it is admitted that that relationship holds good only in certain circumstances. One of those circumstances, for example, is that we continue to use the same definition of intelligence. If we find that blondes are all of "high intelligence" in the areas we investigate, we are assuming that we mean a certain thing by intelligence: school grades, I.Q., the ability to adjust, or some other concept agreed on. Assuming that definition, and assuming the relationship to exist, we may walk into a classroom and, finding the students mostly light-haired, we can say, "This will be an intelligent class." When we say "this *will* be" an intelligent class, we are *predicting* the future performance of that class.

But if we are suddenly transported to another society in which intelligence is differently defined, we cannot predict anything about the class, because our principle was founded on our own definition of intelligence. Suppose, for example, this imaginary society makes intelligence dependent on the ability to play basketball. We have not established any relationship between hair color and that ability; hence we cannot predict anything about the performance of the class under those changed conditions.

Forecasters, fortunetellers, and similar "experts" do not limit themselves in this way. They try to tell us the details of the future regardless of changed conditions. It is well to take note of that fact, since not all forecasters operate with crystal balls, which we might distrust. Some of them pass as business, religious, educational, or other specialists. If we take their kind of prediction seriously, we may do some very foolish things, as we discovered during the long depression of the 1930's and during many other painful periods of our history.

Scientific prediction (again as contrasted with forecasting) is a very useful device. Recall our use of Ohm's law in physics. It not only tells us what the relationships are between current, voltage, and resistance, but it also tells us how to get more current if we want it by varying the resistance or the voltage. If we want a subway train to move faster, we supply it with more current by decreasing the amount of resistance through the motorman's variable controller. That is one aspect of prediction, because what we are actually doing is to say, "If you vary resistance in a given way, then current *will* flow in this amount." We make use of this kind of prediction in operating and controlling all kinds of electrical devices.

So of our sociological principles: they are useful not only from the viewpoint of understanding society, but also in the formulation of plans for societal self-control. If we know that delinquency, or business depressions, or any other social phenomenon is related in a definite way to given social factors, then we can control our phenomena by variation of the factors involved. We cannot control until we know; when we do know, we can predict scientifically; and when we can predict scientifically, we are well on the way toward control.

PRINCIPLES OF SOCIOLOGY

In general terms, then, we have outlined the scientific method as it is used in the development of principles, and we have indicated something of the usefulness of principles in the understanding and control of society. In a beginning course such as this we cannot develop all the principles of sociology. What we can do is to take note of a few of the basic principles in relation to the three factors of our interaction pattern, and thereby arrive at some understanding of societal behavior.

A good many people lack that kind of understanding; and they are often by no means ignorant or stupid people. In fact, very often they are people of highly specialized training. They can, and do, habitually take an intelligent and scientific attitude toward their own specialty—medicine, law, engineering, the physical sciences, whatever it may be—but they are completely unable to observe themselves and their societal relationships scientifically. No matter how intelligent and objective they may be in discussing their own specialty, if the discussion turns to an aspect of society outside that area, they react on the basis of bias, prejudice, and mere current beliefs which may be wholly without validity. When the subject of delinquency, or of labor unions, or of divorce, or of race is introduced into the conversation, they fall victim to the veriest superstitions. The results are unfortunate, since many of these people are influential in their communities and have a great deal to do with the formation of community attitudes and policies. One thing we are trying to do in this book is to widen the general knowledge of sociological principles and of the sociological approach from the scientific viewpoint, and thus to offset the situation we have just discussed.

A good many other people are not entirely without an understanding of society, but their understanding is too general to be very useful. Thus, in relation to the problem of crime, they will say that the environment is an important factor in crime, and that statement is, of course, true. Or they will say that race conflict is in part a matter of differing cultures, a statement which is also true. The difficulty is that they do not know exactly what they mean by the words *environment* and *culture*; and, even more important, they do not know precisely how environment and culture operate in the production of delinquency and of race conflict.

Another thing we shall try to do in this book, then, is to examine in some detail the meaning of such social factors as culture and environment, and to demonstrate how they function in the life of our society and of our times, not only in originating social problems but also in enabling us to meet and to solve those problems. Environment and culture are just as significant in the development of industrial techniques and medical science, for example, as they are in the development of crime and political corruption. They are operative in constructive reactions exactly as they are operative in destructive reactions. We suggested earlier that we are products of our reactions to past situations in terms of the culture we have developed. Let us emphasize the fact now that the "good" aspects of society are such products as well as the "bad" aspects.

SOME LIMITATIONS

We have been describing the scientific method and its applications to sociology with some degree of enthusiasm. Let us now take stock of the limitations of that method, and also issue a warning about the matter of observation.

First, as to the limitations: there are areas of social life in which facts, as facts, are of very minor importance. And since the scientific method is primarily a device by which we gather facts, that method becomes of minor importance in all those areas in which facts themselves are of minor importance. Whenever judgment, evaluation, or some type of appreciation is of primary significance, the gathering of facts is only a part of the total process involved. We may use the scientific method to gather those facts, but beyond that it does not help us much.

For example, the *appreciation* of music or of any of the arts involves the perception of meanings which are to some extent individual and more or less intangible. We cannot lay hold of them and trot them out like race horses on exhibition. Is the excellence of a musical performance to be judged only by such tangible and measurable facts as the number of notes played during a period of time or the relative volume of tone produced? Most musicians would answer that question with a loud and hearty "No!" and most of us would agree with them. "It isn't what notes you play so much as how you play them." But the "how you play them" is a thing we respond to by our aesthetic faculties rather than by our intellectual, scientific, observational faculties.

There are other areas of life in which facts are of minor importance. Much of the area of art, religion, ethics, and philosophy lies outside the realm of pure fact. There are values in connection with all of these which are of significance to many people not only because of what they are but also because of specialized meanings. We can apply the scientific method to a statement of what those values *are*, but their total significance is not measurable by that method.

We are not suggesting, then, that the scientific method must be applied to all areas of life. It would be a dull existence if we chose our friends or our wives according to observational canons only. We are saying, however, that in those areas of social life in which facts are important, in which what we are seeking is primarily facts, the scientific method is our only instrument.

So much for the limitations; now for the warning. Since we often do not use specialized instruments of observation, as the physicist and chemist do, we run the risk of "reading ourselves into" some of our observations. To say the same thing in somewhat different words, we are in danger of confusing *observation* and *inference*. *Observation* is what we actually see; *inference* is a connection we ourselves make between certain aspects of what we see. For example, I *observe* a student run out the door of a college building—and that is all I observe, accurately speaking. Yet almost automatically I will say, "I saw a student running *away from* the building." Actually I did not see him running *away*; I only saw him *running*. The running *away* is not observation: it is my own inference. He may really be running *toward* some other building; or he may be running simply for the sake of exercise with no definite objective; or, of course, he may actually be running away. The point here is that we are not justified in using the term *observation* to include what we infer about our observations.

Sociologists and others who study society have not always remembered that important point. Confusion of observation and inference is one aspect of shallow reasoning which has made popular a good many mistaken theories and which has given such theories a false appearance of validity by making them appear to be ultra-scientific. In the whole field of the inheritance of traits such as criminality, feeble-mindedness, insanity, and similar characteristics, the common assumption has been that, since those characteristics often appear in members of the same family, there must be some hereditary explanation for them. The fact is, of course, that if our beliefs about the significance of the basic interaction pattern are accurate, we should expect similarity of environment and of culture to produce similarity of behavior among individuals without any necessary recourse to hereditary mechanisms as an explanation. But because we confuse what we observe (in this case, the undoubted fact that traits do "run in families") with our own inference about our observations (in this case, the assumption that anything which "runs in families" must be hereditary) we often do not think beyond the surface appearances of our phenomena and the surface explanations.

That this whole difficulty results from confused thinking is evidenced by the fact that we apply the hereditarian explanation most readily to those situations which require some depth of analysis for their understanding. We do not apply it to simple situations. Thus, no one supposes that the fact that American-born students speak English means that those students have *inherited* an ability to speak English. We assume that they simply learned to speak English. If we did inherit an ability to speak English, presumably the task of college English departments would be much simpler than it is.

Again, suppose we observe a number of people coming out of a building during a rain storm. We see most of them raise umbrellas to protect themselves from the rain. Do we then assume that they have *inherited* a tendency to carry and use umbrellas? Not at all: we are quite willing to accept the explanation that their culture has provided them with umbrellas as a protection against rain and that it is customary to use them.

In these simple situations, easily understood and requiring no reasoning beyond the surface reasoning, we are not apt to confuse observation and inference. In more complex situations, such as criminality and insanity "running in families," a good many people are not able easily to separate observation and inference, with the result that questionable social programs and policies are developed.

Now, of course, we cannot limit ourselves to mere observation: we have to draw inferences if we are to understand society. In fact, the hypotheses we discussed earlier in this chapter are themselves inferences, and they are, as we saw, very useful parts of the scientific method. We are not implying, then, that sociologists should not draw inferences: they should do so. What we are suggesting is that sociologists, and all scientists for that matter, must exercise care to distinguish between what they actually observe and what they infer from their observations. If we do not exercise such care, we run the risk of thinking that nature must conform to our own interpretations of it. But nature exists as it is, regardless of what we think about it. And in so far as sociological phenomena are phenomena of nature, they exist as they are, regardless of what we "read into them." It is only as we understand sociological phenomena under those circumstances that we really begin to understand sociology.

READINGS

ASHEN, RUTH N. (Ed.). *Science and Man*. Harcourt, Brace and Company, New York, 1942. A collection of essays of varying quality, presenting different viewpoints on the relationship between science and human activities.

GREENWOOD, ERNEST. *Experimental Sociology*. King's Crown Press, Columbia University, New York, 1945. A discussion of method in sociology, with an analysis of the ex post facto method. Especially Chaps. II, III, and VI.

KAUFMAN, FELIX. *Methodology of the Social Sciences*. Oxford University Press, New York, 1944. A compact discussion of the relationship between the scientific method and general problems of knowledge.

LUNDBERG, GEORGE A. *Can Science Save Us?* Longmans, Green & Company, New York, 1947. A brief and semipopular discussion of the potentialities inherent in the application of science to human relationships.

MACIVER, R. M. *Social Causation*, Ginn and Company, Boston, 1942. Directed toward the problem of how to investigate and interpret the phenomena of social change.

CHAPTER III

SOCIOLOGY AND OTHER SCIENCES

WE SHOULD have now a fair understanding of the material and field of sociology and of the scientific method. We have consistently referred to sociology as a science, one among many other sciences. How is it related to these other sciences?

Perhaps the first point to be made here is that sociology is related in a general way to other sciences through its adherence to the scientific method. The material which we study differs considerably from the material studied by the botanist, the chemist, or the physicist, but we are at one with them in our goal, which is to understand our material, and in our method, which is to gain that understanding by the objective method common to all science. The fact of this basic similarity makes all science one. Unfortunately, a good many of the physical scientists are not yet ready to accord to sociology the status of a science equal to their own. They suspect it of being a rather indefinite collection of unrelated facts and ideas without much claim to scientific standing.

The reason for this somewhat antagonistic attitude towards sociology on the part of physical scientists is twofold.

1. Sociology is a relatively new science and, as we suggested earlier, in the not-too-remote past sociology was not scientific. Its past reputation still clings to it in some quarters. And, in addition to that fact, established bodies of scholars are not willing freely to admit to their company new and, as far as they can tell, untried disciplines. This attitude is both natural and valid; and it is part of the task of sociology to demonstrate that it is a science worthy to be listed with the long-accepted physical sciences.

2. A second reason for antagonism on the part of the physical sciences lies in the misunderstanding by many physical scientists of

what sociologists are trying to do. Many of them confuse sociology with social work or social reform: that is, they view sociology not as a discipline which is trying to understand certain natural phenomena but as an "uplift" movement related more directly to religion and philanthropy than to science. Precisely as the theoretical physicist regards the person who builds electric motors as of a lower status than the scientist (even when the motor builder uses the findings of science to build his motors), so he is apt to regard the "applied" aspect of social work as lower than a science. If he further considers sociology to be simply social work and nothing more, obviously he cannot regard sociology as a science. As the concept of sociology and its field becomes clearer to physical scientists, we may expect wider acceptance of its claim to be scientific.

In addition to these two basic reasons, there are several others of more or less minor importance which are becoming less significant as we understand more about man-in-relationship. One of those minor situations is the superstition that "human nature never changes" and that, in spite of all our efforts at understanding and self-control, we are somehow doomed to failure because men and women act, and always will act, in the haphazard and unpredictable ways that they have in the past. In point of fact, human beings have not acted in haphazard and unpredictable ways in the past, but we sometimes assume that they have because of our own lack of understanding of human motivation. And we now know that *human nature* is a very poorly defined term. In so far, however, as we can define it, we discover that it changes very significantly and sometimes very rapidly. Again, as these facts become more widely known, the superstitions about human nature and human activity will disappear.

Another minor reason for objections to sociology as a science lies in the fact that some otherwise well-informed people confuse sociology with socialism or communism. Actually, there is no more relationship between sociology and communism than there is between sociology and any other social phenomenon. Communism and socialism are both economic doctrines, of interest to the sociologist because economic doctrines are cultural phenomena, but widely different in purposes and methods from sociology. An economic doctrine is essentially a program for economic reform; sociology is essentially an attempt to understand human behavior.

SOCIOLOGY AND OTHER SOCIAL SCIENCES

Other disciplines usually included under the general term *social sciences* are economics, political science, anthropology, and sometimes history and some aspects of psychology. We shall discuss the relationship between sociology, anthropology, and psychology at some length in the following pages. Here we confine ourselves to economics, political science, and history.

1. *Economics and Political Science.* These two areas of study *resemble* sociology in that they share in common with sociology an interest in human interaction as the basic human phenomenon. They *differ* from sociology by reason of their concentration of interest in particular segments of that interaction. Economics concerns itself primarily with man-in-relationship to the problems and procedures of making a living (to use modern terms) or of providing the basic means of subsistence (to use more comprehensive terms). Its subject matter includes the history of techniques of production, with emphasis on contemporary techniques; a discussion of the processes of exchange of goods and of such adjuncts to exchange functions as money, banking, marketing, and business organization; and an investigation of consumption, or the final use of produced goods. These three general topics in turn divide into many specialized and detailed investigations, with the result that economics becomes a very complex study indeed. Complex as it may be, however, it tends to limit its approach to the specialized segment of human relationships we have mentioned.

Much the same may be said of political science: it concentrates its attention on man-in-relationship to the fact of government. And again, the study of government may lead to many specialized investigations in administration, law, international relations, and other fields. It is the specialized interest in government which binds together all these fields.

Recently, both in economics and in political science, there has been a trend towards broadening their fields of interest so that areas of investigation not traditionally included in their disciplines have become matters of interest to them. Thus, economics often includes some discussion of social problems and of problems connected with population; and political science includes such matters as propaganda and something of criminology. In spite of this broadening of their interest, however, they remain essentially sciences which study a particular segment of man's interaction.

Sociology, on the other hand, studies the totality of man's interaction pattern as a general human phenomenon. This does not mean that sociology contents itself with vague generalities. On the contrary, sociology seeks specific information, but it seeks that information as it applies to human activities in a comprehensive, rather than a specialized way. For example, both sociology and economics are interested in the process of competition. Economics stresses competition in the business and industrial areas. Sociology recognizes business and industrial competition as *one example* of the process of competition, but its chief interest is in competition as a general form of human relationship which may express itself in many ways—not only in business and industry, but in a struggle for power and prestige, in certain aspects of family relationships, and in religious life, among many others. The sociologist believes that if he can discover the circumstances which influence competition in all these fields, he then understands one of the important general facts of human existence. The detailed studies of economic competition made by the economist aid the sociologist in the latter's understanding of the general process of competition, but he studies competition in many fields other than the economic one.

So also in the case of political science: both the sociologist and the political scientist are interested in government. The interest of the political scientist is in government as a specific type of human activity; the interest of the sociologist is in government as one example of the general pattern of human activity we call *control*, an activity which may express itself in government, in customs, in moral systems, and in many other cultural devices. Again, the sociologist believes that if he understands this general phenomenon of control he understands one of the important general facts of human existence. ¡ The knowledge he seeks about control is very specific; but it is knowledge about the general pattern that he wants rather than about any one specific expression of that pattern, such as government.

If the distinctions we have given above in relation to economics, political science, and sociology are not crystal-clear, one of the reasons for that lack of clarity lies in the fact that there are very close relationships between the three disciplines. They are all studying human phenomena, often the same human phenomena, but in a different way and with a different approach. We cannot separate one from the other with absolute and final rigidity. There is, in fact, no point in trying to set up absolute boundaries, since the relationships among them should be co-operative rather than antagonistic. If we agree that sociology is, as we suggested above, a generalizing science while the others are specific in their interests, we shall understand the basic differences involved.

2. *History*. The distinction between sociology and history presents a slightly different aspect from that between sociology and the specialized sciences discussed above. History does not study a segmented portion of the human interaction pattern, as do economics and sociology. It is interested in the comprehensive pattern of human behavior, as sociology is, but its emphasis is on the *unique* occurrences in that pattern, while the emphasis of sociology is on the *basic similarity* of the occurrences in that pattern.[1] For example, both history and sociology investigate the several wars which have characterized mankind's relationships at various times. History recounts the unique things about particular wars, that is, history tells us in detail the events that happened during the course of the Revolution, the Civil War, the First and Second World Wars, and so on. Sociology does not seek out the occurrences which differentiate the First World War from the Second World War and those wars from any other wars; sociology tries to discover the phenomena which were *common to* those and to all wars, and which will enable us to understand war as a social phenomenon. We are not interested in the causes of any particular war nor in the result of any particular war. We are interested in the social situations which underlie this behavior pattern that we call war.

Now this is much the same as what we said about sociology in our discussion of its relationship to economics and political science. There, also, sociology was interested in general, or comprehensive, phenomena such as competition and control. In this present discussion, sociology again is interested in a general phenomenon, war, rather than a particular war. We present the relationship between sociology and history separately from that between sociology, economics, and political science, not because the interest of sociology is different in the three cases but because the interest of history differs

[1] P. A. Sorokin, *Society, Culture, and Personality*, p. 7. Harper, New York, 1947.

from that of economics and political science. History, in other words, does not limit its approach to one segment of human existence; it studies all segments of life but emphasizes the unique aspects of the several segments involved, while sociology is interested in the common aspects of the several segments.

Again we must suggest that there is no particular point in rigidly marking off the fields of history and sociology. We are not trying to set up boundaries to our discipline and warning history to keep out. Sociology and history are dealing with the same phenomena. We deal with them in different ways, but our approach should be as co-operative here as in other common fields of effort.

3. *Social Work*. We indicated above that a good many people confuse sociology and social work. The two are actually quite different. Sociology is a science which has for its goal the understanding of human behavior in groups; it studies man-in-relationship to certain aspects of his culture and his environment. Social work is the science which attempts to build up more effective, or more satisfactory, relationships between an individual and his environment, including in the term *environment* the people, the social situations, and the cultural factors which surround him. While it is true that in some aspects of social work special groups are utilized for individual development, as in the case of recreational groups, boys' and girls' clubs, and others, the goal of social work is individual development, not group development. Similarly, while some social workers advocate social legislation and social reforms, the guiding purpose behind that advocacy is individual growth and development.

It should go without saying that when we make the point that social work is "different from" sociology we are not suggesting that social work is "inferior to" sociology. We are simply pointing out a difference, not trying to evaluate the two sciences. To summarize: social work is a therapeautic, or curative, system which, through the technique of *case work*, tries to develop satisfactory relationships between the individual and his surroundings; sociology is a science which tries to understand human behavior and, eventually, to discover methods of societal self-control through which the group may guide its future. Social work makes use of some of the findings of sociology, but its chief source of technical information comes from psychology and psychiatry.

SOCIOLOGY AND ANTHROPOLOGY

There is a very close relationship between sociology and anthropology. Their methods, field of study, and interests are quite similar. The chief difference between the two arises from the fact that, by tradition, anthropology devotes its attention to the study of man and his culture as they developed in times long past, while sociology studies the same phenomena as they are at present. The anthropologist uses the physical remains of long-past peoples for some of his materials, together with the customs and institutions of contemporary peoples now living at a primitive level. Recently there has been a tendency for anthropologists to include contemporary man along with primitive man in their studies. In view of that tendency the distinction between sociology and anthropology is becoming somewhat blurred, but we can still say with a degree of accuracy that the mark of the anthropologist is his interest in early man, while the sociologist concentrates on contemporary man.[2]

There are several divisions of anthropology which are of interest to us here: (1) physical anthropology, which is the study of the bodily characteristics of early man and of our primitive contemporaries; (2) cultural anthropology, the investigation of the culture-remains of early man and of the living cultures among primitive contemporaries; (3) social anthropology, concerned with the institutions and human relationships of primitives of the past and of the present.

Physical anthropology is interesting to sociologists chiefly because of the many studies of race and its relationships to human behavior which the physical anthropologists have made. We shall have occasion to discuss race later at some length, and we shall be very largely indebted to the anthropologists for our material. In addition to these very important racial studies, physical anthropologists have produced many other studies of absorbing interest relating to human evolution, to the development of human physical characteristics and abilities among our remote ancestors, and to the relationship between physical characteristics and crime, disease, and similar patterns.[3]

[2]H. P. Fairchild (Ed.), *Dictionary of Sociology*, p. 12. Philosophical Library, New York, 1944.

[3]E. A. Hooton, *Up from the Ape*, revised 1946. Macmillan, New York. Especially Part II.

Social and cultural anthropology give us many insights into the life of early man which illuminate our own behavior. Early man's life and culture was, in many respects, much simpler than ours. His numbers were few, he did not have an elaborate social organization, and his contacts with cultures other than his own were limited. For that reason anthropologists are able to study his patterns of interaction somewhat more readily than we can study those interactions in the case of complex cultures. This is not to imply that the study of anthropology is easy; for it has many difficult aspects. But those difficulties do not, in general, arise because of the complexity of early society. The comparative study of the interactions of early man and those of our own times often clarifies contemporary situations. What does anthropology tell us about man which is of interest to the beginning sociologist?

1. *Man's Long Development.* It tells us, first of all, that man is the product of a long period of development here on this earth, a period during which he gradually acquired a body structurally and functionally much like ours of today. It demonstrates further that this development is directly related to man's interactions with his environment, his fellow men, and his culture. Not all the details are known, but the general outline is well established.

Early man had no means of transportation which would have enabled him to move about over large areas of the earth and thus escape the effects of a given environment. He also lacked the tools and the techniques which would have enabled him to transform his environment as we do. If, for example, he lived by hunting animals, he enjoyed relative plenty during the season when game was plentiful; but during the seasons when game was in short supply he had to suffer hunger because he could not preserve large amounts of meat from season to season as we can. Similarly, if his environment was very cold at certain seasons, man had to restrict his activities and devote his time and attention to keeping warm enough to survive. He had no elaborate heating systems and of course he had no heated vehicles, as we do, which would have enabled him to move about in spite of the cold weather. He had to accept the conditions of his world for the most part as he found them.

Now, as we might expect in any collection of human beings, some types of men were better able to survive under those conditions than were other types of men. Those who were weaker died at an earlier age than their more fortunate neighbors. There were two results of this general situation. (1) The type of human being which died early in life left fewer offspring than the type which survived to a greater age. As a consequence, there was a tendency for the group to contain more of the type which was adapted to the environment, and of the children of that type, *during any one generation* than it did of the unadapted type. (2) In some cases, and perhaps in many cases, the characteristics favorable to survival were inherited by the children of the adapted individuals. On the other hand, in the case of ill-adapted individuals, not only did they die at an earlier age and thus leave fewer children, but they also tended to pass on to those children their own unfavorable characteristics. Thus the process of maladaptation and early death was carried *to succeeding generations* in the case of the poorly adapted type, and the process of favorable adaptation was similarly perpetuated in the case of the well-adapted type.

In the course of a number of generations, under the circumstances we have just outlined, the "fortunate" type of human being would tend to survive as the *only type* of human being because the "unfortunate" type would tend to disappear completely from the human stock. Now all this may sound like pure biology, but it is something more than pure biology. Remember that we are talking about conditions among primitive men. They did not have an elaborate culture to provide them with tools and procedures by which the physically unfit could be assisted toward survival. For example, they had no knowledge of medicine, drugs, or the healing of wounds. An individual of good physical endowments would "get well by himself," while one of poor physical endowments would die. Cripples, individuals with poor eyesight, and individuals of slow reaction patterns fell victim to enemies and destroyers without any hope of assistance from medical science. Our point, then, is that this whole matter of survival was as much determined by the kind of primitive culture which had been developed as it was by the actual physical make-up of the individuals concerned. The situation is not wholly a matter of biology; it is a matter of biology plus culture.

Thus early in man's existence we find culture assuming increasing importance. We are still considering a stage of human life in which the culture was very simple. In fact, we are suggesting that it was the *lack* of an elaborate culture which permitted the process of selection to take place on a physical basis to a much greater degree than it does in present society. As culture develops, it becomes an increasingly important factor in man's interaction patterns.

The process of the survival and the discontinuance of certain types of human beings on a largely physical basis is called *natural* selection; the process of continuance and survival on the basis of customs, ideas, techniques, and other human products is called *social* selection.

It is important that we understand what selection is, and how it operates. In the case of natural selection, nature does not *create* in certain individuals the characteristics which contribute to survival or death. The fact is simply that certain individuals *have* those characteristics by inheritance or by the appearance of chance *mutations*. The individuals who are fortunate enough to have favorable characteristics survive under the given environmental conditions, the others do not; with the result that in several generations the one type becomes more common than the other. That is, environmental conditions have selected one type for survival. But again, nature did not create the one type "in preference" to the other; natural conditions simply permitted one type to survive more easily than the other.

Much the same may be said of social selection, at least in some of its forms. The complex of customs, beliefs, and other aspects of culture does not *create* a certain type of individual; it simply supplies conditions under which certain types of individuals can attain prestige, power, authority, and cultural status more easily than other types. For example, in our own society *social* selection operates very obviously in the case of the Negro. Our culture assigns to him an inferior place, with the result that not only can he not rise very high in the social scale but often he cannot benefit from such cultural products as efficient medical care, good educational systems, and other developmental devices. Under those circumstances, the Negro is *socially selected* for inferiority, regardless of his actual physical and mental potentialities.

Selection also operates in instances in which there is no racial factor involved, as there is in the case of the Negro. Thus, when the Nazis came to power there developed a set of conditions which favored the less intelligent and which were distinctly unfavorable for the intelligent and sensitive individuals among the German people. The lower type, adhering to the Nazi system, gained power, prestige, and wealth which made available to them superior living conditions, medical care, food, and other advantages. The intelligent and sensitive, who could not accept the Nazi system, became, under the conditions of Nazi domination, the underprivileged, assigned to concentration camps and otherwise destroyed. The Nazi system did not *create* stupidity and brutality in all its adherents, though it undoubtedly did in some. Its chief effect was to provide conditions which selected the already stupid and brutal for superior privileges.

One thing should become clear as a result of this discussion: natural and social selection operate together in modern society. Social selection is the more important because it influences very strongly the conditions under which we live. But within the terms of those conditions natural selection also operates. Thus, within the Negro group, underprivileged because of our cultural attitudes towards them, doubtless the physically more gifted can better survive in the face of deprivation of medical care, poor food, and inadequate housing than can those who are physically less gifted. Similarly, the anti-Nazis were placed in conditions of suffering and mistreatment under which the physically more healthy survived to a greater extent than the physically less healthy. To the extent that physical health is a matter of bodily constitution, then, the conditions imposed by social selection also affected the processes of natural selection. Social and natural selection operate in conjunction with each other.

One other point should be made clear: selection does not operate automatically. The kind of individual who "survives" into the future depends on the kind of conditions we set up in our culture. If we set up conditions which select the stupid for survival and which consistently deny to the intelligent opportunity for survival, then we shall find in our future population an increasing proportion of stupid people. If that should happen, it would be by no means impossible for stupidity to bring about the complete destruction of our culture. In that case, selection would have led not to survival but to destruction. It is well to bear that possibility in mind, because some loose thinkers are apt to give us the impression that natural selection *automatically* leads to progress. It may equally well lead to degeneration and destruction.

The anthropologist, through his studies of selection in simpler cultures, has tremendously aided us in our understanding of selection among ourselves. In this section we have tried to show how man came to be as he is today through the operation of selective forces during his long history on earth. We do not know accurately just how long this history is. It is generally agreed, however, that man had assumed his modern form and acquired some of his distinctive characteristics not less than 100,000 years ago.[4] In the past 100,000 years, then, man's interaction with his environment and his culture, and the selective factors involved in that interaction, have produced contemporary human society. What the future will be depends on our continued interaction and selective processes.

2. *Culture.* Anthropology also deals with the early development of man's culture. Man had not existed very long before he began to create things himself—things which would enable him to survive more effectively in a given environment. As we have suggested before, culture is the sum of man's creations. It includes all his tools, machines, techniques, ideas, beliefs, and customs; his language, and other general "ways of living and ways of thinking." Almost the only things we *exclude* from culture are those which man did not create or transform in some way, such as the ores in the earth, the mountains and seas, the animals, and similar facts of nature.

We are especially interested in culture because it is one of the unique aspects of human life. Animals do not develop culture. It is true that some portions of animal creation, such as the wasps and the ants, build shelters, store food, and even have some division of labor and specialization of activities, all of which *resemble* culture. But all those animal patterns are apparently the result of inherited behavior patterns which remain static and unchanging from generation to generation. Man's culture, on the other hand, is dynamic: it changes and develops from generation to generation through the processes of discovery, invention, elaboration, and other applications of the distinctly human mind to the problems of living. Occasionally writers expound the wonders of "social organization" among the ants and imply that human society should be as well-

[4]Ralph Linton, *The Study of Man*, p. 19. D. Appleton-Century, New York, 1936.

ordered as ant society. They forget that if we did develop that kind of rigid order many of the most outstanding human accomplishments would remain unknown, and human life would become intolerable for all except very limited types of men.

It is also true that some animals, such as chimpanzees, can learn from human beings to use fairly complicated tools in the solution of some problems. They can even "figure out" how to use simple objects as tools without human instruction. In well-known experiments, for example, chimpanzees have piled boxes on top of each other to get food placed out of their reach; or they have used sticks as "tools" to draw food into their cage when they could not reach it with their unaided forelimbs. These examples demonstrate both an ability to learn from human beings and an ability to invent simple devices and processes on the part of chimpanzees.

But neither the chimpanzee nor any other animal in its natural habitat and apart from contact with human beings has commonly invented or used any but the very simplest tools. Nor has any animal spontaneously created new habits, customs, or ways of living. In all the years that animals and man have been on earth (and this must be some millions of years if we go back to early animal life) only man has developed a culture which is not dependent on inherited behavior patterns and which is not tied to the past. It builds on past accomplishments, but, in the very process of building, it outstrips the past by many degrees.

We do not know with certainty when man began to develop a culture. As we have intimated, it was probably very early in his existence as man. Some of his stone tools we find are estimated to be 150,000 years old.[5] His knowledge of fire is at least as old as that, and perhaps he began to wear clothes at about the same period. From then on we find him elaborating his stone tools, developing pottery techniques, refining and using metals, spinning, weaving, and using new art expressions, until he attained a fairly complex civilization a mere 10,000 or so years ago.

By a process of continuing invention and elaboration we reach our own culture with all its complexity. The details of this development lie in the domain of anthropology proper, and we shall not discuss it further. It is, however, interesting to recall once again the fact that we are today the result of a long and, most probably,

[5] L. L. Bernard, *An Introduction to Sociology*, p. 39. Crowell, New York, 1942.

painful process of learning how to live in an environment: a process which involved building a culture so that the materials of the environment could be used for effective survival and could be transformed by ever more efficient tools into more suitable materials. Our civilization is not the product of the past few centuries, nor is it the work of a few "outstanding" individuals of modern time. It is the product of thousands of years and of thousands of individuals who lived as far back as the Old Stone Age, 150,000 years ago.

Our own society is much more complex than primitive society. Its material products, its ideas, its relationships to other groups, are all very confused. Yet we face essentially the same problem that primitive man did: the problem of using the environment, in all its present complexity, for survival. The task we face is much more complex than that of early man; the basic pattern is still the same.

SOCIOLOGY AND PSYCHOLOGY

Anthropology tells us much about the past of humankind; psychology tells us much about our present. As we learn something of the past history of mankind from the anthropologist, we are enabled to understand more clearly our present-day interactions. Similarly, as we learn something of the structure of man's nervous system from the psychologist, we are enabled to grasp more clearly the elements of how and why we react as we do.

Psychology is the science which treats mainly of the internal mechanisms of human behavior. It used to be considered, rather vaguely, the science of the *mind*, or of the *soul*, or of the *psyche*, but today it is very commonly associated with the biological sciences because it studies the structure and functioning of the nervous system, which is, of course, basically biological.[6] We, as sociologists, cannot investigate man's reactions to his environment and culture, or his interactions with other men, unless we know something of the mechanisms by which man reacts and interacts in general. Psychology sheds some light upon these mechanisms.

1. *The Stimulus-Response Pattern.* The simplest of our biological patterns connected with interaction and reaction, though by no means the only such pattern, is the stimulus-response mechanism. We are so accustomed to the fact that we can "feel" in the sense that we react to external influences such as heat, cold, and pain,

[6]Article "Psychology" in *Encyclopedia of the Social Sciences.*

that we sometimes forget the importance of that fact. It is well to recall that, without this kind of sensitivity, many portions of our environment would not affect us at all. The common name for the fact that we can "feel" things and that we react to them is the stimulus-response pattern.

A *stimulus*, from the psychological viewpoint, is any factor, arising outside or within an organism, which impels us toward activity of some kind. The "drives" we mentioned in Chapter I are internal stimuli because they impel us toward activity. Similarly, and for the same reason, heat and cold are external stimuli. Obviously, also, many other aspects of our surroundings, including people, natural facts, and culture traits, are likewise at least potential stimuli. Any aspect of our surroundings which does not impel us toward some kind of activity is not a stimulus.

A *response* is the reaction of an individual to a particular stimulus or set of stimuli. In other words, it is the activity toward which we are impelled by the stimulus. A response may be either internal or external or both. It is internal, of course, when it consists of changes within an organism, such as glandular disturbances, alteration in heart beat, and other bodily reactions. It is external when more overt activity appears, as when we run away, or strike at an enemy, or move our limbs.

Man is not the only animal equipped with a stimulus-response mechanism. Even one-celled animals respond to stimuli.[7] Note this fact, however: the one-celled animal responds with the whole of its body. It has no specialized nervous system. Even some of the simpler many-celled animals tend to respond with the whole of their bodies. But as we go "higher" in the scale of organisms, we find more and more specialization—specialization not only of the nervous system but also of the various parts of the body used in responding to a stimulus. For example, we respond to hunger by eating; but obviously we do not eat with the whole of our bodies. We eat with our mouths, jaws, and so on, not with our legs, feet, and other bodily appendages. It is a great advantage to an organism to be able to respond to different stimuli with specialized organs rather than with the entire bodily system. Not only does it permit refinement of response because it is specialized; it also conserves energy in those parts of the organism not involved in the response.

[7]Norman L. Munn, *Psychology*, pp. 196 ff. Houghton Mifflin, Boston, 1946.

2. *The Reflex Arc.* The *fact* of the stimulus-response pattern enables us to react to those aspects of our environment to which we
are sensitive. The *mechanism* of stimulus-response is a bodily structure called the *reflex arc.* A reflex arc is a linkage between nerves
involved in the reception of stimuli, the transmission of stimuli
within the body to appropriate organs, and the actuation of the
response. This kind of linkage enables us to react with some sort
of appropriate activity instead of at random.

In man and some other animals the structure of reflex arcs is
highly complex. It includes, among other things, a series of *reflex
centers* which sort out the numerous stimuli received and "direct"
them to various actuating nerves. The process of receiving, transmitting, and actuating which results from the impingement of
stimuli on our organisms is called, as a whole, a *reflex* because its
basis is the reflex arc which we have just described.

The reflex arc, then, is the mechanism by which we respond to
stimuli. It is important to us as sociologists for a variety of reasons.
For example, the condition of the nervous system of an individual
obviously affects the kinds of response he can make to stimuli. If
we are deaf (a condition of the nervous system) we cannot respond
to sounds as hearing people do. If there is a defective condition in
any portion of the nervous system, including the brain, that condition may make us incapable of responding in the way that a nondefective person would respond. We may, in that case, be what is
called *feeble-minded*, or *insane*, or *pathological*.

Let us consider some of these facts in connection with our basic
interaction pattern. We have suggested that human existence consists in the interaction of man, his culture, and his environment.
In the instances just cited, the "man" factor is defective, and that
situation of defect influences very strongly the way in which he can
interact with his environment. But there is more to the picture: if
we live in an "advanced" culture, there may exist a number of devices which will enable us to interact with relative efficiency, even
though we cannot attain complete normality of interaction. Thus
Helen Keller, blind and deaf from infancy, cannot possibly react
to the stimuli of light and sound as the normal person can. But she
has been taught to make a fairly effective adjustment. Obviously,
all the methods used to teach her, all the humanitarian attitudes
which made it worth while to teach her instead of killing her as a

baby, all those things are part of our culture. If Miss Keller had grown up in a primitive culture, or if she had been born to parents living in a "backward" segment of our own culture in which those teaching methods were not known and the humanitarian ideals did not exist, her adjustment would have been much less satisfactory.

But the methods used to teach Miss Keller and all the devices of culture brought to her aid are not the only part of her total inter- action pattern which affect the whole situation. In addition to these cultural devices, it is necessary to limit the environment with which she has contact. She cannot drive an automobile; she cannot walk the streets alone; she cannot engage in the ordinary occupa- tions of life. Her environment must be strictly controlled.

Miss Keller's life, then, as she now lives it, is a product of her defective bodily structure interacting with a controlled environment on the basis of culturally provided training. She is an outstanding example of that kind of manipulation of culture and environment, but the same general pattern appears in other areas of life and with other individuals. Thus, a feeble-minded person is, we assume, neuro- logically defective. We care for the feeble-minded by controlling the environment with which they have contact, usually in an in- stitution, and by applying specialized methods of teaching and conditioning, which are part of our culture, for the purpose of training them toward some kind of satisfactory adjustment to life. Many of them can never react as normal individuals do. But a goodly portion of them can live as socially useful citizens after a period of training, provided their contacts are regulated. Much the same thing can be said of the insane, and it could be said of many criminals, if we would seriously apply available treatment methods to criminals, instead of leaving them as we do in prisons with very little intelligent attention.

Here we must plead guilty to the charge of apparently wander- ing away from the main theme of our discussion. We followed that course because our discussion of defective neurological equipment gave us an excellent chance to emphasize again the importance of all three of our interactional factors: man, his culture, and the environment. The existence of a defect or a disease in an individual does not mean inevitably an unsatisfactory adjustment to life. Given an "advanced" culture, and given some control of the en- vironment, we may reach a relatively satisfactory adjustment.

Much the same thing may be said of the nondefective, or "normal," person. The mere fact that we are physiologically normal does not mean that we shall automatically adjust satisfactorily to life situations. We may find ourselves in a culture which hampers us, as in the case of many Negroes, or we may be exposed to environmental influences which will distort our personalities. We are all, in the most real sense of the words, products of the interaction between ourselves, our culture, and our environment.

3. *Kinds of Reflexes.* There are two general kinds of reflexes: (*a*) the *unconditioned* reflex, which is a neurological pattern already established in the individual at birth; and (*b*) the *conditioned* reflex, which is a pattern the individual *learns* or develops as the result of his interactions. In man the number of conditioned, or learned, reflexes is far greater than the number of unconditioned reflexes. Conditioned reflexes are also more important in our adjustment to a complex society than are unconditioned reflexes.

For example, typical unconditioned reflexes are the variation in size of the iris in our eyes in response to varying light conditions, and the fact that an infant sucks when his mouth is stimulated. We are not suggesting that these, and similar, reflexes are unimportant; we are only suggesting that our many *learned* responses are much more important. Our complex surroundings present us with situations to which we cannot react on the basis of unconditioned reflexes. We must learn to react to them, as we must learn to react to new situations. In other kinds of environment we could adjust satisfactorily with fewer conditioned reflexes, and the unconditioned type of behavior would become correspondingly more important.

Man is capable of greater, more complex learning than any other animal. As a result, he develops many significant conditioned reflexes.

4. *Human Motivation.* One danger against which we must guard is the danger of accepting what we have said thus far as the final and complete explanation of human behavior. Any such belief would vastly oversimplify the real picture of man and his relationships. The stimulus-response patterns, the reflex arc, and the facts of conditioned and unconditioned reflexes are all only the *basis* of human behavior, a basis largely rooted in the biological structure of mankind. On that basis is erected a much more complex sociopsychological structure.

If we stop with the stimulus-response and reflex patterns, we picture man as simply a puppet, controlled by mechanisms very similar to those used in manipulating puppets. The desire of the manipulator would be the equivalent of a stimulus; the strings controlling the puppet's actions would equate with our reflex arcs; and the jerking of the puppet's legs would correspond with our responses. Actually that is not the way human beings react. If it were, the study of sociology would be much simpler than it is. Some sociologists, including the famous Vilfredo Pareto, have tried to develop sociological systems which came pretty close to being simply an analysis of human behavior in terms of stimulus and response. The results of their studies are not too helpful, because when they tried to reduce human behavior to a series of responses to stimuli, they had to make the stimuli so complex and the number of responses to any one stimulus so many and varied that their analysis lost coherence and meaning. It is a temptation to oversimplify what we are studying because it makes our task easier and, apparently, holds out much more hope of quick results than we may expect in view of the actual complexity of human behavior.

The stimulus-response pattern, then, is not the ultimate explanation of why we do what we do; it is only the basis on which more significant structures are erected. One aspect of that more significant structure is the modification of the simple stimulus-response pattern by cultural and other factors. For example, many of our experiences leave lasting "records" on our nervous structure and in that way modify the whole stimulus-response picture. Thus, we do not know how a child will react to the stimulus of a bright fire unless we know what his past experiences with fire have been: proverbially, "a burnt child dreads the fire." The child who might be attracted toward the fire because of its brightness or warmth may well be repelled from it or afraid of it if his past experiences with fire have been painful. Similarly, we do not know how an adult will react to the word *fascism* unless we know what his previous experiences with the word, and perhaps with the practices of fascism, have been. He may not react to it at all, simply because he has no idea what the word means; he may react unfavorably because of painful experiences with fascism; he may react on the basis of what he has been taught for or against the fascist system.

A stimulus-response pattern thus *significantly modified by the inner organization of the individual* is called a *motivation*.[8] It is these motivations which lie immediately behind our behavior patterns and which come much closer to describing our behavior accurately than does the stimulus-response pattern.

The examples we have given of the modification of stimulus and response into motivation are socio-psychological in the sense that they arise from interactions either in the form of direct experiences, as in the case of the "burnt child," or in the form of indirect experiences, as in the case of "being taught" about fascism. The most important modifications in a complex culture such as ours are socio-psychological in nature, but the "inner organization of the individual" to which we referred may also contain physiological conditions which modify the stimulus-response pattern. For example, we do not know whether or not an animal will respond to the stimulus of food or water unless we know whether or not he is hungry or thirsty. If his hunger is completely satisfied, the stimulus of food will produce a different response from that which occurs when he is hungry. So also in man, his inner physiological state will affect his responses. If he is very much fatigued, he will not respond as he will when he is not fatigued. Thus, we may be exposed to extreme cold for so long a time that we cannot respond to cold as a stimulus: we lie down and freeze to death.

Motivations, then, inhere in the inner organization of an individual, physiological or socio-psychological. As we have suggested, it is the socio-psychological influences which are of major interest to us here. In order to know how people will react, we must know not only the simple stimulus-response mechanism; we must also know something of their motivations. And we can understand their motivations only through grasping the significance of the culture in which they live, because culture contributes a great deal to the formation of their "inner organization."

Thus, the culture in which we live makes some kinds of experiences common, others uncommon. If we live in a militarized society, we naturally become familiar with military experiences, because we become accustomed to training, marching, manual of arms, militaristic propaganda, and the militaristic outlook. We are subjected to life situations in a military setting, with the result that we tend to interpret life in military terms. Then we begin to in-

[8]Munn, op. cit. p. 263.

terpret what would otherwise be simple stimuli in military terms. We react to the possession of natural resources by countries other than our own as a threat to our own country instead of as, say, bases for trade relationships or some other co-operative organization. We look on a declining birth rate in our own country as disastrous because it weakens us. Finally it becomes impossible for us to accept many of the facts of life objectively and simply as facts. We view them in terms of the militaristic outlook. All this is another way of saying that our experiences in a militaristic culture have become so much a part of our inner organization that situations to which we might not respond at all, or to which we might respond only mildly, become motivations to aggression, attack, or other warlike acts. The simple stimulus-response mechanism is modified into a very powerful motivation. That is the history of Nazi, Communist, and other "police-state" tactics employed in building up aggressive popular opinion in their populations.

In our own culture we are more familiar with stress on the importance of business and industrial activity, that is, we are subjected much more to experiences of an economic nature than we are, in normal times, to warlike experiences. The economic outlook then becomes a major part of our "inner organization," with the result that unconsciously we view life in economic terms. That statement does not mean anything so simple as is sometimes implied: it is not simply a matter of some "profit motive" acting as a stimulus and calling forth definite responses. The motivation is deeper than that. Quite unconsciously we begin to react on the basis of a rather subtle economic coloring in many areas of life. We assume that the man who makes the most money is the "best" man. When we want to study the life of the "upper classes," we more or less automatically look to the wealthy classes for our material. We begin to feel "inferior" (in the psychological sense) unless we can display goods and possessions to impress our neighbors. Even our religion (as witness some of our popular hymns) begins to include ideas of an "accounting" or "balancing of the books" or "bargaining" between man and God.

We are certainly not born with those reactions. In fact, if we examine the Christianity of the New Testament, we find almost the opposite values stressed, the values of sacrifice instead of acquisition, of co-operation instead of competition, and so on. The economic motivation has been developed as a result of our cultural interactions, precisely as the militaristic motivation is developed in Nazi and Communist "police states" because of the cultural interactions common in those states. In both instances, the stimulus-response pattern has been modified by the effects on our inner organization of what we "learn" and what we experience.

There are certain implications of this complexity of motivation for the study of sociology. First of all to be noted is the fact that in an "advanced" culture such as ours there is no single set of motivations common to the whole culture. Motivations differ among the several important groupings which are influential in our society. Thus, certain portions of the Church will respond to religious motivations, industry responds to one kind of economic motivations, labor to a somewhat different economic motivation, "intellectuals" to still another motivation, politicians to still another, and so on throughout a number of other groupings. Obviously it is difficult to secure co-operation among the several differently motivated groupings, as we discovered on the home front during the Second World War.

That difficulty appears not only in wartime. Suppose we want to put into practice a program which will control crime during "normal" times of peace. One of the primary requisites in that case will be to make the prevention of crime seem realistically worth while to influential segments of our society. We cannot make our program seem worth while unless it has some appeal in terms of the motivations of those several segments. To tell a grouping which is strongly motivated from the economic viewpoint that prevention of crime will "save the souls" of the criminals will very probably not have much appeal. On the other hand, to argue to a religious grouping that our program will be economically profitable, or otherwise to our benefit in a purely materialistic sense, will not enlist their co-operation. Such social programs as we wish to bring to actuality, then, must have an appeal not on the basis of any one motivation exclusively but on the basis of several, often conflicting motivations. We are not suggesting that it is impossible to put programs into action; we are saying only that we must understand the significance of motivation in human society if we are to be successful.

We have added, then, to our store of psychological knowledge the very important concept of human motivations. It has carried us beyond the picture of man as a mechanism controlled by stimulus-response patterns to a view of man as strongly modified by the culture in which he lives and with which he reacts.

5. *The Emotions.* Another area of psychological investigation which is of great significance in explaining human behavior is the study of emotions. It is difficult adequately to define the word *emotion* in a way that will be clearly understandable and yet will include all our emotional states. One common definition much used by psychologists runs as follows: an emotion is a disturbance of the individual which is psychological in origin but which affects his entire self, including his behavior, his inner reactions, and his bodily functioning.[9] This definition is useful in that it stresses the psychological origin of emotion and the broad effects of emotion. It is somewhat unsatisfactory for our purpose here, however, because of its use of the word *disturbance.* Some emotions are, of course, disturbing in a more or less violent way, as in the case of fear, rage, and hatred. But there are other emotions much less disturbing, as in the case of the pleasurable reaction associated with relaxation. Sometimes the word *feelings* is used to describe those sensations which are not as violently disturbing in their effects as emotions are. Thus, we are all familiar with the use of the word *feelings* to describe pleasantness and unpleasantness, comfort and discomfort, and other relatively minor pleasurable and painful sensations; while we apply the term *emotions* to such states as fear, rage, anxiety, and love. Feelings, then, are similar to emotions because they may be psychological in origin and they have generalized effects on our total selves, but they are not as disturbing as are emotions. Perhaps, then, we might combine the two terms into the one phrase *emotion-feeling situations* in order to include both concepts.

An additional reason for combining the two terms lies in the fact that the emotions are usually of relatively short duration. We do not hate violently for long periods of time nor do we love violently for long periods of time—romanticists to the contrary notwithstanding. During a relatively short time of acute disturbance the emotions may very powerfully affect our whole reactions. It is important to note that they continue to exert an effect, milder but none the less significant for our purpose here, after the stage of acute disturbance has passed and the emotion has either disappeared temporarily or has passed into a more or less continuous stage of

[9]Munn, op. cit. p. 100.

feeling. For example, after the period of violent and romantic love which often occurs at the beginning of a marriage, there arises, in those marriages which are fortunate, a less disturbing feeling which we call *affection*. The affection one feels for his family may be a strong and continuing influence in his life, and it may therefore be very significant, but it does not quite fall under the definition of emotion as we have given it.

It is precisely this kind of long-time influence in the lives of people (not, of course, confined to family affection or family situations) that we are interested in as sociologists for the most part. Of course, we must take some account of violent emotions in sociological phenomena; but usually we shall be concerned with emotion-feeling, that is, with long-time, continuing influences, psychological in origin and not violently disturbing, which exert an effect on the behavior, inner reactions, and bodily functioning of the individual. Such things as affection, patriotism, devotion to duty, honor, honesty, and similar forces of emotion-feeling become very significant aspects of the "man" factor in our interaction pattern—fully as significant, from the sociological viewpoint, as the more specifically emotional situations involved in fear, hatred, and greed.

Now, if all these emotion-feeling aspects of man affect his interactions with other men, it is obvious that we are not always completely logical and rational beings. If we were, it is possible that the study of our reactions would be much simpler than it is. The fact is that we do not approach situations from a completely logical and rational viewpoint; nor do we, in most cases, approach them wholly from the emotion-feeling viewpoint. We approach them from a combination of these viewpoints, a combination which varies from individual to individual. Thus, some of us may be predominantly logical with relatively little emotion-feeling; others of us may be dominated by emotion-feeling, with few logical controls operating. Again, we may be able to approach some situations largely on the basic of logical reflection, with little emotion-feeling content involved; other situations may be such that our logical faculties tend to be subordinated to emotion-feeling. There are, then, many variations among individuals. Probably it is accurate to say, as we suggested earlier, that most of us approach life from a combination of viewpoints in which logical and intellectual faculties play a part along with emotion-feeling faculties.

Students of society and of man have not always remembered that fact. Sometimes they have assumed that we are always a logical and rational species and that emotion-feeling is unimportant. And sometimes, without overtly making the assumption that we *are* always logical and rational, they have assumed that we *ought to be*, even if we are not. They have assumed that we do, or ought to, consider all the factors involved in any situation we face, and that we then choose the line of conduct which will be to our best interests and best promote our welfare. This theory of human rationality was applied especially in the field of economics, with the result that so-called "economic laws" were drawn up describing how people *would* act *if* they always conducted themselves logically and rationally in economic situations. And then it was forgotten that these were only statements of how people *would* act and it came to be assumed that they were statements of how they *did* in reality act. A realistic examination of people's reactions to economic situations would have indicated that they did not actually conduct themselves in accordance with "economic law." But such a realistic examination was delayed for many years. As a result, we still have with us, in certain areas of popular thinking, the idea that rational self-interest is the only motivation in economic affairs; the idea that "economic laws" drawn up on the basis of how people would or should act are accurate descriptions of how they do act; and a complete neglect of the whole interplay of emotions, feelings, and cultural influences in relation to economics. Perhaps the outstanding example of this kind of mistaken approach is the communist system with its emphasis on the "economic interpretation of history," though the mistake is not confined to communism by any means.

For example, during the period of price control just after the Second World War, there were loud demands for the repeal of control legislation so that "the law of supply and demand could take over" and rectify all our difficulties. Most of the people who made such demands were not thinking of the dozen or so "laws of supply and demand" which modern economists recognize and which take account of a number of changing factors, including cultural and emotion-feeling situations. They were thinking of a single, rigid, automatically operating formula which expresses what people would do if they were rational, but which falls far short of expressing what they actually do under the stress of shortages, a large amount of purchasing power, the emotional-feeling reaction incident to the end of the war, and many other factors. Their idea seemed to be that freedom from controls would permit price rises, which would encourage the production of more goods, which would cause the manufacture of more goods, with the result that large amounts of goods would increase the supply, and cause prices to drop, so that we should all have all we wanted at a low price. It has not worked that way, largely because of psychological factors involved. In other words, the comparatively recent modifications of the earlier "law of supply and demand" common in the thinking of contemporary economists and much more realistic than the earlier "law" have not as yet reached the area of popular thinking.

Economics was by no means the only social science which suffered from the rationalistic approach. The fallacy of believing that what men "ought, logically, to do" is what they actually do has also plagued sociology. For example, it has prevented, until fairly recently, the development of principles in the field of sociology because principles depend on scientific observation and the rationalistic approach prevented objective observation of man. Accurate observation, as we discussed it in Chapter II, is difficult and time-consuming. It was easier to indulge in "arm-chair philosophy" as a result of which we could spin out our theories of what men "must, by the logic of the case, do" and then assume that they did it.

However, it was not only, and perhaps not even chiefly, the difficulty entailed in observation which was significant. It was this very factor of emotion-feeling which we are discussing, but whose importance was not appreciated. Many early social scientists tended to approach the study of contemporary man with a great deal of bias and prejudice—prejudice *in favor of man*, not against him. They "felt" that man was a unique phenomenon and that therefore he could not be studied scientifically as other phenomena could. They "felt" (note the emphasis on emotion-feeling) that man should not conduct himself in certain ways; and when they did observe him conducting himself in those very ways, they could not admit that he did so. It was as though we should feel very strongly that policemen ought to be honest, so strongly that we refused to admit even to ourselves that there could be a dishonest policeman. When we actually saw policemen being dishonest, we would not "notice" it. If we felt that way, we might in general be very useful members of the community but we should hardly be competent to draw up a realistic report on our police department. So of some early students of man: they were very useful members of the community, but not equipped to report realistically on their fellow men.

Let us be clear here: this kind of reaction among some of the early students of man, and among some contemporary students of man, operated without their being aware of it. It was not that they deliberately refused to observe accurately, or that they deliberately distorted their observations. The whole thing was largely unconscious. They did not realize the significance of emotion-feeling, either in their own lives or in the lives of others. Many of us, apart from our own specialties, do not realize the significance of emotion-feeling. We mentioned in Chapter I certain undoubtedly intelligent people who could react objectively in their own special field of knowledge, but lost that objectivity when they discussed some subject outside their own special fields. Their emotion-feeling "runs away with them" in those areas of life, without their being aware of it.

In our attempt to study the principles of sociology, then, we must bear in mind a number of things: the emotion-feeling aspects of our lives are facts, as real as many other facts. They affect our reaction patterns and our interactions with other men. Men behave in certain ways, whether they ought to or not. It is our task to describe their behavior objectively, since principles are only accurate statements of the way people behave under given conditions. We may pass judgment on them for behaving as they do: we may say, "That is right, or wrong, or good, or bad." We may be fully convinced that men "ought to do" and "ought not to do" certain things. In fact, whenever we participate in the working out of a social policy or program we are saying, in effect, "This is what men ought to do." But we must keep our judgment separate from our observations. We must not let our judgments interfere with the clarity of our view of how men actually behave.

SUMMARY

Fortunately for itself, sociology does not have to exist apart from the general body of scientific knowledge and scientific investigation. If it did, its task of studying the basic factors of man's interaction pattern would be almost impossible, since the sociologist would have to investigate directly every phase of the world which has some bearing on his subject matter. This would involve an almost endless amount of observation, classification, and all the other processes of the scientific method. Since we are a part of science as a whole, we have access to the findings of scholars in many specialized areas of investigation. We accept and use their findings in so far as they are available and in so far as we believe them to be scientifically accurate.

Thus we recognize the importance of specialized approaches to certain segments of man's interaction as embodied in economics and political science; we use the historian's materials in a way different from the way he uses them in history, yet we find them very useful.

Anthropology tells us something of early man's development and something of the early growth and functioning of culture. It thus contributes to our knowledge of two of the factors in our basic interaction pattern: man and culture. Psychology reports a great deal of very useful information about the "man" factor, including the mechanisms of stimulus and response and motivation. Its discoveries about the emotion-feeling aspects of man further aid us to be realistic in our own investigations.

With the background available from our discussions of the Field of Sociology in Chapter I, the Method of Sociology in Chapter II, and the findings of other sciences mentioned in the present chapter, we are now equipped to consider more in detail some of the specific materials of sociology.

READINGS

PENDELL, E. (Ed.). *Society Under Analysis*. The Jacques Cattell Press, Lancaster, Pennsylvania, 1942. An introduction to sociology consisting of chapters written by specialists. Especially Chap. 1, "Anthropological Backgrounds," and Chap. 8, "Psychological Regularities."

HOOTON, EARNEST A. *Up from the Ape* (Revised Edition). The Macmillan Company, New York, 1946. Written in a semipopular style. An excellent and outstanding book. Especially Part IV, "Fossil Ancestors and Collaterals."

HERSKOVITS, MELVILLE and FRANCES. *Trinidad Village*. Alfred A. Knopf, Inc., New York, 1947. A good example of a field study in culture.

SOROKIN, P. A. *Society, Culture, and Personality*. Harper & Brothers, New York, 1947. Especially pp. 6–18, "Sociology among the Social Sciences."

MUNN, NORMAN L. *Psychology*. Houghton Mifflin Company, Boston, 1946. A general discussion of psychology. Especially Part One, "Scope and Methods of Psychology."

CHAPTER IV

GROUP LIFE

As a first step in our more detailed consideration of the material of sociology, we emphasize the *man* factor in the basic interaction pattern. We have already indicated something of the characteristics of *individual* man in Chapter III. But man does not live as an individual: he lives in association with other men. What kind of associations does he develop, and what are their functions in his life?

FORMS OF ASSOCIATION

The Aggregate

The simplest kind of association among men is that found in the social *aggregate*. An aggregate is simply a gathering together of people. It is the broadest and most general term applied to association among men because it does not attempt to describe any aspect of that association except the fact of the nearness to each other in space of the individuals concerned. It does not imply that there is present any organization, influence, or other kind of relationship. The people of the United States form an aggregate because they are in proximity to each other. As we shall see later, they may also be more than an aggregate if they develop some kind of organized relationships among themselves. But, however much more they may be, they are at base simply an aggregate.

Aggregate, then, is a convenient term to use when we want to point out the fact of geographical nearness among a number of individuals without attempting to give any further details about the nature of their association.[1]

[1]For the sake of clarity, let us note that groupings of people who are often *thought of* together without their actually being in proximity to each other are called *categories*. Thus, all individuals in the United States under 21 years of age may be classed together for certain purposes into one category. The same may be said of such groupings as "the unemployed," "the criminal classes," etc.

THE COLLECTIVITY

What sociologists call a *collectivity* is defined formally as "a unity of interacting personalities in which those participating possess awareness of more or less homogeneity of composition, of interests, or of joint action. It ranges from the pair [of human beings] to a league of nations."[2] A collectivity may also be an aggregate, if its members are gathered together in some definite bit of geographical space, but it is something more than an aggregate because of several factors. (1) In the case of a collectivity, we discover that there is a degree of *interaction* among the members, which means that they exert some degree of influence on each other as the members of an aggregate do not. (2) In the case of a collectivity there is a degree of *awareness* of some common interests, common purposes, common characteristics, or common activities, all of which are lacking in the case of an aggregate. Note that this is an awareness of approximate similarity. It does not imply that the members of a collectivity are completely similar and without any kind of variation in interests, purposes, characteristics, or action. (3) In the case of a collectivity, both the interaction and the awareness of common patterns of living are psychic rather than physical. They exist and operate even when the members of the collectivity are not in physical contact with each other. We feel the influence of other people whom we do not actually see or touch directly. The ideas, goals, purposes, and beliefs we share with them affect us in many important ways without, in some cases, any first-hand contact with them as people.

In terms of this definition, the people of the United States are a collectivity. So also is the Christian Church in all its branches and denominations. And so also are many associations of the type of labor unions, employers' groups, national Rotary and Kiwanis clubs, and others.

SOCIETY

One special kind of collectivity is called a *society*. The distinguishing mark of a society is its self-sufficiency. A collectivity which can provide all that it needs wholly within itself, and without getting some of its necessities from other groupings, is self-sufficient

[2]H. P. Fairchild (Ed.), *Dictionary of Sociology*, p. 47. Philosophical Library, New York, 1944.

and is therefore a society. It does not necessarily have to provide for itself in actuality; it may establish trade and other relationships with other aggregates or collectivities for convenience or profit. The point is that it could, if necessary, be self-sufficient; it could, if necessary, provide all its necessities from within its own organization. This is not true of collectivities other than societies.

Applying our definitions thus far, we may note that the people of the United States form an aggregate, a collectivity, and a society. The Christian Church is not an aggregate, since it is not necessarily composed of people gathered together in one geographical location; but certain branches of the Church are aggregates, such as the Church in the United States. The Church is also a collectivity because of the awareness of its members of their common purposes and other characteristics. But the Church is not a society because it is not self-sufficient as it is at present organized. The same type of analysis may be applied to the other associations we have mentioned.

THE GROUP

The formal definition of a group reads as follows: "A group is two or more people between whom there is an established pattern of interaction. It is recognized as an entity, by its own members and usually by others, because of its particular type of collective behavior."[3] Obviously, a group resembles a collectivity in many respects, and there is no clear distinction between them in sociological literature. Perhaps the chief differences are three. 1. In the case of a group, the pattern of interaction is more definitely established than it is in the case of a collectivity. That statement means that in the case of a group the purpose toward which its members are working is limited and very concrete. A group usually exists to do one specific thing: to study poetry, or to produce and train children (as in the case of the family), or to influence legislatures (as in the case of "pressure groups"), or to govern a city (as in the case of a city council), or to further some other single and definite interest. Because of this concreteness of group concerns and group functioning, the interaction among members becomes established in the sense that it tends to fall into a definite pattern of influence very strongly exerted in connection with their common

[3] E. E. Eubank, *Concepts of Sociology*, p. 99. Heath, Boston, 1932.

purpose. A collectivity, on the other hand, furthers interests of a more general nature. Thus, labor unions serve all the interests of workers, the Church engages in a number of widespread programs, the Rotary Club's activities are many and various. The members of all these collectivities influence each other in connection with general rather than specific purposes.

The contrast between group and collectivity will become clearer if we examine the significance and the directness of the influence exerted by each. Thus, most of us consider our duty to our family group to be much more important than our duty to, say, the Rotary Club. If the two duties conflict, it is usually the group duty which takes precedence. We do not deprive our families of necessities in order to pay club dues. We would not leave a sick child in order to attend a club meeting. Similarly, in another area of life, students sometimes neglect their studies in order to partici- pate in the program of a sorority, a dramatic club, or some other intimate group. Again the group wins out over the collectivity, the latter being in this case represented by the college as a whole with its general educational purposes as contrasted with the more specific and intimate purposes of the group. The pattern of interaction, then, in the case of a group is more definitely established than it is in the case of a collectivity because the group functions more con- cretely and more directly than the collectivity.

2. A second factor which distinguishes the group from the col- lectivity is the *degree* of awareness of common characteristics, in- terests, and action, admittedly difficult to measure. Both the col- lectivity and the group exhibit this factor of awareness, but the group members have a much greater degree of awareness of their sharing of interests and purposes than do the members of a collec- tivity. As our definition suggests, the group is not simply a col- lection of people—it is a potent influence in the lives of its members, an influence of which they are deeply conscious. "The group member lives in the shadow of the group" in the sense that he feels the power of his association with other people in terms of their common group life.

3. A third point of distinction between a group and a collectivity is that of relative size. Theoretically, a group might be of any size; actually it is usually small, because it is only as it remains small that intimacy of contact, directness of influence, and immediate sharing

of purposes and activities is possible. For example, the whole population of a city cannot govern the city directly because of the numbers of people involved. Such large numbers may function as a
collectivity, but the government of a city demands more concrete
and specialized activity than that which characterizes a collectivity.
Hence we elect a smaller group of city councilmen, or some other
representative body, to do the actual governing. Such a group
functions efficiently in connection with the concrete task of government because it is small enough to form a group and therefore
intimacy of reaction, awareness of purpose and function, and direct
activity become possible. It would be useless to elect a huge body
of representatives to govern. When we do have a fairly large body
of representatives, as in the case of the United States Congress,
much of the detail of government is carried on in designated committees, that is, smaller groups, which then make recommendations
to the larger collectivity.

SUMMARY

We have distinguished several different forms of association thus
far: aggregates, which are based simply on the fact of nearness in
geographical space on the part of their members; collectivities,
which may also be aggregates, but which are distinguished from
aggregates by a degree of awareness of common interests and
common activities; and groups, which are characterized by a very
high degree of awareness of common interests and activities which
exert a strong and direct influence on the lives of their members, and
which are usually composed of a relatively small number of people.
These several forms of association perform different functions and
have different effects on man and on his society, as we shall see
later.

Before considering those functions and effects, however, we must
glance briefly at the origins of association among men.

ORIGINS OF ASSOCIATION

Association among men is a "natural" development—that is, it
developed from the basic pattern of man interacting with his environment. It was not, in the beginning, planned for; it happened.

But it happened not by accident; it happened because of the biological and psychological characteristics of men and the conditions
of the world in which men lived. Man being what he was and the
environment being what it was, the fact of association naturally
resulted.

ASSOCIATION IN AGGREGATES

The simplest kind of association among men, as we have said, is
the aggregate. We note at once that

> *Man's biological structure tends to make him*
> *associate with other men.*

There are a number of things about man's biological nature
which are of interest to the sociologist as factors in the origin of
aggregates.

First of all is the basic fact that man needs suitable food and
a supply of water if he is to survive at all; and the further fact
that all men need pretty much the same *kind* of food. What was
suitable for one man, or for a few men, would, in general, be suitable for all men. As a result, when a certain area of the earth's
surface provided the necessary food and water supply, the tendency
was for numbers of men to settle in that location, thereby forming
the beginnings, at least, of an aggregate. Similarly, areas which did
not provide food and water were left deserted. The simple and
perhaps obvious fact is that men tended to live together in selected
areas because not all portions of their environment provided the
necessities of life.

We must again recall the fact here that early men did not have
techniques for transforming areas naturally unsuitable into something more desirable, as we do today. Early man lived for the most
part in what is called a *collecting* economy. He collected animals for
food by hunting them, and he collected plants for food by gathering
those which grew naturally around him. He did, of course, travel
relatively short distances in the process of collecting animals and
plants, but he did not travel far, with the result that he was de-
pedent on one fairly small area. Group migrations and the migra-
tory way of life were later developments and may be traced to

special situations. In general, early man lived in a restricted location. We can observe some of these collecting economies among our primitive contemporaries, and so gain a fair insight into their way of life and into the potency of the environment in influencing that way of life.

A second aspect of man's biological structure which tended towards the formation of aggregates is the fact of sex. Obviously man's bisexual nature would lead to association with persons of the opposite sex. At first, the associations were probably temporary and possibly polygamous: one male would associate with several females. The male, his females, and their children formed an aggregate of a fair size in itself. Such families would be much larger than our own are, especially in comparison with the present period, when people limit the number of their children and when an increasing proportion of our families is childless.

More significant than the fact of sex itself, however, is a third aspect of man's biology—the fact that human children need care by their mothers for a longer period of time than do the young of other animals. In our own culture this period of childhood has been extended until it now covers the first fifteen or twenty years of life—in fact, an even longer time in the case of students whose education for the professions is prolonged. Undoubtedly the childhood of early man was not nearly so long as that, but it was longer than the few weeks of time required in the case of many animals.

Children, then, had to associate with their mothers in order to survive at all. But there was also a tendency for them to associate longer than was absolutely necessary, as children do in the case of our primitive contemporaries. Certainly there is no evidence that children left their mothers at the earliest possible moment. Association based on necessity, then, tended to continue beyond the period of necessity, thus prolonging the existence of the aggregate.

We find, then, a relationship between the facts of man's biology and the fact of aggregation dependent on the operation of basic needs for food and water, sex responses, and the necessity of caring for children—all of which fostered association in aggregates. We do not know how long a time passed before the development of other forms of association, but we can trace the importance of other than biological factors in that further development.

ASSOCIATION IN COLLECTIVITIES

One of those factors is the growth of culture. Specifically,

*Cultural factors tend to reinforce the trend
toward association among men.*

Once men began to live together in aggregates as a result of their biological structure, the basis was laid for the growth of influential culture patterns. At first, simple imitation was important in creating those patterns. There was little tendency to live apart from aggregates, simply because most men did live in aggregates and it was natural to imitate them. Doubtless this imitation was not conscious and deliberate. Men imitated existing patterns without realizing that they were imitating them and without thinking much about what they were doing. Later, unconscious imitation gave way to the very important aspect of culture we call *custom*. Custom then acquired a compulsive force. Conduct which accorded with custom was approved and rewarded; that which did not follow customary patterns was disapproved and punished. When association became a matter of custom, it was firmly established as an enduring human-behavior pattern.

Somewhere about this point the aggregate lost its significance as the only type of human association, and the collectivity began to be more important. Of course, we cannot distinguish one specific time or one specific attitude as being the sole and only basis of the collectivity. But cultural concepts such as custom, social approval, and social disapproval were significant because they implied some awareness of common interests and some sharing of common attitudes. Group behavior was strongly influenced by this awareness. Men began to think of themselves as belonging to an association of people like themselves.

All of these are the marks of a collectivity.

But it was not only cultural factors that were significant in the development of collectivities. Man's psychological nature, specifically his learning ability, was also very important.

*Man's learning ability tends toward
the establishment and extension
of planned association.*

Planned association means association for a definite purpose and with deliberate intent, as contrasted with the natural association we discussed in connection with aggregates. Man "learned" certain things about planned association which made him value collectivities and extend their functions.

But we must be clear as to what we mean by learning. It is not reading from a book and memorizing its content. Obviously early man could not do that. *Learning* means incorporating the experiences we have into our life organization. As we suggested in Chapter III, the mechanism of learning consists of the setting up of certain responses which did not exist at birth. Early man, then, learned not from books but from his life experiences. He discovered that there were certain relationships among the things that happened to him, and eventually he was able to use this discovery to make some things happen as he wanted them to

At first, doubtless, his discoveries were largely chance and accidental. He found that men working together were useful in repelling an attack by an animal or a human enemy which could not have been met by an individual or by a completely unorganized aggregate. Several people could more effectively kill and transport large animals than could a single individual. People joining their efforts could build a better shelter, and built it more quickly, than they could individually. All these things were matters of discovery for our remote ancestors. They had to experience them before they could realize them as facts.

Very probably, also, some of man's early observations were far from accurate, and some of his discoveries did not mean what he thought they meant. We suggested in Chapter I that man made mistaken connections between what he did and what subsequently happened to him. When he had good or bad luck after eating a certain kind of food, he assumed that his eating of the food brought him good or bad luck. His assumption may have been wrong, but he was not aware of that fact. Much the same thing happened in connection with man's discoveries about his life in association.

Thus, people tended to crowd together into a more or less compact mass in fear of some such natural event as a storm, an earthquake, or an eclipse. When the event passed by without harming them, they assumed that they had escaped harm *because* they had crowded together. When they gathered together, they had to stop whatever work they were doing; very probably they also moaned, cried out in fear, or otherwise made a noise. These activities became connected with the passing of the threat. After a number of repetitions, man "learned" that in the face of a natural catastrophe he "had to" stop his work, crowd together, and make a noise. This procedure was, of course, very effective in the case of the "threat" inherent in an eclipse because there was no real threat. It might not be as effective in the case of earthquakes and of storms; yet many of those would also pass without doing appreciable harm. So the custom became established, as we find it among our primitive contemporaries, of greeting natural "threats" by crowding together and making a noise. Once this practice became established as a custom, and once it was formalized into a ritual, its authority and influence became widespread, and we have the beginnings of *magic*.

As a matter of fact, we can still find survivals of such magical practices in our own culture. We make a great deal of noise at times without knowing just why we make the noise—we have forgotten what our remote ancestors "discovered," but we still follow their routine. At the New Year (a dangerous time because devils may gain power then which will last throughout the year) we make a huge racket in order to assure our happiness by driving away the evil spirits. Until recently, a newly married couple would probably be subjected to a *charivari*, which consisted of a noisy and most inharmonious demonstration carried on by their "friends." The custom of *charivari* has passed because it degenerated into a form of blackmail: the new husband, or some other person, had to dispense gifts to bribe the charivarists to leave. Originally, however, the whole thing was done with the best of intentions, namely, to scare away devils who might otherwise assume control of the marriage and make a good deal of trouble. Our funeral customs also reflect early man's reactions. After a death it was customary, until quite recently, to dress in a special and extraordinary way so that the ghost of the dead person would not be able to recognize us and harm us. Black was customary for funerals in the United States, the women also wearing a long mourning veil. In some Oriental countries white is the appropriate funeral dress. Whether the color be black or white, the change from the usual mode of dress, and especially the long veil, made it impossible for the ghost to recognize the wearer.

Remember we are not suggesting that we in our times did all these things because we were afraid of ghosts or devils. We did them as a matter of custom, even after we had forgotten the beliefs in ghosts or devils which were originally responsible for the custom. Whatever our reasons for following the customs, they enable us to understand something of the reactions of early man. They may have done him no more actual good than they do us, but he could not recognize that fact.

Man learned a good many things about association, then, some right and some wrong. He applied his learning to the establishment of planned associations. In effect, he said, "When you are threatened by enemies, then you must act in this way; when you are threatened by natural catastrophes you must act in this other and special way; and when your game animals are too big to handle effectively alone, you must get together and handle them."

One point must, however, be clearly made: all of this was the result of a learning process, the result of experience. Man did not reason in some abstract way about what he should do in situations that never happened to him. He learned what to do in the case of any happening by having it happen to him a number of times and by gradually discovering what he thought was the effective thing to do in case of that happening. Then he made plans to do that same thing in the case of future occurrences of the same kind.

This point is important because some students of society used to believe that associations originated in a *social contract* or agreement among men to establish collectivities for the purpose of their mutual benefit and welfare. When it was later demonstrated that human reason does not operate in such a way as to make it at all likely that there ever was any such original agreement as that implied in the social-contract theory, there was a reaction against the idea that reason could have played any part in man's early associations. It became fashionable to believe that human association was wholly a matter of stimulus, response, and chance. We suggest here that the abstract type of reason which would be necessary to plan in advance an elaborate scheme and purpose of social organization very probably did not play any part in the origin of collectivities and planned association. But the concrete type of reasoning involved in learning did play a part. As man drew elementary conclusions, right or wrong, about his association with other men, and began to apply those conclusions, he learned to plan his associations.

One caution: In the nature of the case, we can know very little about man's activities 150,000 years ago. Not everyone agrees with the outline here given of our early development, but our approach has this to recommend it: it does not assume the presence of any factor that we cannot observe and, to some extent, measure in the life of contemporary man. We know the facts of man's biological needs; we know that culture is important in its influence on human behavior; and we know that man learns slowly perhaps and incorrectly at first, but he does learn. From the interaction of all these factors, association develops. Until some more authoritative explanation of its origin and growth displaces this naturalistic theory, we suggest that it be accepted.

ASSOCIATION IN GROUPS

As human population grew in size and as man's relationships to other men and to his surroundings became more complex, groups became functionally important. An increase in the number of people making up the collectivity was accompanied by differentiation into specialized groups. Instead of each man being self-sufficient in the sense of himself producing all that he needed, men began to exploit their special abilities. One became a woodworker, another a metal worker, another a specialist in defense, and another a specialist in the affairs of the spirit world. Woodworkers formed a specialized group with interests common to their trade, and so did the metal workers and the medicine men. They remained members of the collectivity, but were differentiated from the general membership on the basis of their function.

Accompanying this kind of functional differentiation was the growth of a system of exchange. When each individual no longer produced all that he needed or wanted, it became necessary to devise some means by which the products of specialists could be "bought" or otherwise acquired. Systems of direct barter operated successfully in some areas; in others money, or a substitute for money, facilitated the exchange process. All this introduced a greater complexity of relationships at the same time that it assisted the growth of even more functional differentiation. And, in turn, dependence on specialists for certain products increased the importance of the subgroupings through which specialization was carried on.

On the whole, the growth of economic specialization meant increasing efficiency in providing for the survival needs of the population. With increasing efficiency goes increasing leisure for certain members, at least, of the population. This increasing leisure, coupled with the fact that the number of people itself was increasing, led to a divergence of interests not directly connected with the economic life. Recreational interests, art interests, scientific interests, and many others appeared, and again the collectivity became differentiated into groups to further such specific interests.

In all these ways, the increase in numbers of people, together with the differentiation of individual abilities and interests, led to the formation of many different kinds of groups. We find much the same thing in our urban civilization of today. Locality groupings such as the community and the neighborhood, which used to be significant aspects of our social organization, have become of decreasing importance. More and more they are being replaced by special-interest groups which attract individuals from many different localities. One result of this trend is that, in modern society, the group is of paramount importance as the shaper and influencer of our individual lives. We shall stress the importance of groups in this respect as we discuss the functions of association.

FUNCTIONS OF ASSOCIATION

Our consideration of the origins of association has been of necessity primarily historical in the sense that it is related to past occurrences. We now turn to a discussion of a more contemporary matter, the function of association.

The general function of association today is simply to assist the survival of the aggregate and of the individual. Exactly as man learned the strengths of association in the remote past, so we have learned the strengths of association in the present. We can exploit our environment to obtain food, shelter, protection, enjoyment, self-development, and all the other things we want, much more efficiently in the aggregate than we could as individuals. Some individuals, of course, would be able to survive at a low level of living apart from association with their fellows. But what most of us want is survival for large numbers of individuals and at a high level of living. We do not want to live on roots and in sod houses; we want to live in modern dwellings, to eat tasty food, to dress impressively, and to enjoy life. In order to do all those things, we must live in association with other men. Association, then, functions to give us the things we want, or, to speak more accurately, we believe that association gives us more of the things we want than we could get in isolation.

As a result of that belief, we have developed great systems of production, of distribution, of control and regulation, of education, and of family living. We call these systems the *institutions* of society, and they form the subject matter of Part II of this book. Our institutions correspond roughly to collectivities, since they include large numbers of people, they subserve very general purposes, and yet there is a degree of awareness and of similarity among the people composing them, so that they are more than mere unorganized aggregates. These institutions are largely organizational in function: they co-ordinate the activities and the efforts of many different individuals in such a way that they contribute to a general goal or purpose. As such, they are necessary adjuncts to associational living.

But they are only part of the associational aspect of society. Groups, as distinct from institutions, also play a very important part. As institutions organize societal functioning, so groups organize and otherwise influence individual personalities. If institutions are to function effectively in our complex society, if association is to be in any sense co-operative rather than simply an area of conflict, we must somehow assure ourselves of a supply of certain necessary *kinds* of individuals. They cannot have the habits of cave men and the outlook of primitives. The association itself and the type of men who live in that association must be in relative harmony. How do we bring that about? Briefly, we do it by modifying the human animal in such a way that he is fit to live with in our kind of society. The chief instrument of such modification is the group.

The fact is that we are not "born human" at all. We are born "biohoms," a word coined to describe purely biological man, unmodified by any cultural influences.[4] The "biohom" has a human

[4] E. E. Eubank, *Concepts of Sociology*, Heath, Boston, 1932.

physiological structure and organization. He has all the organs which will enable him to learn to be human (except in the case of some obvious defectives). What society does is to take this biological organism and make it into a human being. Implied in this statement is the further idea that different cultures give widely different meanings to the words *human being*. Actually, a human being is one who acts in accordance with our standards of human conduct. He speaks our language, knows our traditions, is skilled in the areas of life we consider important, follows (more or less) our moral systems, and responds as we respond. He can communicate words, thoughts, feelings, to us in a manner we understand and appreciate. He lives as we do. If he does not do all these things, we call him a savage, a "Hun," or some other derogatory name such as *brute* and *beast*, both of which imply a contrast to *man* or *human being*.

But obviously other cultures, with other values, would describe a "human being" in terms of their own values; and, if those values differed from ours, the description would also differ. It is literally true, then, that

> *Man becomes human only in association*
> *with other men,*

because it is only as he associates with other men that he learns to modify his behavior in such a way that they will accept him as human.

Consider again the "biohom." He has a hunger drive, a sex drive, and a few other drives. If he expressed these drives in unmodified form, he would eat anything, approach any sexually attractive object, and act in such a way as to further his own self-preservation without reference to any social controls. In order to become human, he must learn the prescribed discrimination in food habits; he must learn to control his sexual impulses so that he expresses them only in socially approved ways; and he must learn to direct his impulses towards self-preservation in such a way as to harm others as little as possible. All of this may be difficult for some individuals to learn, but actually these are only the very elementary and basic modifications necessary. In a complex society the techniques of living and the proprieties of social relationships go far beyond the areas of our basic drives.

Now undoubtedly the institutional organization of society functions to set the general framework of processes by which the "biohom" is modified into a human being. But the actual agent of humanization is the group, because its small size, its concreteness of purpose, and its directness of contact all permit its influence to operate very strongly on the individual. We may say, then, that

> *The social group is our most effective*
> *humanizing agent.*

Thus, it is our family group which begins to modify our original structure and functioning in very significant ways. Not only are we trained in habits of cleanliness and physical care. We are also trained to adjust to other people. We learn that we cannot live in terms of our own wants and our own satisfactions. We must live in terms of our relationships to other people; we must exist as participants in a number of groupings. These are the first steps toward becoming "human" in the sense of being able, eventually, to live in a series of relationships to a larger society. When we acquire that ability in the amount that characterizes most of our fellows, we become *adult*. Those of us who do not acquire it remain childish, no matter how old they may actually be, and we refer to them as *infantile*.

Familiar as we may be with that process, we sometimes overlook another very important aspect of family life: the family not only teaches the child certain concrete patterns of behavior, it also lays the general foundations for his "human nature" in the sense that it sets up certain positive and negative attitudes towards life. It thereby strongly influences the way in which he will react to future associations. If, for instance, our family life as children is such as to create in us attitudes of fear, anxiety, and worry, we tend to react to new situations primarily on the basis of fear, anxiety, and worry. We have no other "equipment" with which to face such new situations; the only basis on which we can react is the complex of attitudes we have developed in the process of growth. This approach also implies, of course, that if our family life is such as to give us attitudes of confidence and security, we tend to react to the rest of society in a confident and secure manner.

For example, a child approaches the experience of schooling with the background of attitudes toward life which his early family associations have given him. If he is anxious and insecure, he will not get from the experience of schooling as much constructive benefit as the confident and secure child will. So of other experiences.

We are not suggesting that the equipment we get from our early lives as family members is forever unchangeable. It, in turn, may be modified when necessary by other agencies of society, such as the school, the church, psychiatric treatment, and so on, but their task will be more difficult because of the failure of our first intimate group, the family, to give us a sound foundation for the future.

We implied in the preceding paragraph that many societal agencies function in the general process of modification. That is, of course, true. Here we are concerned with emphasizing the fact that these other societal agencies function as *groups* in their efforts to modifiy us. Take education as an example. In one sense, education is an institution, one of the great systems to which we referred earlier as organizing the framework within which the processes of modification take place. The institution of education is important because it organizes the whole process of instruction in a more or less standardized way. But the educational institution *functions* through the intimate, personal activities of the classroom—that is, it functions through a group. The essential part of the educative process is the interrelationship between teacher and pupils.

This interrelationship exhibits all the characteristics of a group: pupils and teacher are part of an established pattern of interaction, characterized by a great deal of awareness of common interests, purposes, and activities. That statement may cause some smiles among those who remember that such is hardly the traditional conception of a little boy in a classroom. Yet the traditional conception is by no means wholly accurate in modern schools. And, to the extent that it is accurate—that is, to the extent that pupil and teacher are not part of a group pattern—education fails to accomplish its purpose. Thus the situation supports our belief that the modifying agencies of society operate as groups when they operate effectively.

Part of the difficulty with American education at present is that we have not realized that fact. We have stressed buildings, equipment, organization, administration, and other materialistic aspects of education. We have forgotten that all these must function through the personal relationship of teacher and pupils. One of our contemporary problems in education is to attract the kind of person into teaching who will be able to make education effective through his influence on children.

It is not education alone which functions through groups; other institutions, such as religion, government, and recreation, actually carry out most of their functions through small groups in which the relationships and influences are intimate and therefore effective.

The group, then, is our chief humanizing agent. It has always functioned as such, but it is even more important in our own times than it was in simpler societies because our type of social organization involves a great deal of dependence on other people. We specialize in our own vocation. Outside of that vocation we depend on firemen, policemen, doctors, lawyers, merchants, and all the rest to function for us. As "biohoms," they would be completely undependable and erratic. As human beings they become much more dependable. They function as important parts of the whole social organization in at least a relatively satisfactory manner.

In addition to this primary fact about groups we must note that they also perform other important functions in our society. They are a means of self-expression in the form of special-interest groups; they are a means of exerting influence on the larger aggregate, as in the case of pressure groups; they act as agents of the collectivity, as in the case of city councils and Congressional committees mentioned earlier. They function to develop resources, natural and human. They may, in short, function in many specialized ways in and for the collectivity.

But we must emphasize again the fact that the primary function of the group is to act as the humanizing agent for the collectivity. If we, as a society, forget that function—as we have recently— and permit certain fundamental groups such as the family to degenerate (as we have done recently), the results quickly appear in such "unhuman" conduct as delinquency and other social problems. We do not usually refer to the conduct characteristic of problem individuals as "unhuman" conduct; we usually call it *antisocial* conduct. In whatever way we refer to it, it is a serious problem. And its roots lie in the failure of groups to act as humanizing agents.

READINGS

PENDELL, E. (Ed.). *Society Under Analysis*. The Jacques Cattell Press, Lancaster, Pennsylvania, 1942. Chap. 10, "Human Groupings—The Cradle of Human Personality."

SOROKIN, P. A. *Society, Culture, and Personality*. Harper & Brothers, New York, 1947. Chap. 8, "The Organized Group as a Collective Unity"; Chaps. 11 and 12, "Differentiation of Human Population into Sociocultural Groups"; Chap. 21, "How Social Groups Originate and Become Organized."

LANDIS, PAUL H. *Social Control*. J. B. Lippincott Company, Philadelphia, 1939. Chap. 5, "The Role of the Group in Socialization."

LUNDBERG, GEORGE A. *Foundations of Sociology*. The Macmillan Company, New York, 1939. Especially Chap. IX.

THE ENVIRONMENT

As WE HAVE SUGGESTED, the environment is the total surrounding of an individual or of an aggregate. That definition is somewhat too general, however, to be of much assistance in our analysis of society. Actually, the sociologist is interested not in the total surroundings of an individual as such, but in those aspects of his total surroundings which influence him in some way, directly or indirectly. For example, a symphony orchestra, a number of libraries, and several colleges are all part of the total surroundings of everyone who lives in New York City. But there are many people in New York whose lives are not in the least affected by any of those things. In that case, they do not form part of the significant environment of those people. There are other individuals in New York whose lives are affected only very indirectly by orchestras, libraries, and colleges. For them, the environmental influences emanating from musical and educational organizations are relatively insignificant parts of the environment, subordinate to such other influences as business, politics, the radio, and the newspapers. It is, then, in the significant environment that the sociologist is interested.

Let us analyze somewhat more deeply the meaning of *the environment* to the sociologist and its functioning for man-in-relationship-to-man.

THE MEANING OF ENVIRONMENT

THE KINDS OF ENVIRONMENT

Our first point is that the total surroundings of an individual are differentiated into several kinds. In ordinary speech, *the environment* means the physical or geographical environment, that is, such things as climate, soil, terrain, wind, and weather influences. Agreeing with ordinary usage, the sociologist recognizes the physical surroundings of man as part, but part only, of his total environment. By analogy, perhaps, we should also speak of a "biological environment," to include the animals and plants which form part of our total surroundings. Usually, however, we include animals and plants in the physical environment, thus avoiding the use of another and separate term.

The *physical* environment was, as we suggested in Chapter I, a very significant part of early man's interaction pattern because it supplied him with the materials for food, clothing, shelter, tools, and other necessities. Natural resources are, of course, still very important, but in modern times other kinds of environment than the physical are more significant in their influence on our lives.

For example, the *cultural* environment (a second kind of environment for the sociologist) is of great importance. It includes all the human creations which surround us: material *artifacts*, such as buildings, tools, machines, and all the other host of products we have created; and immaterial "mentifacts," such as beliefs, customs, laws, and systems of thought.[1] Often the two are mixed. Education, for example, is an important part of our cultural environment. Obviously it includes not only such artifacts as buildings, books, typewriters, and other tools but also such "mentifacts" as techniques of instruction, educational goals, and codes of regulation.

We are influenced by our cultural environment in the same way that we are by our physical environment. In fact, in complex societies the cultural environment is much more important than the physical environment.

A third kind of environment is the *social* environment, by which we mean the people who surround us. Both the numbers of people, and the kind of people they are, influence us. For example, the fact that an individual lives in a crowded urban center of heavy population density affects his behavior patterns: he must adjust in some way to the presence of large numbers of people. But he also reacts to the fact of whether the people who surround him are, say, saints or sinners or some mixture of the two. We "react" to them because they exert some influence on our behavior.

But when we say that they influence us, we do not mean that we

[1]E. E. Eubank, *Concepts of Sociology*, p. 357. Heath, Boston, 1932.

automatically imitate them. The net result of our reaction to them may be to make us not resemble them at all. We may react negatively and refuse to have anything to do with them; or we may react positively and favorably towards them; or our reaction may be so mild that they really have little influence of any kind on us. How we react depends on the previous influences in our lives. For example, we cannot accurately say that an individual becomes a criminal "because of his environment." If that were so, everyone living in given environments would become criminal, a situation that obviously does not exist. The social environment is one factor in the total development of criminals; another equally important factor is the individual's whole background which influences his reaction to that social environment.

We must bear in mind this threefold division of the environment if we are to understand its operation in our basic interaction pattern. When we say that modern man "interacts with the environment" we do not mean only his physical surroundings. We mean in addition that he interacts with the whole of his cultural creations plus the many kinds of people with whom he has contact.

THE "SEGMENTED" ENVIRONMENT

Our picture of man in his environment is even more complex than we have thus far indicated because of the fact that the environment, physical, cultural, and social, is different for different segments of the population. Perhaps the simplest illustration of this fact is the contrast between the rural and urban segments of our own society, a contrast we will discuss at some length in a later chapter. Here we cite it simply for purposes of illustration. Until comparatively recently, at least, the rural dweller in the United States was influenced chiefly by the physical environment. His primary contacts were with the land, animals, crops, and the facts of soil and climatic variations. They were the significant aspects of his environment because they affected him directly. Of course, other things were important also: the cultural environment, for example, because it conditioned the food habits of the nation and because it provided techniques of marketing farm products. But his daily life was lived largely in terms of the physical environment; other aspects were a secondary influence.

In the case of the urban dweller, the environment is primarily cultural, that is, man-made. Apartment houses, subways, factories, newspapers, and all the other creations of man are more important by far in the city than are animals, plants, and the facts of geography. The things to which the urban dweller reacts in the significant areas of his life are far different from the things to which the rural dweller reacts.

One result of this is a difference in the ways of living which characterize our cities and our farms. People live differently in the two areas. Related to this difference of living are differences also in motivations and in attitudes: the two segments "think" differently in the sense of reacting differently to the same stimuli. Thus, for many years farmers and city dwellers had different ideas about politics, morality, the goals of life, and many other things. They were not "born different"—they developed differences in the process of interaction with different kinds of environment.

Yet obviously they are both members of one society and there must be a degree of co-operation if that society is to function adequately. Divisions of opinion in such matters as government, education, religion, and family life based wholly on rural-urban differences tend towards the disorganization of society. In recent times the differences in ways of living between farmer and city dweller have become much less marked than they used to be. The farmer has shared to a much greater extent in the cultural environment of the city through the functioning of radio, movies, periodicals, travel, and other means of contact. One result of this increasing similarity is increasing unity between the two segments we have been discussing.

The rural and the urban segments of society, then, furnish us with one example of reaction to differing environments and the results of such reaction. But those two segments are not the only ones which interact with different environments. Another sharp division, for instance, has been that between what we may call the "privileged" and the "underprivileged" segments. Thus, the wealthy person has contact with a far different cultural, social, and even physical environment from the poor person. He has access to the very highest developments of our own civilization; he can indulge in foreign travel and thus know other civilizations; he has the opportunity to study the cultures of the past. For the poorer person, most of these contacts do not exist. In fact, the poorer person may not even have access to necessities, such as the improved medical techniques which characterize our own times, many industrial products, and constructive leisure-time activities. All these simply are not a part of his environment because they have no significance for him. And again, differences of attitude, of motivations, and of ways of living accompany these differences of environmental significance.

There are, of course, a good many degrees of privilege based on wealth in our own times. It is not only the very wealthy and the very poor classes for whom the environment differs. It also varies for the many income groupings between those two extremes.

And wealth is not the only kind of differentiation. Race, nationality, religion, intelligence level, education, and many other factors also affect the realities of the environment with which we have contact. Naïve people sometimes ask, "If the environment is so important in the development of ways of living and ways of reacting, why aren't we all the same?" In the light of much of what we have said thus far in this book, that is rather a foolish question. But a *partial* answer to it is, "Because the environment is not the same for all of us, even though we live in the United States, in the same city, and even in the same neighborhood."

We have tried thus far to give some concrete meaning to the term *environment* by describing the kinds of enviroment, the fact of segmentation in the environment, and some of the results of segmentation. Let us now analyze more definitely *how* the environment operates as a factor in our basic interaction pattern.

ENVIRONMENTAL INFLUENCES

We are familiar with the fact that the environment, physical, social, and cultural, does exert an influence on human behavior. We *react* to that influence in various ways on the basis of our previous life experiences. Thus, we alter our conduct to avoid some influences and to make use of some other influences. New inventions, material and immaterial, affect us by permittting new ways of living. People with whom we associate stimulate us in various ways. Our problem now is to investigate some of the relationships between the number and kind of environmental influences to which we are subjected and certain aspects of man's life in association.

THE ENVIRONMENT AND SOCIAL DIFFERENTIATION

Social differentiation is the process whereby variations in our ways of living arise: variations in the cultural backgrounds which characterize the members of society, variations in social status, in social relationships, in achievements, in interests, and in many other factors. A society is *undifferentiated* when all its members follow pretty much the same way of life, are very similar in cultural background, believe the same things, and share many customs in common. Most of man's early groupings were undifferentiated aggregates. Some more recent groupings also exhibited very little differentiation; for example, the rural social organization characteristic of our own society a few generations ago was largely an undifferentiated type of organization. Yet differentiation is one of the outstanding facts of our contemporary way of life. How did it arise?

One very important factor in its development, though not the only factor, is the fact that our environment has presented us with an increasing variety of influences. Generally it is true that

> *An environment which provides a variety of influences tends to foster social differentiation.*

Considering first one of the physical aspects of the environment, suppose that it does provide several different kinds of food in abundance. Apart from some group conditioning strongly against or strongly in favor of one type of food, the tendency will be for some members of the grouping to like one kind better than another. They may like it better for any number of reasons: because it tastes better to them, because it is easier for them to prepare, because it looks better, or because it is scarce. Other members of the aggregate are attracted to other types of food. As these various segments of the population habitually use different kinds of food in different ways, they become differentiated from one another. Now this fact of differentiation in food habits may be of no particular significance in the case we have cited. We are simply using the situation as an example. The fact that the physical environment provided several kinds of food in abundance makes differentiation easier than if it had provided one kind of food only.

Suppose that the environment provides the possibility of several different vocations, as in the case of an aggregate living near the sea in a tropical climate. Vocations connected with the sea, with the forest, and with simple agriculture are all possible ways of life. Different segments of the aggregate develop different interests and follow varying occupations. There is no compulsion about this. There are, for instance, groupings which live near the sea which do not develop any seafaring way of life. The fact is that potentially different occupations are present, and the possibility of following different ways of life is inherent in the total situation. As the several occupational groupings become established, we have social differentiation based on specialization.

From a somewhat different approach, there is, of course, one biological fact of differentiation which leads, in turn, to social differentiation: the fact of sex. Women bear children and care for them. In early cultures childbearing did not produce the serious physical disablement in women which it often does in our own culture, with the result that usually it did not interrupt the course of the mother's way of life to the extent that it does in our times. But whatever specialized activities were connected with childbearing, they obviously became the specialized activities of women, not of men. Similarly, activities connected with suckling children and otherwise caring for them became the special work of women. We have, then, social differentiation based on a biological fact, a social differentiation which continues to the present day in the differing ways of life we think proper for women as compared with those we think proper for men. As the different "proprieties" for men and women become established in culture, they also become a type of influence emanating from the cultural environment.

So of certain other kinds of biological differentiation such as variations in skin color, in physical strength, in emotional organization. They all contributed to the adoption of different ways of life by different segments of the collectivity. Note that we are suggesting only that they *contributed* to differentiation. They are not the sole cause of differentiation, nor did they inevitably and in all instances lead to differentiation.

As society became more advanced, the variety of influences emanating from the cultural environment was tremendously increased through the process of invention. One important effect of invention is to bring to the surface potentialities inherent in the environment which were not utilized in simpler cultures. If, for example, a collecting economy existed in which hunting was the chief way of life, the potentialities of the environment for agriculture would be neglected. When techniques of agriculture were invented, the agricultural potentialities of the environment become active stimuli toward cultivation as a way of life. In this case it is the cultural environment as developed through invention plus the potentialities of the physical environment, that is, its suitability for cultivation, which combine to produce differentiation.

Much the same thing may be said of inventions relating to the herding and breeding of animals, together with other aspects of animal domestication. Domestication is a much more efficient use of animal life than is hunting, because domestication involves the creation of animal life, with some assurance of a relatively stable food supply, whereas hunting involves the destruction of animal life and an unstable food supply. At least three possibilities of economic development, then, exist in the aggregate: hunting, agriculture, and the herding of animals.

Sometimes this differentiation was so marked that it led to conflict and the splitting of the original aggregate into several groupings. The story of Cain and Abel in the Old Testament is an echo of the conflict between the agricultural and the herding ways of life. But conflict and the splitting of the aggregate were not inevitable: differentiated ways of life could, and did, exist in the same groupings of people.

Invention, then, is one very important factor tending to increase the number and variety of influences operating through the cultural environment. Its effect is to increase the complexity of that environment. Of equal importance with invention, during the later development of mankind, is the factor of culture contact. As one grouping establishes contact with another grouping, the result is a broadening of the cultural environment. Instead of the influences of our own culture operating as the chief influences, we find those of the contacted culture also producing an effect. This statement is true whether the culture contacts were antagonistic, resulting in conflict, or whether they were friendly. In either case, some new influences were introduced. Of course we do not mean to suggest that all these new influences were enthusiastically welcomed and forthwith adopted. As we noted earlier, the power of our own customs is often strong enough to create attitudes of superiority, fear, or superstition which prevent our learning new ways of life. The process is more subtle than outright adoption or rejection. One grouping *reacts* in some way to the customs of the contacted group: it rejects some of their practices, adopts others, and permits a gradual "seepage" into its own way of life of still others. Very often new ways of life penetrate the old without our knowledge. And even if we determine to reject the new, that very determination, and the agencies we set up to assure rejection, themselves become new parts of our own culture.

The influences emanating from culture contact, then, do not mean that inevitably we shall imitate the new culture. They do mean that we may set up new patterns of reaction which differentiate us from our ancestors. And they also mean that there may be differentiation in our own grouping because some of us will accept new ways, others reject them; some will support our determination to prevent the acceptance of new ways, others will oppose that determination.

The significance of the cultural and physical environment in all this is obvious: it provides varied influences in great number, and the reaction of segments of our society to these influences fosters social differentiation. We can apply this same general analysis to differentiation in specialized fields. Thus, our environment has expanded tremendously in the last few generations through the invention of new techniques and through expanded contacts with other groupings. Resources in the physical environment of the United States which were all here before white civilization reached these shores had very little influence on the culture of the Indians. Because of our new techniques, they have become very important to us. Knowing how to use them is, of course, a prerequisite to using them; as we use them, we elaborate our techniques in many specialized ways; specialization in industry grows almost beyond our capacity to understand it; and specialization in industry leads to social differentiation of many kinds.

Similarly, contact with other cultures in our times is commonplace: the interchange of knowledge, customs, artifacts, and "mentifacts" is a daily occurrence. Immigrants, the children of immigrants, long-time "native" Americans, Negroes, Jews: the people who make up our population are vastly differentiated in background. Influences of many different kinds thus characterize our contemporary cultural environment.

It is not surprising, then, that our urban civilization presents the spectacle of a huge amount of differentiation. We shall discuss some of the results of this differentiation in Part II. It affects the functioning of a number of institutions in the social organization and raises a number of other problems.

THE ENVIRONMENT AND SOCIAL CHANGE

The environment is related to social change in somewhat the same way in which it is related to social differentiation. *Social change* is a term used to describe variations in, or modifications of, any aspect of social processes, social patterns, social interaction, or social organization.[2] It is both a broad term and also a neutral term because it does not imply that the change is either good or bad. It implies nothing about the quality of the change; it simply takes account of change as one of the facts of social life.

The relationship between the environment and social change is somewhat as follows:

> *An environment which provides a variety of influences*
> *tends to increase the rate of social change.*

If there are few influences arising from the environment (both physical and cultural environments are included), there are few occasions for changing the established ways of living and ways of thinking. Whatever adjustments and group behavior patterns have been established in reaction to a few influences tend to continue with relatively little modification. Very probably there never was an environment with no influences towards change whatsoever; nor was there ever a culture which did not modify its ways of living to some extent. The point about an environment rich in stimuli is that it tends to hasten the *rate* of social change; in a simpler environment, the rate of change is slower. The several factors we discussed in connection with social differentiation are also important here. Thus, the development of new techniques through invention, contact with differing cultures, and differentiation itself within the

[2]Adapted from H. P. Fairchild (Ed.), *Dictionary of Sociology*, p. 277. Philosophical Library, New York, 1944.

aggregate, are all factors which expand the cultural environment with which the aggregate has contact. In that way they increase the number of influences to which it is exposed, increasing the rate of social change as a consequence.

For example, if we assume a group to be entirely agricultural in its way of life, we should not expect it to respond to stimuli relating to commerce and industry. Those stimuli would not be significant because they relate to an area of life not germane to the chief interests of the group concerned. But a group which was both agricultural and industrial would be subjected to, and would be responsive to, influences related to both fields of activity. Differentiation of vocational interest within the group broadens the significant environment in the sense that it makes important more different kinds of stimuli in the environment. Consequent adjustments to the newly significant influences increase the rate of change.

Again, it is commonly said that every group is *ethnocentric*, that is, convinced that its own way of life, limited as it may be, is the best way of life. Ethnocentrism retards the rate of change by setting up a barrier between the group and certain environmental stimuli. On the other hand, groups which have had a great deal of prolonged contact with "foreign" cultures are much less ethnocentric than groups with limited contacts.[3] Contact with other cultures, which, again, is a form of expanding the cultural environment, since new elements from foreign cultures become part of the group cultural environment, offsets the ethnocentric factor.

Our own society is characterized by a very rapid rate of social change. The reasons for that fact should now be obvious: invention, differentiation, and contacts with other cultures have all reached a high point. The resulting effects on social change are what we should expect.

Our rapid rate of social change also raises problems for social organization which we shall discuss at length in Part II. Let us content ourselves here with noting the fact that we cannot have the advantages of invention, differentiation, and culture contact without also having the disadvantages, temporarily at least, of instability and social disorganization which follow a rapid rate of change.

[3]H. E. Barnes and H. Becker, *Social Thought from Lore to Science*, Vol. I, pp. 13–17, 141–149. Heath, Boston, 1938.

The Environment and Social Control

Because the environment influences the process of differentiation and the rate of social change, it also influences the need for social control.

An environment which provides a variety of influences tends to increase the need for social control.

We have already mentioned the fact that there are two kinds of social control: (1) control exercised by one grouping over another grouping by force or the threat of force; and (2) self-control or co-operative control of a group by itself, in accordance with an accepted plan or system of ideals. The second kind is also referred to as societal self-control or societal self-direction. Conditions of environmental influence strongly affect the need for both these kinds of control.

The *first* type of social control, embodied in the control of one group or portion of a group over another group, in turn has two forms: *repressive* social control and *co-ordinative* social control.

Repressive social control exists when the controlling segment tries to prevent deviations from what it considers the "right" or the "best" forms of conduct. We try to prevent the appearance of the conduct of which we disapprove. Thus, we try to control crime by preventing the existence or appearance of criminal conduct. If we were successful, the whole category of criminals would disappear from among us. When we try to enforce laws relating to the driving of automobiles, we do so in the hope that the reckless and dangerous driver will disappear from our midst. So of every program of repressive social control: its aim is to cause the *disappearance* of the conduct controlled.

Co-ordinative social control, on the other hand, has quite a different purpose. Its aim is to enable various behavior patterns to *continue in existence* with a minimum of conflict. It does not attempt to eradicate those behavior patterns from society: that is the aim of repressive social control.

For example, we have different religions, different political parties, different interest groups, and many other examples of differing behavior patterns existing in our own culture. Without some kind of co-ordinative social control, conflict among these would be almost inevitable. We therefore establish general regulations which in effect set up a framework of rules applying to all the different ways of life, restricting them in some respects and guaranteeing them rights in other respects. This is, of course, control of one group in the society by the society itself; it is control exerted by one grouping over another grouping by force or the threat of force. But the purpose of the regulations is not to cause the disappearance of the conduct characteristic of one or the other of the controlled groupings; it is to enable that conduct to exist along with many other types of conduct.

Both repressive and co-ordinative social control are related to environmental influences. Thus, a totalitarian state sets up a very complicated system of repressive social control. Its purpose is to isolate the people of the totalitarian state from different stimuli which might reach them from other areas. If the program goes further, and other nations are destroyed or subjugated, stimuli leading to any other type of conduct or thought than the approved type disappear.

On the other hand, a democratic state which permits, and in some cases welcomes, differentiation in ways of living and ways of thinking is thereby fostering variation in stimuli. The people of a democratic state can think and act as they will, within broad limits, and they can contact other aggregates freely. Rapid social change is one result of such free contact. Another result is potential conflict between different segments of the population which follow different interests and ways of life. Avoidance of much of that conflict comes when we set up systems of co-ordinative social control.

Within the past fifteen years or so we have observed a great increase in co-ordinative social controls in the United States, even apart from the specialized controls of the Second World War. Legislation has given to the Federal government increasing powers over business, industry, and organized labor. There has, of course, been a great deal of opposition to such increase in government control. Much of that opposition has arisen from a misunderstanding of the fact that the major portion of our recent government control has been co-ordinative rather than repressive. People who have insisted that the United States was "becoming fascist" because of the admitted increase in government control have been especially guilty of that misunderstanding. Most of us would object very strongly to any degree of *repressive* control by the government which had for its object the destruction of business or of labor unions. In the case of *co-ordinative* control, which has for its aim not their destruction but the establishment of a framework within which they can both continue to exist with a minimum of conflict, our objections ought to be less violent. We may not be enthusiastic for control, even of the co-ordinative type, but we can understand its necessity in a highly differentiated and rapidly changing society such as ours is.

Another source of objection to government control is simply the fact that it is relatively new in the United States. People who are by no means senile can look back to the time when we did not have such a thing, a time toward the close of the period of our predominantly rural social organization. In a rural type of organization no great amount of co-ordinative social control is necessary because of its relative stability and its general lack of variation in environmental stimuli. Many of the processes of rural life are essentially repetitive in nature, and were common to a large majority of the rural population. Hence the doctrine of *laissez faire*, which advocated as little government regulation as possible, could be almost literally applied. The processes of social life could be left with little formal control, precisely because they were repetitive, well understood, and widely accepted. There was little conflict between different ways of living and thinking.

But we no longer live in that kind of rural environment. We may have benefited by our transition to an urban way of life. We have more comforts, a higher standard of living, a higher level of education, and so on. Together with these benefits, however, have inevitably come problems, one of which is the conflict, actually now in evidence and potentially even more bitter, among differentiated segments of our society. We cannot have the benefits without also suffering from the problems, unless we take appropriate steps to control the problem situations. An increase in government control and in other kinds of co-ordinative control is one device by which we attempt to do this. To object to it simply because "our ancestors had no such thing as this" is to think in a shallow manner.

So much for our first general type of social control: the control of one group in society or one segment of society by another segment. The second general type of social control, called variously societal self-control or societal self-direction or societal planning, is also related to the type of environment. We can develop programs for societal self-direction only when we have some understanding of how society reacts to environmental influences, some understanding of the significance of such influences, and some understanding of methods by which we can work together to control our reactions. We must have not only people capable of understanding all these things, but also a cultural environment which will provide us with tools of understanding, an environment whose techniques of production permit us to have leisure and freedom from the necessity of constant effort simply to get the bare means of subsistence; and we must have a society in which orderly and intelligent processes of behavior have been developed. Above all, we must have people who are motivated in the direction of individual and societal self-control.

It is not at all clear that our society has all these prerequisites for self-direction. If not, they are a goal toward which we may work.

THE CONTEMPORARY ENVIRONMENT

Before closing our general discussion of the environment, it would be well to consider some aspects of our contemporary environment.

First, what kinds of environment most affect us? Our discussion up to this point should indicate that both the cultural and the social environment are significant. The geographical environment affects us only indirectly, because we have developed a number of devices which shield us from contact with the bare facts of climate, weather, animals, and the other physical facts of our surroundings. Changes in weather, both seasonal and occasional, are of little importance to us because we automatically take advantage of such cultural devices as clothing, heating systems, specialized foods, medicines, all-weather vehicles, and many other things which permit us to follow the normal course of living in spite of weather changes. We may suggest, then, that

In contemporary society the geographical environment tends to be of decreasing importance in influencing man's ways of living.

As to the relative significance of the cultural compared with the social environment, it is difficult to generalize. Certainly, as we have suggested before, the people who surround us in infancy and childhood exert a powerful, if often unconscious, influence on us. Doubtless also this influence of people continues to a great extent throughout our lives. On the other hand, our culture has developed so many means of mass influence, such as the radio, the movies, periodicals, books, and others, and these means are so efficient and so widespread, that their influence is often greater than that of our immediate associates. In fact, our immediate associates are themselves affected by the attitudes and the values disseminated by such means of mass influence, with the result that the people who surround us often simply reinforce the influence of impersonal cultural devices.

For example, it is currently fashionable to blame parents for the delinquency of their children (an example we shall use several times in this book). Such placing of blame assumes two things, both incorrect assumptions.

1. It assumes that the pattern of family living is of the isolated type common in the rural social organization of a few generations ago when the family was almost the sole source of influence on children. Physical separation from neighbors and the absence of the means of mass influence mentioned earlier meant that the children acquired most of their behavior patterns from their parents. If, in that case, children were delinquent there was some logic in tracing the fault to their parents, although even then the logic was not absolutely unquestionable. In our own times, when the urban family lives not in isolation but in close physical contact with other families; when organizations, such as the school, the informal "gang," and more formal clubs of various kinds, begin early to influence the child; when patterns of behavior are disseminated by popular entertainment and other mass-influence devices,—in such times the parents soon lose direct control of their children. Under such circumstances it is hardly accurate to blame parents exclusively for the wrongdoings of children.

2. The second incorrect assumption is that the modern parent should be so motivated "by nature," or in some other mysterious way, that he will make his children the center of his existence and will make every effort to "bring them up in the way they should

go." Certainly he is not so motivated by the cultural influences of our contemporary society. On the contrary, current mores stress the importance of display, ostentation, sophistication, money, possessions, entertainment, and almost anything else *except* devotion to and care of children. If the cultural environment does not provide the parent with motivations in the direction of child nurture and care, where shall he get such motivations? Obviously many parents get them nowhere at all, with precisely the results we should expect. To blame parents for neglecting their children and thereby conducting themselves in precisely the way that our culture insists is the smart way to conduct themselves is pure thoughtlessness. Parents are children themselves—children of their culture and their times.

All this is to indicate very strongly that the cultural environment is a very powerful influence among us today—perhaps more powerful than the social environment, since the people who surround us reflect the cultural environment. The implications of that situation for societal self-direction are obvious.

ADAPTATION TO THE ENVIRONMENT

The idea of adaptation to the environment, and its accompanying doctrine of the "survival of the fittest," has become part of the folklore of America in the sense that it is an idea commonly cited as a pseudoscientific justification for existing conditions. Because it is one of the beliefs which characterize our culture, we must pay more attention to it than the doctrine itself might warrant.

Let us first make the point that there is no doubt whatsoever that human beings, as well as animals, adapt themselves to the environment. But they adapt themselves in radically different ways, and the environments to which they adapt themselves are very different. These statements deserve further discussion.

We are using the term *adapt* in its usual meaning of "to make suitable." Similarly, *adaptation* means simply "the process of making suitable." In connection with the phrase *adaptation to the environment*, the term means that the animal or human organism and the surroundings within which that organism lives become mutually suitable to each other. Adaptation, then, implies some modification in the organism, or in the environment, or in both. A good deal of the confusion apparent in our folklore arises from the fact that we are not always clear as to what these modifications are, or in what they take place.

In the case of animal evolution, including human evolution in the dim past, it is the animal itself, the organism as such, which is modified so as to be made suitable to the environment. Without some such change in the animal itself, it would not survive. If it does not modify or cannot modify, it dies. As we suggested earlier in this book, that is what happened to certain manlike forms a million years or so in the past. It also happened to many animal forms. Some millions of years ago much of the intermountain region of the United States was a tropical forest. We find the fossils of forest animals and of marine life which lived in tropical seas where mountains and arid plains now stand. The animals which we now know only as fossils were once suited to the environment of this area. When the environment changed, they could not modify their form, structure, and biological habits to meet the new conditions and so they ceased to exist.

We call this kind of animal adaptation *passive adaptation*, implying thereby that the organism more or less passively accepts the facts and the influences of the environment. Passive adaptation leads to natural selection, the mechanism of which we discussed in Chapter III. Let us summarize briefly that mechanism. The physical environment presents certain conditions of climate, food supply, and animal life. Some animals are more favorably endowed than others in terms of the given environment: their physical equipment is such that they can meet the conditions of the environment more effectively than can other animals. They therefore live longer than those less favorably endowed and they produce more offspring. With the passage of time the number of well-endowed animals increases and the number of poorly-endowed decreases. Thus the proportion of the one type tends to exceed very greatly the proportion of the other types; in fact, the other types may disappear entirely. If that happens, we have the situation referred to as the "survival of the fittest," a term which quite accurately describes the mechanism of natural selection *under the conditions of passive adaptation and in subhuman species.*

But when the term is applied to human adaptation and to contemporary human association, it becomes relatively meaningless because of the different type of adaptation and the different environment involved in contemporary human association. The concept of the survival of the fittest applied to contemporary society appealed to the individualism of the later nineteenth-century Victorians in England. We can, perhaps, follow their line of reasoning: they had "survived" in the sense of having reached the point of wielding a great deal of power and prestige. If it were true that the fittest survived, then obviously the nineteenth-century Victorians were the fittest, since they had survived. It was a pleasant thought, no doubt, and incidentally one which has occurred to many other groupings at a good many different periods of human existence, though it was not always expressed in just the terms we have used.

Their mistake lay in assuming that the word *fittest* in the phrase "survival of the fittest" meant something like "absolutely the best possible kind of human being." Much the same idea motivates advocates of "survival-of-the-fittest" doctrines today. But unfortunately the phrase does not mean that, even when it is applied to animal species. All it means is "best adapted to a given environment," or fittest *in terms of a given environment*. The mechanism of passive adaptation will produce the fittest in that limited sense; but it will not produce the ultimate and finally "most fit" animal or human being *in terms of every possible environment*. An individual adapted to the liberal intellectual atmosphere of the later Victorian environment would hardly be adapted to our own environment. And there is no point in arguing which environment is "better." We may, if we wish, insist that the Victorian environment was better than our own. But we are not discussing the relative worth of the environments. We are discussing the mechanism of the "survival of the fittest."

To approach the matter from another direction, most of us would agree that the Nazi environment, which, incidentally, we should also evaluate as "worse than our own," was an efficient selective agent. It is, of course, an example of a cultural environment rather than the natural environment which is operative in the case of natural selection. We use the term *social selection* to refer to the selective process when it is the cultural or social environment, or both, rather than the natural environment which is significant in the process. In modern society, social selection is so much more important than natural selection that we can almost neglect the factor of natural selection entirely. When we speak of the "survival of the fittest" in modern society we must mean survival through the operation of the cultural and social environments if we mean anything at all, which is sometimes doubtful. The Nazi cultural environment, then, was a very efficient selective agent.

The Nazis found a good many people in Germany who were adapted to the democratic environment and way of life. This adaptation to democracy was not confined to the people of any one class: they were workers, students, intellectuals, artists, politicians, and many others. They refused to adapt themselves to the new Nazi environment of stupidity and brutality. As a result, many of them were killed, either outright or through confinement in concentration camps. If this process of social selection had continued for a generation or so, there would have been "selected" for survival a type of human being much changed from the one we associate with the intellectual, democratic way of life. But that new type would have been the "fittest" in terms of the Nazi environment because it would be the net result of social selection in terms of the Nazi environment. We should hardly, however, call it the fittest in the sense of the highest type of human being, because it would have lacked the elements of intelligence, altruism, emotional balance, and many other characteristics that we cherish.

This close relationship between the term "survival of the fittest" and the specific type of environment is not understood clearly by those who use the term loosely. For example, we sometimes hear people deplore the existence of social-welfare programs in our culture on the grounds that such programs "enable the unfit to survive" and thereby weaken our population. The implication is that if we did away with all social-welfare programs the processes of selection would operate, and we should presently have the "fittest" population in the world. But fittest in what sense? Unfortunately the idea is usually presented in the form of a very general statement without concrete details. We cannot, therefore, be sure of just what is meant by the term *fittest*. Usually the impression is given that the fittest would all be highly intelligent, moral, and physically well-developed specimens. But there is no evidence that the free operation of selection in society would produce that kind of person. It might, for example, produce a physically healthy person who had survived because he was without any morality in the sense that he had little or no regard for his associates and hence did not hesitate to survive at the expense of the weaker people around him. If he survived through lack of morality, there seems no reason to believe that he would automatically develop morality after he had survived. If he did not, we should have a society completely disorganized by the constant conflict among strong men without the controls of ethics.

Again, the selective process might produce a type of men who were "intelligent" in the narrow sense of being more clever and more self-interested than their fellows, since the clever man often wins out over the merely strong man. But intelligence, in the sense of cleverness, without morality is even more dangerous than is physical strength without morality.

In short, we do not know what kind of person selection would produce; but we doubt whether it would produce a "perfect" individual, given the present conditions of our cultural environment and the present pattern of interaction among human beings. Would the free operation of selection produce a better population group than we now have, considered as a grouping rather than as individuals? Very probably not, since, under present circumstances, we manage to produce some people who are physically excellent, others who are morally excellent, and others who are of a very high grade of intelligence and of skill. Sometimes, in fact, we even find these characteristics present in the same individual. The *society* obviously has these human characteristics of intelligence, physical health, and morality as part of its total population resources, even though not every individual exhibits them. It would appear that what we need is a program which will develop all these characteristics in more individuals, as we have developed them in the aggregate. But such a program implies more planning, not less; it implies a greater degree of intelligent and deliberate action and a lesser degree of reliance on unguided processes of selection.

Another interesting point in connection with this whole question of survival of the fittest rests in the fact that we do not know what our surroundings will be like in the future. Any plan that we set up must take that fact into account; any advocacy of unguided selection must also face it. Conceivably an atomic bomb or some other destructive agency might leave large portions of the world a wilderness with the result that the qualities of physical health, individual initiative, disregard of the rights of weaker men, and other "animal" characteristics would be very important for survival. On the other hand, no such catastrophe may occur, and we may continue much as we are at present with some elaboration. In that case, intelligence, co-operation, and skill will be much more significant than the animal characteristics. Again, there may be quite unforeseeable changes in our surroundings.

Our problem, then, in relation to survival really is to develop an individual who has as many different qualities, abilities, and skills as possible, so that he may be equipped to survive in any kind of environment. Until such individuals are developed, human co-operation in which the stronger assist the weaker to survival is a definite necessity.

Throughout this long discussion we have been dealing mostly with the concept of *passive* adaptation, which has been characteristic of animal evolution. There is, however, another type of adaptation through which the environment is made suitable to the organism rather than the organism to the environment. We call this type of adaptation *active* adaptation, since essentially what happens is that the environment becomes a stimulus to activity on the part of the organism, and that activity is adaptive in nature. Instead of permitting the conditions of the environment wholly to control our actions or to change our biological organization in some way, we proceed to develop techniques which will enable us to control the effects of the environment and to live pretty much as we wish in spite of the environment.

Of course we are all familiar with this process of active adaptation. We do not grow coats of heavy fur in winter; instead we put on some kind of protective clothing. We do not hibernate in caves during cold weather; instead we erect houses with elaborate heating systems, and invent means of transportation which will operate in all kinds of weather. We do not confine ourselves exclusively to the fertile areas of the earth; we live where we will because we can make all areas suitable.

Active adaptation is characteristic of the human aggregate, as it is not characteristic of any other aggregate. When we suggest that we must all adapt ourselves to the environment in some way, we refer to this kind of active adaptation, not to the passive type of adaptation which involves complete submission to environmental conditions. The geographical environment as a *limiting* factor is relatively unimportant; its function as a *stimulus* to invention is much more important. Invention elaborates the cultural environment and, as we noted earlier, it is the cultural environment that is the most significant type of environment in our times.

PROBLEMS OF ADAPTATION

We have already shown that our contemporary environment is a complex one. Contact among cultures, inventions, differentiation of population, all increase this complexity. It is also true that all these go beyond the confines of any one nation or any one society. It is literally true that we live in a "world environment." With the exception of a few primitives who live in isolation, the world population forms one vast aggregate. It is not as yet a society because it is not characterized by unanimity of purpose or wide sharing of common ideals and ways of living. But its segments are in such close contact that it does form an aggregate. Rapidity of travel, exchange of goods, other relationships both friendly and antagonistic, all force us into contact.

Before the First and the Second World War there was some tendency to believe that this contact would automatically have good results. It was assumed that the closeness of nations, brought about by such factors as the airplane and radio, would somehow become the "neighborliness" of nations. In spite of the Second World War, some remnants of that attitude remain. Its mistake lies in its belief that technological progress also implies social progress. Technological progress is neutral and impersonal; it may have good or ill results. An airplane which can reach our shores in a few hours from a foreign country may be used as a weapon of attack or as a means of transporting friendly ambassadors. The fact that the "shrinking of the size of the world" makes us nearer in space to foreign nations does not mean automatically that we shall understand those nations or that they will understand us better. It may mean conflict as well as co-operation.

Potentially, of course, our nearness to other nations is an important step toward co-operation with them. But it is only an instrument which we and they can use for co-operation, if we will. In addition to that instrument, there must be motivations which will actually bring us into closer co-operation. We are in process of adjusting fairly well to the complexity within a nation. We are now faced with an even more complex world environment. Again, the problem is the same; it is only the pattern which is different.

READINGS

PENDELL, E. (Editor). *Society Under Analysis*. The Jacques Cattell Press, Lancaster, Pennsylvania, 1942. Chapter 4, "Geographic and Geological Regularities."

TOYNBEE, ARNOLD. *A Study of History* (Abridgment by D. C. Somervell). Oxford University Press, New York, 1947. Chapter VII, "The Challenge of the Environment," a discussion of the results of environmental stimuli.

HUNTINGTON, ELLSWORTH. *Mainsprings of Civilization*. John Wiley & Sons, Inc., New York, 1945. Discussions of "the role of biological inheritance and physical environment in influencing the course of history."

CULTURE

WE HAVE MENTIONED culture a number of times up to this point, and we have discussed in a very general way its meaning and functions. Our purpose is now to analyze it more in detail.

THE FACT OF CULTURE

ORIGINS OF CULTURE

A summary statement, in the form of a principle, of the origins of culture reads as follows:

> People living in association for an extended period of time
> develop standardized and generally accepted ways
> of living and ways of thinking.[1]

The totality of these ways of living and ways of thinking makes up the culture of a people. This definition of culture differs from that used in ordinary speech. In the social sciences, culture does not mean *only* music, art, literature, and the "finer things of life," though they are included in the concept. Culture includes all the products of the interaction of a group with its environment, the "bad" products as well as the "good." It includes all the creations of man, material and immaterial, constructive and destructive.

These things, however, must be generally accepted by the grouping in order to be part of its culture. Ways of living and ways of thinking which are characteristic of isolated individuals only or of very small segments of a larger grouping are not part of the culture of that grouping. We usually refer to them as *deviations* from the general culture.

[1] J. E. Cuber, "Are there Principles of Sociology?" *American Sociological Review,* June, 1941.

111

Culture is one of the products of association among men. Recall the discussion of the effect of association on the *individual* in Chapter IV. Briefly, we suggested there that association in groups transforms the individual from biohom to human being by developing in him what we call "human nature" or "personality." The effect of association on the *aggregate* is somewhat similar: it gives rise to a standardized way of reacting common to all members of the aggregate. The "humanized" individual is one whose patterns of behavior have been modified so that his habits are "human" in terms of our own definition of "human." As the individual becomes more human through association and thus integrates the several aspects of his personality, so the aggregate becomes more integrated through association and the consequent development of culture.

It is also a fact that culture, while it is a product of people's living in association, also becomes a reality apart from those people. It acquires and maintains an existence in its own right.

The culture of an aggregate tends to acquire an existence independent of that of the members of the aggregate.

For example, we are born not into a bare physical world but into a cultural world in which we are presented with a number of ways of living and ways of thinking which exist as independent facts. They are as much facts as are the facts of the physical world. We must adjust to them, precisely as we must adjust to the facts of the physical world. We may modify those ways of living and ways of thinking in the course of our lives, but we do not create them. This heritage from the past appears in the form of artifacts and of "mentifacts," in the form of buildings, of books, of symbols, and of everyday customs. Thus we do not create language in the sense of discovering that meanings may be given to certain sounds. We use a language which has been passed down to us from people who have lived before us. As we use that language, it changes gradually through the addition of new words and the dropping of some old words, by developing different customs relating to grammar and pronunciation, and in many other ways. The point is that what we have done is to "work over" a heritage from the past, not to create a wholly new tool of communication.

The same thing may be said of other aspects of culture. We do not create our customs and laws; they come to us from the past and they bind us to the past, even though we may gradually change them. Even in the field of mechanical invention, an area in which we believe that we differ a great deal from our ancestors, our products have been developed from and built on the investigations, the knowledge, and the machines of our fathers. We are not, of course, completely unoriginal. We are original, but our originality consists in large part of elaboration of past products. That is true even of the atomic bomb, basic foundations for the development of which were laid many years ago.

We are sometimes prone to overlook the importance of this heritage from the past. We are apt to become so much immersed in our own times that we miss the significance of our cultural heritage. A great part of the stability of any society comes from this body of material which has been passed down to it. A great deal of the leisure which we have and which enables us to devote our time to scientific investigation, art, and similar activities, comes to us because our ancestors have given us a high level of cultural advancement. When we break completely with our past, or when it is destroyed in war and revolution, we appreciate something of the difficulty we should have in starting over with no heritage whatsoever.

One of the tasks of present-day education is that of making young people more conscious of their cultural heritage, a factor which should bind us together into a more strongly unified society, in spite of surface differences. Our present specialized ways of life, the rapidity of social change, and the differentiated backgrounds of our population all tend to have dividing or segmenting effects. To the extent that we appreciate and share in not only our American culture but also the culture of those European countries which have been important in shaping American culture, we can offset some of the segmenting effects of our present way of life.

TRANSMISSION OF CULTURE

Inherent in what we have been saying is the principle that

> *The group transmits some portion of the basic content of its culture from one generation to the next.*

Formal methods of transmission exist in every group. Examples are educational systems, religious institutions, historical societies,

traditional exercises, written constitutions, and so on. One definition of education commonly used by sociologists is "the system
which transmits knowledge to be learned and behavior patterns to
be imitated." Similar purposes are part of the program of such
organizations as the Daughters of the American Revolution,
American Legion, constitutional leagues, and similar bodies. In so
far as these programs are effective, they are part of the formal means
of transmitting culture.

Our own civilization has at its command a number of devices for
the formal transmission of culture which were not known in earlier
societies. Two of these are an elaborate system of writing and the
printing press. Without them, many of the detailed cultural products of the past few generations, such as mathematics, results of
scientific discoveries and investigations, legal decisions, and historical material, would not have come down to us in as complete
form as they have. Similarly, without them our own culture would
be available to the future only partially. As for our own times being
less susceptible to past influences than other times, the reverse is
true; we are more susceptible because of our more efficient means
of recording and transmission. This situation has not been apparent
to any great extent in the less important details of culture such as
customs and fashions; it has, however, had a great deal of effect in
the important areas of industry and scientific research.

Informal methods of transmission also exist in every culture.
They range from simple word-of-mouth advice passed on by older
to younger members of the aggregate, to newspapers, periodicals,
the movies, and the radio. In addition, much unconscious imitation
also takes place and operates to transmit behavior patterns. The
"customs of the country" attract us, and we follow them in many
areas of life.

There are also, of course, in most cultures some influences which
tend to break down the transmission of culture unmodified. In the
past, as we noted in connection with our discussion of the environment, one of the most potent of those modifying influences has been
contact with other cultures. Since the commercial way of life
greatly facilitates culture contact, it has tended toward relatively
full and easy modification of culture patterns. Much of the progress
of ancient Greece arose from the fact that it was a commercial
country.

These same factors are important in fostering cultural change in our own times. To them we may add a third, namely, the special interests of certain segments of our society. Advertising, a very potent influence, often helps toward the adoption of new ideas and new modes of conduct. Other pressure groups exert influences in the direction of their own interests and thus also may lead to changes in our reaction patterns. It is interesting to note in this connection the way in which smoking and drinking by women have come to be accepted as "right" or at least "permissible." Liquor and tobacco advertisements at first showed women only near cigarettes or liquor, then touching them, then holding them, and finally using them. Some length of time, of course, elapsed between the successive stages. We came to accept the new ideas gradually, a little at a time, until we were agreeable to the whole pattern, even though it was a significant change from past habits and standards.

In a somewhat similar way the idea that it was important to be sophisticated was gradually foisted on us. The dictionary definition of *sophisticated* still emphasizes as meanings of the word such things as "adulterated," or "deprived of original simplicity," or "made artificial," all of them meanings with a "bad" connotation. We usually do not think of sophistication in those terms, however, because modern advertising has long used the word to mean "highly cultured" or "well-informed as to the most civilized modes of conduct." When we are told that we are sophisticated, we take it in a complimentary way; we do not assume that it means we have been made artificial.

Advertising, then, not only has changed the meaning of a word, which is a fairly common occurrence, but it has made us value a behavior pattern which our fathers would have criticized as unnatural and artificial.

We find, then, that there are tendencies in our own culture, as there have been in most cultures, which operate to further the transmission of some behavior patterns unmodified, and others which operate to modify our behavior patterns. That situation brings about a condition under which

Not all culture content is transmitted unchanged;
there is some tendency toward modification.

The mere process of continued association itself leads to culture modification in some areas. New inventions appear with great rapidity and are quickly accepted in modern society. We have come to like new models of automobiles, refrigerators, radios, houses, and other cultural products. This ready acceptance of new mechanical inventions was not generally characteristic of past cultures. We can find in our own recent history a good many examples of skepticism regarding new inventions. The steamboat, the locomotive, the telephone, and the radio were all regarded as amusing eccentricities not so very long ago. Much of this past skepticism came from a lack of information and from a lack of imagination. Thus it is said that when the telephone was first demonstrated to one of the Presidents of the United States, he said, "It is interesting, but of what use will it ever be?" Not a very imaginative outlook!

Our own ready acceptance of new mechanical inventions springs partly from the fact that we have become accustomed to new things which actually function efficiently, and partly from the fact that we, as an aggregate, have a widespread, if superficial, knowledge of mechanics. We have also been led to expect great things of science, an expectation that offsets whatever lack of inherent imagination we may have.

This proneness to the ready acceptance of mechanical invention tends very strongly in the direction of culture modification. For we not only accept a new invention, but also adjust our way of life to the existence of the new invention after we have accepted it. The automobile has worked a change in our highway system, in our occupational distribution, in our police system, in our attitude towards law, in our beliefs about the proper way to spend Sunday, and so in a widening circle of influence until many seemingly unrelated aspects of existence have been affected. Much the same thing may be said of new ideas and their effects on culture modification; new theories of education, of government, of religion, all produce something in the way of reaction.

The mere fact of continued association, then, tends in the direction of culture change as it gives rise to invention and elaboration. In addition to that factor, expansions of, and developments in, the cultural environment with which we interact may compel some modifications of our general patterns. We noted in the preceding chapter that our expanding environment has brought us into contact with nations and peoples far removed from us geographically. We are now in the process of adjusting to that fact. Our traditional American emphasis, since the early days of our nation, has been on "isolationism," on "keeping out of foreign entanglements." A good many people would like to see a policy of isolationism maintained if we can maintain it. If we cannot, and European and Oriental affairs are forced upon our attention, a readjustment of behavior will be necessary which may involve a drastic change from the isolation of the past. Our new environment is thus apparently forcing us in the direction of an important culture modification.

Culture, then, is not a fixed entity. Some portions of it change; other portions persist with little modification. Can we analyze this process further?

MODIFICATION OF CULTURE

How is it that some portions of culture resist modification to a greater extent than others? In general,

> *Those portions of its culture which a group believes to be related to survival are more resistant to modification.*

The term *survival* is complex in meaning. Basically, it denotes simply "continuing existence as an organism," a meaning we may refer to as *biological survival*. If a group believes that the continuing existence of its members depends on the preservation of any culture trait unchanged, there will, of course, be a strong resistance to change.

Every aggregate develops some kind of food-getting techniques which are obviously important to biological survival. Any attempt to interfere with food-getting techniques or with the environmental resources on which the techniques operate will arouse strong opposition. It does not make much difference what the real effects of interference would be; it might, in fact, actually improve the food situation. If the group *believes* that such suggestions threaten its food supply, it will react adversely to them. Often religious or magical authority is invoked to maintain the system of food-getting.

Thus in the Old Testament, the prophet Amos, together with other Hebrew prophets, denounced the growing commercialism of the Hebrews on the grounds that the nomadic way of life was the only one pleasing to Jehovah, who would withdraw his favor from a people following the commercial way of life. This is an example of religion defending the traditional food-getting techniques. It was not fully effective, since some of the Hebrews did follow the new way of life, but some others maintained the traditional mores.

Most aggregates also develop a family system which assures the biological survival of the group through reproduction. The same resistance appears toward innovations in the family system that we have noted in connection with the food-getting system. In our own times, admittedly, there have been great alterations in our patterns of family living. The size of families has declined, divorce has become more common, and parent-child relationships have become less formalized and less stable. In spite of these changes we often speak as though we were still a family-centered society. We tend to react negatively to suggestions for deliberate and planned changes in family living. The changes we have cited took place without a readjustment of our thinking about the family. We accept them partly because they have already happened and partly because we are not willing to believe that they will have any effect on our biological survival. But we do not like the idea of deliberately introducing family changes in the future, because we mistrust the outcome. Religious authority, which favors the traditional family pattern for the most part, is also of significance in our attitudes towards the family.

We fear the two great threats to biological survival: famine and sterility. Our patterns of living in connection with those two problems change slowly.

But biological survival is not the only kind of survival. We want to survive not merely as biological organisms with our food and shelter limited to bare necessities. We want to survive in terms of a set of standards which we erect; we want a specific *kind* of food and shelter, together with satisfactory surroundings and means of self-expression. In fact, apart from those conditions and standards, "life would not be worth living," which is another way of saying that we believe biological survival as such would not be worth the effort. We will go to war to maintain our standards and the meanings of our way of life, even though war brings death to many of our group members. That is what we did in connection with the recent war. The Second World War was partly a matter of biological survival, of course, because we had before our eyes the spectacle of what had happened in areas subjugated by our enemies. But it was also more than biological survival; it was a matter of our wanting our own "freedoms" and the opportunity of living in accordance with our own standards and our own way of life.

Much the same is true of individuals. We will, on occasion, sacrifice our lives to maintain our ideals. If we really value honesty, we shall be honest even when we suffer for it. And so of other virtues.

This second type of survival is rather hard to designate by any one term. If, for example, we call it "social survival," we may leave the impression that we mean only some such thing as "group survival" or the survival of an aggregate. If we call it "psychic survival," with the implication that we mean survival of an integrated personality to which maintenance of standards and of values is necessary, we run the risk of confusion with "spiritualistic doctrines" relating to life after death. Possibly the most acceptable term is *psychosocial survival*, because it includes both the idea that the aggregate or individual will resist changes which threaten its standards and the idea that the survival in question is not wholly biological, since it includes all the values which, we say, "give meaning to life."

Modification of culture, then, will be slow in the areas of living which the group believes relate to its psychosocial survival, as well as in those areas which it thinks are related to biological survival. The whole field of religious beliefs is one example of this tendency. Religion changes, but it changes slowly except in times of general social upheaval. So of other patterns which we think express the distinctive meanings of our culture. One important factor which influences the relative resistance of a culture trait to modification is the significance of that trait for survival in the thinking of the aggregate concerned.

On the other hand, rapidity of change may also be affected by conditions other than the basic one of survival. Thus even apart from survival considerations, modifications will tend to be rapid in culture traits connected with areas of life which are of major interest to the aggregate. Take the field of industry in our own society as an example. It is true that we resist very strongly any proposals for changes in the fundamentals of the capitalistic system because we believe that the meanings inherent in that system are necessary for our psychosocial survival. But within the framework of capitalism we have welcomed change; changes in techniques, in methods of production, in job analysis and job placement, are all important for our industrial system. We welcome them because they do not alter the fundamental framework of capitalism and because our major cultural interest is economic and industrial. As long, then, as our biological and psychosocial survival is not involved, modification takes place rapidly in those portions of our social pattern which are major interests of the society.

By way of contrast, in medieval society the major cultural force was religion. We are not surprised, therefore, to discover a great deal of activity in connection with religious affairs: architectural, artistic, and legal elaborations which led to the flowering of a religious civilization. The basic tenets of Catholicism, which were held to be necessary for both biological and psychosocial survival, remained long untouched. Within the framework of Catholicism elaborations were welcomed.

Cultural change is affected, then, by two factors: survival, both biological and psychosocial, and the orientation of interest on the part of the aggregate. Both of these are operative in our own culture and they explain many of the details of cultural change.

Turning to a somewhat different aspect of our topic, we may note that, as a result of modification at different rates in different aspects of culture, we find a mixture of old and new ways of living.

The tendency is for older culture traits to persist together with modified traits.

When this situation promotes conflict and maladjustment between the old and the new, or between areas of culture which have changed and those which have not changed, it is described as "cultural lag." Cultural lag is formally defined as "retardation in the rate of change of some one part of an interrelated cultural complex, the lack of synchronization producing maladjustment."[2]

[2]H. P. Fairchild (Ed.), *Dictionary of Sociology*, p. 170. Philosophical Library, New York, 1944.

Cultural lag characterizes all societies to some extent, but it is especially significant in complex cultures such as our own is.

One cause of cultural lag in our own times lies in the fact that some areas of life have been investigated by science and are at least relatively well understood, while other areas are still almost wholly within the domain of emotionalism and ignorance. We know a great deal about physical science and the problems of industry, but very little, comparatively, about social science and the problems of human relationships. We can control machinery, but we cannot control crime or prevent criminals from themselves using our machinery. We can treat many physical diseases, but we cannot effectively combat social problems. We conduct ourselves with relative wisdom in some aspects of our national affairs, but we are often at a loss in the field of international affairs.

There is, however, another aspect of cultural lag in relation to science in a complex society. That is the length of time necessary for scientific ideas to penetrate from the "inner circle" of scientific investigators to the circle of popular knowledge and opinion. In a democracy such as our own, social policy is strongly influenced by the mass of the people; the wisdom of any policy depends ultimately on the wisdom of the people; and wisdom, in part at any rate, depends on the knowledge the people have. In a simple type of social organization the knowledge characteristic of the general population may be adequate. We have reached a point, however, at which the understanding of our common life is a matter of highly specialized investigation. Accurate knowledge of human relationships demands some background of specialized training. It takes a long time for such knowledge to reach any major portion of our population. Therefore our behavior often shows a lag between the knowledge on the basis of which we act and the knowledge actually available to specialists.

For example, a good many of the programs for the sterilization of the "unfit" which are currently proposed rest not on the latest scientific knowledge of heredity but on popularizations of discoveries in the field of heredity made a generation ago. It has, in other words, taken a generation for the ideas of scientific investigators to become common knowledge. But during that generation scientific investigators, in turn, have not been idle; they have been accumulating new facts, often at odds with the facts held to be true a generation ago. Their new facts will not become part of popular knowledge until a generation from now, if the spread of scientific knowledge proceeds at as slow a rate as it has in the past. A generation from now the mass of the people will be influencing social programs on the basis of ideas now current. Some lag is inevitable, unless we turn the control of society completely over to boards of specialists in the several fields of scientific investigation, and that procedure would have its own difficulties.

Somewhat the same thing has occurred in the area of family relationships. Scientific students of the family and marriage know a great deal about their subject, but they are hampered in their attempts to apply their findings to family problems because of opposition from the mass of the people due to lack of knowledge on their part. Scientists are met by the old superstitions that everyone knows how to get along in marriage, that a mother inevitably knows what is best for her own child, that the father should rule the home, and so on. Our policies with regard to family relationships lag, not because specialists do not have a fund of scientific knowledge, but because specialists cannot make their knowledge immediately available to large segments of the public.

And so with other social problems. We are fumbling in our approach to them, partly because we do not know enough about them and partly because the specialist cannot apply the knowledge he has. Cultural lag is obviously not always the symbol of a backward society; it may be the symbol of an increasingly complex society. Whatever it symbolizes, it raises problems of maladjustment. These problems are properly dealt with in a book dealing with social pathology. Here we make only the obvious suggestion that the chief means of combating problems inherent in cultural lag are (1) the wide dissemination of accurate factual knowledge, and (2) the creation of motivations which will make the mass of people interested in acquiring and applying that knowledge.

CULTURAL RELATIONSHIPS

In addition to the somewhat detailed aspects of culture that we have been discussing, it is necessary for us to recall some more general facts about our relationship to culture, and to point out some of the implications of those facts.

Cultural Differences

Differences in cultures arise naturally from the basic interaction pattern of human association:

The process of association of different groups in different environments produces a culture content which varies widely from group to group.

If we have grasped the material hitherto discussed, we shall have no difficulty in understanding the origin of cultural differences. Since culture originates in the process of association in a given environment by a given grouping, then a variation either in the grouping concerned or in the environment would tend to produce different results. Much as we may understand that elementary fact, we do not always apply it intelligently in our contacts with other cultures. Many of us, for example, assume that the members of a less complex culture than our own are necessarily and inherently biologically, emotionally, and intellectually inferior to us. We overlook the fact that the environment in which they live may not have provided any stimulus toward the development of a complex society. Dwellers in a fruitful tropical environment, in which a plentiful food supply can be obtained with little effort and with little organization, may not develop a complex economic institution. Why should they? There is no inherent "instinct" in human beings which sets toward "progress" or complexity. If human wants are satisfied simply in an environment of abundance, the natural tendency is to remain content with a simple culture and simple techniques.

Now, of course, we may hold that the simpler way of life is inferior to ours. But we are not justified in holding, as we sometimes do, that the people who follow that way of life are an inferior race or cultural grouping. We may discover, on further examination, that if they are subjected to environmental stimuli similar to ours they become much as we are. Our point is that the mere existence of a different and simpler culture than our own is no proof of the inherent and inevitable inferiority of the people who have developed that culture. This is a point which will be of great significance when we come later to discuss racial, cultural, and nationality groupings now living in the United States.

Evaluation of Cultures

If we turn from this kind of evaluation of people to an evaluation of differing cultures, we meet a somewhat different situation. All of us are prone to pass judgment on cultures other than our own. How shall we approach this matter of culture evaluation more logically?

First, let us agree that it is hard for us to appreciate the individual satisfactions which people find in the many cultures that differ from ours. Every way of life has inherent in it meanings for the "native" which may escape the outsider. To the person who has grown up in the culture those meanings are real, and they provide many kinds of satisfactions. It is foolish to suggest that no one can enjoy himself, or do constructive work, or live an effective life unless he does it in the way we do. It is a familiar fact that some Europeans criticize the people of the United States for a number of things which seem to us quite acceptable, but which to outsiders seem naïve and possibly destructive. Obviously a European who has grown up in the privileged classes of an "old" culture can hardly grasp the satisfactions we find in newness and in efficiency. On the basis of that lack of understanding, he may describe us as uncouth or worse. Critics of that kind overlook the fact that they are without a sympathetic background which would enable them to evaluate us. In precisely the same way, some Americans are very critical of the stability, routine, and "unprogressive" aspects of European culture. We also forget that we are without the background which would enable us adequately to evaluate those and other features of the European way of life. It is common for all of us to find difficulty in appreciating the meanings that other cultures have for individuals who have grown up under the influence of those cultures.

So much for the individual meanings of the cultures we try to evaluate. We are also somewhat hampered in our attempts to judge the collective meanings of other cultures because it is impossible to approach such judgment except from the viewpoint of our own values and other specialized meanings, and it is very important to bear that fact in mind. We may, however, suggest a few criteria of evaluation which are to some extent useful.

1. We may ask, "To what extent do the cultures we are judging promote biological survival through the utilization of the resources

of the environment in which they exist?" How many people could those resources support, given other techniques, in comparison with the number it does support, given the techniques actually used? There have been cultures which have had to limit drastically their populations because they could not support large numbers of people. In so far as this inability results from defective techniques, the culture is judged to be defective.

2. We may also ask, "To what extent do the cultures we are considering promote psychosocial survival through the development of a social organization which leads to constructive rather than destructive relationships?" The type of culture which is unstable and characterized by conflict relationships is judged to be inferior to the stable and developmental type of culture.

3. We may then inquire, "To what extent do the cultures we are considering promote 'individual' survival, in the sense of the development of individual capacities, as a life goal?" Here, again, our assumptions are strongly conditioned by our own values. We tend to be individualists; other aggregates do not. In answering this question, we should have to discover to what extent the individual is permitted and encouraged to develop his individual potentialities and to use those potentialities for his own benefit as well as for the benefit of the group. In so far as a group insists on complete uniformity of behavior, we judge it to be inferior to a group which encourages differentiation and utilizes differentiation as a tool for the development of human life.

These three criteria are, of course, not the only ones which might be used. But they do give us some logical basis on which we may evaluate differing cultures. They are not completely objective because they are tinged with our own cultural valuations. They must be used with caution and restraint.

The Individual in a Complex Culture

One of the characteristics of life in a complex culture is that we become progressively more dependent on the culture.

As a culture becomes more complex, the tendency is for individuals to become more and more dependent on it for continued existence.

Most of us could not survive at all apart from the framework of our culture. We are all admittedly to some extent independent of *certain aspects* of our culture; and admittedly some individuals may approach complete independence much more closely than others. But most of us rely on culturally provided instrumentalities to such a degree that they become "second nature" to us. Because of this fact, we forget at times how closely we are dependent on cultural developments. It becomes such a "natural" situation that we are not aware of it.

For example, consider our dependence on other people and their skills for the variety of specialized services we use daily. We rely on the police for protection, on doctors for medical aid, on skilled workers for the products of their skill, and so on to the last degree of complexity. It is very probable that we could, if we were given time enough, develop in a crude way many of these skills for ourselves. In simpler cultures people are forced to develop many of them for themselves or they do not survive. Our point here is that we do not develop them because we do not have to. The conditions of our association are such that it is easier and more efficient to depend on others for their products, as, of course, they depend on us for ours.

This fact of actual interdependence is not, however, the only influence toward a more or less complete reliance on culture. Consider the further fact of simple familiarity. We know our own language, our own customs, our own beliefs, our own behavior patterns, and our own symbols. When we see a building of certain proportions and of a given type of architecture, we know at once what its function is; it is a church, or a school, or a post office. When we see a man approaching dressed in a certain blue uniform and wearing a badge, we know that he is a policeman, and the word *policeman* calls up in our minds his function, status, and relationships in the community. Because we are familiar with all these facts, and many others like them, we come to take "for granted" and without thought a good many situations with which we come into contact in our daily lives. As this process continues, we are more and more bound to our culture and its devices.

We have only to consider how we should fare in the midst of a completely unfamiliar culture—say, that of the interior of Tibet— or in some area in which there was no human culture at all. Many of us would die shortly; those of us who did not die would face many difficulties and would have to live a very limited kind of life. Obviously the modern urbanite is not equipped to survive in a wilderness.

We may freely admit that we should hardly be able to survive in the Tibetan culture, an admission that brings no shame to us and very little criticism of us. But if we admit our dependence on our own culture, we very often meet with criticism from people who point out to us that our ancestors in pioneer days survived without all the adjuncts of our civilization. Our ancestors were more self-sufficient than we are—obviously because they had to be—and it is sometimes suggested that modern Americans have degenerated because we are not as independent as our ancestors were. And yet the mere fact that we are less independent than they were does not indicate in itself that we have degenerated. It indicates only that we are provided with many cultural devices that our ancestors did not have, that we naturally make use of them, and that one result of those situations is more interdependence and less independence.

Recall our discussion of the development of a simple culture in the tropics. There is little incentive in such an environment to develop a complex industrial and economic system, because the environment provides satisfactions without complex transformations of natural resources. In precisely the same manner, there is no great incentive in our own culture to develop the pioneer type of self-sufficiency, because our environment encourages interdependence and co-operation. In fact, we can go even further and suggest that, valuable as the pioneer type of self-sufficiency was in early America, and much as we owe to the pioneers, what we now need is a greater measure of co-operation rather than a greater measure of self-sufficiency. Given the circumstances of our own type of association, co-operation is a greater virtue than self-sufficiency.

Undoubtedly not everyone will agree with that statement, because it is still part of our ways of thinking to glorify individualism of a crude type, with its independence and drive towards self-sufficiency. But we must soberly ask whether those things are as valuable in our own times as they were in pioneer days. Can we conserve the values expressed through self-sufficiency and yet develop the further co-operative relationships necessary for life in our complex society? It is part of our common task to do exactly that.

INSTITUTIONS

It is a fundamental principle of sociology that

Every culture develops institutions
of some kind.

An *institution* is a standardized reaction pattern common to the great majority of people living in a culture. When we say that an institution is a standardized reaction pattern, we mean that it is a way of behaving which develops in order to meet certain situations and which is approved by the great majority of group members as the "right" way to meet those situations. Obviously, according to this definition, institutions are a part of culture. Let us see in more detail how they develop.

There are certain life situations which are repeated time after time, and which are common to all the members of a particular aggregate. For example, hunger is such a situation. We become hungry repeatedly; the satisfaction of hunger is always a temporary satisfaction. And *everybody* gets hungry repeatedly. It is not an experience confined to any minority of individuals. So of many human needs—shelter, clothing, and such other things as we consider basic necessities of life. They are common to all members of the aggregate, and they are recurrent. Under those circumstances, aggregates living in given environments develop standardized ways of providing the basic necessities of existence through the use of environmental resources. Naturally, the ways vary from group to group, from environment to environment, and from time to time. Some will be elaborate, others simple; some will occupy a position of dominance in the social organization, others will be of subordinate importance; some will function efficiently, some will be inefficient. But of whatever kind they may be or however efficient they may be, we call this standardized reaction to the recurrent and common situation of basic human needs an *economic institution*.

Another recurring and common situation occurs in connection with sex, reproduction, and the necessity of providing adequate care for young children. Obviously this occurs among all aggregates and is common to all individuals. All children require care; it is not a case of one child requiring it while other children can develop without it. So a standardized way of meeting this common and recurrent situation develops. This we call the *family institution*.

But in addition to needing care during childhood, children must learn something of the way of life of the aggregate in its environment. Some of this learning is provided in connection with family patterns, but even in unelaborated cultures there are facts which traditionally must be learned outside the family. The ways of men must be taught to boys and the ways of women to girls. As cultures become more elaborate, the learning process becomes formalized, and we have, in response to the common and recurrent necessity for all children to learn, the growth of *educational institutions*.

From a very early period of his history man also had contact with an unseen world. It is not, especially in the case of early man, a world of ghosts and spirits that are vastly different from man himself. In fact, the inhabitants of the unseen world are assumed to be much like man himself except for the fact that they *are* unseen, invisible. Thus, a falling tree is often assumed to fall deliberately in an attempt to "catch" a man passing under it. The current of a stream represents the attempt of the stream to seize a man and drown him. Tree and stream are not invisible, of course; but the motive power is invisible. There are also such true invisibles as the wind, storms, and thunder. Their effects, or what primitive man interprets as their effects, are visible enough; the things themselves are not. Man, then, faces the recurrent and common situation of dealing with the invisibles. He cannot approach them as he does man because they elude his attacks and avoid his friendly overtures. He therefore develops specialized reaction patterns to be used in dealing with the unseen world. These we call *religious institutions*.

Finally, all aggregates sooner or later face the necessity of developing systems of control. At first this may be an unorganized and informal type of control; later it may be part of the family institution; but eventually there comes a degree of complexity in human relationships which demands some specialized vehicle of control over recurring situations. Men kill game together. If the strongest insists on getting the most, the situation may become very unpleasant. Perhaps defense against an enemy becomes necessary; haphazard leadership may bring disaster. For situations such as these, a formal system of control develops which we call a *political institution*, or government.

These five institutions—economic, family, educative, religious, and governmental—are the *basic* institutions of any culture. Others may develop, as they have in our own times—institutions connected with recreation, with science, and with the arts, for example—but they are always in addition to the basic five. In Part II we shall discuss at some length each of these institutions as they exist in our own social organization.

Institutions have complex patterns. They include beliefs, customs, ideas, penalties for infringement, and above all, people. Institutions are essentially people following accepted modes of behavior in the face of given situations. They behave in those ways because cultural factors and social pressures strongly influence them. Thus when a child reaches a certain age he goes to school. This seems to us such a very natural reaction that we often fail to realize that when we send our children to school we are indulging in an institutional mode of conduct. So it is in the case of other institutions.

The interrelationships between institutions will be more fully treated in Part II.

READINGS

LINTON, RALPH. *The Study of Man*. D. Appleton-Century Company, Inc., New York, 1936. An introduction to some of the concepts and methods of anthropology. Chaps. V and VI, "Backgrounds and Distinctive Aspects of Culture"; Chap. XVII, "The Qualities and Problems of Culture."

LINTON, RALPH. *The Cultural Background of Personality*. D. Appleton-Century Company, Inc., New York, 1945. Especially Chap. II, a discussion of the nature of culture.

GOLDENWEISER, A. *Anthropology*. F. S. Crofts & Co., New York, 1945. Especially Chap. IV, "From Mind to Culture."

CHAPTER VII

INTERACTION IN OUR TIMES

WE HAVE DISCUSSED in some detail the three factors of the basic interaction pattern of human association. Let us now examine some of our current interactions as illustrative of the operation of that pattern.

URBANISM

One of the outstanding phenomena of our times is urbanism, which means, of course, the tendency of people to live in cities rather than in country areas. At present somewhat more than one half of our population lives in cities.

Studies of the population of the United States indicate that there is very little innate difference between urban residents and rural residents. We are not able to discover any major differences in physiological structure, physiological functioning, native intelligence, capacities for emotional adjustment, health, or any other inborn characteristic when we compare urban and rural residents. Let us make this clear: There are many differences between urban and rural residents in intelligence, behavior patterns, skills, abilities, and other characteristics. Those differences exist, but there is no evidence that they result from *innate* differences in the two populations. There is no evidence that urban people are *born* more intelligent or more capable or otherwise different from rural people. The "native equipment" of the average urban person seems to be much the same as that of the average rural person, allowing for individual differences which occur in some members of both groupings. We find individuals of outstanding abilities in both urban and rural areas, and we find individuals of subnormal abilities in both areas. But as aggregates the two populations differ very little in their constitutional equipment.

131

In view of the fact that the inborn characteristics of both populations are much the same, and in view of the further fact that there
are significant differences actually existing between the two populations, the conclusion seems warranted that the differences we observe spring from interaction with different kinds of environment.
We have already noted the fact that the urban and the rural environments differ in many ways, even at present when the similarity
between city and country is much greater than it has been in some
past periods of history. What are some of the details of the urban
environment which apparently are so effective in producing distinctive traits among the dwellers in our cities?

THE URBAN ENVIRONMENT

One major characteristic of the urban environment is its intense
concentration of population. In some crowded city areas there may
be as many as 35,000 persons per square mile. A comparison of
this density of population with that of some Western states, which
may reach as low as 2 persons per square mile, indicates something
of the difference. These two figures are, of course, in the nature of
extremes. But there are Eastern states in which the average density
of population is 600 per square mile for the state as a whole, with
considerably higher concentration in their urban areas. Close
physical contact with people, crowding together, and mass movement characterize much of our metropolitan life and to a lesser
extent our small-city life.

The urbanite not only is in close contact with large numbers of
people, but also meets many different kinds of people. Foreign-born
and native-born, black, yellow, and white, Protestant, Jew, and
Catholic, workers, artists, professional men—all sorts of people surround him. The urban population is much more highly differentiated than is the rural population. The potential stimuli are much
more varied.

Because of this close contact with many people of different ways
of life, the urbanite tends to develop a "shell" of indifference toward
most of the people he meets. He does make some close friends. In
fact, he probably has more close friends than the rural person, who
may be isolated from other people by long distances. But toward
those who are not his intimates the urbanite must, because of the
very fact of numbers, hold to only superficial contacts. He does not

know intimately his hundreds of neighbors in a large apartment
house, because if he were, or could be, personally interested in the
manifold details of their lives he would be overwhelmed by divergent interests and would literally be unable to pursue any interest
of his own. As a result, the urban *system of interaction* tends to be
indirect and impersonal in many areas of life. The urban dweller's
contacts become casual, formal, and superficial. This behavior
pattern is not an inborn trait of the urbanite; it is the result of interaction with an environment characterized by the press of large
numbers of people around him. In the rural environment people
are scarce; in the urban environment they are plentiful. Hence
different attitudes toward people tend to develop.

Another characteristic of the urban environment is its diversity
of occupational activity, as a result of which the urban aggregate
develops different skills from those of the rural aggregate. Mental
work, agility at figures, the need for skill in human relationships,
all characterize the urban commercial life; specialized mechanical
skills, routinization, and the necessity of being a "cog in a machine"
are typical of much of urban industrial life. The farm dweller
develops skills of quite another sort.

Finally, the surroundings of the urbanite are almost entirely
man-made or man-related. Buildings, subways, factories, libraries,
people, ideologies, are the important factors in urban life. The
rural dweller has contact more predominantly with the facts of
physical nature.

We may, then, describe the typical urban environment as one
in which there is a high concentration of population, a highly differentiated aggregate of people, various types of occupation, and
an indirect and formalized system of interaction. Is there any relationship between these facts and typical urban people?

Typical Urban Attitudes

Specialists in urban sociology have described a number of attitudes as typical of contemporary urban dwellers. This is not to
imply that these attitudes characterize every individual who lives in
our cities; there are many exceptions, but the predominant type is
clear. It also appears probable that there is a close relationship between the size of the city involved and the definiteness of these at-

titudes; the larger the city, the more definite the attitudes. In general,

> *The urban dweller tends to be more dependent on his culture*
> *than the rural person.*

This is another way of saying that the urban dweller tends to be less self-sufficient than the rural dweller. Recall our discussion of self-sufficiency a few pages back. As we said there, the statement that an individual is dependent on his culture must not be taken as a criticism of that individual. It does not indicate that he is a less desirable type than the self-sufficient person.

One aspect of the urbanite's lack of self-sufficiency is found in his tendency to rely on other people in a good many situations which the farm dweller is compelled to meet through his own resources. Obviously, the urban environment fosters such reliance, simply because of the fact that in cities we are in contact with many people. Those who live on an isolated farm or ranch do not develop the habit of relying on assistance from other people. Again, it is not only the fact that large numbers of people surround us in the city which is important; it is also the fact that they have specialized skills appropriate to the various situations we face. The urban environment, then, not only permits the growth of an attitude of dependence on specialists; it actually encourages such an attitude by making available the services of specialists.

In many rural areas all the cultural apparatus of doctors, policemen, firemen, bus drivers, preachers, teachers, and others is not readily available at most times; and at certain seasons of the year it is literally out of reach. The tendency, therefore, is for the rural resident to make some attempt to meet the situations he faces through the use of his own resources. He is more self-reliant than the urban person, not because he is born that way but because his interaction patterns develop his potentialities in that direction.

In addition to being more dependent on his culture than the rural person, it is also true that

> *The urban dweller tends to be more humanistic*
> *than the rural dweller.*

He tends to center his activities and his thinking chiefly on human interests and human values, as contrasted with religious or other worldly interests and values. The urban dweller is impressed with the human achievements in his surroundings. Doctors save his life, lawyers get him out of trouble, policemen catch his burglars, firemen extinguish his fires, captains of industry employ him, architects build sturdy and convenient shelters, psychiatrists soothe his mental anguish. Man is not, admittedly, universally powerful; there are some situations with which he cannot cope. Human beings are not efficient at all times and under all circumstances. Yet in the daily life exigencies of the urbanite, man's skills and man's achievements are of vast significance. Hence it is natural to respect human abilities and to believe that man as he develops will progressively assume more and more control over the changes and chances of this mortal existence. There seems to be singularly little scope for supernatural or superhuman intervention.

The rural resident, on the other hand, is much less inclined to trust to the devices of men. His contact with the facts of nature, of seed and growth, of storm and drought and the inevitable swing of the seasons, all of which man is still to a large degree unable to control, may encourage in him a religious outlook; or it may lead to a bitter and fatalistic philosophy. In either case, it is not a humanistic philosophy.

It is also true that

The urbanite tends to be more sophisticated than the rural person.

He is apt to ascribe the success of his fellows to "pull," influence, luck, or some factors other than the merits of the individuals concerned, factors which have no effect on the natural processes characteristic of the farmer's environment. He doubts the disinterestedness and the good will of many of his associates; he likes to consider himself worldly-wise and "pretty hard to fool."

The source of the urbanite's sophisticated outlook is in his interaction with the typical urban environment. It is quite true that some people secure advancement and preference by "pull," luck, and similar means. It is also true that some men will gladly cheat their fellows on very slight opportunity—true in the rural as well as the urban environment, but there are more of them in the cities! The urbanite is not imagining these things. He is mistaken only when he attributes them to all mankind on the basis of his own limited contacts.

It is also true, of course, that the sophisticate is socially acceptable in certain urban groups in spite of his shallowness. Again the urbanite is not inaccurate in his interpretations of city life. His mistake comes when he attributes to the value system of those groups a universal validity; when he assumes that because the sophisticate is one typical urban type, he is also the ideal type which all men should imitate.

The attitude characteristic of popular songs, popular literature, much of modern drama and the movies, and many other commonplaces of the urban environment is such as to increase devotion to sophistication and to spread the vogue of sophisticated behavior. That vogue does not exist to any great extent in rural areas except where they have been subjected to urban influence. The farmer, as we said, distrusts men not because he has been disillusioned about them but because he believes that they are important in the face of natural forces. Sophistication in the face of nature is apt to be a barren and unrewarding behavior pattern!

The urbanite values conspicuous consumption to a greater degree than the rural dweller.

Conspicuous consumption is a behavior pattern described long ago by Thorstein Veblen in a classic of American social science.[1] Briefly, conspicuous consumption implies that goods are purchased for their "display value" or their "impression value" rather than for their "use value." The person who "consumes conspicuously" is interested in enhancing his reputation in the eyes of his associates by possessing elaborate, expensive, and scarce goods. When a number of people engage in this practice, we have "competitive consumption," each person striving to outdo the others in buying lavishly and wastefully.

Presumably, conspicuous consumption, in so far as it is a successful vehicle for impressing one's associates, gives a great deal of psychological satisfaction to those practicing it. It has characterized urban areas and some urbanites for a considerable time. More than two centuries ago, Bernard Mandeville, living in London, remarked that "handsome apparel" is a very important adjunct to life, that "fine feathers make fine birds," and that people are judged chiefly

[1]Thorstein Veblen, *Theory of the Leisure Class.* Vanguard, New York, 1899.

by their clothes, with the result that they have the satisfaction of being esteemed by a "vast majority" not "as what they are, but as what they appear to be."[2] He attributes this situation to the impersonality of the urban interaction pattern, its superficiality, and its tendency to judge people by externals. Conditions are not much different in some sectors of urban life today.

We have selected these four characteristics from many alleged to be typical of the urban attitude. The strong presumption is that they result from interaction with the environment, especially when we recall the fact that we have not been able to discover any innate differences between urban and rural people which would account for the appearance of such characteristics among urbanites.

We may check that proposition by attempting to discover whether or not there exist generally any situations in our contemporary society which we might expect to accompany the growth and spread of the attitudes we have mentioned. Thus if the outlook of our times is increasingly interdependent, we should expect to find an increase in "collective action," that is, an increase in proposals for the solution of life problems by group action instead of individually. We do, of course, find such an increase in co-operative approaches to social action, in the form of labor unions, employers' associations, public-education projects of increasing scope and inclusiveness, and public and private social-work projects. All these are examples of attempts to solve individual problems, such as attaining security, getting an education, etc., through social programs rather than through strictly individual initiative. One difficulty with some of them at this particular time is that they tend to be group rather than societal programs, with the result that co-operation within the group exists to a large degree but co-operation between groups is not always typical. Thus labor unions further the interests of labor, and employers' associations further the interests of employers, but in only a few cases do they attempt to go beyond their own group lines and co-operate with each other. One reason for this lack of intergroup co-operation is doubtless the fact that the whole program of meeting life situations through collective action is relatively new. We may expect, as the idea becomes

[2]H. E. Barnes and H. Becker, *Social Thought from Lore to Science*, p. 406. Heath, Boston.

more securely established, a larger measure of intergroup co-operation, with a corresponding decrease in such conflicts as that between
labor and capital.

Similarly, if our outlook is increasingly humanistic, we should
expect a decline in the authority and prestige of traditional religions which emphasize otherworldly goals and supernaturalism.
There is some evidence that there is such a decline, although we
cannot be absolutely sure. Statistics of church membership and
church attendance indicate that the traditional churches are barely
"holding their own," both in membership and in donations of
money.[3] The decline in interest in traditional religion may be
temporary, the result of the relative newness of the humanistic outlook. Possibly future developments will replace the present lack
of interest in religion by a growing interest in religions which balance this-world and other-world goals in some manner which will
include the distinctively humanistic values.

Again, if the urban personality is sophisticated and concerned
with conspicuous consumption, we should note an increasing preoccupation with technology, display, production, money, and all
the other appurtenances of a mass-production system, without
which conspicuous consumption is impossible. Here also we find
what we should expect to find.

We cannot, of course, say that urbanism in itself caused all these
phenomena. The most we can say with finality is that they have
accompanied urbanism. We do not know which caused which.
Probably neither causes the other in any simple way; they may
both spring from some more general complex of causative factors.
However that may be, the development of the urban way of life in
general is an apt illustration of the basic interaction pattern which
we study in sociology. Man, culture, and environment interact to
produce these and other contemporary phenomena.

We do not know what the future of our urban civilization will
be. We are too familiar with the "problem" aspects of city life to
share the enthusiastic views of the early 1900's, which held that the
city was the "hope of democracy" and that it was an instrument
which would automatically improve the educational, economic, and
cultural status of our population. In fact, some contemporary

[3]See Chapter XIV.

students of man are apt to go to the other extreme and to regard the city as degenerative of people and destructive of democracy.[4] Such a view is as little warranted as the overoptimism of the 1900's.

The fact is that our urban civilization does present problems of attitude and of behavior patterns not known in rural civilizations—which did, however, have their own problems. On the other hand, our city civilization has developed resources of intelligence, skill, and co-operation which also are not known in rural civilizations. The city as we know it is both problem and opportunity, as are many other social phenomena. What results the city will have for our future civilization depends on how clearly we see and grasp the opportunity. City life represents a vast change from the rural life common in America a few generations ago. Change, as we have several times suggested, is characteristic of cultural and social phenomena. We may accept that fact theoretically, but life in the midst of change may present so many problems that we do not accept it emotionally. Perhaps part of the function of sociology is to insist on the reality of change and on the necessity of using it constructively, in this area of city living as in other areas of life.

INTERACTION AND WORLD PROBLEMS

Many of the most pressing immediate problems which face our civilization are those concerned with world relationships. National problems are also important, but it is increasingly apparent that we can solve those national problems only in a world setting. A significant point here is that the general interactive process has been important not only in creating problems but also in providing potentialities for the solution of those problems.

INTERACTION AND CONFLICT

We have already noted the obvious fact that conflict is one possible result of contacts between differing cultures. As aggregates with varying customs, motivations, and attitudes come into closer contact, the differences may, and often do, arouse antagonisms.

[4] L. Mumford, *The Condition of Man*, Harcourt, New York, 1944; P. A. Sorokin, *The Crisis of Our Age*, Dutton, New York, 1944; Karl Mannheim, *Diagnosis of Our Time*, Oxford University Press, New York, 1944.

We are mistrustful of the different, we tend to consider it inferior and possibly dangerous, and we find it hard to establish easy and effective relationships with people who differ from ourselves.

It is also increasingly true in our own times that similarity of goals, attitudes, and motivations may produce conflict. If several nations have the same, or very similar, ambitions—for example, to dominate the world or to get possession of raw materials—such similarity may lead to conflict. Our problem, then, is not only the reconciliation of differences of custom, language, and outlook; it is also to make some constructive disposal of our similarities.

This problem, in both its aspects, is related to the interactive process and to the cultures which result from that process. It is not the actual possession or lack of such valuable items as raw materials so much as it is the attitude which nations take toward raw materials and the motivations implicit in those attitudes which is significant in promoting conflict. If we considered oil, coal, ores, and similar natural products to be of very little importance, we should hardly go to war abut them. Our culture makes them very important and of great value because we have developed a highly mechanized industrial system. Without that system our attitude toward such natural products might well be neutral or even negative, as it is in some segments of Oriental cultures which have asceticism as a life goal. The point is that there is no necessary and inevitable sequence between war and lack of raw materials or other natural resources. The important factor is a cultural one, namely, our attitude toward raw materials.

Much the same is true of sectional differences in the United States. It is not chiefly the possession of different types of resources or the suitability of one region of the United States for manufacturing while another region is more suited to agriculture that causes the West and the South to look with suspicion on the East. In fact, the situation ought to be quite the reverse; diversity of resources and of natural equipment should permit the different sections of the country to specialize in those occupations to which they are best suited and to work in co-operation with other specialized areas of the country to their mutual benefit. The sources of the antagonisms and suspicions are cultural; they rest in attitude on such factors as varying economic techniques and values, and in custom.

Precisely the same situation characterizes the conflicts that exist between different racial and cultural groupings. Here in the United States the source of race conflict is not in what the Negro actually is, and only to a very slight extent in what he actually does. It is in what we feel about the Negro, in the attitudes we have developed toward him, in the groundless fears that we entertain as to what he might be and what he might do. Those Negroes who insist that it is inaccurate to refer to a "Negro problem" because the whites are the predominant group and that therefore we should call the whole situation a "white problem," may be exaggerating or oversimplifying facts, but there is a basic soundness in their view. It is what the whites think about the Negro that is important; and what we think about the Negro is a cultural product, a matter of custom, of attitude, and of motivation.

We can carry this analysis still further. Conflicts between labor and capital, between various religious denominations, and between other groupings in our society are all basically cultural phenomena. They spring for the most part not from what we know about our opponents but from what we do not know about them. And the fact that often we know very little about them is, in turn, affected by cultural barriers which isolate one grouping from another.

One significant point about this discussion is that, if all these factors in conflict are cultural and are the product of interaction, then we can have much more hope of solving conflict problems than we might under other conditions. If, for example, there were some kind of instinctive hatred between Negro and white, or some kind of innate dislike between capital and labor, or some kind of inborn antagonism between Protestant and Catholic, our task of solving conflict problems would be much harder than it is. But if the conflict is basically cultural, then new cultural developments, such as accurate information about one another, actual contact with one another, and revision of values and attitudes introduced into the interaction pattern will produce new patterns of behavior, and conflict may gradually be replaced by co-operation. The process of introducing new developments into the interaction pattern is much more complicated than we have made it sound here, and results would certainly not be immediate or automatic, but in the long run the only solution of conflict that will be effective is along the lines we have suggested.

WORLD CONDITIONS PROMOTING CONFLICT

Granting that conflict is primarily a cultural rather than a geographical or a racial phenomenon, what are some of the world cultural conditions which promote conflict? In general they are conditions in which the fact of difference is important. Differences of language are, perhaps, the most familiar impediment to understanding and co-operation; differences of custom, belief, and ideology are also familiar. Especially significant are the social effects of different religions. The Mohammedan finds our doctrine that women are the equal of men complete nonsense because his religion teaches him that they are not the equal of men. The Hindu, with his belief in vegetarianism, his attitude toward cattle as being sacred beasts, his disregard of sanitation and public health, finds us not only a people queerly concerned about unimportant things, but religiously repugnant because we eat animals, insist on sanitation, and think it important to study such matters as birth, death, and disease, instead of leaving them to the inscrutable wisdom of God. Other religions differ from ours in equally striking ways.

This is strictly something more than a difference in religious belief. The actual difference of belief results in differences of behavior and of standards which, in turn, express themselves in patterns of group living. We sometimes speak as though we could carry democracy "on a platter" to the rest of the world, to the immense delight and gratification of all the world's inhabitants. It is indeed important that we set an example of democracy for the rest of the world; but we may find that our example is not readily accepted by the world, because democracy conflicts with certain religious beliefs which are firmly held by a large portion of the world's inhabitants.

It is not only, of course, religious ideas which are in conflict with democracy. Political, social, and racial ideas are in some segments of the world just as antagonistic to the basic democratic way of life as are religious ideas, and just as firmly held. Areas in which totalitarian, or police, states have been established may well be impervious to example or precept in the matter of democratic patterns of behavior.

Another important difference is that of the intelligence level of some of the populations of other areas of the world. We are not implying that those populations are innately less intelligent than our own. Their cultural milieu, however, has not been such as to promote the development of their potentialities.

But differences are not the only aspect of conflict. In so far as there are similarities of goals, in so far as nations want the same natural resources, the same territories, and the same population resources, conflict may result. It is not sufficient merely to establish similarity of goals and purposes. We need goals and purposes which are truly common, that is, shared by all the peoples of the world. Our goal then becomes not simply the same as that of another aggregate, in the sense that both want the same resources and seek them in a competitive spirit. Instead, we have a goal so genuinely shared in common that as one aggregate advances that goal it also advances the goal of all other aggregates. We sometimes find this commonness of goal among writers and artists: the significant fact is not competition among them with the intent that one may excel at the expense of others; the significant thing is the advancement of writing and painting, a goal generally shared, so that the excellent work of any one of the group is valued as a contribution to the general goal rather than to individual ends. The transfer of this kind of attitude to world relationships and international goal is a necessity if we are to avoid increasing conflict.

All this implies that we must re-examine and revise our own way of life in the light of the example of democracy it sets to other nations. We should hardly want to "give" other nations the problems inherent in our urbanism, our race conflicts, our undue emphasis on materialism. If we can demonstrate some of our ideals, and revise our own way of life to express those ideals more clearly, we shall give the world something worth having.

WORLD CONDITIONS PROMOTING CO-OPERATION

As a matter of fact, there are a number of cultural forces now existing in world relationships which are integrative rather than disintegrative. They are not limited to the culture of any one nation. They are common to many segments of European-American culture generally; and there is some hope that they are becoming more common in some areas of the Orient. They are potentially much more than similarities. They are shared attitudes and goals of the kind we have just discussed.

For example, modern technology has in it potentialities of integration. Raw materials from all over the globe are used in industrial processes. Of course this situation may, and possibly will, lead to conflict, but it is also a potential basis for specialization and co-operation. The financing of the industrial process, which has become an international matter, also contains potentialities for co-operation. During the period of colonial exploitation of large areas of the earth by so-called "mother" countries, industrial and financial relationships were largely matters of one-sided benefit. Colonial exploitation is, however, rapidly becoming a thing of the past, and, in any case, it is a far different relationship from that involved in the mutual investment in one another's resources by the populations of different nations.

International labor unions are another potential force for world integration. Again, this is a development which may lead to the oft-predicted "capitalist-proletarian struggle," and it can, therefore, result in disintegrative patterns. But emphasis on the essential similarity of labor throughout the world is a powerful cohesive force which can be perverted only by stupidity and selfishness.

Let us turn from economic and industrial aspects of our social order. There are other aspects of human life which are potentially constructive and integrative. One such aspect is the whole area of science, philosophy, and education. Scientists and intellectuals of the Western world are in general agreement as to the aims and purposes of their respective activities, which implies that a common goal, shared internationally, is already in existence for that grouping. That they do not always, or cannot always, assert the validity and the superiority of that goal over other lesser goals is painfully evident in the subservience of scientists and intellectuals to other groupings in all countries of the world. But they are becoming increasingly vocal in their insistence on certain common values inherent in the intellectual life. International journals of science and of philosophic investigation expressing this emphasis circulate with some degree of freedom in most nations of the Western world.

There exists also a body of doctrines regarding the "rights of man," to use a somewhat old-fashioned term, or the essential worth and dignity of human beings, to speak in more modern terms. That body of doctrines is, admittedly, mostly limited to Western civilization as yet, and even to certain limited sectors of Western civilization. But it is not limited to any one *nation*. It has still to reach many sections of the Orient, but any body of beliefs based on the essential worth and dignity of man, and shared in common by an increasing number of people in the world, is a strong potential force for world integration.

What we have, then, is a mixture of forces, some tending in the direction of conflict, others in the direction of co-operation. Neither the one result nor the other is inevitable. But both the problems and the solutions for those problems, both the disintegrative and the integrative factors, are cultural phenomena. As we understand more about societal living, and as more people understand the significance of cultural differences and of cultural products, we shall approach the solution of our problems more intelligently.

INTERACTION AND POPULATION "PROBLEMS"

Approaching a different aspect of interaction, we come to the point that the very foundation of our society and of its subaggregates is the people who compose them. Man is a highly significant factor in the interaction pattern we have been studying. As we have suggested in our discussion of urbanism, the *number* of people involved in the pattern has a definite effect on the products of interaction. It is also true that the *kind* of people involved in the pattern affects vitally the products of interaction. This whole area of the relationship between the people who make up the "man" factor in our interaction pattern and the two other factors in the pattern has traditionally been studied in sociology under the heading *population problems*. We retain that phraseology, although there is no real reason for referring to the study as "problems" any more that we refer to the study of association or of culture as "problems."

As we might suspect, the two great fields of population study are (1) the study of variations in the number of people who make up a population, and (2) the study of variations in the kind of people who make up a population. The first is referred to as the study of *population quantity*, the second as the study of *population quality*. How are these related to the phenomena of interaction?

POPULATION QUANTITY

INCREASE AND DECREASE OF POPULATIONS

We do not have sufficient data to make any accurate statements about population increase and decrease throughout the world for the major portion of its history. Even today we lack such data for the populations of much of the world. Large sections of the Orient do not keep any population statistics. It is only within the past generation that facts about population have been compiled for all the states in our own country. The most that we have, then, is a fairly accurate knowledge of present population conditions in certain countries of the world. If we are to study population trends, that is, the changes which have taken place in specified populations over a period of years, we are forced in some cases to use estimates of doubtful validity.

As far as we can tell, the population of the world has shown a tendency to increase with some degree of consistency. For the period from about 1600 to the present we may be somewhat more specific. The white race has increased about sixfold in the period from 1750 to the present time, that is, from about 175,000,000 to about 675,000,000.[5] At the same time, the culture of the white race has been such that that race has dominated an increasing area of the world. Estimates of future growth indicate that the increase will not be nearly so rapid in the next three centuries as it has been in the past three centuries if the European-American members of the white race and their descendants continue to follow their present reproductive pattern.

The present world population is slightly more than two billion people. About 55 per cent of this total lives in the Orient, that is, outside Europe, Africa, and the Americas. Thus a slight majority of our population lives in that portion of the globe about which we have relatively slight information.[6] The non-Oriental population of the world is distributed in such a way that Europe has approximately 25 per cent, North and South America about 13 per cent, and Africa about 7 per cent.

In the United States our early history was characterized by very

[5]Paul Landis, *Population Problems*, pp. 18 ff. American Book, New York, 1943.
[6]Ibid.

large percentage increases in population. We should naturally expect this to be true since the early white population was small, and the addition of even a few newcomers from Europe would mean a great deal in terms of percentage relationships. The two hundred years from 1650 to 1850 showed increases of from 30 to 40 per cent each ten years. In the period from 1850 to 1950, the percentage of increase per decade has declined, with especial rapidity toward the end of the period. Thus the increase from 1850 to 1860 was about 35 per cent; that from 1930 to 1940 was only about 7 per cent, with the increase from 1940 to 1950 estimated to be also about 7 per cent. It has been estimated that the increase in the decade from 1970 to 1980 may fall to as low as 1 per cent if present trends continue.

These changes in the rate of population increase reflect, of course, changes in the reproductive pattern of the population of the United States. One measure of that change which is very commonly used is the *crude birth rate*, that is, the number of children born per thousand people in the population. This is not an adequate measure, because it takes no account of the kind of people that make up the population: their age, their sex distribution, their economic and social status, and so on. If the population of a community is made up largely of people over the age of sixty-five, we should not expect the birth rate there to resemble that of another community of the same size in which the majority were around twenty-five. Similarly, if a population consists predominantly of men, as it does in some mining communities, we should hardly expect the birth rate to compare with that of a community in which the sexes were evenly distributed. The crude birth rate takes no account of differentials such as these; yet we have to make use of it in a good many instances because we do not have the information which would enable us to analyze the composition of the populations involved.

When we do have such information, we may use the *refined birth rate*, which makes comparative use of the age and sex composition of populations, and sometimes of other factors. Thus a comparison between the birth rates of two communities is more accurate when expressed in terms of the number of married females within certain age groups.

Actually, however, the birth rate, whether crude or refined, is used only when we cannot compute another and much more realistic figure called the *net reproduction rate*. The advantage of the net reproduction rate is that it makes allowance for changing trends in birth and death rates, in the age and sex composition of the population, and in other significant factors. It measures population increase or decrease on the basis of the relative number of women of childbearing age there will be in the future population, as indicated by the number of daughters born to women of childbearing age in the present population.

A population which has a net reproduction rate of 100 is one in which the number of women of childbearing age in the future will be about the same as at present, with the result that the population should neither increase nor decrease. Any rate of less than 100 indicates that the population will decline; and one of more than 100 indicates that it will increase. All these predictions are based on the assumption that there will be no drastic change in the trends of birth and death rates or in the sex composition of the population.

In the United States the net reproduction rate for the country as a whole has declined from 116 in 1920 to 96 in 1940. This means that if we had been writing in 1920 we should have predicted a population increase of about 16 per cent in the generation following 1920. Writing today we should predict a decrease in population, on the basis of the net reproduction rate of 96, of about 4 per cent in the coming generation.

Of more interest than the net reproduction rate for the country as a whole are the rates for some of the different segments of the population. Thus in 1940 the rural farm population—those actually resident on farms—had a net reproduction rate of 144; the rural nonfarm population—those living in rural areas but not on farms—had a rate of 114; and the urban population had a rate of 74.[7] Interpreting these figures, we might expect a drastic decrease in the population of our cities in the coming generation if those cities relied only on their native-born children for future residents. Actually we do not find a decrease in city populations, because the rural areas furnish a surplus of population which tends to migrate to the cities.

What we have, then, is a picture of reproductive behavior on the part of the population of the United States which varies with the

[7]Ibid. pp. 59, 95.

type of cultural environment. The rural-urban relationship noted above is one factor in that variation. Others are religion, occupation, social status, immigrant status, and race, only the latter being a biological factor. There have been a number of attempts to state a universal "law" of population growth, but none has been particularly successful. Until further definitive studies are made, we must confine ourselves to the statement that variations in population growth and decline result from the interaction of man with his culture and his environment, and to an indication of some general factors which are apparently of importance in affecting population.

In our own times the increase of urbanism has been accompanied by a decrease in the net reproduction rate. Either the life goals of the urbanite do not include raising a family as a value, or the circumstances of his surroundings discourage him from raising one. Conditions of urban housing are notoriously not conducive to large families. Standards of child care, including education, health care, recreation, and dress, are set at a point so high that many people cannot afford more than one or two children. The fact that urban women can find many opportunities for employment doubtless makes childbearing appear in some instances as an interference with a career. The vogue of sophistication does not include any great emphasis on home and family values. All these cultural factors, more common in the urban than in the rural areas, militate against reproduction.

Of course, the increasing knowledge of birth control and availability of birth-control devices in urban centers accounts for much of the actual decline in the birth rate. But simply to point to the practice of birth control as a cause of changes in our reproductive behavior is superficial. We must ask the further question "Why do people practice birth control? Why do they limit their families to one or two children?" We cannot know the reason in every case, but, in so far as family limitation is a group phenomenon, and in so far as it does accompany urbanism, we are led to suspect that the urban environment is such as to encourage it. We can find no other important factor at work. Urbanites are not, as far as we can discover, biologically more sterile than ruralites. The reason for the decline in the birth rate is not a decline in the marriage rate. The proportion of people married per 1000 of the population has varied only slightly over a long period of years. In fact, as Professor

Landis points out, the long-time trend of marriage rates in the United States has been such that the birth rate should have increased.[8] Both the proportion of the total population married and the proportion of those in the younger age groups who are married have increased somewhat.

Of course, it is not only the "life goal" factor in the urban environment which has caused a decrease in the net reproduction rate. Other factors are doubtless important, such as the increase in divorces and desertions, and the breaking of families through other causes. Increase of leisure time has perhaps also had some effect. Many people spend that leisure in purely recreational activities, often in commercial recreation of some kind, with the result that our culture is very strongly oriented toward pleasure. Family responsibilities interfere with pleasure.

Our discussion thus far has indicated that the interaction process has brought about a decline in the net reproduction rate, and along with that a potential decline in our population. All this was largely undeliberate; it was not "planned that way." It was a natural product, resulting from the interaction of natural factors. We shall return to a further examination of some of these points in our discussion of the family in Part II.

THE COMPOSITION OF POPULATION

The *composition* of a population means the number of people it contains of certain age characteristics, sex characteristics, occupational characteristics, status characteristics, and so on. Obviously this topic verges on a discussion of population quality, since age, sex, and the other characteristics mentioned are measures of the kind of people we have in our population. We discuss it here, however, because population quality has traditionally been more concerned with other characteristics than age and sex composition, as we shall discover presently.

SEX COMPOSITION

What is the relationship between the number of men and the number of women in our population? The male birth rate is higher than the female birth rate, with the result that there are about

[8]Ibid. pp. 64 ff.

105.7 males born for every 100 females born. Since the death rate of males in early life is somewhat higher than that for females, the excess of male births is to some extent counterbalanced. The death rate for males continues somewhat higher throughout the middle and older age groupings. Thus a female born in 1944–1945 had a life expectancy of almost 69 years, which means that she might expect to live to that age, though many females would, of course, die at a younger age, and others might live to be older than 69. A male born in 1944–1945 could look forward to about 63.5 years of life, although again many individual males would die at younger and older ages.[9] In spite of the higher birth rate of males, then, the tendency in our population in recent years has been toward equality in number of males and number of females in the total group. In 1940 there was in the general population an average of only 101.1 males for every 100 females.[10] Very probably since 1940 the ratio has become about equal, so that in the whole population we now have about 100 males to every 100 females.

While these figures for the population as a whole are interesting, greater significance attaches to the sex ratio in certain segments of the population. Still using the figure of the 1940 United States Census, the last general census taken, we find the following distributions:

1. The ratio of males to females in the urban areas of the United States was about 95.8 to 100.

2. In the rural nonfarm areas of the country there were 104.5 males to every 100 females.

3. In the rural farm areas of the country there were, on the average, 112.1 males to every 100 females.

Perhaps even more significant than the urban-rural distribution of the sexes is that distribution in relation to age. If we take the ages 25–34 for males and 20–29 for females as the most common age for marriage, we find the following ratios hold:

1. In those specified age groups of the total population there are 91.2 males for every 100 females.

2. In those specified age groups of the urban population there are 87.7 males for every 100 females.

[9]*Fortune*, December, 1946, p. 250.
[10]Sixteenth Census of the United States, 1940.

3. In those specified age groups living in rural areas, both farm and nonfarm, there are about 96.6 males for every 100 females.[11]

The interesting point about these figures is the fact that there is a deficiency of males in the marriageable-age groupings in all the segments of our population, the deficiency being largest in the urban population, smallest in the rural population.

Specifically, in the urban population of the United States and in the inclusive age grouping of 15 to 49 years, there is a consistent deficiency of males. It ranges from a deficiency of about 12 males in the group 20–24 years of age to a minimum deficiency of about 2 males in the age group 40–44. There is also a large excess of females in the urban population above the age of 60.

Now, are there any relationships between the cultural environment and the age composition we have been describing? One obvious relationship lies in the fact that the urban environment provides a much greater number of jobs for women than does the rural environment. There is, therefore, a migration of females in a greater proportion than males from the rural to the urban areas. They become associated with commerce, the entertainment business, fashion magazines, artistic endeavors, and many other typical urban activities.

Aside from the opportunities to earn a living, women are attracted to the city by our prevalent belief that the city is the best place in which to live. In addition to that fact, the city provides an opportunity for professional women to practice their professions. A woman physician is more generally acceptable in the city than she is in the country, and the same may be said of other women in professional life. The urban surplus of women is almost wholly a matter of the kind of cultural environment the city provides.

It is interesting to speculate on the possible results of the excess of females in our cities. Under present conditions it is the cities which are most influential in the origination and spread of standards relating to "good taste," the proper clothing to wear, the proper music to listen to, the proper books to read, and so on ad infinitum. Through the medium of the radio, periodicals, newspapers, the movies, and similar devices these urban standards of behavior and belief are transmitted to rural areas. If the urban standards are developed by, or in response to, a predominantly female population,

[11]Landis, op. cit. p: 260.

they may very well reflect female attitudes. The "feminization of the country," for better or worse, then becomes a possibility!

For example, Los Angeles, with a total white population of some two million, has about forty thousand more females than males; New York, with a white population of seven million, has almost sixty-eight thousand more females than males; and Boston has an excess of about twenty-five thousand females in a total white population of about seven hundred and fifty thousand. These cities are all important centers of trade, entertainment, and education. Interesting results of the discrepancy in sex composition in these and other cities may appear, though it would be extremely hazardous, in more ways than one, to attempt to predict those results.

The predominance of females in the United States may also have an effect on politics. If there are more females within the voting ages than there are males, they can, by organization and combined effort, change the policies of the country as they wish. There is no evidence that they are doing this; it is simply a possibility.

In fact, all our suggestions as to the possible results of the surplus of females are in the domain of speculation, since we cannot predict what will happen. But we can see plainly the relationship between the environment and our changing sex composition.

AGE COMPOSITION

The age composition of the United States population also shows a definite trend in that the proportion of our population in the older ages is increasing and has been for some time. In 1900 the per cent of the total population of the country 65 years of age and older was 4.3; by 1945 about 7.2 per cent of the population was 65 years of age and older. If present trends continue, we may expect that about 10 per cent of our people will be in the "over 65" group by the end of the present generation. Similarly the proportion of people in the age group below 14 years has been decreasing. Naturally this decrease will be reflected in a decreased proportion of young adult and middle-aged individuals in the coming population.

One important factor in the increasing proportion of older people among us has been the decline of our death rate. In 1900 the crude death rate was about 17.2 per 1000 people; by 1945 it had decreased to about 10.6 per 1000 people. Of course not all this decline took place in the older age group. A good portion of it, for instance, is due to the decrease in infant mortality. But that portion of the decrease which has affected older people naturally tends to influence our population composition in the direction of increasing the older groupings.

That this decrease of death rates is a cultural factor is obvious when we consider that medical and sanitary engineering developments have been very important in bringing it about.

The increasing proportion of older people in our population may have some interesting results for our way of life. For example, we cannot care for aged members of our families in large family homes as we used to, because our pattern of living does not make large houses common. Most of us live in small apartments or small houses. Either our aged relatives must have money enough to pay for their own housing, also in small units, or we must increasingly provide specialized institutions to care for the aged. We are, in fact, doing both. Modern homes for the aged, having a great degree of comfort and some degree of luxury, already exist; and we are providing old-age pensions and other forms of assistance to the aged, which will permit them to live in foster families or otherwise independently of their own families.[12]

The fact that many of our people no longer care for elderly parents in their homes is sometimes considered unfortunate because it seems to indicate a moral decline. The inference is that we have less affection and respect for parents than we used to. It is very doubtful, however, that the change in our methods of caring for the aged constitutes any moral decline on our part—quite the reverse is, in fact, a possible interpretation if we wish to argue the morals of the case. Cultural changes have been such as to discourage large family aggregations, as we suggested on page 149 in our discussion of the net reproduction rate. This statement applies to the inclusion of parents in family aggregations as well as to the inclusion of large numbers of children in family aggregations. The "natural" adjustment to the situation is to care for parents in some location other than the family home.

Similarly our occupational patterns have shifted from farming to industry. The farm provided opportunities for useful work by older people which made them a distinct asset rather than a burden; and the farm also provided resources of food grown

12*Fortune*, December, 1946, pp. 250 f.

and preserved at home. Industry, on the other hand, offers less opportunity for the aged to work—though they are by no means incapable of industrial employment, as our experience in the Second World War demonstrated. The typical pattern of industrial employment, however, provides one money income to a family, with the result that the nonworking aged may be a liability rather than an asset to the family constellation. It is natural, then, that we should initiate systems of old-age pensions and other means of assistance. The whole situation does not mean that we like old people any the less; it simply means that, given our way of life as it has developed, old people do not function as they did in our past way of life.

Of the approximately 9,000,000 old people in the United States in 1946, about 39 per cent (3,930,000) lived by means of some kind of public or private assistance, distributed about as follows: Old-age assistance and other government subsidies, 2,070,000; friends, relatives, and church organizations, 1,650,000; cared for in institutions for the aged, 210,000.[13] Another 34 per cent of the 9,000,000 total lived by employment of some kind: 2,000,000 on wages and salaries; 1,400,000 on self-employment (business, professions, and other skills); and 10,000 by means of unemployment insurance and compensation for sickness. Another 18 per cent of the total, or about 1,800,000, lived on pensions, government and private. Only 9 per cent, about 920,000 people, lived on income from investments.

These figures indicate that only about one third of our people 65 years of age and over are functioning in our economic system. Assuming that there are others who perform significant functions not directly connected with the economic system, we may suggest that at least one half our people over the age of 65 do not perform any significant function in our society. This statement does not mean that they cannot perform such functions, or that they could not under other conditions of association. Part of our program of societal planning must include plans for active functioning by the aged in our social order, or for providing constructive ways in which they can use their leisure. A group of nine million people is a resource which we ought to be able to use instead of letting it deteriorate. Moreover, a group as large as the one we have been discussing can exert a great deal of influence on society if it is organized to do

[13]Ibid.

so. In other cultures which have experienced an increasing proportion of people in the older age groups that influence has been predominantly in a conservative direction. The aged are interested in security rather than in a free chance to make their own way in life; their own way has already been made—or perhaps has not been made, as the case may be. A conservative influence in society, with its emphasis on security, may be desirable, unless it becomes so reactionary that it leads to stagnation. One important way to prevent development of a completely reactionary attitude among the aged is to provide them with functionally important or constructively developmental activities.

It is quite beside the point to suggest that the aged people of some generations ago did not have to have any such things provided for them. Our own times differ from those past times in many important respects, with the result that our patterns of behavior also differ from past patterns of behavior.

POPULATION QUALITY

Problems of population quality relate to the kind of people we are developing in our population and to programs for improving the quality of the population.

THE DATA OF POPULATION QUALITY

In approaching our discussion of population quality, let us suggest that there are certain facts about our population which are undoubtedly true, much as we may disagree about the meaning and interpretation of those facts. The first fact is referred to as *differential reproduction*, which means the tendency of certain segments of our society to produce more children per marriage than are produced by certain other segments. For instance, if we classify families according to their income level, putting in the lowest category those living on government relief and therefore without income, and in the highest category those families with an income of $3000 or more per year, we find that the families on relief have, on the average, a net reproduction rate almost three times that of the families receiving $3000 or more per year. Between these two extremes there tends to be a definite general relationship: the higher the income class, the lower the net reproduction rate, though there are exceptions to this rule.[14]

We find much the same relationship in families which have varying educational backgrounds: on the average, and with some exceptions, the lower the educational level, the higher the net reproduction rate. Obviously, there may be a connection between the educational level and the money income; it is still true that only people of a certain level of income can send their children to college.

Again, when we arrange families according to occupational level, we find that the lower the occupational level, in the sense of skills and training required, the higher the net reproduction rate.

Similarly, we may contrast the native-born and foreign-born populations, with the result that we find the fertility of the foreign-born considerably higher than that of the native-born stock.[15] It was this particular aspect of differential reproduction that especially troubled some past investigators of population quality. Thus Professor Huntington refers to the situation as a "war of smokeless decay" in which our native stock is gradually being replaced by a decadent foreign stock.[16] Mr. A. E. Wiggam holds that the "low foreigner" will continue to be our chief national problem as long as we foolishly think we can "Americanize him," because he is constitutionally incapable of learning our ways.[17]

These last instances illustrate one interpretation, though by no means the only interpretation, of the admitted facts of differential reproduction we have cited. Those who follow that interpretation classify certain segments of our population as "superior" and others as "inferior" on the basis of their income, education level, occupational class, and place of birth. They then view with alarm the fact that the "inferior" (according to their classification) are reproducing at a much more rapid pace than the "superior," with the inevitable conclusion that the nation is headed for ruin and decay.

[14]J. K. Folsom, *The Family and Democratic Society*, pp. 277 ff. Wiley, New York, 1943.

[15]This statement refers to the true foreign-born, that is, those born in foreign countries. American-born children of foreign parents, and descendants in succeeding generations, follow the native rather than the foreign-born pattern.

[16]E. Huntington and L. F. Whitney, *The Builders of America*, Chap. 3 et passim. Morrow, New York, 1927.

[17]A. E. Wiggam, *The Fruit of the Family Tree*, p. 7. Bobbs-Merrill, Indianapolis, 1924.

The prime mistake in this interpretation is perhaps obvious. America has been noted for its *social mobility* and *social circulation*. Those terms mean that many, perhaps most, people refuse to stay in the "inferior" classes to which they may have been relegated by sociologists. The son of the immigrant becomes the small business-man of the next generation; his son in turn becomes the business or professional leader of the third generation. Children of low-income families do not necessarily remain in low-income occupations; they often rise to business and professional status. From the viewpoint of education, grandfather graduates from the eighth grade, father goes on to high school, and son finishes college and professional school. All this is perfectly ordinary and commonplace in our society.

How is it that this obvious fact of social circulation was over-looked in the interpretation we discussed just above? In large part the reason was that students of these matters a generation ago were imbued with the idea that the major portion of an individual's life equipment is hereditary. This statement brings us to another obvious and admitted fact about people, which is simply this: that certain traits tend to run in families, a fact familiar enough to most of us. People in the same family tend to look like one another, they tend to act like one another, to believe the same things, to resemble each other in many respects. No one doubts that. Once more, it is not the fact itself which is in question—it is the interpretation of that fact.

Earlier students of man, observing that traits do tend to run in families, assumed that the explanation of that fact lay in heredity. They were familiar enough with hereditary mechanisms in the case of eye color and other physical manifestations. What could be more natural than to assume that attitudes, beliefs, intellectual capacities, emotional instabilities, and many other characteristics were in-herited? Some of them did make that assumption with a vengeance. In such a case, of course, the future was very dark. If the lower classes were so limited by inheritance that they would always be "lower," and if they were reproducing at a much more rapid rate than the upper classes, then obviously the future population of America would be predominantly lower-class with presumably dis-astrous results.

Most sociologists today see little reason to agree with that as-sumption of a generation ago, but it is still a part of our popular folklore. We mentioned on page 121 that new scientific ideas, developed in the investigations of specialists, require almost a generation to reach the mass of the people. The whole popular attitude toward heredity is one example of that kind of lag.

In contrast, the sociologist today doubts very strongly whether all aspects of "inferiority" are inherited. It may be said that many traits "run in families" because the cultural environment in which the several members of the family live is very similar and because the interaction patterns among family members are very intimate. Children do not habitually live in isolation from their parents and their brothers and sisters. If the cultural environment provides similarity of stimuli and of influences, we should expect a large measure of similarity in behavior patterns to result, quite aside from the operation of hereditary mechanisms.

Furthermore, if the cultural environment is varied, as it is under the operation of social mobility and the circulation of individuals from class to class, the results of that expanded environment will be reflected in varied behavior patterns. The pattern of the son who has received a professional education is much different from that of the grandfather who did not complete the eighth grade. The real problem in connection with differential reproduction, then, is to make available to the people of all classes a type of cultural environment which will provide information, knowledge, skills, wisdom, income, and whatever else we believe characterize the "higher classes," and to encourage motivations which will impel the people of all classes to make use of what is so provided. Such a program will not turn all the "lower classes" into geniuses, nor will it automatically make them good citizens in the mass. Perhaps it will make them into citizens as good on the whole as the members of the "higher classes," and raise the level of intelligence and of skills among the majority of the "lower classes" to the point where the latter will be indistinguishable from the "higher classes."

The difficulty is that we often expect our programs for human betterment to make every individual into an outstanding person. No program will do that for all members of the "lower classes." But it is yet to be demonstrated that every individual in the "higher classes" is outstanding.

It is interesting to note what is actually happening to our population quality from this viewpoint of the changing cultural environment. We have been providing educational and other facilities for some time now. They should be having perceptible effects by this time. Actually, we find the following situation:

From 1930 to 1940 the population of the United States increased about 7 per cent. We do not know what the increase has been since, but presumably it has not been greatly in excess of 7 per cent. If we assume a 7 per cent increase in population, then

1. The number of college graduates in the population has increased about six times as fast as the population itself.

2. The number of high-school graduates has increased about fourteen times as fast as the population itself.

3. Increases in "higher-bracket" occupations have been as follows:

Salaried professionals (designers, reporters, musicians, nurses, etc.) have increased twice as fast as the population.

Manufacturing executives (proprietors, officials, managers of industry) have increased about five times as fast.

Industrial engineers have increased about ten times as fast, lawyers twice as fast, chemists three times as fast, engineers something more than twice as fast.[18]

If the number of people in these occupations is increasing at a more rapid rate than the population itself, we must conclude that more people are being drawn into these occupations from the existing population. Also, if the "lower classes" have been reproducing at a more rapid rate than the "higher classes," a large proportion of the occupational increase noted has been supplied from the "lower classes."

The point is that the provision of environmental opportunities and environmental stimuli is already having its effect. The "lower classes" are becoming the "higher classes." The fears of earlier students of society are not justified.

Other implications of differential reproduction may, however, be disturbing. Thus if, as is the case, the "higher classes" on the average do not reproduce at a high rate, and if more and more people are drawn into those classes by means of social circulation and follow their patterns of reproduction, we may presently face a declining population. The results of such a development for business, defense, and other aspects of the social organization may be disintegrative, and under such circumstances major readjustments

[18] *Fortune*, December, 1947, p. 228.

in our social life may be necessary. The real focus of our attention, then, need not be on the threat of differential reproduction from any hereditary viewpoint, but on plans to increase the net reproduction rate of the population in general.

In conclusion, let us note that there is some evidence that the "higher classes" have failed to reproduce because of temporary circumstances. At present it appears that the more successful sectors of these classes have more children than the less successful sectors of the same classes. The future, then, may see a stabilization of our reproductive patterns.

SUMMARY

The undoubted facts of differential reproduction are not now interpreted as indicating a hereditary tendency toward degeneration in our future population. Population policies intended to improve the quality of our future population rely strongly on environmental instrumentalities. There is evidence that these instrumentalities are becoming effective in producing a change in the kind of people we have from the viewpoint of intellectual, occupational, and behavior levels.

READINGS

MUMFORD, LEWIS. *The Condition of Man.* Harcourt, Brace and Company, New York, 1944. A survey of present trends in urban civilization, with historical backgrounds. Critical of urbanism.

MANNHEIM, KARL. *Man and Society.* Harcourt, Brace and Company, New York, 1941. A discussion of contemporary society from the "problems and planning" aspect.

"World Population in Transition." *Annals of the American Academy of Political and Social Sciences,* Vol. 237, January, 1945. A discussion, by a number of specialists, of world demographic trends, regional studies of population, aspects of population change, and issues of population policy.

Minority People in a Nation at War. *Annals of the American Academy of Political and Social Sciences,* Vol. 223, September, 1942. A discussion of the position of minority peoples in war times which illuminates their position in peace times.

CHAPTER VIII

RACE

THE SIGNIFICANCE of race in human interactions is often considerably overemphasized. It has some importance because it tends to influence the interactions of certain segments of populations; and it is of somewhat more importance for our purposes here because beliefs and superstitions about race and attitudes relating to race have become cultural forces in our times. We must therefore examine certain aspects of the race question.

DEFINITIONS

It is important at the outset to have in mind clearly what we mean in sociology by the term *race*, and by certain other terms associated with racial discussions.

THE MEANING OF RACE

In scientific discussions the word *race* has a very definite and restricted meaning. It is often used with quite another meaning in popular discussions, as we shall presently see. Let us agree on the scientific meaning.

> *A race is a category of human beings who share certain definite, measurable, heritable physical characteristics.*

This definition stresses certain facts.

1. The characteristics by which we distinguish one race from another are *physical* characteristics. Any traits which are cultural in origin are excluded. Such phenomena as customs, languages, beliefs, "intelligence level," and reaction patterns that are not exclusively biological are not racial phenomena. We exclude them from the scientific definition of race because there is no evidence

that any of them are related to biological racial characteristics. A man with a black skin may be as intelligent as a man with a white skin. A black man may conduct himself in exactly the same way as a white man. He may respond to the same influences in precisely the same manner. Actually in many instances it is impossible to distinguish a "light black" from a "dark white" by superficial observation, because they act, believe, and live in the same way.

2. The characteristics by which we distinguish one race from another are *definite* and they are *measurable with accuracy*. The fact that they are definite means that we can describe them with precision so that we and other people know exactly what we are talking about. Thus when we speak of *pigmentation* we mean the presence of certain coloring material in the layers of the skin. When we mention a *cephalic index* we know precisely that it describes certain measurements of the human head, made in a certain way. If one investigator has measured the cephalic index of an aggregate, every other informed investigator knows exactly what his procedure was, and every other informed investigator can repeat the process if that becomes necessary.

This criterion of definiteness excludes from any distinction between races such concepts as "relative artistic ability," "emotional make-up," and "relative ability to carry through a job," though these and similar qualities are mentioned in some loose and inaccurate popular treatises on the subject of race.

Even on the basis of definite and measurable physical traits it is often impossible to distinguish *individual* members of one race from individual members of another race because of the shading of one trait into another, and because of the overlapping of racial traits. It would be simple if Race A exhibited one series of cephalic indexes, and Race B quite another series. Actually there is an area of overlapping, with the result that certain measurements will be found in some of the members of both Race A and Race B. The same is true of other physical characteristics.

3. Finally, the traits which distinguish one race from another are heritable, that is, they are passed on from one generation to another *by the mechanism of heredity* and not otherwise. We shall have occasion to refer again to heredity. Let us note here simply that *heredity* does not mean the existence of mere resemblances among

people. Resemblances may be cultural or accidental in origin. Heredity implies resemblances which occur because of a definite mechanism which we understand, and whose operation we can demonstrate in connection with the trait we are discussing. We can demonstrate that operation very clearly in the case of some physical characteristics; we can demonstrate its operation in the case of only a very few mental traits, and we cannot demonstrate its operation at all in the case of cultural traits. A great deal of confusion in racial discussions has resulted from failure to adhere to accuracy of meanings in connection with the terms *heredity* and *hereditary*.

Such, then, is the meaning of the term *race* in sociology and anthropology. Because the term is loosely used with quite different meanings in popular discussions, we are compelled to pay a good deal more attention to the subject of race than it deserves. What are some of these other meanings?

Sometimes the word is used loosely to mean any aggregate or category that differs from ourselves. Thus people speak of the "Italian race" or the "English race" or the "Jewish race," although actually there are no such things. What they mean is the Italian nation or nationality group, the English nation or perhaps the British Empire, the Jewish people or the Jewish cultural group. All these are, of course, distinguishable from one another. They differ in a variety of ways, but they differ on some other basis than that of race.

In other instances the word is loosely used to describe certain characteristics of a true race, such as the Negroes, but it is applied to nonracial traits such as their relative degree of literacy compared with whites, or their crime rate in our culture, both of which are cultural rather than racial factors.

The Meaning of Racism

Most commonly of all, the term *race* is loosely used in connection with *racism*. Racism is a collection of doctrines, beliefs, and superstitions *about* race and its assumed significance for social and cultural life. It is a mixture of fact and fancy, with a tinge of deliberate deception, but it has enough of the appearance of accuracy to deceive a good many people. Unfortunately, examples of racism abound in our times.

Thus the Nazi attitude toward the Jewish people was based on misconceptions of the meaning and importance of race in influencing behavior patterns and was supported by a number of deliberate misrepresentations. In spite of all these facts, Nazi racist doctrines appealed to some segments of the German people precisely as similar doctrines have appealed to other peoples in other nations. The history of our own relationships with the Negro is not too dissimilar to the instance we have just cited. The truth of racist doctrines is secondary to their influence. Part of their attractiveness lies in the fact that the branding of an aggregate as an inferior species of human being on a racist basis not only inflates the ego of those who so brand it but it also justifies exploitation and other forms of mistreatment by the self-styled "superior" species.

Perhaps the most familiar and widespread racist doctrine is the belief in "Nordic superiority." Nordics are a subclass of the white race, distinguished by such physical characteristics as light hair and blue eyes, relative tallness, and a certain type of bony structure in the head and body. We can sometimes distinguish Nordics from other branches of the white race with some degree of definiteness, but they are not in themselves a separate race. They are, to repeat, a subclass of the white race, as are, incidentally, the Jewish people also.

The mistake of the proponents of Nordic superiority lies in two directions. (1) They assume that certain aggregates constitute what they call a "pure" Nordic stock, that is, Nordic unmixed with any other race or any other subclass of the white race; and (2) they assume that this allegedly pure and unmixed stock has produced the "highest type" of civilization in the world because of its racial background and characteristics. Both of these assumptions are mistaken. The Nordics are not an unmixed racial stock. In fact, except among primitives who have had no contact whatsoever with other groups, we do not know of any pure, unmixed racial stock.

Whether or not the Nordics have produced the highest type of civilization depends on how we define that term. Their civilization usually has been characterized by militarism and industrialism, neither of which is an unmixed blessing to mankind. Whatever they have produced, however, has been produced by a mixture of Nordic and other populations, since there is no such thing as an unmixed Nordic group.

But not even all Nordics or all whites have developed industrial civilizations. In northern Africa certain of the Berbers who have lived in relative isolation from Europe for many centuries are of predominantly Caucasian, or white, stock. But they live at a very primitive level, with only the simplest kind of agricultural and industrial techniques. In fact, their culture is less advanced than that of some Negroes who live farther south in Africa. The mere fact of membership in the white race is not a guarantee of cultural superiority.

In fairness we should note that ideas as to the superiority of their own race are not limited to whites. Some Negroes hold to the doctrine of black superiority; many Japanese are convinced of the entire truth of the assertion that the Japanese are the most highly developed "race" in the universe; some Chinese smile in superiority at the vagaries of the white race and white civilization. No one racial group has a monopoly on race prejudice.

Aside from the widely held belief in the "Nordic myth" which we have been discussing, there are other beliefs which form part of racism. They are not organized into a comprehensive system, as the Nordic myth is, and they are often applied in a more or less haphazard fashion to particular instances of race conflict. But in those particular instances they may have serious effects. Thus in the United States there are those who assume that all Negroes are lazy and inefficient; in Britain there are those who assume that the "natives" of British colonies are all incompetent and inefficient; currently some Hollanders are convinced of the general incapability of all Indonesians. Many other examples might be cited. They may be silly, or they may be pernicious, or they may be unimportant, but they are all mistaken. What man is in the aggregate is the result of his basic interaction with his culture and with his environment. Race may be one factor in that interaction, but it is a minor factor.

ANOTHER VIEW OF RACE

We insist that it is a minor factor for the very important reason, among others, that in modern times we cannot distinguish one racial group from another with any degree of certainty. Anthropologists distinguish certain large categories of mankind which we call races, according to their different physical characteristics; and in primitive or otherwise simple cultures it is possible to point out certain predominant traits which indicate that the populations composing those cultures belong to one or another of the inclusive racial groupings. But in modern complex societies we cannot make those simple distinctions, precisely because of the complexity of the groupings involved. There has been so much contact of cultures and so much intermixture of populations that racial distinctions which originally may have existed are now blurred. In regard to this, Professor Linton makes the following comment:

There is no human group whose ancestry is known for even five generations in the exact terms necessary for racial determination. In fact, there is not even a family line for which we have satisfactory information over this brief period. Most genealogies are simply lists of names, and even the family portrait gallery fails to yield information on many important points. All that we can do is to classify human varieties as we find them today. Any conclusions as to their relationships which may be based on these classifications are merely conjectures with varying degrees of probability.[1]

Professor Alexander Goldenweiser points out that even the anthropologist studying primitive cultures finds race an unimportant category; that, in fact, it is often an encumbrance which the anthropologist disregards. He suggests that "What the anthropologist finds is man to whom nothing human is foreign" because "all the fundamental traits of the psychic make-up of man anywhere are present everywhere."[2]

Professor Ashley-Montagu in a recent book strongly criticizes the anthropological definition of race *even in the accepted scientific form, as we have given it,* on the ground that it is really a meaningless concept of little or no use in our study of human groupings.[3] He agrees in this respect with Linton and Goldenweiser, but is somewhat more forthright in his statement.

It is interesting that these three outstanding anthropologists, among many who might be cited, agree in their judgment that race is an unimportant factor in human life and that we cannot in modern times distinguish one race from another with sufficient accuracy

[1]Ralph Linton, *The Study of Man* (Students' Ed.), pp. 36–37. Appleton-Century, New York, 1936. Quoted by special permission of the publishers.

[2]A. Goldenweiser. *Anthropology*, Chap. II, especially pp. 20 and 32. Crofts, New York, 1945.

[3]M. F. Ashley-Montagu, *Man's Most Dangerous Myth, The Fallacy of Race*, pp. 27 ff. Columbia University Press, New York, 1942.

to use the concept for the analysis of human groupings in any significant way.

Very possibly the reader by this time will be inclined to agree with Professor Goldenweiser that race is an encumbrance, and that it would be much better to neglect the whole thing in our studies of man. Unfortunately, we cannot do quite that because, as we intimated earlier, certain ideas characteristic of racism have so penetrated our culture and our thinking that we must meet them with more accurate statements. The principles which follow reflect the current scientific view of race and its relationship to human affairs.

RACE DIFFERENCES

First of all, at the risk of elaborating the obvious, let us be clear about one fact: there are differences between races. We may put it this way:

There exist observable racial differences in cultural and personality traits as well as in biological traits.

The reason for making such an obvious statement is that racists are apt to falsify the whole position of social science with respect to race. They are apt to insist that we hold to the belief that there are no differences at all between races. Uninformed persons who are told that this is the accepted belief have only to look at a Negro and then at a white to see that the one has a darker skin than the other; there is at least that difference. They come to the conclusion that sociologists, who are represented as saying that there is no difference at all between the two, must be deliberately promulgating false doctrine, and hence they tend to reject all that sociologists have to say on the subject of race.

Moreover, our uninformed person can look at the way in which Negroes live in segregated areas of our cities; he can observe the type of occupation that Negroes follow, almost universally the "lower" and less skilled kinds of occupation; he can discover with little effort that educationally Negroes in the aggregate are not the equal of whites in the aggregate. The differences go beyond mere skin color or any other purely biological fact. There are also cultural differences between white and Negro. The conclusion is that if sociologists cannot see all these differences they must be lacking in the very elements of observation.

The point is, as we stated in the preceding principle, that of course these differences exist. By all means emphasize the fact that they do exist. But we must also go further and try to discover *why* they exist. Is it because of the race of the Negro and the race of the white, or are there other important factors? The racist assumes, without putting much thought on the matter, that race is the cause of the difference. But that is a shallow kind of thinking. It is on much the same level as the primitive thinking we mentioned earlier in the book. Primitive man makes a hideous noise when an eclipse appears, and when the eclipse passes without doing any harm he assumes that it passed away harmlessly *because* he made a noise. We in our wisdom know that noise-making had nothing to do with the passing of the eclipse. But we sometimes, in our unwisdom, assume that a black skin or some other racial characteristic is the sole cause of the cultural differences between Negroes and people with a white skin. Some segments of our society are by no means free of such primitive reasoning processes.

There are, then, racial differences. What are the causes of those differences?

RACE, CULTURE, AND ENVIRONMENT

In a complex culture the biological facts of race are of little or no importance in the creation of cultural and personality differences.

Cultural differences are those differences in *aggregates* which are expressed in varying customs, beliefs, languages, techniques, and ways of living generally. Personality differences are differences in *individual* traits and characteristics such as intelligence, skill, cleverness, emotional balance, habits, and behavior patterns. Even though the members of an aggregate may be subject to the same cultural influences, individual personality traits may vary widely. Thus Negro groupings in the United States may exhibit very similar culture traits in whatever section of the country they may be, but there are individual Negroes who are intelligent, other individual Negroes who are stupid, some who are skilled, others unskilled, some who are lazy, others ambitious, and so on.   That is, of course, precisely the situation we find among the whites.   As an aggregate, they tend to follow a common way of life;   as individuals they differ from one another in many traits.   The one is culture, the other personality.

We shall discuss personality at some length in the next chapter. What we wish to emphasize here is that in a complex culture the biological facts of race are relatively unimportant in the creation of both cultural and personality differences between aggregates.

Thus if we investigate the intelligence of Negroes and of whites, or of the members of any other contrasting racial categories, by any of the accepted methods of testing intelligence, we make some interesting discoveries.   First, we discover that there is in general a tendency for the average intelligence of the white aggregate to be higher than that of the Negro aggregate.   But if we compare selected segments of the respective aggregates, we find that there are exceptions to that rule.   Suppose we compare Negro college graduates with white tenant farmers, a class who are economically underprivileged and undereducated.   The average intelligence of the Negro college group will be higher than that of the white tenant-farmer segment.

Some readers will protest at once, "But that is to be expected, since the one group is college-trained and the other is not."   Implicit in that very protest is agreement with the suggestion that race, as such, is not a guarantee of low-grade intelligence, which is precisely the point we have been making!   If some black-skinned people can be made more intelligent than some white-skinned people by such a purely cultural factor as college training, the biological characteristic of race becomes of minor importance.

Now it can be argued at this point that it is the Negro with some admixture of white blood who is superior intellectually.   All that we can reply to that contention is that there is no evidence that it is true.   We cannot prove that it is wrong.   But would we reverse the statement and imply that unintelligent whites are those who have some admixture of Negro blood?   There is no evidence for any such statement as that either; and, in fact, it would hardly occur to most whites to make any such suggestion because, while it might suit the purposes of their racial argument, it would be considered "degrading."

The first thing we note, then, in our investigation of intelligence and race, is that there is a great deal of overlapping of intelligence levels between the two racial groups. This statement is not only true of violently contrasted segments such as Negro college graduates and white tenant farmers; it is true in general of the two racial aggregates. While the *average* of white intelligence may, for cultural rather than racial reasons, be higher than the *average* of Negro intelligence, there are some Negroes more intelligent than whites, and there is an area of intelligence which characterizes members of both groups.

In the example just discussed we compared two racial segments in which the cultural environment was markedly different because one segment had college training while the other had a very limited background of education. Let us now compare two segments in which the cultural environment is similar. If we match the Negro inhabitants of any large city with the white inhabitants of the same city, we discover that there is very little difference in the average intelligence levels of the two aggregates, provided educational and other cultural facilities either are common to both whites and Negroes or, if the Negroes have special schools, are truly equal in equipment and staff. This will not hold true when special Negro schools of an inferior kind are provided. In the case of actual equality, cultural factors far outweigh racial factors in significance.

Another point to note is that there are many individual Negroes who have developed specialized skills and abilities, and have become musicians, dramatists, lawyers, physicians, teachers, or clergymen. These individuals are admittedly as much of an exception in the Negro aggregate as are those whites with specialized abilities the exception in the white aggregate. We are not by any means suggesting that people like Mr. Paul Robeson and Miss Marian Anderson prove the inherent ability of every Negro to develop unusual talents, any more than similar special cases among whites indicate the ability of every white to develop unusual talents. But if, in those individual cases, race in itself was no bar to accomplishment, it is a further indication of the relative unimportance of the biological fact of race.

We are really faced with two questions here: (1) What was the stimulus to accomplishment present in the case of these unusual Negroes? (2) Is that stimulus present for the aggregate of Negroes? Unfortunately, we cannot answer those questions with finality because it is difficult to analyze the motives of individuals and it is not easy to trace the significant motivations in the patterns of an aggregate. We may, however, say this much: the individual Negroes cited, and others who might be cited, did have the advantage of certain cultural factors which are not generally available to all Negroes.

Most Negroes in the United States find that the color of their skin closes to them many of the advantages which are generally open to whites even of moderate economic position. In addition to cultural differences between the Negro and the white, there is another factor: the stimulus to attain advanced goals through hard work. The Negro in the United States is forced into an inferior position and into inferior activities. Even if he becomes a professional person, he will most probably have to practice his profession in a position far less attractive than that of whites in similar professions. How much of a motivation toward study and advancement is there in this prospect of subordinate rating and opportunity, regardless of individual qualifications? May not the Negro ask if it is, after all, worth the effort involved?

Of course we, from our more favored position, may advance the idea that the Negro with talent should develop his potentialities, if he has the opportunity to do so, even in the face of all his difficulties, because the helping of his people, the raising of their position in society, should be a strong enough motivation. As a matter of fact that motivation is present in the case of a good many Negro leaders. Very probably it is as common among Negroes as it is among whites, some of whom enter vocations which will reward them principally by giving them the opportunity of serving their fellows. In the case of the Negro, however, this goal is much less likely to be realized than in the case of the white, given our present social organization.

A further question of interest is this: If the Negro had the same type of cultural environments as the white, would he approximate the white in cultural and personality characteristics? There is some reason to believe that this might be the case, because of the following fact:

When members of the same race interact with different environments, significant differences in cultural and personality traits develop.

Compare, for instance, the Negro living in Africa, in those areas in which he has been only slightly influenced by white culture, with the Negro living in the United States. Obviously the way of life of the two aggregates differs in almost every significant detail. Somewhat the same thing may be said of Negroes inhabiting different sections of the United States: the Northern Negro lives on a different level and in different ways from the Southern Negro. Similarly, we may compare Negroes in the United States at different periods of history. Negroes today have "progressed" beyond the Negroes of a hundred years ago. So, of course, have whites. The point is that the Negro does not remain fixed at some inferior stage of development beyond which he cannot go. In all of these cases, the importance of the cultural environment in producing differences of behavior in members of the same race is obvious.

RACE CONTACTS

Our belief in the relative unimportance of racial factors in social life is further strengthened by those instances of race contact which we can observe. In general, the following principle is true:

> *When different races are in close contact, there is a tendency*
> *toward the development of similarities in cultural*
> *and personality traits.*

If we discovered that the similarity was wholly the result of one race borrowing from or imitating the way of life of another race, we might assume that this very fact was evidence of the inferiority of the borrowing race. Actually the similarities develop through a process of mutual borrowing. In the United States the Negroes have very largely borrowed from the whites, but it is also true that whites borrow from Negroes. Much of our modern popular dancing is of Negro origin, as is much of modern popular music. Modern religious denominations which involve exaggerated emotional expressions show some relationship to Negro types of religious behavior. Again, we have borrowed some Negro foods and ways of food preparation, some Negro turns of language, and some superstitions.

There is no doubt of the fact that most of the borrowing has been by the Negro from the white. That is natural in view of the fact that the whites are by far the majority and in view of the fact that white industrial ways are much more advanced than those of the Negro. The Negro had to adjust himself to the dominant culture in order to survive.

The well-known cases of the assimilation of one race into the culture of another furnish even more conclusive examples of the effects of close contact on cultural and personality traits.[4] They indicate very strongly that the culture of any race is responsive to the influences of the environment.

We may go a step further, and say that apparently even the *physical* traits of race are responsive to environmental influences. Professor Franz Boas, some years ago, investigated changes in the cephalic index and in certain other purely physical traits of children born in this country of European parents, with whom he compared children born in Europe of the same parents. He eliminated in this way any factor of intermarriage or interbreeding with other than the parent racial stock. The parents of the children were the same; the only different circumstances were the place of birth and the environment in which the two groups of children grew up. His conclusion was that the American children of these immigrants differed in physical type from their parents and from their brothers and sisters who were born in Europe. The changes are also cumulative: they were more marked for children born two years after the arrival of the mother than for children born one year after her arrival, and so on.[5]

The only possible conclusion seems to be that the environment— in the inclusive sense of physical, cultural, and social environment —was an important factor in causing changes in the physical aspects of the individuals involved. Obviously, this finding tends to support Dr. Ashley-Montagu's belief that our whole concept of race, even when it is defined in accurate and measurable terms, is a more or less meaningless concept. Races change, not only as the result of interbreeding and intermarriage with other racial stocks but also as the result of a changing environment.

[4] A. Goldenweiser, loc. cit.
[5] See ibid. p. 17, for a summary of Boas's study.

RACE PREJUDICE

It is unfortunately true that no matter how careful our discussion of the facts of race, culture, and environment may be, it will have little effect on those people who suffer from an exaggerated form of race prejudice. It would not be surprising if there were a few people who were victims of prejudice. We can discover almost any behavior pattern characterizing some portion of an aggregate. The surprising thing is the considerable amount of favorable response to the propaganda sent out by various racist groups. Small as these groups may be in themselves, they nonetheless exert a disproportionate amount of influence. Why do so many of us respond to such propaganda? Why do so many of us demonstrate race prejudice in our own individual contacts with members of other races, even though we may be perfectly aware of the facts about race?

There are doubtless many reasons. Perhaps the most common one is our liking for, and our ease with, individuals with whom we are familiar and who are the same as we are. We all tend to feel ill at ease in the presence of the unfamiliar and different. Our native culture surrounds us with a whole galaxy of familiar things—a familiar language, familiar customs, familiar artifacts, familiar beliefs. This nexus of familiarity enables us to move through life taking a good many things for granted, because a mere glance tells us what their place and function in our culture is. We become accustomed to this complex of familiar things, and aside from it we feel ill at ease. Since we do not particularly like to feel this or any other painful sensation, we tend to avoid the unfamiliar and the different. A person of a different race or cultural background, then, beocmes a person to avoid. He does not fit into our familiar scheme of things. We do not associate with him.

In addition to this refusal directly to associate with him, we attempt to make him fit into our familiar scheme of things somehow. We may do this by assigning him a definite and restricted locale and function in our culture, as we do with the Negro in the United States, and as some European cultures have done with the Jewish people through the use of the ghetto system. Or we may force him into our scheme of things by building up a stereotype about him, that is, a mental image which describes him to our satisfaction, whether it is accurate or not. Thus, all Chinese are assumed to be laundrymen. The stereotype of Chinese as laundrymen satisfies us because it is familiar and because it forces the Chinese into our own cultural forms. Even if we do not assume that all Chinese are laundrymen, we assume that they all have the characteristics of laundrymen, which serves equally well to "place" them in our conceptual scheme. We thus avoid considering the Chinese to be intelligent, thoughtful individuals, and we do not have to worry about understanding what the Chinese is thinking; possibly, even, what he is thinking about us. We suspect dimly that what he thinks may be different from what the average member of our own group thinks, and we avoid the different.

We do not limit this kind of reaction to different races, of course. We apply it also to different cultural and nationality groups. We assume that all Frenchmen are constantly preoccupied with sex, that all Englishmen are snobs, that all Jews live only that they may acquire more money, preferably by dishonest means, and that Italians do nothing aside from eating spaghetti and singing operatic arias. We forcibly shove them into some kind of stereotype which is familiar. Of course it is also true that foreign populations have a variety of stereotypes about us, equally inaccurate and ludicrous. What we have been describing is a common human reaction pattern, not limited to any one nation or population.

Obviously stereotypes and the assignment of restricted roles to alien races and culture groups do not contribute to any great understanding of the members of those groups as human beings. Anyone interested in creating race or cultural prejudice can make effective use of that fact.

In addition to this more or less amorphous feeling of discomfort in the presence of other races, there is the factor of fear of other races and of the different generally. Sometimes we fear them on more or less logical grounds; at other times our fears are baseless and absurd. Whites in the lower occupational and economic brackets often express the fear of competition from the Negro. To some extent this fear is more or less logical; the Negro may actually be forced to work for lower wages, and he may be just as useful industrially and agriculturally as the unskilled white. But from another viewpoint the fear is misdirected, since the large reserve of unskilled white labor is just as much of a threat as the relatively small group of Negroes. In any case, the solution of the problem of the unskilled laborer lies in the direction of development of his skills, stronger unions, social legislation, and other constructive devices. Transferring economic fears and insecurities to the Negro or to any other minority group is a foolish procedure.

Finally, we may feel antagonistic toward other races because many of us are basically insecure in the whole area of our social relationships. This has doubtless always been true to some extent, but it is even more so at present, when we are told of threats inherent in the atomic bomb, of increasing labor-capital strife, of the possibility of a third world war within a few years, and of the "certainty" of another depression in the not-too-distant future. We cannot approach the question of race contacts and race prejudice except in terms of our basic personality components. If insecurity is one of those basic components, we can hardly approach members of minority racial and cultural groups with confidence.

The implication of all that we have been saying is that problems of race prejudice cannot be solved quickly, and that they cannot be solved as isolated problems. They will become more amenable to solution when we develop a greater understanding of ourselves and of the society in which we live, and when we develop more skill in societal self-direction which will enable us to predict with some degree of accuracy what future trends will be. Both of these will increase our feelings of confidence and security.

Specifically, in the field of race relations we must develop (1) a greater knowledge of the facts of race and of the significance of race in cultural and personality developments; (2) a further realization of the importance of the cultural environment in affecting the totality of race and group contacts; (3) an understanding of the significance of individual and group feelings of inferiority and insecurity in conditioning human behavior; and finally, (4) a greater realization of the ultimate value of people as human beings, whatever their racial or cultural characteristics may be, and the incorporation of that emphasis on human worth and dignity into our social goals.

READINGS

ASHLEY-MONTAGU, M. F. *Man's Most Dangerous Myth: The Fallacy of Race.* Columbia University Press, New York, 1945. A discussion of the meaning of race by a trained anatomist and anthropologist.

BENEDICT, RUTH. *Race, Science and Politics* (Revised Edition). The Viking Press, Inc., New York, 1947. The exact meaning of *race,* and the relationship of race and racial concepts to various areas of life.

HUSZAR, GEORGE (Ed.). *The Anatomy of Racial Intolerance.* The H. W. Wilson Company, New York, 1946. A collection of reprints from sociological and other journals dealing with intolerance and suggesting remedies. The book goes beyond "racial" intolerance to include cultural and other prejudices.

LOGAN, RAYFORD W. (Ed.). *What the Negro Wants.* University of North Carolina Press, Chapel Hill, 1944. A direct and realistic presentation of the Negro's aims, with suggestions for policies to achieve them.

JOHNSON, CHARLES S., and associates. *Into the Main Stream.* University of North Carolina Press, Chapel Hill, 1947. A comprehensive study of the "better practices" in race relations actually existing in the United States.

CHANDLER, ALBERT R. *Rosenberg's Nazi Myth.* Cornell University Press, Ithaca, New York, 1945. A critical analysis of a recent racist doctrine.

CHAPTER IX

PERSONALITY

PERSONALITY is another important trait of man which vitally affects his interaction pattern. We meet life with such equipment as we have developed. A very important part of that equipment is our personality. Personality is, in turn, influenced by our interactional life. It develops and changes as we meet new situations. This complex fact requires some further interpretation and examination.

DEFINITIONS

THE MEANING OF PERSONALITY

The term *personality* is used in our study with a meaning different from that which it has in ordinary speech. When we speak ordinarily of an individual's personality, we usually mean the relative amount of *charm* he has, or the relatively good or bad impression he makes on people. In sociology we very definitely do not mean that sort of thing. Instead, we use the term in two senses, closely related to each other but with slightly different emphases.

1. In one sense the sociologist means by personality the total resources of the individual; or, to put the same statement in other words, the total physical, intellectual, and emotional organization of an individual. Your personality is all that distinctly characterizes you as an individual: your mental equipment, your emotional balance, your attitudes, your skills, your capacities, and your physical make-up. You not only possess a distinctive combination of all these traits, but you also use them in a distinctive way. Someone else may have precisely the same kind of skills, exactly the same intelligence quotient, and much the same attitudes and beliefs. But his personality will differ from yours because he has organized all

these things in a way different from that in which you have organized them. They mean different things to him; he uses them
in ways different from your use of them.

From this viewpoint, then, your personality is the real "you."
It is the "you" which meets varying life situations and reacts in
some way to those situations.

2. From another, somewhat more dynamic viewpoint, an individual's personality is the total result of all his past experiences and
interactions. He has learned certain things, he has developed certain attitudes and habits, he has come to believe certain things,
and to react in definite ways. Thus when we are born we consist
very largely of potentialities and little else, aside from our purely
physical organization. We can make a noise with our vocal cords,
but we cannot articulate words. Soon that ability to make a noise
is modified by our surroundings, and we begin to put various
sounds together in such a way as to make them understandable to
other people. Presently we are speaking some kind of language.
No one should be particularly surprised that a child speaks Chinese
if he has grown up in a family which organizes sounds into the
Chinese language. We are not born with a specialized ability to
speak any one language; we are born only with the potentiality of
organizing noises into coherent speech. What brand of speech it
will be depends upon the culture in which we live and upon the
intimate groups with which we associate.

The same is true of other potentialities. We can move our arms
and legs, for instance. Infants move them in a series of random
motions. Presently some degree of organization enters into these
motions; they become related to one another so that we can creep
and then walk. We are also born with certain "mental" potentialities, that is, with latent abilities to establish relationships between
happenings that affect us. We hear a noise, another noise, and then
we feel very comfortable because we are taking in food. At first all
these are disconnected occurrences. Then we learn to connect these
specific noises and our feeling of comfort. The first noise is the
closing of a door, the second, footsteps, then the comfortable experience of bottle or breast. Later, when we hear the noise we expect
the food. That is one example of the establishment of relationships
between occurrences which had been unrelated.

Our personalities have begun to develop. We are organizing

sense impressions (the noises, the satisfaction of nursing); we are co-ordinating our own abilities (to move our arms and legs, to make a noise ourselves); and we are establishing relationships between ourselves, the things that happen outside ourselves, and some of the things that happen within ourselves. This process of personality development continues long after childhood. In some cases it continues as long as the individual lives, since he continues to learn and learning is, essentially, the discovery of relationships. Thus, if we are learning a language, we discover the relationships between sounds, words, grammar, and meanings. If we get a new job, we must discover the effective relationships between our own capacities and the skills required in that particular kind of work. When we marry, we must learn to establish a new system of relationships to the presence of another person, to new responsibilities, to a different status in life. As we organize our reactions to these various experiences, our personalities develop.

There are several implications of this general theory which we must note. For one thing, we may organize, or integrate into our developing personalities, destructive as well as constructive experiences. Our interactions may make fears, anxieties, and worries into important parts of our personality structure. We may develop antagonistic and domineering attitudes as well as co-operative attitudes. All these then become part of the equipment with which we live our lives. They may make it very difficult for us to adjust ourselves adequately to some life situations unless we are aware of their significance and take some steps to counteract them.

Another implication is this: the two definitions of personality we have been discussing are not mutually exclusive or contradictory. The first one dealt with personality from the short-time viewpoint. At any particular moment, how shall we describe you? What organized group of resources represents you? The second one dealt with the formation of personality from the long-time viewpoint. What experiences contribute to the "you" as you now are? The first approach to personality is static, the second dynamic. The first views personality as organization; the second views it as process; both are valid views. Human beings are, in fact, both static and dynamic, both organized and developing. We stress one or the other of these aspects, depending on the focus of our interest.

A third principle which should be clear is that the total environment within which an individual develops is of great significance in the formation of his personality. We suggested a moment ago that we ought not to be surprised that an individual speaks Chinese if he has grown up in a family which organizes sounds into the Chinese langage. Similarly, we ought not to be surprised to find that attitudes and behavior patterns develop from the interaction between our potentialities and the total environment in which we live. For example, consider the development of a criminal personality. A good many people think of criminals as sneaking individuals who are ashamed of their way of life and who long to be law-abiding. But it is not that way at all. The criminal's way of life is as full of satisfactions for him as the way of life of the law-abiding man is for him. The attitudes accompanying antisocial conduct are just as much cherished by the antisocial person as our own are cherished. The antisocial person is just as proud of his achievements in crime as we are of ours in other areas of life. His personality is organized about a different system of values, but it *is* organized. He was not born a criminal; he developed into a criminal as the result of the interactions of his constitutional potentialities with this total environment. His potentialities were, on the whole, very much like ours at the beginning of his life. His criminal career becomes more than a mere habit with him; it becomes the pattern through which he attains life satisfactions, biological, psychological, and social. The whole problem of repressing crime would be much simpler than it is if all criminals went about secretly longing to be honest men.

Much the same thing may be said of psychoneurotics and the "insane." In the great majority of cases they were not born with these defects. They were born with much the same potentialities that any of us has. Somewhere and somehow those potentialities became actualities, not like ours, which we call "normal," but sufficiently unlike ours so that we call them "abnormal." The environment is not the only factor at work in creating either "normal" or "abnormal" people. The environment is never the only factor in any situation. There is always a true interaction, that is, a mutual relationship, between man, his potentialities, and the total environment in which he lives. It will contribute greatly to our understanding of ourselves and of our fellows if we can grasp that fact.

Finally, personality resembles culture in that both are products of man interacting with his environment. Culture is the product of an aggregate; personality the product of an individual interaction. In our diagram of the advanced form of interaction on page 5 we have shown a group interacting with its environment through the medium of its culture. If we replace the group in that diagram by a single individual, we shall then have the pattern of personality formation.

SOCIOLOGICAL SIGNIFICANCE OF PERSONALITY

We have already indicated in the course of our previous discussion something of the sociological significance of personality. In addition to what we have said, let us advance the following ideas:

1. Personality is of significance for the sociologist because the kind of personality which characterizes any large number of individuals in an aggregate will affect the totality of the ways of living and the ways of thinking of that aggregate. For example, an aggregate which has a large number of immature individuals in it, that is, individuals with immature personality patterns, will as an aggregate exhibit immature reaction patterns. The individuals whom we call *immature* have not been able to establish realistic relationships between themselves and the world. It is typical of young children that they view themselves and their own comforts as the primary facts of life. If they are uncomfortable, they cry about it. They grab for the things that they think will make them comfortable. Most of us, as we mature, are able to organize ourselves more satisfactorily in relation to reality. We learn that we cannot have all we want when we want it, and that it is not the thing to do to "yell" about the situation. We learn that we cannot persistently grab the things we want in a relatively well-organized social group without disturbing the organization.

But some people reach the stage of adulthood without ever completely learning that. They remain able to view the world only in terms of their own comforts, they consistently grab for things, and they "yell" with vexation when they are frustrated. Naturally, an aggregate which had many of that kind of people in it would not be able to establish stable relationships either within itself or with other aggregates. The Nazi society is one of our most recent examples of this kind of self-centered type of immaturity. Organized crime, racketeering, and political corruption are other examples closer to home.

2. Personality is also significant for the sociologist because group processes, group beliefs, and other cultural developments have much to do with the formation of the individual personality. We have here, again, a true interaction, with influences operating in both directions: from aggregate to individual, and from individual to aggregate. The personality patterns of the individual members of a grouping affect the aggregate behavior patterns; and, in turn, the culture of the aggregate is a powerful influence in the shaping of the individual personality.

Let us now analyze somewhat more in detail certain aspects of the relationship between personality and society.

FORMATION OF PERSONALITY

As our first principle we suggest that

The human personality is a product of the interaction of the individual human being and the total environment with which he has contact.

In one sense this is simply a summarization of what we have been saying. But let us emphasize one point. No individual has equally significant contacts with all his surroundings; some of his contacts are more influential in personality formation than others. The intimate groupings to which we belong "screen out" some aspects of our surroundings, with the result that stimuli originating in those areas either do not affect us at all or affect us only slightly. For example, suppose that an individual is born into a family living in a backwoods area of our nation. Suppose further that his family does not have a great deal of interest in the "intellectual life," as is somewhat natural in those surroundings. He has no contact with newspapers, periodicals, or books. Suppose further that the family members make fun of any interest he may show in such things. The result will be that during important years of his life not only will he have very little contact with the "intellectual life" but he may develop attitudes which are distinctly antagonistic to intellectualism. He may go to school under compulsion, but that antagonism will be part of the equipment with which he faces the experience of schooling. Naturally, he does not take to learning very readily. And unless he has a wise and competent teacher he may never take to it. By the time he is adolescent, he may well be to all intents and purposes moronic.

But he was not born a moron. He was born with average potentialities. What happened was that his intimate family and other groups screened out all favorable stimuli connected with the development of the intellectual life. This may be rather a drastic illustration, but the general pattern is by no means uncommon. Religious groupings, for example, sometimes screen out certain aspects of the environment, such as the evolutionary theory or the study of science. Other intimate groupings function in similar ways.

Personality, then, develops from the interaction between the potentialities with which we are born and *those portions* of the environment with which we have close contact. Individuals with precisely the same constitutional equipment may develop into quite different personality types because of influences from different segments of their environment. To an outside observer of the situation, it might appear that the environments in the two cases were identical. Actually the two environments may have been quite different because of the "screening" process of the respective intimate groups.

In some cases, of course, the constitutional equipment, that is, the potentialities with which an individual is born, may be defective. Persons are born blind, deaf, or with some portion of the nervous system not functioning. Defective constitutional equipment is very significant in simple societies because it affects the interaction pattern in vital ways. It is not so significant in complex cultures. As we mentioned earlier, Helen Keller, born blind and deaf, has been able to develop a relatively satisfactory adjustment because of the culture in which she lives. If she had been born in a primitive culture, she would very probably have died as a child or, if she had lived, would not have been able to develop anything resembling a "human" nature. The sense organs, by means of which she would interact with her culture, are missing.

So of other individuals born with other defects, mental or physical. We suggest, then, that

> *In a highly developed culture the constitutional equipment*
> *of the individual tends to be of minor significance*
> *in personality development.*

Much more significant than the constitutional equipment as such is *what the culture can do with that equipment.* That depends, in turn, on such factors as how much is understood about human potentialities, what devices are originated to make effective use of human potentialities, and what motivations exist to influence the culture to interest itself in the use of such devices. We are speaking here not only of individuals born with defective equipment, though the statements do apply to them; we are speaking also of individuals born with average and with better than average equipment. The moron in an undeveloped culture may well become the "village idiot," whose antics amuse what we are tempted at times to call his fellow morons, although they pass as being of average mentality. The moron in a highly developed culture may, through proper training and care, become a useful member of his group, performing helpful, if limited, tasks. At the other extreme the genius in a simple culture may be regarded as eccentric, or even a familiar of the devil to be destroyed. In an advanced culture, means exist to make constructive use of his better-than-average equipment. Such a culture, through its understanding of the human personality and through its specialized activities, is able to use the average equipment in a much more effective way than can the simpler culture.

We are not implying that differences in constitutional equipment are wholly without significance in contemporary interaction patterns. They are significant. Even in our own culture, for example, we are not able to do very much for the lower grades of the feeble-minded, the idiot, and the imbecile. We can doubtless give them better care than was available in the past, but we are still limited in our devices for developing whatever potentialities they may have. It is commonly said that they are "hopeless" cases; and they *are* "hopeless" under our present conditions of understanding and of techniques. But it is somewhat provincial to imply that we can never in the future develop any techniques which will make them something other than hopeless. We do not know what we shall be able to do in the future. Objective as we may try to be, we are still apt to fall into the error of assuming that our present state of knowledge is the most advanced that can ever exist. It is well occasionally to remember that we may not, in the future, suffer from some of the limitations which characterize us now.

However that may be, the fact is that the constitutional equipment of most individuals is less important for their development than are our cultural devices for assisting the individual toward growth. This whole discussion brings up once again the question of "heredity versus environment" to which we have referred briefly before. A good deal of confusion reigns in that whole area. In order to clarify our own approach to the question, let us suggest again that mere resemblance is not sufficient to establish the hereditary nature of the traits in which the resemblance exists. Similarity of environment, similarity of culture, and similarity of the interaction pattern in general may account for resemblances, without any hereditary process being involved. In order to establish a resemblance in traits as hereditary, we must be able to demonstrate that their transmission occurs in accordance with a definite mechanism, whatever that mechanism may be,—and it is almost certainly a much more complicated mechanism than the simple Mendelian formula which to most people explains heredity in its entirety. Most sociologists are inclined to believe that no individual is born with a "criminal heredity," or with a "criminal constitutional equipment," whatever that would be. Similarly, we doubt very strongly the influence of heredity in producing such pathologies as insanity, alcoholism, narcotic addiction, and suicide. We doubt very strongly that in the majority of cases individuals are predestined by the facts of their heredity to develop any of these behavior patterns *regardless of what their environment may be*. The evidence points very strongly to the general interaction pattern as being the originating factor in all those conditions.

Nonetheless, belief in the hereditary nature of many of our behavior patterns is very strongly intrenched in popular thinking, and there is a definite tendency to defend the hereditary viewpoint with some belligerence. Doubtless there are attractive features about it. In the case of favorable characteristics, pride or self-complacency might tend to make us claim for ourselves the good points appearing in our children, a claim validated by reference to "heredity." In the case of pathologies and other unfavorable characteristics, one attractive feature of hereditarian theories is that they apparently offer us an easy, almost magical, way of solving our problems through sterilization of the unfit or some similar process. Additionally, the belief in heredity frees us from responsibility for our actions;

we are, presumably, inevitably "doomed" by the facts of heredity to do whatever we do. A third attractive feature about the theory is that heredity represents science to many people, and our age reacts positively to science and scientific knowledge.

There is also, of course, the fact that resemblances in physical traits are inherited apparently according to a fairly well-established pattern. It is natural to assume, therefore, that nonphysical traits are also inherited. Yet the fact remains that even physical traits may be drastically modified by such environmental factors as food, occupation, medical practices, and other cultural devices. True, these modifications are not themselves inherited by succeeding generations, but they influence the development of the individuals in whom they occur.

We must also bear in mind the fact that not all traits which appear in an individual at birth are inherited. They may be *acquired*. Thus a baby born blind as the result of a gonorrheal infection did not inherit his blindness, even if his mother is also blind. Similarly, children who suffer from certain childhood diseases at a very early age may become deaf or otherwise defective as a result. Obviously they did not inherit the defect; it would not have appeared without the interaction of the child with the disease.

To repeat, the whole area of heredity versus environment is one in which we are not very well informed. Much more investigation is necessary. But rigid adherence either to hereditarianism or to environmentalism will prevent any useful investigation. An objective approach to the problem is one of the prime necessities.

DEVELOPMENT OF PERSONALITY

One of the things which distinguish human beings from animals is the fact that we can make choices through the use of our imagination. We do not have to engage in a particular course of action in order to discover what its results will be. Instead, we think things over, we imagine ourselves doing certain things and then we imagine what the results would be if we actually did them. If the results we foresee are undesirable, obviously we can avoid them. Our ability to make this kind of choice saves us a great deal of time, effort, and the hard knocks which might come from experiencing in reality what we experience in imagination. Of course, the process is not infallible; our decision as to what would result if we did certain things may be a wrong decision. In addition to that fact, our ability to apply the process to concrete situations is conditioned by emotional reactions, cultural beliefs as to right and wrong procedures, and lack of motivations. But on the whole the processes of choice are productive of more accurate results than would be possible if our mentality were so limited that we were dependent wholly on direct experience.

The ability to choose wisely between possible courses of action depends on a number of personality factors: on knowledge, on intelligence, on attitudes, on emotional balance. The more knowledge we have, and the more intelligently we are able to organize and to use that knowledge, the more accurate our judgments will be. In other terms, the more highly developed our personality is, the more accurate our judgment will be.

The development of personality is conditioned by both the amount of knowledge we have and the kind of knowledge we have. These, in turn, are related to the culture in which we live.

> *The development of personality is directly related*
> *to the complexity of culture.*

A complex culture enables us to develop the distinctively human characteristic of choice to a much greater degree than does a simple culture. How?

1. The total fund of knowledge available to the individual is largely a matter of cultural development. We cannot predict the results of our actions unless we have a relatively large amount of knowledge both about human beings and about the world in which we live. No individual by himself ever gathers all the necessary knowledge. He gets much of it from the accumulated labors of his fellows, who have worked over a long period of years. In simple cultures there is not a sufficient fund of knowledge about human reactions and about the world to predict future happenings except under very limited circumstances. Direct experience, which may be destructive in its results, is necessary. Thus the possibility of choice is limited.

To take a very obvious illustration, primitive man could not construct a motorless glider because he knew nothing of the physical laws of gravity and nothing of the principles of flight. He could not, in other words, say, "If I construct a glider in this fashion, it will carry me safely where I want to go; if I construct it in this other fashion, it will not be safe." He simply lacked the knowledge to make any such prediction. Of course, primitive man did not think in terms of gliders. But he did think about many other things: about crossing streams, about approaching animals, about disease, about ghosts. Lacking a fund of knowledge relating to all these things, he could not make adequate choices. He lived largely by "hit or miss." In fact, very often he died because what he did was not the result of accurate previous judgments.

In our own times we also suffer from a lack of knowledge which would enable us to make relevant judgments in certain fields. Perhaps the most spectacular recent instance of that situation is the atomic bomb. When the first trial was made, there was no agreement as to what the results would be. It is said that at least one prominent physicist was willing to bet, on the eve of the trial, that "it would not work." Others were not sure of what the outcome of the trials would be.

Less spectacular than the atomic bomb, but equally illustrative of our current lack of knowledge in certain fields, is the situation with regard to industrial depressions. It is doubtful whether we know enough about all the factors concerned with the phenomena of depressions to prevent them. We still, apparently, have to experience them and to do what the occurrences of the moment require, on an empirical basis. When we do build up a fund of knowledge about all the factors, economic factors and others, connected with depressions, we should be able to predict what will happen under various conditions and then to take the wisest course in view of the conditions existing at any particular time.

The complexity of culture, then, affects the development of personality in accordance with the relative amount of knowledge that we have accumulated. We suffer at present from the fact that our own culture has accumulated such a fund of knowledge only partially, and only in certain fields of investigation.

2. The possibility of choice in the case of any individual is limited by the contact he has with differing segments of his culture, regardless of what the fund of knowledge in the culture as a whole may be. The "uneducated" individual, who has no contact with the advances of his civilization, receives little benefit from the cultural

accumulation of knowledge. We say that he "acts rashly," or "does foolish things," or "is stupid about what he does," all of them expressions indicating lack of foresight, which in turn implies lack of choice. A culture which does not develop means to enable a majority of people to share in the advances of civilization stunts the personality growth of many individuals.

3. Finally, the number of possible choices of action is itself limited by culture patterns, apart from the fund of knowledge available. We may indulge in any number of choices and we may come to any number of perfectly valid conclusions as to the wise thing to do under certain circumstances. But if that thing is culturally unacceptable, we shall have great difficulty in doing it. Superstitions, taboos, habitual valuations, are all cultural forces which condition our course of action. These are of less significance in complex than in simple cultures.

The more developed the individual's personality is, the more "human" he is in the sense that he can make more and wiser choices. Complexity of culture contributes, potentially at least, to the development of personality. One of the tasks of our own culture is to spread developmental factors to wider segments of the population.

READINGS

PENDELL, E. (Ed.). *Society under Analysis*, Chap. 9, "Personality—What Am I?" The Jacques Cattell Press, Lancaster, Pennsylvania, 1942.

SOROKIN, P. A. *Society, Culture, and Personality*, Chap. 19, "Sociocultural Structure of Personality." Harper & Brothers, New York, 1947.

MUNN, NORMAN L. *Psychology*, Chap. 25, "Personality." Houghton Mifflin Company, Boston, 1946.

GROVES, E. R., and MOORE, H. E. *An Introduction to Sociology*, pp. 144–203, "The Development of Personality; The Psychoanalytic Interpretation of Personality; The Social Expression of Personality." Longmans, Green & Co., New York, 1941.

BROWN, L. G. *Social Pathology*, Chap. IV, "Human Nature." F. S. Crofts & Co., New York, 1942.

CHAPTER X

PRELUDE TO SOCIAL ORGANIZATION

ALL these various aspects of man-in-relationship which we have examined—man himself, his environment, his groups, his culture, his race, and his personality—do not exist primarily as separate and unrelated phenomena. They exist as coherent parts of an integrated whole which we call *social organization*. It is our purpose now to discuss certain aspects of social organization. In Part II we shall deal in more detail with the institutions and the processes which are important in contemporary social organization.

MEANING OF ORGANIZATION

The word *organization* always refers to an *arrangement* of the component parts of an object. When a thing is organized, its parts are arranged in a definite pattern with reference to each other. When it is unorganized, the parts have no definite arrangement; they fall into haphazard patterns.

For example, when an assembly dismisses at the university or when a crowd emerges from a theater for an intermission, the lobby gradually fills with people. Many of them pass on through the lobby and outside to their own concerns. But others, who have no immediate affairs of importance, stand about talking in small groups, moving from group to group, lighting cigarettes, and gazing around. If anyone wants to pass from one side of the lobby to the other under those circumstances, he finds his trip by no means an easy one. He bumps into people who are wandering around, he has to circle groups of conversationalists, he has to dodge this way and that. The difficulty arises from the fact that the people in the lobby are not arranged in any special way. They happen to be in that location temporarily. They form a haphazard pattern. In other words, they are an unorganized grouping.

192

The situation is somewhat different during intervals between classes in a university, when students are passing from one class to another. True, some of them have no immediate purpose, and do manage to impede the progress of others by simply wandering around. But most of the students are moving in masses toward certain objectives: the exits of the building, various classrooms, and so on. Confusion is still present to some extent, but there is more evidence of organized movement. Since the people involved have definite objectives, there is less haphazard movement and more of a tendency toward definite patterning. They are partly organized, partly unorganized.

If we enter a classroom while a class is in session, we find quite a different picture. There is little confusion, arrangement is definite and patterned, functions and relationships are prescribed. The class is organized because the relationships between the various members are definite and coherent.

Organization, then, is nothing mysterious. It simply means the arrangement of the component parts of an object, or of a group of people, in relation to each other. This arrangement is influenced by the purpose of the object or grouping. Thus, when we study the organization of a grouping already in existence, we try to discover what the arrangement of its parts is. If we propose to describe the organization of a university, for example, we draw a chart indicating at the top the head official or board, below that the subordinate executive officers, then the teaching faculty, and so on. What we have done in thus describing university organization is to point out how the several boards, departments, and individuals are arranged with reference to one another.

Similarly, the organization of an industrial plant may be indicated by describing how the product flows from one department to another, through a series of processes. We carry it from raw material through various stages to finished product, following an arrangement of the several divisions of the plant with reference to one another and to the whole process of manufacture.

It is important to bear in mind this concept of organization as being, fundamentally, an arrangement of parts. It is also well to remember that organization may be of two kinds: it may be the result of deliberate planning, or it may be natural and largely undirected in its development. For example, we may decide to organize a new enterprise in the business, industrial, or educational fields. We mean by that statement that we plan the arrangement of component parts, individuals, groups, and materials with reference to each other and with reference to the kind of work we want to do. This is an example of planned organization.

On the other hand, a community may, through the course of the years, develop a set of relationships which come to be a more or less fixed pattern of arrangement but without any over-all planning. It starts as a small aggregate; population increases, and specialized activities develop; new enterprises are formed to serve the increased population and to provide special services; the simple form of government has to be changed to meet needs that arise; more police, better fire protection, other services become necessary; new real-estate developments come into being; and so the process continues in many forms and through various steps. The point is that at the end of the process we have an organized community, but the organization has developed not in accordance with any plan laid down at the beginning. It has developed as a series of reactions to changing situations.

Very often in such a case elements of disorganization are also present. There may be, for example, conflicts of laws resulting from the passage of new legislation without modification of that already in existence. There may be conflicts between racial groups, business groups, nationalities, and other aggregates. Slums may arise as buildings originally intended for one purpose come to be used for another purpose, or as the original inhabitants of once favored areas leave those areas for residence elsewhere. Concentration of population may lead to such conditions of traffic that the whole community life is interrupted.[1] All these things are elements of disorganization because they introduce chance, haphazard relationships among the people who are the basic parts of the community. Such disarrangement of those parts with reference to each other and to the whole community promotes disorganization.

Much of what we study in the following chapters will be naturalistic, unplanned social organization, and much of it will have important potentialities for disorganization present.

[1] "The Traffic Outrage," *Fortune*, October, 1946, p. 123.

MEANING OF SOCIAL ORGANIZATION

Thus far we have been discussing chiefly the general meaning of the term *organization*, but our illustrations have carried us beyond the simple meaning of that term into the meaning of *social organization*. We suggest as a definition of social organization the following:

> *Social organization is the system by which the parts of society*
> *are related to each other and to the whole society*
> *in a meaningful way.*

We have already defined a society as a collectivity which is potentially self-sufficient.[2] In our future discussion of social organization we shall have in mind for the most part the organization of a society, although subaggregates may also be organized, of course. For the sake of accuracy, if we refer to the organization of any aggregate less than a society, we shall use such terms as community organization, group organization, or some other specific reference.

For a time in sociology there was a reaction against the use of the term *society* on the ground that it was too general to have any recognizable meaning. The trend then was in the direction of studying social groups instead of society, because it was held that social groups are definite, concrete entities which we can analyze with some degree of accuracy. The emphasis on groups is undoubtedly a very useful one, and it has produced a fund of extremely valuable knowledge about man-in-relationship. But we suggest here that study of groups need not be the only emphasis. Group life is only one form of association. Groups function within a larger collectivity which we call a society. Apart from that larger collectivity, most groups could not exist. This is especially true of modern times, in which groups have come to have functions restricted largely to specialized interests of the group members.

Our definition of a society as a form of collectivity implies that there is a degree of interaction among the members of a society. This emphasis is in line with other recent definitions of the term. Thus one writer states that a society is a group of people who have lived together and worked together long enough to get themselves organized and to think of themselves as a social unit with well-

[2]Chap. IV.

defined limits.[3] Another stresses the common set of habits, customs, and ideals which characterizes the members of a society, and adds that they are often set off from other groups by attitudes of difference or antagonism.[4] A third finds the basis of society in commonness of customs, traditions, and attitudes, plus the fact of a "feeling of unity."[5] A fourth adds to these the concept of self-sufficiency, since the true society is not dependent on some other aggregate for its existence.[6]

These characteristics are those of a collectivity. Now it may be said that our definition lacks something of concreteness. It may be hard to determine with finality whether or not a particular collectivity is or is not a society. But we are not primarily concerned with the determination of whether or not a particular collectivity is or is not a society. We are concerned with the processes of arrangement of parts in those collectivities which resemble societies, as we have defined the word *society*.

The parts of the society which are related to one another may be of several different kinds: individuals, groups, institutions, or aggregates. For a society to attain self-sufficiency these several varieties of parts must function together with some coherence. If the activities of individuals or aggregates are haphazard and wholly unrelated to the society, no organized social life is possible. Manufacturing becomes meaningless without the sale of the manufactured goods; willingness to buy goods means nothing unless the goods are actually manufactured; railroads which operate rolling stock not adapted to carrying the particular type of goods manufactured would be useless. On the other hand, unless the family institution functions to produce children the society falls to pieces. But the family institution cannot function without business, government, and education. In some way the separate activities of all these aggregates in our society must be arranged, co-ordinated, organized.

It is that sort of thing we have in mind when we say that the parts of a society must be related to each other in a meaningful way. They must so function in relationship to each other that what they

[3]E. E. Eubank, *Concepts of Sociology*, pp. 120–130. Heath, Boston, 1932.

[4]Ralph Linton, *The Study of Man*, p. 91. Appleton-Century, New York, 1936.

[5]Kimball Young, *Sociology*, p. 19. American Book, New York, 1942.

[6]J. L. Gillin and J. P. Gillin, *An Introduction to Sociology*, p. 19. Macmillan, New York, 1942.

do is significant, not only for themselves but for the whole society. One of the problems of contemporary society is to balance meanings for the individual, for the subaggregates of society, and for the whole society.

As individuals we all tend to be more or less self-centered. We tend to view the world in terms of our own interests. It is a good world if we find that it treats us well, satisfies our needs, and lets us do what we want to do. Similarly, groups and aggregates tend to be group-centered. They regard the world in terms of their own specialized functions and activities. It is a good or a bad world chiefly to the extent that it encourages, or at least permits, the group to carry out its own purposes. This group-centeredness becomes obvious in the attitudes of labor unions, business groups, recreational associations, or any other kind of special-interest group.

That kind of meaning is perfectly valid for the individuals and aggregates concerned. But in addition to that meaning, there is another meaning which is of interest to us here: the meaning which the whole society finds in the activities of individuals and of subgroups. Granted, for example, that pressure groups of various kinds operate to benefit themselves, we must then ask, "What are the results of their activities on the functioning of our society?" a question we are coming to ask more and more at the present time about labor organizations, industrial monopolies, and varieties of politically active groupings. In any statement of those results in answer to such a question, we find inherent the societal meanings of the several organizations mentioned.

Societal meanings may differ considerably from individual or group meanings. From the viewpoint of society, for instance the family must perform one necessary function: providing future citizens who are trained in the basic ways of the society. The meaning of any particular family for the society lies in how well it performs that function. The values that individual family members may get from their life together (such as happiness, self-fulfillment, or pleasure) are, from the societal viewpoint, of secondary importance unless they affect the reproductive function of the family group.

Similarly, society places a value on the activities of a business or industrial group in terms different from those of the group itself. A corporation is apt to be well satisfied if its profits are large, its competitors few, and its customers many. Society, on the other hand, is not particularly interested in those aspects of business and industry except in so far as they may provide tax resources. Society is interested in the results of the total functioning of the specified grouping on the whole people. If its profits are made from the sale of adulterated goods, society interferes, even if such interference means the total loss of customers, profits, and business itself. If a corporation is monopolistic, controlling the major supply of its product, either actually or by agreement, society reserves the right to dissolve the monopoly on the grounds that it may adversely affect the whole people.

To repeat, a major problem of our society is to organize the parts which compose it in such a way that the relationship among the parts and to the whole society will be meaningful, not only for those parts but for the society also.

During the years following the First World War, and up to the depression of the 1930's, many people in America formed the habit of overlooking entirely the fact that there were societal meanings of importance involved in our individual and group activities. "Rugged individualism," which meant the right of the individual to act entirely for his own benefit within the rather wide limits of the law, became the creed of the day. We were impatient with any suggestion that society had any rights in the matter.

Toward the middle of the long depression of the 1930's we began to see the necessity of modifying our doctrine of "rugged individualism." The Second World War compelled many of us to make even more drastic modifications of that doctrine. As the war progressed, it became obvious that societal meanings had to take precedence over individual meanings. Individuals and aggregates "meant something" only in so far as they could contribute, or it was thought they could contribute, to the war effort. Selective service operated with very little regard for the individual's wishes; manufacturers found it necessary to convert their plants for war work; rigid price control, and other kinds of controls intended to serve the interests of society, were forced on us. We had reached the point of an almost complete emphasis on societal meanings, with individual meaning definitely secondary.

We are now in a stage of readjustment after the war. There is some evidence that at least certain groupings in the country would willingly return to the rugged type of individualism which would leave very little scope for societal meanings. There is some evidence that other minorities would like to see a system in which certain special interests would have the dominant voice in national affairs, with the interests of the whole group secondary to their own. And there is some evidence that a few would like to proceed to a totalitarian organization in which the societal interests would completely dominate individual interests.

All these have within them the seeds of disorganization. Our task is to balance individual, group, and societal meanings so that the parts of society, in all their variety, will be related to the whole in a meaningful way which will include individual, group, and societal interests. We shall note further something of the conflict among those interests, and the disorganizing results of such conflict, in Part II.

PROCESSES OF SOCIAL ORGANIZATION

Social organization takes place in terms of two important processes. Even when it develops naturally and without over-all direction, we can trace the influence of these two processes in the whole pattern.

The first is the process of *differentiation*, by virtue of which the parts of a society become distinguishable from one another because they perform different kinds of functions, because they are characterized by different backgrounds, because they have different aims, goals, and programs. If we were all identical, either as individuals or as groupings, we should be indistinguishable one from another, and any particular arrangement of parts would be the same as any other arrangement. It is only as we differ from one another that organization becomes significant.

The second is the process of *integration*, that is, the process through which the differentiated parts are brought into harmony with each other. It is important to remember that integration does not mean making the parts more like each other. On the contrary, integration enables dissimilar parts to function together effectively.

Because these two processes are more or less constantly at work, social organization is not a static and unchanging arrangement. It is the net result of the processes of differentiation and of integration interacting with each other. For example, over a period of years the urban way of life came to be differentiated from the rural way of life in the United States, so that there was a significant contrast between the two. That contrast might have had a disorganizing effect because it might have prevented the two segments of our society from functioning in harmony. There is still some difference between the two, and there are still echoes of "agrarian revolt" and of other potential conflicts. But we have gone far toward the integration of both our rural and our urban segments into our whole society, largely by the process of "rurbanization," that is, by the development of an integration between the urban and the rural ways of life. The residents of rural areas have come to function in terms of a primarily industrial civilization. The total result of "rurbanization" may not be entirely beneficial, but one of its results has been the avoidance of the disorganization which might have arisen from a complete differentiation of the two ways of life with no integrative forces.

Many of the problems of education, the family, government, and other social institutions arise from progressive specialization and a lag in integration. For example, our schools now have to provide for students with many different backgrounds and interests, a situation which did not exist in our rural type of social organization. In the fact of this differentiation, the schools have responded by setting up specialized departments and curricula in large numbers. But by so doing they have lost the oppostunity to create an effective common bond among their specialized graduates. They have, in other words, educated specialists without integrating those specialists into the meanings of our common citizenship in one society. Education is now trying to develop general courses which are intended to have this kind of integrating effect.

Somewhat the same situation has arisen in connection with problems of the family. Specialization of activities has become characteristic of family members. Parents and children live to an increasing extent outside the home; their work is outside the home, they find their recreation outside the home, they belong to special-interest groups of many kinds outside the home. One result of this situation is that the home has lost many of the meanings that it had in the past, for the simple reason that we do not find as many significant satisfactions in the home as we used to. Hence the tendency of the family to "break down." Since we as a society cannot exist without some kind of family organization, our problem becomes a twofold problem of integration. First, we have to integrate the individual family members into the life of the family; and second, we have to find some means of reintegrating the family as an institution into our social organization.

ARRANGEMENT VERSUS PROCESS

The processes of differentiation and of integration are so important in social organization that, from one point of view, we may say that social organization itself is really a process. It is, in fact, a *changing* arrangement of parts. If we analyze it at any one time, the pattern of arrangement impresses us; if we examine it over an extended period of time, the changes that have taken place during that period impress us. This approach to the study of social organization is interesting and useful. It would be a mistake to emphasize exclusively either the static or the dynamic aspects of our social institutions. It is just as important to know something of the history of the family as an institution as it is to know something of the current problems of the family. In fact, we cannot understand the current problems of the family without some knowledge of its history, because it is only as we know its history that we can understand how the problems came to exist. The same is true of other social institutions.

This whole approach again illustrates the importance of the basic interaction pattern of human association. Our present social organization, like every other social phenomenon, is the result of our reactions to past situations. Social organization is both a product of our past interactions and a fact important in our contemporary interaction patterns.

READINGS

PENDELL, E. (Ed.). *Society under Analysis,* Chap. 13, "Social Structure—Mostly Mind-stuff but All Real." The Jacques Cattell Press, Lancaster, Pennsylvania, 1942.

SOROKIN, P. A. *Society, Culture, and Personality,* Chap. 3, "Generic Structure of Sociocultural Phenomena." Harper & Brothers, New York, 1947.

PANUNZIO, CONSTANTINE. *Major Social Institutions,* Chap. 1, "The Social Institutional Order." The Macmillan Company, New York, 1939.

BARNES, H. E., and REUDI, O. M. *The American Way of Life,* Chap. IV, "Human Needs and Social Organization." Prentice-Hall, Inc., New York, 1942.

ZIMMERMAN, C. C. *The Changing Community,* Chap. VII, "Community Life Organization." Harper & Brothers, New York, 1938.

THUS FAR

As a result of our discussions thus far, we should have gained something in the way of information and also some insight into the methods and the approach of sociologists. For our present purposes, the latter is the more important gain. Mere factual information changes with the changing times. Tables of statistics, charts, and similar materials are useful and interesting, but they soon become outdated. By contrast, an understanding of the methods of sociology, its approach to its field of study, and its insights into the facts of human life in association is of more permanent value. We suggest the following as a summary of sociological attitudes.

1. Sociology looks on contemporary man and his culture as a product—a product of his long history embodying the results of his past experiences modified by his contemporary and continuing interactions. Man was not always "human" in our sense of the term. He has attained humanity, or a measure of humanity, over an immensely long period of years.

It is sometimes objected that this view of mankind as product degrades man. It is difficult to agree with that objection. Quite the reverse, in fact, seems to be true. Thus if we hold that man was once created perfect, we must regard the whole course of his history as one long process of degeneration, for the obvious reason that he is very far from perfect now. If, on the contrary, we view man as a development from a much simpler and less "human" being than he is now, then it is apparent that man has slowly improved rather than degenerated. "Imperfect" as he may be now, he is more intelligent, more civilized, more human than he was in the past. Fumbling as many of his adjustments may be now, they are definite achievements. They all represent patterns that do not exist in nature. Man literally created them as he interacted with his physical environment and with his growing culture. Man as product of his progressive utilization of his surroundings is by no means a wholly disappointing creature. To view him as such a product is not to degrade him, it is to appreciate him.

2. Sociology views the individual human being also as a product of his interactions. It is not only man in the aggregate who has developed humanity; man the individual must also develop humanity. Recall the fact that this statement does not mean that we are completely passive. It is not true that the individual is an inert product as manufactured products are. Man results from *interaction* with his surroundings, that is, he influences his surroundings in many vital ways as well as being influenced by them.

Again, conservative people may object to this statement because they misunderstand it. It does not imply that we are automatons. We are active agents in building into our personalities the modifications we create in the process of interaction. Personality as well as culture is an achievement.

3. Sociology emphasizes the importance of life in association, and especially of life in groups, recognizing the fact that groups are very important elements in the interaction pattern from which personality results. "Man becomes human only in association with other men," and the social group is the most significant intimate factor in the humanizing process. One very important implication of this belief relates to co-operative control in society, also called "societal self-direction." Intimate groups such as the family are the substance of the humanizing process. In complex societies, such as our own is, there is a tendency to overlook that fact and to emphasize instead the more impersonal systems we call institutions, with the result that the integration which comes from similarity of intimate conditioning is lost. That loss of integration is, as we noted, one of the problems of our own times.

4. Sociology stresses the significance of the cultural environment in the interaction pattern from which comes man the individual and man in the aggregate. It is a fact that all human beings have very similar drives, and that we are strongly impelled to seek satisfactions for such drives. We find those satisfactions in terms of our total surroundings for the simple reason that there is no other place in which we can find them. As those surroundings

differ in major ways, so also man the individual and man in the aggregate tend to differ.

Once more this belief has not only a theoretical significance in the sense that it explains man; it is also of interest to those who are concerned with the planned development of human resources. The total surroundings of individuals and of groups may be regarded as agencies for this development. Projects for slum clearance, for the improvement of living conditions in general, or for the spread of education find their logical justification in the fact that the cultural environment is very significant in the conditioning of human beings. Now all that may seem very obvious. In fact, Mr. G. K. Chesterton was fond of saying that psychology and sociology both "announce as tremendous new discoveries the things that our grandmothers knew anyway." Granting the wisdom of our grandmothers, it is still a fact that a good many people regard the programs we mentioned not as significant instrumentalities for development but as "crackpot schemes" of visionary idealists. As sociology demonstrates the importance of man's total surroundings, there will be less justification for dismissing social-welfare projects on the grounds that they are unimportant bits of "fancywork" embroidered on the fabric of society by well-intentioned but unrealistic people.

The whole concept of man's interaction with his surroundings is also valuable for those who are concerned with understanding "problem" individuals whose patterns are deviations from the average and approved conduct of the aggregate. If their environment provides the major satisfaction of life in a socially disapproved way, it is natural that they, as individuals, should tend to become antisocial in behavior. Why should we expect anything else? It is not necessary to bring into the picture any dark doctrines of the inherent moral depravity of man, as theologians used to, or any mysterious and ghostly force called heredity, as some of our contemporaries do, in order to explain crime, narcotism, insanity, and similar patterns.

5. Sociologists spend a great deal of time in the examination of human culture. Culture is a product of man's interactions in the aggregate and it also becomes an important factor in that interaction. Cultures differ the world over because they are products of interaction patterns which contain differing factors. The simple

cultures of the tropics differ from the complex cultures of other, more temperate areas because of the difference of *natural factors*, which in turn condition the development of cultural techniques. The fact that human aggregates find satisfaction in living under the conditions of a simple culture does not indicate that they are inferior species of human beings. Similarly, the fact that the cultures of other nations differ from that of our own does not imply that the inhabitants of those nations are different species from ourselves.

6. The sociologist, in common with the anthropologist, is unable to discover any evidence for *racist* theories. The differences between races are physical differences, unimportant for the development of personality and culture except in so far as social factors artificially based on racial characteristics assign an inferior position to given races.

7. Finally, the sociologist is committed to the belief that the scientific method is the only basis for the discovery of fact, sharing this belief with physical and biological sciences. There are areas of life in which fact as such is of minor importance, giving place to emotional and appreciative faculties. Even in those areas the scientific method may be used to ascertain facts, though it is limited to the extent that facts are only part of the total pattern.

We now proceed to apply this approach to the areas of social organization and of social processes.

PART TWO

SOCIAL ORGANIZATION AND PROCESSES

INTRODUCTION

SOCIAL ORGANIZATION is the system by which the parts of society are related to each other and to the whole society in a meaningful way. Essentially, this meaning lies in the functions which the several parts perform, both for themselves and for the aggregate. In turn, the function performed is based on the satisfaction of some human drive, psychological or physiological. The basic human drives are probably very few in number—physiological urges such as the need for food, for shelter, for sex; and psychological urges such as the need for security, for response, for new experiences. Even though the drives themselves are few in number, the means of satisfaction may be varied and elaborate. Thus the basic food drive gives rise not only to the food quest as such, but also to patterns such as varying means of cookery, mealtime practices, and economic aspects of food handling in an elaborate society. The sex drive gives rise to family organization, dancing, courtship, prostitution, concubinage, and other institutions. The security drive is important not only in matters such as defense but also in religion, in certain kinds of mass rituals, and in patterns of superiority.

Each culture maintains recognizable standardized group-reaction patterns through which the basic drives common to all human beings find formal and approved satisfaction. These standardized reaction patterns are called *institutions*. They function in social organization by relating common modes of human expression to socially approved and commonly held beliefs and ideas.

In the following five chapters we consider the five basic institutions of society. Our arrangement is based on the drives in relation to which the *primary* function of each institution arises. Since, as we suggested in the case of the family institution, important secondary functions may be added to the primary function of any institution, a discussion only in terms of the originating drive situation would be partial and incomplete. As we deal with these institutions, then, we may be led far afield from mere human drives as such to the elaborations incident to a complex culture.

We discuss the family first, since it is based on the very important sex drive. This statement does not mean that the family is wholly a sex institution. It has many other functions. But it is very significantly an expression of what varying cultures have done about the elemental fact of sex. Next we deal with the economic institution, primarily concerned with basic subsistence needs, but secondarily significant in many areas of life. Then we take up the religious institution, ministering particularly to the drive for security, but also affecting the ideational life of the aggregate, its system of controls, and many other areas of association.

Finally, we discuss two institutions appearing as separate institutions somewhat later in time than the others, though their functions were earlier performed by other institutions. These are government and education. They are responses primarily to certain conditions of association rather than to any single basic drive.

The particular arrangement of our chapters is not of great importance; our goal is to understand the functioning of institutions in social organization.

Following our treatment of institutions, we deal with certain of the social processes which are important in their effect on social organization. As we suggested in Chapter X, organization is both arrangement and process, both static and dynamic. It is necessary to understand both these aspects. Again we do not propose to deal with all the social processes which have been described by sociologists. We choose only those most important for a basic understanding of sociology.

THE FAMILY AS A SOCIAL INSTITUTION

IT IS RELATIVELY SIMPLE to distinguish the family from other institutions and from other patterns in our own society because we are familiar with our own way of life and the functioning of various groupings in that way of life. Our own family pattern is only one type among many which have been developed in different cultures, just as our own society is only one among many societies which have existed or now exist. Sociology is the study not only of our own society but of those other societies as well. The question then arises, "How shall we determine what the family institution is in some other society with which we are not familiar?" We cannot select the pattern which most closely resembles our own because there have been major differences in family organization, not only in different cultures but in our own culture at different times. In practice, we find it necessary to determine what function the group which we call the family has performed and is performing, regardless of variations in external patterns of behavior. On the basis of the performance of that specific function we can distinguish the family in any culture with which we may have contact.

We discover at once that there is more than one function involved in family patterns. The first of those functions is the channeling of sex expressions, a function which is perhaps obvious. But we must point out here that the family is not the only group which has operated to channel sex expressions in a socially approved way. We in our own culture and at this particular time may not approve of those other modes of sex expression; but the fact remains that other cultures have approved of them and that in past segments of our own culture they have been approved. Prostitution, for example, is now socially disapproved in most areas of the United States in the sense that it is both illegal and immoral. But in some

European countries it has been licensed and has operated under official supervision. In one state, at least, of the United States the same system is now in vogue. Under those circumstances, it becomes legal, though it may still remain immoral. The point is that prostitution as a sex institution is to some degree socially approved in some cultures, but it is far different from the family as an institution.

Similarly, concubinage is at present both legal and moral in some countries of the Orient. The keeping of mistresses is permitted in the sense that punishment is very seldom meted out for the practice and that, in certain sectors of our society, the practice is not criticized.

Our point here is that, while the family is one of the sex institutions, and in fact is the one sex institution that meets with universal approval, it is not the only sex institution. We must distinguish it from other sex institutions. Again we find the basis of the distinction in the specific functions of the family which the other sex patterns do not perform. One of those other functions is the production and the nurture of children. True, of course, children may result from other sex contacts and provision for their care may be made, but it is only the family which has as its stated function the production and nurture of children.

Another function of the family common in many cultures and still to be found in our own culture is the transmission of property through inheritance formulas. We find remnants of this function in our own legal system; *dower* rights which guarantee certain shares in family property to the widow are still common, as are laws protecting the rights of legitimate children. Perhaps this function is less important among us than it has been in some other societies because our property is not primarily in land and real estate, as it used to be. Freedom to will personal property is greater than freedom to will landed estates. In England, where land ownership has always been significant in the creation of wealth, the freedom of the owner to bequeathe his land as he pleases is still restricted in some cases, and was formerly very definitely restricted.

These points are perhaps sufficient to indicate that our definition of the family must include more than the mere sex-institution functioning. Stressing the two functions which are of universal importance, and omitting the property-transmission function as less important now than it used to be, we may define the family as:

The social institution based on the fact of sex which has for its function the production and nurture of children.

Admittedly, some of our families may not be fulfilling this function in so far as the production and nurture of children are concerned; but that is still considered an important family function, and it has universally been so considered.

One point should be made clearly. The fact that the family is based on sex and that its stated function is the production and the nurture of children does not mean that family relationships are limited to those two situations. Many other significant human relationships arise in the process of family living, and many other human values are served by family contacts. Companionship, for example, is one of the contemporary values of family living, along with affection, response, and security. Our definition of the family, then, is intended to distinguish it from other institutions on the basis of function, not to limit the area of family interaction in any way.

Implicit in the preceding paragraph is the point that family living is an area of human relationships. The family is an associational form, within the terms of which human beings interact with each other. Perhaps that point is too obvious to be made; yet we sometimes overlook it because we regard the family as only a standardized group operating through legal norms. It is a standardized group, as other institutions are, but it is something more. It is also an area of interpersonal relationships, of relationships between individual human beings. The man-to-woman relationship, the parent-to-child relationship, and the child-to-child relationship are all extremely important in the "humanizing" process which is inherent in the nurture of children.

Because of these interpersonal relationships, the family operates as more than an institution; it operates also as a social group, with all the characteristics of a social group. An older approach to the study of the family used to stress almost exclusively the institutional aspects of family living, very probably because those aspects were very important in the past. Recently the trend in family studies has been toward an emphasis on the interpersonal aspects of family living, again because the interpersonal aspects are of great significance in our contemporary culture.[1] In a society, such as ours was a few generations ago and such as some European societies still are, which places great emphasis on institutional aspects of the family, interpersonal relationships are *relatively* unimportant. Strong societal sanctions enforced these institutional regulations. An individual who violated them was sharply criticized.

The whole matter of status, and the other aspects of the institutional family, are of much less significance today. Our ideas as to the rights and duties of husband and wife vary from one segment of our culture to another, and even within segments they are not explicitly codified in detail. Where they exist, they are general "feelings" on the subject rather than explicit rules. As a result, individual desires, aims, goals, ability to adjust, and similar matters are more important in determining the quality of family life than are institutional regulations.[2] This fact has raised certain problems for family members, and it has also somewhat shifted the interest of sociologists in the aspects of family living which engage their attention. We shall include both institutional and interpersonal aspects of the family in the discussion which follows.

One further point preliminary to our discussion. The terms *family* and *marriage* are used by sociologists to describe two different aspects of our family patterns. Marriage is the institutional relationship which inaugurates the family; and a group which includes husband and wife but which does not produce children remains a marriage rather than a family. The family proper is a group which includes parents and children; a marriage does not include children.

Actually, most of us are members of at least two families, our parental family and our marital family. We are members of a family based on *kinship* and of another family based on the *assumption of roles* towards a spouse. Professor Gillin uses the term *family of orientation* to describe the kinship family, because kinship *places* the individual in a series of relationships and hence *orients* him to the

[1]E. W. Burgess and H. J. Locke, *The Family*, Part II, "The Family and Personality Development." American Book, New York, 1945.
[2]Ibid.

larger society. He uses the term *family of procreation* to describe the marital family.[3]

MATES AND MATE CHOICE

One of the areas of marriage in which there has been considerable variation in custom is that concerned with the number of spouses an individual may have and the method of choosing spouses.

THE NUMBER OF MATES

In general, we may distinguish two types of marriages on the basis of the number of mates permitted:

1. monogamy, which means, literally, "one marriage," and which implies that only one mate at a time is permitted; and

2. polygamy, which means "many marriages," and implies that more than one mate is permitted at a time. Polygamy is, in turn, subdivided into two categories:

   a. Polyandry, meaning literally "many men," and describing the situation in which a woman has several husbands; and

   b. Polygyny, meaning "many women," and applied to those situations in which one husband has many wives.

There would perhaps be little point, in an introductory text such as this, in discussing the several kinds of mate systems from a purely historical approach. But we are interested in something more than history; we are interested in discovering how these patterns of behavior arose from man's interaction pattern, and in applying such information as we get to a tentative explanation of contemporary changes in marriage.

What factors in the interaction pattern, then, account for the differing systems regulating the number of mates permitted in marriage? There are at least three: (1) the balance numerically between males and females in the population, or a lack of balance in one direction or the other; (2) the condition of the primitive economic system; and (3) the fact that the family group performed a wide variety of functions later taken over by specialized institutions, in that it had an important place in religious rituals, admin-

[3] J. L. Gillin and J. P. Gillin, *An Introduction to Sociology*, p. 209. Macmillan, New York, 1942.

istered justice, and performed other government functions. All these factors made it important for each individual in the group to be recognized as a member of a family.

Especially in the case of women, life apart from a family was difficult if not impossible. Even men found it hard to live comfortably in the primitive economic system without a wife and a family to help them. Women faced not only this economic problem but also the difficulty of getting justice, of taking part in religion, and of assuming any kind of status in the aggregate. Even in a monogamous society such as our own rural aggregate was, we found it necessary to provide for unmarried females by permitting them to be members of a family, though they were not, of course, spouses. The traditional old-maid aunts who helped around the house or farm are examples of the provision of family care in an economic system which did not permit them to support themselves. They are less common now, not because marriage has increased, but because the rural way of life has become less common. In an industrial society a woman can support herself in a fair degree of comfort apart from family relationships.

In view of the economic conditions under which primitive peoples lived, and in view of the generalized functioning of family groups in early society, it was important to set up some family system which would include as many as possible of the population in some kind of family grouping. In other words,

> *In primitive societies marital customs regulating the number of mates in marriage are such as will include the maximum number of individuals in some kind of family relationship.*

The number of males and of females tended to be about equal in most early groupings. This was true except in those instances in which there was destructive contact with another aggregate, as in the case of war or conquest. Hence throughout most of mankind's history monogamy has been the most common mating system in the sense that monogamy was, and is, permitted in all cultures that we know of, even when other systems were also permitted. When polygamous matings were encouraged, or allowed, they were almost never absolutely required. In fact, they were often practiced by certain individuals or certain classes only. This holds true even today among polygamous groupings.

Monogamy did not always carry the implication of permanence, however. For instance, it has not always included the assumption of a lifelong relationship between one man and one woman, as our own type of monogamy has. There is much evidence that divorce was relatively easy in primitive society, such things as desertion, a change of fancy, or simple agreement to disagree being enough to sever a monogamous relationship. Property and prestige factors might complicate the separation, and some settlement in the nature of balancing gains and losses in both fields might be necessary. But sex and marriage relationships were, by and large, not questions of morals among primitives. They were matters of physiology and of custom, and were looked on from that point of view.

There was also, of course, little sentimentalism or *love* (as we use that term) involved in marriage. Often in the case of the death of a male partner in marriage the female partner was expected to find a new mate as soon as possible. Among some primitives, including certain of our American Indians, it was customary to require male prisoners taken in war to marry a woman of the tribe who was a widow. If he refused, he was put to death.[4]

We should also make the point again that polygyny often existed in the same society that permitted monogamy. This variation in mating systems comes into being when differentiation of strength, of hereditary power, or of social class makes it possible for some individuals to claim more than one wife. The extra wives often represented, in a very real sense, power, prestige, or wealth. They were also an economic resource in the sense of being additional labor power for the husband.

In general, however, the tendency is for a monogamous system of marriage to function as long as the number of men and women is approximately equal, and as long as most individuals can be included in a family grouping of some kind through the monogamous system.

But there are situations in which the number of individuals of different sexes is not approximately equal. Sometimes, for instance, it becomes necessary to limit the population, which means, in effect, to limit the number of people who can be born. Conditions of the physical environment, of the economic system and hence of the food supply, and defective social organization are all factors that may

[4] L. L. Bernard, *An Introduction to Sociology*, p. 93. Crowell, New York, 1941.

produce situations in which limitation of the population is necessary. For whatever reason, a society is sometimes able to support only a limited number of individuals.

A simple and effective way for the unmoral, in our sense of the term, primitive to reduce the population is to reduce the number of potential mothers. The practice of *female infanticide*, that is, the killing of some proportion of the female infants born, is one common way of assuring that there will not be too many mothers in the aggregate. Since this practice is seldom accompanied by a reduction in the number of male infants, the tendency then is toward an unbalance between the number of males in the group and the number of females. In turn, this unbalance produces a polyandrous system of marriage, admittedly a rare type of marital organization, but one which is found usually in connection with extreme poverty and a simple type of economic organization. Professor Bernard also connects polyandry with a grazing economy that required the absence from home for long periods of men engaged in herding, since they had to follow their flocks over a relatively wide area. In that case, he explains, another man remained at home in order to keep the household functioning and protected, with the result that more than one husband was necessary.[5]

Very probably there is no single reason which will account for the appearance of polyandry wherever and whenever it is found. It is a response to a total situation in which poverty and the discrepancy in numbers between the sexes were important factors, perhaps in addition to other factors which are not obvious to us. Whatever its causes, it functions in such a way as to include a large majority of the population in a definite family group, since it allows the surplus males, who might otherwise be "unattached," to be common husbands of one wife.

Polygyny is much more common than polyandry. Again we must remark that there is probably no single cause for polygyny. It also is a reaction to a total situation in which several factors are significant. In some cases it is related to differentiation of strength, social class, and other factors, as we suggested above. In other cases it is related to a surplus of females in a given population, together with an economic system in which unattached females find it difficult to function. Among primitives this kind of unbalance re-

[5]Ibid. p. 95.

sulted from the higher male death rate incident to such occupations as hunting and war. We have already noted the fact that a woman whose husband had died was expected to find a new husband as soon as possible. If men were scarce a polygynous marriage was the natural result.

In some cultures it was the duty of a male relative of the deceased husband to marry the widow; and if he refused to do his duty he was subject to punishment. A familiar illustration of this system occurs among the Hebrews of Old Testament times. A specific Old Testament provision orders the brother of a deceased husband to take the widow as wife, though there the provision is limited to a widow without children. The purpose was not only to give the widow a place in a family system but also to "raise up seed" to the deceased brother. Punishment is provided for refusal to perform this duty.[6] Obviously, if the brother were already married, a polygynous marriage would result.

MATES IN MODERN MARRIAGE

Turning now to a discussion of mate systems in modern society, it is evident that there is a much less direct connection between our mate system and the factors we have suggested as being important among simpler peoples. In our own times marriage has acquired meanings not connected with the societal functioning of the family institution. Mates are usually chosen with reference to characteristics which will promote individual goals rather than societal goals exclusively.

It is a fact that

> *In contemporary society legal regulations controlling the number of mates permitted in marriage are traditional rather than functional.*

We are, in our own times, technically a monogamous society, since polygamy is illegal. There are, of course, a number of ways by which sex satisfactions are attained outside the family system, but, because they are outside the family system, we still remain monogamous as far as our marital system goes. On the other hand, the kind

[6] *Time*, February 17, 1947, p. 56.

of monogamy we now practice differs from that of a century ago in the United States, when monogamy was assumed to mean the lifelong marital partnership of a man and a woman.

Divorce has, of course, become much more common. In 1946 about one marriage in four resulted in divorce, and it is estimated that by 1980, if present trends continue, one marriage out of two will result in divorce. Custom now permits the changing of mates to a much greater extent than it did formerly. We no longer look on the person who has been divorced as being thereby automatically disgraced. Perhaps, then, it is desirable to use some other term than monogamy to describe our contemporary marital system, in order to stress the fact that, while it is still technically monogamous, it is a different kind of system from that of the past. We suggest the term *successive polygamy*, meaning thereby the marital system by which legally we may have only one mate at a time, but may have as many mates in succession as we can acquire.

Of course not everyone in our society practices successive polygamy. It has until recently been confined to certain segments of our population, notably the wealthier segments and those which are on the fringe of respectability. As Professor Zimmerman suggests, our system of strict monogamy "has broken down from the top." The upper classes have been the first to adopt the new system.[7] But it is spreading to a good many other segments of our population which are by no means wealthy or on the fringe of respectability. Doubtless the Second World War helped to disseminate the pattern of easy marriage and easy divorce, but the war did not originate that pattern. It was already in existence; the war simply accelerated a process that was already taking place.

It is a matter of judgment or of prejudice whether we want to say that successive polygamy has become common enough to be called the typical marital system of contemporary America. It is by no means the only system. "Old-fashioned" lifelong monogamy still exists and is still a vital marital arrangement, but the newer arrangement is becoming more common among the influential and semiprominent middle-class people who set the pace for lower social classes. In that sense we must admit that successive polygamy is at least becoming typical of our times.

[7]Ibid.

Our Future Marital System

It is difficult to predict what our future pattern as to the legal number of mates permitted in marriage will be. This is one aspect of the general problem of social organization we mentioned in Chapter X—the problem of balancing individual meanings and societal meanings. From the individual point of view, a family which is not providing individual and personal satisfactions is not functioning adequately. According to that viewpoint, we have every right to change mates if we are personally and individually unhappy. But from the societal viewpoint the family which does not provide children for the future population is not functioning adequately. In so far as easy divorce permits the setting up of temporary relationships which do not contemplate children, a rapid change of mates is undesirable for the society.

There is, of course, no inherent reason why the family should not perform both societal and individual functions. The experience of the past demonstrates clearly that parent-child relationships may provide great satisfactions both for the children and for the parents. The emphasis on individual happiness as the chief goal of life to the exclusion of more social concepts is probably a temporary and passing emphasis, at least in its extreme form. We tend, in many segments of our population, to believe that we are happiest when we are free from responsibilities. We dislike the assumption of obligations. Since children and other family relationships increase responsibility, it often appears to unthinking people that child care is incompatible with individual happiness. Again this shallow view is probably temporary, incident to the current phase of disorganization apparent in much of our institutional life.

If we should continue toward a complete domination by the happiness motive, there is every reason to believe that divorce will increase, with the result that successive polygamy will become our established system. If we can balance the contemporary heavily individualistic goals with social goals, a more stable marital system will result in the future.

There is little reason to suppose that the traditional type of polygamy, which permits a number of mates at the same time instead of in succession, will become legal. We have a surplus of women, particularly in the marriageable-age groups, and a surplus of women has, in times past, been one of the factors encouraging polygamy.

On the other hand, we also have a complex economic system in which the unmarried woman can find a significant place with relative ease. In earlier societies the simple and masculine type of economic system was fully as important as a surplus of women in promoting a polygamous marital system. There is no particular necessity in our times for a woman to be a member of a marital group in order to support herself.

More likely than the establishment of legalized polygamy is a future decline in morality which will permit extramarital sex relations to a greater degree than is even now common. This situation will, if it occurs, be reflected in the functioning and organization of the family as a social unit. If the family seems likely to become completely disorganized, we as a society will in all probability institute drastic reforms in our whole concept and practice of morality. We will then once again have a foundation for a societally functioning family group.

Trends toward family disorganization as they appear at present are cultural facts which become significant for the future of our population aggregate. Precisely as the different marital customs of the past have arisen from the interaction of aggregates with a total environment, so the marital customs of the future will arise from our interaction with our own changing environment. One very important distinction, however, between our own times and those of the past is this: we have a much more complete equipment of knowledge about human behavior than past societies had. We can recognize the trends which are taking place, and we can trace their causes. We can also predict what the future will be if present trends continue. There is no real reason why we should not undertake some form of societal self-control which will offset trends toward disorganization. We shall return to this question of a program for marriage toward the end of this chapter.

Mate Choice

Societies not only develop customs as to the number of mates permitted in marriage; they also develop regulations regarding the kind of mate who may be chosen. There are three general types of mate-choice systems.

1. The *parental* system is that in which some authoritative member of the kinship families of the proposed partners in marriage controls the choice of mates. Often it is the head of the family, either the ruling male or the ruling female, or some other person arbitrarily designated as family head. The control exercised is not always absolute in the sense that the future marital partners are not consulted at all in the matter, though there are systems in which no volition is allowed them. But control is stringently exercised and generally approved by the aggregate. Even when there is some consultation of individual wishes, the societal meanings of the family are the important aspects of mate choice. Individual happiness is either wholly unimportant or at least secondary. What we think of as love does not enter into the actual choice. It is, however, one of the goals of marriage, since the expectation is that affection will develop between the spouses after their marriage. The parental system of mate choice has been very common in the past and it is still widely practiced in Oriental societies. In general, it flourishes in relatively simple cultures in which the family is the chief basis of social organization.

2. The *restricted* system is that in which young people are not bound by parental control, but in which there are certain well-established rules relating to mate choice which are strongly sanctioned by the aggregate. Some societies, for example, have developed a system of marriage called *endogamy*, which means that the marriage must take place "within the aggregate." The well-known attitude of orthodox Jewish people is an illustration of the endogamic system. Marriage with non-Jews is discouraged at present, and in the past was not countenanced at all. Gentiles who frown on marriage with Jews are exhibiting their own form of endogamic predilection. Until recently it was expected in our own society that people would marry somewhat within their "own social class," another form of endogamy. Parental control in the strict sense was not exercised; the restriction was societal in origin, and was enforced by societal approval or disapproval rather than by parental dictum. It controlled mate choice in an effective manner.

Other aggregates developed the system called *exogamy*, a custom whereby individuals married someone outside their own group. In its origin exogamy appears to be related to the belief in totemism, a form of ancestor worship that traced the beginnings of a human aggregate either directly to an animal ancestor or to the special favor of some animal ancestor given to the original pair of human beings. The members of one totemic clan were all related, and thus marriage within the clan would have been a form of incest. Our own laws relating to incestuous marriages are one aspect of an exogamic system. We do not marry close relatives, not because our parents forbid it but because custom and law forbid it.

Other aspects of the general restricted system of mate choice may be found in our laws relating to the age at which marriage is legal, in our religious doctrines regarding marriage with those who are not members of our own religion, and in antimiscegenation statues, which forbid intermarriage between races.

3. The third common system of mate choice is the *spontaneous* system, in which mate choice is very largely a matter of individual inclination, with the minimum both of parental control and of societal restriction. This is, of course, by and large our own system. It is common now for young people to announce to their parents the fact that they intend to marry a certain individual; or, sometimes, to announce the fact that they have already married that person, rather than to ask permission for the marriage. Of course, in many cases consultation with and confidence in the parents exists before "anything serious" is undertaken. But this is properly a consulting situation, not at all the same thing as parental domination of the choice.

The growth of spontaneous choice systems is related to the increase in complexity of an aggregate. With the differentiation in ways of life that accompanies complexity, the family assumes less importance than it did in earlier societies. We have already mentioned as an example of this situation our own family organization, in which family members have developed differentiated ways of life and differentiated interests. Fewer of our satisfactions are found in the home now than was the case in the past. Relationships between parents and children are less formalized than they were in the past. It is not surprising, then, that young people do not expect or welcome parental choice of mates.

Another aspect of societal complexity which affects the growth of spontaneous choice systems is a rapid rate of social change.

Under conditions of rapid change older people do not have, or are not believed to have, the accumulated wisdom of experience which, in a stable and unchanging society, enables them to function as advisers and counselors to the younger generation. When social change occurs at a relatively slow pace, the life situations faced by young people are similar to those which have been faced by their elders. Advice from elders becomes then a valuable adjunct to effective living. At present the situations faced by young people differ in many respects from those faced by their parents, or young people believe that they differ, with the result that the experience of parents seems somewhat irrelevant. In general,

> *As a society becomes more complex, mate choice*
> *tends to become more spontaneous.*

MODERN CHOOSING OF MATES

The modern system of mate choice, then, is the spontaneous system. Aside from incest regulations and such specialized areas as interracial marriage, individuals are relatively free from societal and parental controls in their choice of mates. Some analysis of this system and its results for contemporary American family organization is in order.

1. *The Anatomy of Choice.* First of all, it is desirable to have some understanding of the processes involved in what we refer to as a *choice.* Choice in itself is the selection of one item in preference to another. Such a selection is a behavior pattern; we are behaving in a definite way when we make the selection. Like all behavior patterns, it is a reaction to a total situation by a total personality— a reaction which an individual can make only on the basis of such personality equipment as he has built up from his past experiences. This is very largely a cultural matter. The kind of personality we can develop and the limits of its possibilities depend on the cultural fund of knowledge, the value systems, and the life goals which characterize the segment of our culture with which we have most intimate contact, as we pointed out in Chapter IX. Further, cultures tend to develop certain kinds of individuals, so that the available supply of individuals from which we select will be influenced by culture patterns.

What we have, then, in a choice situation is an individual selecting one from a number of items, the basis of the selection being
very heavily influenced by culture. A marital system based on
spontaneous choice produces the kind of mating which reflects
culture patterns. If, on the basis of that system, marital and family
organization is held to be unsatisfactory, as it is, for example, by
some students of our culture, the situation is not the result of individual stupidity or willfulness in the great majority of instances. It
is basically a cultural product. Programs for the betterment of
marriage must deal not only with marriage as such, but with the
whole cultural organization.

2. *The Conditions of Choice.* In our contemporary society the conditions under which spontaneous marital choice is made differ
markedly from the conditions existing in simpler societies. In such
societies, which were largely rural in organization, the conditions
of living promoted intimate, first-hand contacts with the people
from whom selection of a mate was to be made. The small size of
the aggregate, the relative social isolation of the community, the
difficulty and unusualness of travel, all tended to create a life pattern in which one individual knew most of the other individuals of
his aggregate with a degree of accuracy no longer possible. In our
contemporary social organization the size of the population, the
casual type of contact, and our general mobility contribute to the
growth of superficial contacts with other people. Such contact
does not permit a choice to be made in the same way that it was
made under the conditions of rural social organization.

It is also true that our contemporary society is highly differentiated, whereas the rural culture tended to produce individuals
of a similar background, or similar goals, and of similar reaction
patterns in general. There were, of course, individual differences
in the rural aggregate, but the differences were not nearly as marked
as they are in our own population. The choice of a mate in contemporary society, then, becomes a matter of selecting on the basis
of a limited number of facts, with a large area of ignorance in relation to other facts. In the rural type of social organization selection
was often also made on the basis of a limited number of facts, but
the conditions of association were such that similarities between the
partners in many important areas of life could be assumed.

One interesting development of our own times has been the growth of "marriage counseling services," which are devices intended to give the prospective partners a fund of knowledge about each other and an understanding of the realities of marriage in our culture. In so far as such services change the conditions under which the spontaneous choice system operates from conditions of ignorance to conditions of knowledge on which judgment may be based, they are very significant. They are an example of a societal adjustment to the complexity, superficiality of contact, and differentiation of background in the population.

3. *Cultural Influences and Values.* The influences and values of our own culture which affect the operation of the spontaneous choice system are many and varied. We shall mention some which are of admitted importance.

First of all, perhaps, is the emphasis on romantic love as the only basis for marriage. As Professor Linton points out, our culture is one of the very few which have placed a strong positive value on romantic love.[8] We have developed an intensely sentimental attitude toward romantic love, as a result of which we have come to look on it as a species of magic which will infallibly ensure marital happiness. Experience indicates that it does not operate that way. If marital choice is made wholly on the basis of this deeply emotional and sentimental experience, as many of our cultural instrumentalities tell us it should be, the resulting marriage can hardly be stable. Romantic love is quite a different thing from a mature affection between spouses. Such an affection rests on a complete appreciation of another individual's total personality, including the physical, emotional, and intellectual aspects of the other individual. It is more stable because it is not completely emotional. We are not suggesting that there should be no affection between spouses. We are pointing out that our culture strongly influences us toward a type of love which is apt to be temporary and changing. Mate choice is exercised by a large proportion of our population in terms of that type of love.

A second cultural influence affecting marital choice lies in the fact that emotional maturity and the development of permanent life goals are apt to be delayed by the conditions of our contem-

[8]Ralph Linton, *The Study of Man*, p. 175. Appleton-Century, New York, 1936.

porary association. It is a familiar fact that the more "civilized" cultures, our own included, tend to prolong the period of childhood. We have, for example, erected a complex educational system which carries over into the twentieth year or later, and we are progressively spreading participation in this expanded educational system among a larger proportion of our population. We no longer assume that the majority of children can leave school after they have finished the eighth grade. We assume that most of them will finish high school, and we are coming to assume that most of them should continue to college. In itself this is, we believe, an excellent thing. It does, however, prolong the period of childhood and adolescence in the sense that it delays participation in adult community activities for many of our young people. Since they do not experience realistically the adult patterns of their community, emotional maturity is delayed. Marriage is also, of course, delayed in some cases. One result of this general situation is that the mate chosen in terms of the restricted patterns of adolescence may not prove to be the mate desired when emotional maturity develops.

A third cultural influence affecting marital choice results from our long-time taboo against the dissemination of factual information regarding sex, with consequent confused attitudes towards sex. This is only partially a matter of actual sex instruction in the sense of knowledge of the details of sex relations, the conception and birth of children, and so on. More important than that, it is a matter of our total reaction to the fact of sex. Individuals whose attitudes toward sex are influenced either by pornographic devices or by well-intentioned misinformation, and for whom there is little or no counterinfluence directed toward a realistic appreciation of sex in adult life, will find it difficult to approach sex in marriage constructively. We are most unwise as a culture when we permit this significant area of life to become the property of groups which exploit it, directly or indirectly, in manifold ways. Since the taboo is apparently becoming less stringent, our attitude toward sex should become more balanced and realistic, with the result that we should be able to integrate it constructively into our cultural patterns of living. A mate in marriage is not exclusively a sexual object, and mate choice based on sex alone is certainly not a desirable system. But the sexual aspects of a mate, considered as part of a total personality, are important. To the extent that we do not take some such objective attitude toward the fact of sex, our spontaneous system of marital choice is defective.

Another cultural influence on our system of mate choice is the position assigned to women in our culture. The weight of evidence is that there is very little *innate* difference between men and women in intelligence, emotional balance, or potential skills and abilities. Such differences as do exist are culturally produced. They arise through limited or specialized types of interactions permitted women as compared with the broader interactions permitted men. If, for example, women are excluded from institutions of higher learning, as they have been in our past history, they will not develop the attitudes characteristic of higher education. If they are excluded from certain vocations, they will not develop the skills incident to those vocations. If female artists and musicians are held to be not quite "respectable," the majority of women will not develop artistic or musical abilities except as amateurs. Since we have, as a culture, withheld from women experience in many areas of life, the superstition has arisen that women are innately inferior to men, a superstition widespread even today and very hard to combat. Obviously an individual imbued with this attitude, which, in effect, asserts that women are an inferior species of human being, will choose his mate not as his actual or potential equal but as his assumed inferior. The resulting marriage will not be stable unless the wife agrees in this estimate of her status. An increasing number of women are refusing to agree to such an estimate.

We are now, of course, permitting considerably more freedom to women than we did formerly. As they exercise their prerogative of interacting with the totality of our culture patterns, it will become increasingly evident that women as an aggregate are not an inferior species but are, in fact, the equal of men as an aggregate. Under those conditions, our system of spontaneous choice will produce more stable marriages.

These examples are sufficient to indicate something of the influence exerted by culture patterns and cultural values on the spontaneous system of mate choice.

4. *Evaluation of the Spontaneous System.* Undoubtedly our system of mate choice raises a number of problems both for individuals and for our culture. It certainly does not operate automatically to

further either individual or societal goals for marriage and the family. It operates only under the general conditions of association current among us, and only in terms of our cultural values and other influences. Yet it does have within it such potentialities for effective marital choice that we can hardly conceive of a return either to the parental system or to the restricted system. Spontaneous choice permits adjustments, both individual and social, which make it an effective instrument for family and marital stability. If modification in our marital system is necessary, as some people firmly believe, the modification will come not in the spontaneous aspects of the system but in the conditions under which it functions and in the cultural values which influence it. There is reason to believe that current disorganizational aspects of the family are temporary and incident to our transition from a primarily rural culture to a primarily urban and industrial culture.

SYSTEMS OF DIVORCE

Exactly as most cultures have developed systems of marriage and family regulations, so most cultures have developed systems of divorce as a means of dissolving certain marriages. Throughout historical times men have divorced their wives; and, as Professor Elmer notes, their right to do so was seldom questioned, though the wisdom or the ethics of the procedure in a particular case may have been a matter of doubt.[9] We stated earlier that sex and marriage among primitives were apt to be considered matters of custom rather than of morals. Systems of divorce were set up in accordance with the beliefs of the particular aggregate concerned. Reasons considered valid for divorce tended to be largely personal, with the societal attitudes codified in the direction of whatever customs had developed.

In complex societies divorce shows a tendency to return to its earlier status. We find that condition in our own times, and it appeared also in the Greek and the Roman societies during the period of their most complex development.[10] Thus in Roman society about 100 A.D. divorce was easy, rapid, and "causeless," that is, permitted

[9]M. Elmer, *Sociology of the Family*, p. 352. Ginn, Boston, 1945.
[10]C. C. Zimmerman, "Family Crisis," *Rural Sociology*, December, 1946.

for no particularly important reason other than the inclination of the persons concerned. There was also a decreasing number of children, a rise of theories of "companionate" marriage as a solution for family problems, a rise and spread of juvenile delinquency, a revolt of youth against parental control, and other situations with which we are familiar in our own times. All these contrast with the Christian agricultural society of the Middle Ages and with our own rural society of some generations ago in America. It is generally true that

In complex industrial society both marriage and divorce
tend to become personal rather than societal matters.

THE NUMBER OF DIVORCES

According to the *Statistical Abstract of the United States*, there were almost 28,000 divorces in the United States in 1887 but by 1940 the number had increased to an estimated 264,000. These figures indicate that a large number of persons are affected by our patterns of divorce.

On the other hand, the figures as to the increased number of divorces may be misleading unless we also take into account the fact that the population of the country has also increased, as has the number of marriages. One simple way to take account of the increase both in population and in the number of marriages is to express the number of divorces as a "rate," that is, to express it in terms of some stable figure. Thus, we find that the rate of divorce *per thousand population* in the country has increased from 0.5 in 1887 to an estimated 2 in 1940. Since the total population of the county includes children and others who do not participate directly in divorce proceedings, the rate per 1000 population is inaccurate. It is, however, a useful device for comparative statistics in those years for which we do not have more accurate information.

For certain years we do have more accurate information. Thus for 1940 we find that there was a divorce rate of about 4.3 per 1000 of the United States population *15 years of age and over who were married*. In this segment of population more directly concerned with marriage and divorce, therefore, the rate is higher than it appears to be when we use only the population in general as the basis of our computation.

Another comparison often made is that between the number of marriages and the number of divorces. In 1940 there were about 1,565,000 marriages in the United States and about 264,000 divorces. This is a rate of about one divorce for each six marriages. Estimates, the accuracy of which we do not know, for the year 1946 indicated that during that year about one divorce was granted for every four marriages celebrated.

Most of our figures are chosen for the year 1940, partly because that is the last year for which we have full census data, and partly because we want to avoid possible disturbing factors introduced by the Second World War. On the basis of past experience, such disturbing factors may exist as a result of war. Thus in 1938–1940, a period when we were preparing for the Second World War and which also, incidentally, was a time of great business prosperity, the divorce rate reached the point of one divorce for each five marriages, the high point up to that time. During the same period divorce reached a peak of one divorce for each two marriages in some "boom" communities.[11] After the First World War the divorce rate increased by about 40 per cent.

There is no evidence as yet to indicate that the trend of rising divorce will be reversed. We may therefore expect that there will be more divorces in the future than there are now. As we said earlier, some statisticians predict that if present trends continue a rate of one divorce for each two marriages will become the prevailing rate in the United States.

ATTITUDES TOWARD DIVORCE

The increase in the number of divorces has been accompanied by changed attitudes toward divorce. Not only is it much less unusual than it used to be, but it is regarded much less seriously. The *grounds* for divorce have been increased in some states; and in other states the interpretation of existing grounds has been so broadened as to include many kinds of conduct not literally comprehended by the terms used in statutes. For example, "intolerable indignities" may mean almost anything from the worst kind of cruelty to the mildest kind of criticism of trivial things. "Incompatibility" may refer to anything from situations involving actual friction of per-

[11] E. M. Duvall, and R. Hill, *When You Marry*, p. 250. Heath, Boston, 1945.

sonalities in important areas of life to minor disagreements about unimportant things. Other terms are similarly interpreted in an inclusive manner.

Standard grounds for divorce, accepted in most jurisdictions for a number of years past, include adultery, cruelty, commission of a felony, habitual intoxication, and similar acts. In addition to these long-accepted causes, the following occur in at least one jurisdiction, some of them in several: living apart, absence, divorce out of state, excesses, joining religious sect, violent temper, public defamation, intolerable severity, misbehavior, and wickedness.[12] In terms of these vague grounds, it is not difficult to believe that most people have erred sufficiently to permit their spouses to divorce them, if only on the grounds of "intolerable severity" or "joining religious sect." As to misbehavior and wickedness, the opportunity for a broad interpretation is obvious.

It is interesting to note that only about 7.5 per cent of divorces are granted for reasons of adultery. This figure does not reflect the real situation, since there is a tendency to cite the "least disgraceful" cause for divorce, adultery often being deliberately avoided even when it does exist. But the figure cited does indicate the significant use of other grounds in divorce proceedings.

It is also interesting to note that only about 20 per cent of divorce cases are "contested." In the others, whatever the reason, one party to the divorce does not enter any specific defense or denial of charges, thus permitting the divorce to take place without active opposition.

We do not know whether the "easy" interpretation of grounds for divorce has caused the increase in divorces, or whether the increase came first and the easy interpretation followed under pressure. They are probably related in some more complex way than simple cause and effect. Possibly both are symptoms of changes in our general social organization rather than in marriage and family customs alone.

WHO IS DIVORCED?

It is difficult to generalize about the kind of person who is divorced, because relatively little attention has been paid to the study

[12]Elmer, op. cit. p. 363.

of participants in the cases. Some courts have social workers, psychiatrists, and other officials who attempt to make a study of each case and report to the judge. But in most "domestic affairs" courts the legal aspects of the case are the only areas of emphasis. In those cases in which there has been at least an attempt at analysis of the total personal and social situations involved, there is a strong indication that "personality difficulties" are very important factors in divorce. What this statement means, usually, is that one or the other of the parties to the case has not matured emotionally or that the tastes, attitudes, values, and other aspects of the personality organizations of the individuals concerned differ in some way.

Often causes other than personality factors as such are actually cited as the basis of disagreement, such things as financial difficulties, disagreements over sex, presence of relatives in the home, or simply the desire to marry someone else. There is no doubt that all these situations are present in many marital disturbances, but it is doubtful whether they are the really important factors in the difficulty. Almost every family has, at one time or another, faced one or more of the tension situations listed above, and yet far from every family meets them in such a way that divorce results. Certainly the great majority of families have "money troubles" at one time or another, and a reasonable number of families meet serious money problems. Yet by no means all those families seek divorces.

It is, then, not the mere fact that we encounter problems that leads to divorce. It is our *attitude toward* the problems and, ultimately, our attitude toward life itself. Attitudes are a very important part of personality structure.

If, for example, an individual believes that he has a right to a completely happy and untroubled existence, he resents anything that interferes with his happiness, whether it is financial, sexual, kinship, or otherwise. He makes little or no attempt to meet and solve his difficulties. He simply resents them. But, since it is hard to resent such an impersonal thing as "difficulties" or "life in general," he is apt to transfer his resentment to some individual, to some person who comes to represent the cause of his unhappiness. This process of transfer happens outside as well as inside marriage, of course. But when it happens inside marriage, the most convenient person to whom the resentment can be transferred is the spouse. "If I hadn't married you—" becomes a phrase of bitterness and reproach as well as a rationalization of failure to approach problems realistically. The implication is that if the marriage had not taken place, or if the spouse were a different kind of individual, the difficulties being experienced would not have arisen. In certain cases that implication may be true. In many other cases, it is purely imaginary. If this kind of tension occurs frequently, the marriage breaks.

It is the immature personality which is apt to be able to do nothing about problems except resent them. The childish individual who tries to organize his life completely about a pleasure principle acts like a child in trying to destroy whatever he thinks interferes with his pleasure. Often he succeeds, and another divorce takes place.

There are other aspects of immaturity on the part of adults that affect the whole marriage-divorce situation. For example, the immature person may indulge in childish fantasies of a magical way out of his difficulties. He may visualize another person as the center of his fantasies. Then that other person becomes the "other man," the "other woman," or the third member of a "triangle," who figures so prominently in divorce news. Or the immature person may seek a substitute for his parent, who solved all his difficulties in childhood. Again, the "other man" or "other woman" may function in fantasy as the lost parent who used to be so dependable a source of help. It is difficult to meet immaturity and its accompanying attitudes in any rational way.

We do not mean to imply that every person who is divorced suffers from a serious personality defect. Two people at least are concerned in every divorce. It is possible that a perfectly normal and well-adjusted person might marry an individual whose personality was not matured. It is also possible for personality defects to develop after marriage, with the result that a normal person finds himself married to an increasingly abnormal person. Under those circumstances, one person involved in a divorce may well be a normal personality, whatever the other may be.

There are many more complex situations than those we have thus far described, but the discussion has been sufficient to indicate that if we are to understand the causes for divorce, we must go more deeply than the externals of marital difficulty. We must understand something of personality, of attitudes, of motivations, and the formation of all these traits in the individual. Such matters belong properly to a book devoted exclusively to marriage and the family.

PROGRAMS FOR MARRIAGE AND THE FAMILY

A number of students of the family believe that very grave societal results may spring from present family trends. Professor Zimmerman, for example, suggests that the American family system will not outlast the twentieth century if present trends continue. He also traces historically a connection between our complex industrial society and the antifamilism which has developed.[13] The term *antifamilism* refers to the growth of a set of attitudes and values which are antagonistic to the family. It includes not only patterns such as divorce, which are directly antagonistic, but also such other patterns as our materialistic emphasis and our pleasure goals which are indirectly antagonistic. Since no society can survive without some kind of family system, it becomes necessary under those circumstances to consider what steps we can take either to rehabilitate our older system or to control the changes which are taking place so that they will result in a constructively functioning new system.

Whether or not Professor Zimmerman's rather extreme view is accurate remains to be seen. However that may be, the fact is that a number of programs for the improvement of marital and family living have been suggested. We note below the general approach of such programs.

LONG-TIME PROGRAMS

Significant goals in a long-time program for marriage and family living include the lowering of the divorce rate, the lessening of marital tensions, the exercise of greater care in marital choice, and the decreasing of the number of childless marriages. These are goals which cannot be attained in a few years, and so they become properly steps in a long-time program. Three specific suggestions follow.

1. The first proposal is for the dissemination of information about marriage and family-living patterns. This is an area in which there is a good deal of factual information, but we have tended to leave

[13]Zimmerman, op. cit.

its dissemination to journalists, feature writers, and similar people who often cannot escape the temptation to be sensational on the subject and therefore to distort it. It is only recently that a number of sober and yet readable books dealing with the facts of marriage and of family living have been published.

Information is of course not the only prerequisite to more appropriate behavior in relation to marital patterns, but it is a very significant prerequisite. The areas of information to be disseminated include facts about personality characteristics and personality formation, discussion of the mechanisms of choice and of all the factors that affect those mechanisms, specific examples of the operation of personality and cultural factors in relation to marital problems, and some concrete concepts of adult behavior and attitudes toward life.

If this program is to be followed, the information should be imparted as early in the individual's life as he is able to absorb it. Certainly it should be no later than the first year of high school. It should be continued beyond formal schooling in periodicals, newspapers, books, and other instruments of adult education. If the average individual has this kind of information, and has it soon enough, he will be less bewildered in the face of marital maladjustments.

2. In addition to information, important as that may be, most long-time programs include some appeal to people which will influence them from the viewpoint of motivations. We defined motivations in Part I as the stimulus-response pattern significantly modified by the inner experiences of the individual. They are the immediate bases of human behavior. A marriage program, in order to be effective, must discover motivations which will make the average person not only acquire information about marriage, but also apply that information to his own life situations.

It is difficult to erect new motivations in a culture which has developed strong systems of belief and attitude, but existing motivations may be applied specifically to a marriage program. In our own times the economic motivation and the happiness motivation are probably the most powerful motivations, in the sense that they affect our total response to a variety of stimuli in important ways. Happiness is widely held to be the end and aim of existence. Obviously, then, happiness is a generalized motivation which is

already established in our culture, and one which may be made to
serve as a motivation in connection with a marriage program. It
is, on the whole, true that the person who has some acquaintance
with the facts of marriage in our culture and who will apply those
facts to his own behavior will be happier in marriage than the person who neglects both the facts and the application. As part of a
long-time marriage program, that fact must be demonstrated.

There will, of course, be many difficulties in this aspect of any
marriage and family program. The great insistence on the romantic-
love approach which pours constantly from the movies, the radio,
periodicals, and other sources of mass influence is directly at odds
with the type of factual information we have been discussing. In
addition, the orientation of interest in large segments of our population is not in the direction of serious individual and societal analysis. Taboos against certain kinds of information in connection with
marriage and certain marital problems are very strong. All these
will prevent any sudden and spectacular success in the field of marriage and family education, but there are indications that patience
and persistence in such education will be rewarded.

3. But the dissemination of information and the development of
motivations will be of little significance unless they are reinforced
by changes in our general cultural patterns. It is a fact that, at the
present time, childbearing and child care, along with many other
aspects of family living, are unnecessarily burdensome for middle-
class parents. Such parents are at a disadvantage, financially and
otherwise, in comparison with childless couples. Any program for
improvement in marriage and the family must include modifications of those culture patterns which react to the disadvantage of
parents. For example, we can undertake to remove some of the disadvantages under which parents labor as compared with the nonfamily person. We can erect houses specifically for families with
children, possibly government-owned, but certainly renting within
a range which will make them available to those with limited incomes. If we are to believe the claims of popular writers on marriage and the family, another necessary step in a family program
lies in the direction of providing help for the average middle-class
mother. Such help in the past was available from female relatives
or inexpensive domestic servants, sources which are no longer
plentiful. Government or other financial aid toward the purchase

of household machinery and toward the operation of inexpensive community-housekeeping services is a suggestion to be considered.

It is alleged that in the intellectual and financial middle class "motherhood is a sentence to years of drudgery, confinement, and responsibility," because the cares and complexities of family life fall exclusively on the mother.[14] If it is such, or if a number of women believe that it is such, we can hardly hope for an enthusiastic acceptance of parenthood by the members of that class.

A third co-operative step is the provision of inexpensive but good nursery schools, co-operative community enterprises in child care and the performance of family tasks, and neighborhood entertainment projects on a co-operative basis. The mother who has special interests, specialized education, or special abilities may thus be freed from some of the unnecessary burdens of family care and permitted to live a more satisfying life than she now does in many cases.

These and similar suggestions have been made by the Population Committee of the National Economic and Social Planning Association.[15] They may serve as an illustration of a program for marriage advanced by a serious and influential group.

Most of our discussion thus far has related to economic aspects of contemporary family life. There are, however, other aspects equally important. For example, standards of child care are higher than they have been in the past. We no longer assume that children should be self-supporting at the age of fourteen. We propose to give more children an education which they may not complete until they are twenty or more years old. The question then arises for the middle-class family as to how many children it can have and still give them standard advantages, educational and otherwise. Certainly the large families of the past will not be possible under our present high standards. As a society we could go far toward solving that problem by making education and other advantages either actually free or very inexpensive. The difficulty is that we have assumed that free education meant education open to all students, regardless of their capacity or lack of capacity to benefit from it. One result of that belief has been that education has lost much of

[14]"This Business of Parenthood," anonymous, *Harper's*, January, 1931.

[15]J. H. Folson, *The Family and Democratic Society*, pp. 288 ff. Wiley, New York, 1943.

its meaning as a developmental agency. It has geared its program to the actual capacities of the less able student rather than to the potentialities of the more able student.

We have outlined in this section some of the important suggestions common to current programs for marriage. To conservative people, the whole project may well seem nonsense because they do not realize the changed position of the family in our contemporary social organization. A more objective attitude demands that we evaluate the programs in the light of current situations instead of wholly rejecting them or uncritically advocating them.

SHORT-TIME PROGRAMS

Programs for marriage and the family also include plans from which more immediate results may be expected. Important features of such short-time programs include the following.

1. An important feature is the reliance on marriage-counseling services, which are directed toward the prevention of marital tensions and toward the relief of tension situations which have already arisen. Marriage-counseling operates through trained personnel who, by using specialized techniques, analyze the total situation involved in specific difficulties and try to help the individuals concerned to understand themselves and the forces at work in creating the situation. Their aim is to establish more satisfactory relationships. Such services have not functioned long enough to permit an accurate evaluation of their results. In the case of a few outstanding centers, results are reported to be very satisfactory.

The prevention of family separations is not always practicable. In fact, separation is sometimes the only solution of existing tensions. But one goal of counseling services is to prevent *unnecessary* divorce. They also function in the area of premarital advice, a service somewhat harder to evaluate, since we do not know what might have happened in the case of some marriages if the counseling factor had not been present. It is very probable, however, that in so far as unwise marriage is prevented through the activities of counseling agencies, divorce is also prevented.

2. Instruction in marriage through schools, churches, and other community agencies is another aspect of short-time programs. It is a relatively new venture, with goals much like those of marriage-counseling services.

3. Intelligent court procedure is a third aspect of the short-time programs. It differs from marital counseling and from marriage instruction in that it operates after a decision in favor of divorce has been made by the marital partners, and official steps in that direction have been taken. Under present circumstances, however, it is as necessary as counseling and education, because not all persons in potential or actual marital difficulties are reached by those services.

Intelligent court procedure, in terms of a marriage program, means the attachment to domestic-relations courts of social workers and of other specialists skilled in the analysis of personality and in the investigation of social situations. They are often able to discover the basic realities involved in the divorce situation, instead of permitting the proceedings to be simply a matter of legal relationships. The court official is the last resort of a short-time program. He interviews people only after serious decisions have been made. He must function with the other agencies in the program; he cannot replace them.

SUMMARY: THE FAMILY IN SOCIAL ORGANIZATION

Social organization is the system by which the parts of a society are related to the whole society and to each other in a meaningful way. The meanings involved derive very largely from the functioning of the parts. What the institution does for us, and our view of the importance of what it does for us, very significantly influence its meaning for us.

The family has had two outstanding functions in past society: the channeling of sex and the production of children. As our patterns of morality have changed, and as our population over a period of years has vastly increased, both these functions have been of declining importance.

Other family functions of the long past—impartation of religious instruction within the family group, economic services rendered by the family to its members, recreation within the family group, the beginnings of education—all these have been assigned to specialized groupings and thus to a great extent have ceased to be family functions.

One important result of this loss of function has been a decrease in the meaning of the family, both for the society and for the individual family member. The family does fewer things, provides fewer satisfactions. This situation is reflected in the orientation of our cultural interests away from the family as an institution and toward other institutions. It is also reflected in the instability of family groupings.

Programs to remedy this situation are hampered by the fact that the loss of societal function by the family makes such programs appear unimportant to large segments of our population. In addition, individual marital programs, such as those involved in marriage counseling, can meet the difficulties of only a relatively few individuals. The cultural orientation remains much the same.

There is reason to believe that the present disorganization of the family, incident to its loss of function, may be temporary. The family is an old institution. Our recent development of the economic system is new and impressive, even though the economic institution as such may be as old as the family. As the economic institution in all its ramifications becomes stabilized, along with the other institutions which we have developed in such a spectacular fashion, the family will probably again assume its functioning place in future society.

READINGS

ELMER, M. C. *The Sociology of the Family*. Ginn and Company, Boston, 1945. An excellent discussion of the family as a social institution.

NIMKOFF, M. F. *Marriage and the Family*. Houghton Mifflin Company, Boston, 1947. A competent study of the family in its institutional aspects, and of modern marriage.

TRUXAL, A. G., and MERRILL, F. E. *The Family in American Culture*. Prentice-Hall, Inc., New York, 1947. An outstanding volume dealing with the American family and contemporary American marriage.

DUVALL, E. M., and HILL, REUBEN. *When You Marry*. D. C. Heath and Company, Boston, 1945. A practical discussion of contemporary marriage written for the average reader.

BOWMAN, HENRY A. *Marriage for Moderns*. McGraw-Hill Book Company, Inc., New York, 1942. Another practical discussion of modern marriage, especially from the viewpoint of preparation for successful marriage.

JUNG, MOSES (Ed.). *Modern Marriage*. F. S. Crofts & Co., New York, 1940. A symposium by specialists, dealing with the problems and adjustments of contemporary marriage. Somewhat more advanced in treatment than the two preceding references.

CHAPTER XIII

THE ECONOMIC SYSTEM

THE CONTEMPORARY economic system includes not only industry and commerce in all their ramifications, but also the complex of agricultural activities we have developed. A sociologist, approaching the economic institution as a part of the social organization, is primarily interested in the relationships between economic activity and other aspects of our common life. He is not particularly concerned with the internal functioning of the system. Such matters as the operation of demand and supply, the functioning of monetary and credit systems, problems of production and of management, all are the concern of the economist, not of the sociologist. Leaving them to the economist, we shall ask such questions as, "How does the economic system affect the total social organization? What are its effects specifically on other institutions in a society? To what extent does it influence our ways of living and our ways of thinking in general?" In answering such questions, we make clear the relationships between the economic institution and our life patterns. The economic system in social organization then becomes our first general topic.

THE ECONOMIC SYSTEM IN SOCIAL ORGANIZATION

As in the case of the discussion of the family in the preceding chapter, we may suggest that it is fairly simple to recognize and to define the economic institution in our own culture. We are not, however, interested in our own culture only, but in human society in general. It therefore becomes desirable to delimit the boundaries of the economic institution. Again we find that the simplest way in which we may so delimit them is by discovering the functions which characterize economic activity in human culture.

DEFINITION

In every culture we can trace a system of techniques which has for its purpose the exploitation of the environment for the satisfaction of subsistence needs—the need for an adequate food supply, for shelter, and for clothing in those areas in which clothing is a necessity. The sum of those techniques is the technological aspect of the economic system, a very important part of the economic institution, and one which may have very significant effects on many aspects of social organization.

Technology in itself, however, is only part of the economic institution. Equally significant is the collection of customs, ideas, superstitions, and beliefs which grow up about the techniques. These relate to the proper manner in which techniques may be used, to the ownership of tools, to the distribution of the products of technology, to inheritance, and to many other situations related to technology but not technological in themselves. In our own times many of the problems that trouble us are basically related not to technology as such but to the effects of technology on economic custom and belief. So it has been in other cultures.

It would be a mistake, then, to regard the economic institution as a collection of techniques only. It is that plus a complex of customs and beliefs. An inclusive definition would run somewhat as follows:

The economic institution is the complex of techniques, ideas, and customs relating to the exploitation of the environment for the satisfaction of subsistence needs.

As we might expect, the details of economic systems vary from one culture to another, depending on the interaction of a given group with a given cultural and physical environment. Thus we find some economies based primarily on hunting and fishing, others on agriculture, others on the herding of flocks, and others on industry, commerce, and transportation. Often we find a mixture of these various kinds of economic activity.

Much as the specific details may vary from culture to culture, we may classify economic systems in relatively few general types.

1. The *collecting* economies are those in which the basic economic activity consists in the utilization of products existing naturally in

the environment. Hunting, fishing, and the use of plants native to an area without cultivation or other agricultural operations, are all examples of collecting economies. In general, they are characteristic of simple cultures.

2. *Simple-transformative* economies are those in which natural products are modified in a simple way. Agricultural economies and those which domesticate and breed animals are among early types of simple transformative economies. Unpretentious as they may appear to us, they are very important in human development. They go far toward freeing mankind from a dependence on natural supplies of food; and they introduce an element of control over nature, based on understanding of natural processes and forethought applied to the relationship between present and future supplies of food. Included also in simple transformative economies are those which develop the beginnings of manufacture, thereby making the environmental resources more suitable for use under the given circumstances of association. The modifications introduced by handicraft and other uncomplicated processes begin the relationship between the economic and other institutions which develop in later society into a complex interdependence.

3. *Complex-transformative* economies are those systems which utilize natural products largely as raw materials, performing a number of elaborate operations on these natural products or on combinations of natural products, with the result that the finished goods are far removed from the state of nature. Our own economy is, of course, an example of complex transformation, as have been the economies of other civilizations. We now use almost nothing for food, shelter, clothing, or any other purpose, in its unmodified form. One result of this development is that the economic system assumes a greater importance in the total social organization because tastes, standards, and wants are of such a nature that we are not satisfied with unelaborated products.

4. *Mixed economies* are those in which there are a number of different kinds of economic activity, some simple, others complex. Examples of mixed economies may be found in some of the earlier civilizations in which agriculture of a simple kind was carried on by one segment of the population, while other segments engaged in manufacturing and commercial enterprises of some degree of complexity.

Both complex-transformative and mixed economies are apt to include areas of life much beyond the mere subsistence needs of the group concerned. As we suggested earlier, a great deal of our own economic activity is in the nature of elaboration, and much of our economic energy is taken up with the production of other than strict necessities. Doubtless we could survive without the many kinds of goods we now have. But, much as we may elaborate, the core of our economic system deals with basic subsistence needs. In fact, it is because our system is efficient in supplying those subsistence needs that we are able to spare time and energy for elaboration. Our many accretions to basic subsistence activities should not blind us to the fact that subsistence is the mark of the economic institution, as we state in our definition.

The influence of an economic system on the rest of the social organization is conditioned by the kind of system it is, in terms of our classification above. We shall now consider that influence in more detail.

ECONOMIC RELATIONSHIPS

In what ways does the economic system relate the parts of a society to the whole society, and thereby function in social organization? In answering that question, we must distinguish between the complex-transformative systems and the systems of simpler cultures.

In simpler economic systems, the institution functioned for the individual chiefly by providing him with accepted techniques so that he, as an individual, could provide food and other basic necessities for himself. In such cultures, each individual had to be more or less self-sufficient. Each learned from the culture in which he grew up the methods of making and using tools, methods of harvesting and storing crops, and techniques for breeding and using animals. Some individuals improved on existing techniques through the process of invention, but the average individual was content merely to learn their use. As he learned from his group and as he engaged in the search for subsistence along with his group, he became identified with that particular association of people and with its ways of living. His relationship to the whole was largely based on similarity of life pattern, economic and otherwise.

Under those circumstances the binding of an individual to a group through the economic institution is no stronger than the binding through other institutions, such as the family and religion. Economic ideas and economic processes do not dominate the social organization as they do in our own society. We may suggest that

In simple cultures the economic institution is not the dominant institution in society.

This situation arises from two facts: first, the fact that the individual is related to the economic institution primarily as a learner of its rather simple methods; and second, the fact that after he has learned economic techniques he becomes largely a self-sufficient economic agent. There is no great specialization of tasks or division of labor, with its resulting dependence of one individual on another. Almost every person in the aggregate has to know how to do almost every job necessary for survival.[1] He learns how to do these jobs from the folkways of his group, but he uses them as an individual.

Circumstances are quite different in our own society, as in any complex society. We still learn how to perform the operations necessary to a particular job partly *on the job*, and hence partly from the economic institution. But we can, for the most part, use the skills we learn only as part of a complex organization. This is certainly true for many industrial occupations. It is becoming more applicable also to the professions. A physician, for example (who, by the way, does not learn from the economic institution but from an educational institution), no longer practices as a solitary individual; he uses hospitals, clinic facilities, and other community agencies as a matter of course. In our times a teacher does not set up as instructor of the young apart from some kind of organized school system. Musicians are employed by orchestras, radio concerns, and similar organizations.

There are, of course, exceptions to these statements, as in the case of skilled artisans and of outstanding professional people. But, by and large, the average individual in our times must use his skills in conjunction with some organized effort rather than as a self-sufficient economic agent. Apart from the co-ordinated effort of a group of men, of whom any individual, particularly in industrial

[1]A. Goldenweiser, *Anthropology*, Chap. II. Crofts, New York, 1945.

processes, may be only a relatively unimportant unit, there can be no sale of product, no income for producer, and no wages for labor. We have become dependent on other people for the successful and co-operative exploitation of the environment through which we as individuals get our own means of subsistence.

This fact of interdependence, of course, goes beyond any one *production line*. Raw materials for one process and production line come from other processes and other production lines. In some instances not only raw materials but finished products come from outside sources. Automobile manufacturers often get parts from other specialized manufacturers. The surgeon does not make his own instruments and other supplies. The teacher uses equipment made for his profession but not made by him. If there is a breakdown or a slowing down in any of the supplying plants, the users of their products must also slow down or close. It is this fact which makes the strike such an effective weapon for labor.

Interdependence does not stop even there, however. We have specialized beyond the production line itself to the extent that one group—the employing group, or *capital*—owns the machines, while another group—the employed group, or *labor*—provides the man power to operate the machines. These two groupings are also, of course, interdependent. The fact that most laborers do not have a skill which can be utilized apart from costly machines makes labor dependent on capital. The fact that machines which are not operated do not produce a profit makes capital dependent on labor.

There is one aspect of this whole situation that is sometimes overlooked by enthusiasts for a machine civilization. Our skill at mechanical invention might well enable us to create machines which would be so nearly automatic in operation that labor would become progressively functionless and therefore unnecessary. In fact, we have already approached that situation in some manufacturing operations. Automatic machinery does not, however, free capital from its dependence on labor, for the simple reason that the mere production of goods is not the only aim of manufacturing. Goods must be sold as well as made. One important source of buying power is the wages paid to labor. To the extent that we replace men by machines we also tend to reduce the buying power of the population. Machines produce, but they do not consume their own products. Both labor and capital are dependent on the consumer of their goods. It is not a question, then, of a one-sided dependence. It is a situation of true interdependence.

We may go even further than this, and point to instances of interdependence outside the manufacturing field. In our money economy, as in any money economy, we have grown accustomed to paying others for services we performed for ourselves in the not too remote past. We *demand*—that is, we are willing to pay for—the services of physicians, lawyers, teachers, professional entertainers, launderers and cleaners, restauranteurs, and a host of other specialists. Doubtless we could dispense with the services of some of these people in case of necessity, but we have become accustomed to having them and we are unwilling to do without them. Some of them, of course, we could not dispense with, for example, physicians, lawyers, policemen, and firemen. We cannot perform their functions and our own also, partly because of our specialized training and partly because we lack the time. We are dependent on them and they, in turn, are dependent on us.

In effect, then, economic relationships have changed. Because many of us cannot function with the skills we have as individuals but must use those skills as units in a system, the system becomes of much more importance than it was in simpler cultures.

> *In complex societies the economic institution tends*
> *to be the dominant institution.*

In such societies the individual is related to the social organization from the economic viewpoint, not by a process of learning simple techniques but through the process of increasing interdependence. This kind of relationship tends to be impersonal. Feelings of friendship, loyalty, and enthusiasm are reduced to a minimum. They are replaced by the hard pressure of necessity. Certain situations in our own times arise from economic dominance of the interdependent type, which will be discussed below.

RESULTS OF ECONOMIC DOMINANCE

1. *Growth of Class Consciousness.* One of the results of the dominance of an impersonal and interdependent economic system in our own times is the growth of class consciousness, based not on inherited

rank or blood but on economic functioning. Individuals of like economic status and function join together with their fellows. They develop sympathetic attitudes toward others in circumstances similar to theirs, even when those others are not members of their immediate grouping. Labor unions are a familiar example of this kind of development. Unions are countered by associations of employers and manufacturers who try to advance the interests of their own class. Both labor and employing groups exert pressure on legislative bodies, with the result that the conflict is carried far beyond the domain of purely economic activity into that of political maneuvering. There is also a growing movement to have *consumers* organized, so that both unions and employers would be held to account by those who buy the goods produced by labor and capital.

The significant thing here is that these three groups are, for the most part, primarily interested in advancing their own interests and in opposing the interests of other groups, when such opposition appears to be desirable. They have not organized in order to increase co-operation among the three classes, though that may well be one by-product of their activity in the future. Class consciousness has developed in this case partly from the actual fact of interdependence and partly from attitudes taken toward that fact. Interdependence is a relatively new phenomenon in our economic history. Many of us fear and resent it; to many its evil results seem certain. With that attitude it is natural that there should be attempts to coerce other classes than our own to "do their duty" in order that our own comfort may be assured. Co-operative behavior will hardly spring from that kind of attitude.

We are not suggesting that there should be no unions or employers' groupings or consumers' organizations. All these can function as powerful instruments of mutual understanding and co-operation, thus making constructive use of the fact of interdependence. If complex and impersonal relationships characterize an economic system, some medium is necessary through which the several segments involved in the relationships can officially approach one another and negotiate with one another. The disturbing aspect of our present situation lies in the fact that the net result thus far of much of their activity has been oppositive rather than co-operative.

One effective way of offsetting the conflict situation is to stress the fact of *inter*dependence instead of dependence. There is the tendency for one group or the other to insist that it is the really vital and necessary factor in production on which the other factors depend. For example, Marxists hold that labor produces all value and that the capitalistic class is a parasite on labor. Some employers' groups, on the other hand, are fond of propaganda to the effect that the only real source of production is "the money which provides the machines to make the goods." Neither of these views is correct. Goods and wealth come only from the co-operative effort of many different individuals who are members of the various different social classes we have been discussing.

2. *Economic Coloring of Attitudes.* Another effect of the dominating position of an impersonal and complex economic system in a complex society is the coloring of our attitudes toward noneconomic aspects of society. Money and financial values tend to become the sole measure of all values. Literary, artistic, and similar productions are measured by financial returns from sales, regardless of any other standards of judgment. In addition, there is a tendency to conclude that size, number, and other quantitative expressions are the only terms in which reality may be described. Truth tends to become simply what "most" people believe, without regard to the processes of thought by which they may have arrived at their opinions. Democracy is held to be simply "the will of the majority," with no reference to the ideals on which democracy is based or to the method by which the will of the majority is exercised. Wealth is believed to be the true estimate of an individual's worth. This emphasis on quantitative measurements is typical of the economic outlook; it characterizes our business and industrial activities.

It is, of course, a very useful attitude in some aspects of our economic life, but when it is carried over into other areas of living it may have narrowing results. It is perhaps the more dangerous because it is not a deliberate attempt on the part of business and industry to influence the population. We tend to develop the attitude unconsciously because we are so strongly associated with the economic institution and because its position is such a dominating one.

This kind of coloring of other institutions by the economic outlook is very probably a temporary phase of our social organization, incident to the fact that we have developed the economic institution to an unusual extent, and it may be some time before it is restored to a balance with the other institutions of our social organization.

3. *Population Influences.* A third effect of our economic institution in social organization lies in its indirect influence on population. Because it is efficient, it can provide not only goods in abundance but also leisure time for the major portion of our people in a degree never before possible. In turn, leisure time enables us to develop ourselves educationally and otherwise to an extent never before possible for a large proportion of any population. A population so developed may form the basis for an intelligently controlled social organization in which they can participate as full members rather than as mere units.

Obviously our economic system has not yet done all these things, and the situation we have envisaged is far from actuality. But the difficulty is not in the ability of the economic system as such to produce goods and leisure time; it is in the distribution of those goods and in the human relationships involved in such distribution. In turn, distribution and human relationships go far beyond the confines of an economic system; they are political and social. It is doubtful if changes in the economic institution as such will have the results hoped for by some of our radical groups. More to the point would be an increase in understanding of the social factors involved.

It is a fact that the incomes of many people are, and will remain for some time, inadequate. Even in 1944, a year of war prosperity, estimates indicate that nearly one half of the income recipients in the United States received less than $2000 per year; while only one tenth of 1 per cent received more than $25,000 per year. Not all these income recipients were heads of families. Those, however, who were heads of families could not provide for them a comfortable standard of living at a rate of income of $2000 or less per year.[2] In 1947 money income in the United States was at an all-time high, but we were in a period of inflation, with the result that the purchasing power of incomes received was less than during the war years.

We are, then, a wealthy nation, but not, on the whole, a wealthy population, even though we are wealthier than most past popula-

[2] Estimates from Treasury Department, *Congressional Record*, March 19, 1945, p. 2480.

tions. We may expect the situation to improve as we learn how to adjust the economic system to the rest of our social organization.

Furthermore, the economic institution affects not only the kind of people through its distribution of goods and of leisure time; it also affects the number of people. Thus an efficient system permits a given quantity of natural resources to support a larger number of people than does an inefficient system, other things being equal. In the case of our own population we could, from the production viewpoint, support a larger number of people than we now have.

This relationship between population and natural resources has been studied extensively over the past two hundred years or so. Thomas Malthus was among the first in recent times to codify his views on the matter. Writing about 1800, he pointed out that the means of subsistence were limited and that population tended to increase more rapidly than did those means of subsistence, with the result that "natural checks" to population increase came into operation. Important among these natural checks were starvation, vice, disease, and other destructive factors. He viewed our collective life as the maintenance of a precarious balance between food supply and people. He did not foresee contraception as interfering with this relationship. He did, however, view migration as only a temporary solution for the problem of food supply in any one area. If there was any great movement of people from one area to another, the resulting plenty for those who remained would lead to a higher birth rate, with the result that in a generation or so population numbers would again "press" on the food supply. He saw no permanent solution to the problem.

The solution which has appeared in our own times is twofold in nature: first, population has not increased as rapidly, in Europe and America, as it could if reproduction were uncontrolled and unaffected by cultural factors; and second, our agricultural processes have so improved that the productivity of the soil is much greater than it was in 1800. This situation is one example of the relationship between an efficient economic system and the number of people who may be supported. Recent developments in *soilless agriculture*, a system whereby plants are grown in gravel and are supplied with concentrated chemical nourishment, promise even greater productivity for the future.

There are, however, some students of population who regard our present situation as in itself only a temporary solution to the pressure of people on food supply. Followers of the basic ideas of Malthus, though not of his specific doctrines, they are called Neo-Malthusians. They claim that Malthus was fundamentally correct, since the amount of arable land is limited and, if population were to continue to increase, a point would be reached at which there would be insufficient food for all. They are, of course, correct in this somewhat academic doctrine. More to the point is their insistence that the Malthusian problem has been solved only in a relatively small area of the world, that is, Europe and America. Starvation, famine, disease, and death still operate in much of the Orient and apparently will continue to be important, since the difficulties of introducing Western economic methods to Oriental countries are admittedly grave. Finally, Neo-Malthusians point out that the essential correctness of Malthus is shown by the fact that we have had to limit our population, even with all our technological advances. Our rate of increase is much less than it was a century ago, and they suggest that it is that fact rather than our efficient economic system which has made the effect of the cruder Malthusian factors less obvious.

We cannot decide, on the evidence available, whether the contentions of the Neo-Malthusians are sound or not. The whole matter is one which requires further study and investigation. It is by no means a theoretical bypath in sociology, because many of us assume that the spread of our Western economic methods to other areas of the world will solve not only population problems but many other social problems. That basis for social programs becomes of doubtful validity if the Malthusian viewpoint is accurate.

CONTEMPORARY ECONOMIC PROBLEMS

There are many economic problems concerned with the internal functioning and relationships of the economic system which are the direct concern of the economist. We are interested here not in that type of problem but in the more directly sociological problems based on attitudes toward the economic system and relationships between the economic system and other institutions.

THE PURPOSE OF THE ECONOMIC SYSTEM

One area of disagreement to which we must pay considerable attention relates to the purpose of the economic system. At first glance this question might seem highly theoretical and remote from the realities of social life, but a brief consideration will indicate that it is at the very core of some of our economic problems. By way of pointing up the differing views in relation to the purpose of our economic institution, we may note two contrasting approaches, agreeing that there are many variations in viewpoint lying between those two extremes.

1. *The Production Viewpoint.* According to one approach, the economic system is very largely, if not exclusively, a system for the production and marketing of goods. Those who hold to this viewpoint look on the economic system as self-contained—that is, they look on it as a system which has wholly completed its function when it combines the traditonal factors of "land, labor, capital, and management" in a way so efficient that it produces a high quality of goods at a reasonable price. Economic problems then become problems of production and of technology, and the system should be judged on that basis. Beyond those matters, the economic system is without responsibility, though, of course, individuals engaged in economic activities may, as individuals, assume responsibility for the welfare of their employees, for community improvement, or for any other matters that interest them.

2. *The Security Viewpoint.* Another, and contrasting, group of people holds that the purpose of the economic system is not *only* to produce and to market goods but also to provide security for at least the majority of people. Those who advocate this approach assert that in our complex money economy security involves having money enough to provide the requisites for a reasonable level of living, not only during the working life of the individual but also after his working days are over. They also assert that this kind of security comes to most of us only through our connection with the economic system. Most of us as individuals cannot attain security—not because we are inferior or "bad" individuals, but simply because of the fact that we are born into a society whose method of exploiting the environment is such that we are forced to become a "cog in a machine." In other words, according to this school of

thought, security has become more and more a collective, or group, product and less and less an individual product. The agent of the group in providing security is the economic system. Therefore, they suggest, since we cannot escape the system, that the real test of it should lie in how well it provides security for the great part of our population.

We must not be confused here. The "security advocates" agree that an economic system can provide for security much more readily if it is technologically advanced than if it is technologically backward. They do not by any means oppose technological advances, but they insist that mere technology is no guarantee that the system actually will provide security, and they call upon it to assume wider responsibility in this direction than it has in the past. Obviously from this viewpoint our economic institution is not a self-contained system which can limit its activities to its own internal interests. And equally obviously this is an *economic* problem which carries us into the field of government and many other aspects of social organization.

If we examine the conflicting judgments passed on our economic organization at the present time, we shall discover that the basis of much of the conflict lies in differing ideas as to the purpose of the system. For example, legislation with regard to wages and hours, the right of labor to organize, fair employment practices, and the control of prices seems logical and desirable to those who hold to the security view of the purpose of economic activity. On the other hand, if labor is primarily a factor in production, much like any other factor, then attempts to secure a standard of income or to prevent discrimination against minority groups in the employment field is quite beside the point. Proponents of the self-contained economic viewpoint believe that the price paid to labor will be sufficient to compensate the laborer for his actual contribution to the economic process in which he is involved, and such compensation is considered to be a fair compensation.

To this attitude the "security" proponents reply that labor is something more than a mere factor in production and that minority groups, as part of our social organization, must be assured of the requisites of a reasonable level of living. Hence discrimination against minority groups is important not only to those groups, but logically it is the concern of the economic system. The proponent of the production viewpoint is unable to accept such statements as making sense.

In general terms, we may suggest that those who espouse the "security" view are apt to be critical of our present economic and industrial system. They point to poor housing, inadequate incomes, inadequate provision for old-age and health needs, and similar admittedly pressing problems. Those who hold to the "production" view feel that these are problems for individual solution through individual savings, individual insurance programs, and wise use of income. They insist, again, that the real function of the economic system is to produce high-quality goods at a reasonable price; and they ask, "Why should the economic system be expected to provide security any more than the educational institution, the religious institution, or the family institution?"

The "security" approach is the more recently developed of the two, and hence it is often identified by its friends with liberalism and progress, and by its enemies with radicalism and revolution. Whichever of the two attitudes may be correct, it is a fact that if present trends continue we may expect a much greater emphasis on the security approach. The Federal Social Security Act, with its provisions for taxation for old-age and survivors' insurance will probably be extended to include more kinds of people than it now does. Union labor is, rather naturally, interested in the security approach and tends to favor political measures which will permit a broader redistribution of income through differential taxation of various kinds. In addition to the interest shown by labor, there is a growing acceptance of the "security" view among white-collar workers and among some consumers' groupings. Under present circumstances, then, it appears that we may expect a period of continuing disagreement about the purpose of the economic system, with proponents of the "security" view gaining more influence. If this should prove to be the case, it will require a readjustment of thinking in regard to economic matters on the part of many people in the United States.

CONTROL OF THE ECONOMIC SYSTEM

The question of controls applied from outside the economic system by government and other agencies of the community is related very closely to the purpose of the economic system we have just discussed. There is, however, another aspect of control that merits attention. What group or groups *within* the system shall control it? That question also is the center of some controversy at the present time, and it also has its implications for social organization.

There are four groupings within the economic system which we may differentiate for our purposes here. 1. Those who furnish money, that is, stockholders, bondholders, and financiers, constitute one group. 2. Those who perform management functions, both those who set policies and those who plan for the co-ordination of labor, materials, machines, and markets, form a second group. Members of this group are often hired employees of the stockholders or of officers designated by the stockholders to operate the company. 3. A third group are the technologists, that is, employees of the company in the higher wage and skill brackets, who devote their attention to the improvement of machinery and of manufacturing processes. 4. Labor, that is, employees of the company in the lower wage and skill brackets who do the work necessary to the actual processing of goods, form the last group. Within each of these four groupings there are various levels of importance to the total process, but, omitting differentiation within the groupings, we may distinguish these four on the basis of general type of function. Our question then is, "How shall the control of economic activity be divided among these several groupings?"

In the not too distant past such a question would have admitted of one answer only, an answer delivered with some degree of positiveness. It would have been asserted dogmatically that management controlled the enterprise, subject in the case of corporations to the vote of shareholders, but in no case subject to the wishes of labor, technologists, or any such class of persons. Without intimating that such an attitude is correct or incorrect, we may note that it is now being widely questioned. In a recent and prolonged labor-management conflict the management of the enterprise published newspaper advertisements asserting that labor wanted to examine the account books of the company, not in order to demonstrate the ability of the concern to pay higher wages but because labor wanted to participate in the management of the company. The implication was that such a desire on the part of labor was a monstrous invasion of a field in which the working man had no legitimate interest. Labor advertisements published in reply denied that such was the specific intent of employee demands in this particular instance, but also asserted that if it were the real intent there was nothing monstrous about it since labor had every reason to interest itself in the management of any concern. This kind of statement amounts to a denial of the right of management to operate an enterprise without reference to the opinion of labor and, by implication, of other groupings. Within the past two years labor's right to take part in the management, and therefore in the control, of industry has been reasserted.

It is not only labor which has concerned itself with policies of production and the control of industry. Technologists have their own dispute with those who finance industry. They hold that some of industry has been operated chiefly for financial profit rather than for other, and allegedly better, reasons. The technologist maintains that his interest in the improvement of industrial processes has been blocked in some instances because the immediate application of new technological developments would not be profitable, or because new and improved developments would result in the scrapping of older processes with consequent financial loss. New inventions are "put on the shelf" and older processes continued in use for the sole reason that the older type of product can still be sold at a profit and that newer processes can be introduced at some later date when there is some necessity for a stimulus to sales.

In the field of automobile manufacture, for instance, it is alleged that new devices such as the automatic clutch and steering-post gearshift lever were first put on the more expensive cars not because they were too costly for the cheaper cars but because putting them on expensive cars added artificially to "swank" and reputation. When they were put on the cheaper models, an increase in the price of such models was justified, though not necessary. The technologist would like to be free of this kind of control so that he could produce literally the most mechanically perfect product at the best prices possible.

The financial interests reply to the technologists that it is the large-scale organization of modern industry which permits the technologist to exist and function. Without this organization he would not have the opportunity to do his research and to perfect his inventions. They point out that large-scale industry demands the use of huge amounts of capital, and that money must come from some source in large quantities. They believe that the necessary funds will flow into industry only if there is a reasonable chance of good profits. Financially interested persons also insist that the criticism directed at them is based on a confusion between the legitimate financing of industry and the manipulation of stocks, bonds, and other instruments of finance. They hold that such manipulation, admittedly unsound, is relatively uncommon, though it is apt to be sensational when it does occur and therefore to occupy a great deal of space in newspapers. They object to having their policies "tarred with the brush" of mere speculation and identified solely with money-making devices.

A third area of internal conflict in the economic institution arises from the role of the stockholder in modern industry. In the case of corporations the stockholders are legally the owners of the enterprise, since they have bought shares which represent shares of ownership. Meetings of stockholders are held by most corporations at least once a year, but in the case of large enterprises with thousands or hundreds of thousands of stockholders it is almost an impossibility to secure the attendance at such meetings of any great proportion of the stockholders. The custom of *proxy* voting has therefore become common, that is, by signing a designated form the individual stockholder gives some person who will attend the meeting the right to cast the stockholder's vote for him *by proxy*. He may transfer this right to any other stockholder who is to be present, but in the case of large corporations the common custom is to suggest to a voter unable to attend that he make over his right to vote to a specific person, often an officer of the company. Obviously such a procedure, to the extent that it is followed, gives the holder of many proxies a measure of control over policies far greater than his actual ownership of stock might warrant. In addition, it tends to place control of the company more or less completely in the hands of the officers of the concern, rather than in the hands of the stockholders. This is a somewhat anomalous situation, since the officers of the concern are actually the employees of the stockholders, theoretically under the control of the stockholders.

There is no question as to the existence of the situation we have just described, but there is some disagreement as to the reasons for its existence. On the one hand it is alleged that most stockholders do not want to assume the responsibility of attending meetings and determining company policies. It is stated that the share of stock has become, to all intents and purposes, not a share of ownership of an enterprise carrying with it certain rights of control, but merely a piece of paper which gives its legal owner the right to share in company dividends, if there are any dividends. As such, it is simply a potential source of income, in the eyes of most stockholders, which has the advantage that it can easily be sold to someone else whenever it seems to the owner's advantage to dispose of it. In proof of this assertion it is stated that not only do stockholders not attend annual meetings, but many of them do not take the trouble even to send in proxies. They are apparently quite content to leave the matter of policy determination to a small group of "insiders" as long as dividends are forthcoming. In fact, it is even said that the average stockholder would be amazed if it were suggested to him that he shares in the responsibility of company management.

Certain militant stockholders reply to the above contentions that the small group of "insiders" who actually run the company do not want stockholder interference with their activities. They declare that a stockholder who innocently assumed that he was supposed to attend an annual meeting and attended it prepared to exercise his rights would certainly not be welcomed by the "insiders," who are comfortably keeping things in their own hands. Because of the nonparticipation of stockholders in policy-making, whatever the reason, the officers of a corporation may actually control it, even though they have relatively little money invested in it. Not only may they vote themselves large salaries and other advantages, but they really have little interest in whether or not the concern functions as efficiently as possible, unless their own salaries are threatened. It is further alleged that they may, without much interference or risk, make a good many "deals" in company funds which will be to their own advantage rather than to that of the company.

It is not easy to evaluate these two different contentions. Certainly there have been instances of dishonesty and manipulation on the part of officers of corporations, and certainly details of such unsavory dealings have often made newspaper headlines. On the other hand, there are many instances of able and honest management in the face of stockholder indifference, and these do not often make newspaper headlines, with the result that they are apt to be not nearly so impressive as the manipulative "deals." In any case the disagreement is one more instance of conflict over the question of the internal control of the modern economic system.

We have noted three general areas of such conflict: (1) that between labor and capital; (2) that between financier and technologist; and (3) that between stockholder and "insider" in the corporation. All these conflicts are closely related to the complexity and the impersonal relationships which characterize modern industry. The individual workman is merged into the impersonal labor group; the individual employer is engulfed by the impersonal management; the individual owner disappears in the midst of the impersonal stockholding group; and the old-fashioned inventor at his basement workbench becomes the technologist on the research staff. All these developments may increase the actual efficiency of a going concern, but they also raise problems of relationships among the several groups. The "boss" cannot negotiate directly with the "hand." Instead management, which represents a grouping of functions, must treat with labor, which represents another group of functions. Since these two groupings cannot actually treat with each other as groupings, they choose representatives to treat with other representatives, with the result that there is an increasing loss of direct contact, understanding, and mutual good will. The process of *collective bargaining*, that is, bargaining as groups rather than as individuals, is apt to be a slow process, even when it does attain some satisfactory results. Work stoppages during the period of bargaining are common, so that, however efficient our impersonal organization may be for the going concern, it also has the effect of not permitting the concern to "go" at all for certain periods.

The implications of this total situation for our social organization are chiefly in the area of increasing conflict, in the area of the subordination of the economic system to special interests rather than to the interests of the entire society, and in the area of malfunctioning of the economic system in general. We shall refer to some of these again in our later discussion of economic reorganization.

RESTATEMENT OF ECONOMIC IDEALS

A third area of importance in contemporary economic problems which has strong social implications is concerned with the relationship between our traditional American economic ideals and contemporary economic practices. Our economic ideals have been, and are, strong influences in our culture. They were developed in connection with one type of economic practice which is becoming progressively less typical of our economic system. Their application to newer forms of economic organization is not clear. The ideals are a value which we wish to conserve. Some restatement of those ideals as they apply to present economic situations is therefore desirable.

1. *Our Past Economic Organization.* Our economic organization of a hundred years ago was characterized very largely by individual enterprise. That means that most of our products were made and sold by concerns which were owned by a single individual or by a few partners; which were small in size, employing relatively few laborers; and which required small amounts of capital as compared with the large sums accumulated today. Industry was largely localized, using raw materials, labor, and other resources available in the immediate locality. The market for most factories was likewise within a limited area. Adjuncts to sales such as advertising, specialized packaging, and elaborate campaigns were lacking. Much of the success of the enterprise depended on the initiative, honesty, and ability of the individual owner.

Competition was a real "competitive effort" to win patronage through the production of a high-quality product, and it was *free competition* in the sense that there were large numbers of small producers who operated as individual concerns, avoiding combinations, secret agreements, price-fixing, and similar practices which are common today. Free competition was a powerful stimulus to production. It also operated to raise the quality of goods produced, since the customer would, in the absence of monopolistic pressures, buy the best available goods in his price range. The simplicity of the economic system, the directness of transactions, and the practical utility of most goods sold, all permitted the consumer to judge the relative quality of products with a degree of accuracy not common today.

Undoubtedly the economic system of the past functioned very imperfectly and had many faults. Fraud was certainly not unknown; products were adulterated; inferior goods were produced and sold. The point here relates not to the "perfection" of the economic system of the past, but to the fact that producer and consumer were differently related to each other than they are at the present. The consumer was more likely to be capable of accurate judgment of the quality of goods than he is now, and the producer of an inferior product was more likely to meet competition than he is now.

One reason for that likelihood lay in the fact of *free enterprise*, which also characterizes our economic organization today. Enterprise was "free" in the sense that any individual was at liberty to establish any kind of lawful business he might wish to undertake. The fact that relatively little capital was required and that monopolistic combinations were few made the establishment of new enterprises relatively easy. The individual entrepreneur made use of his own skill and initiative to raise money, secure equipment, and manufacture his product. He chose his labor force from a small, very probably unorganized, local grouping on the basis of his needs and their capacities. He assumed the risk of losing his money and he retained whatever profits there were without accounting to anyone. He had to survive economically through his own ability to manufacture a superior product to sell at a fair price. Only very seldom could he drive a competitor out of business through the exercise of sheer power given him by concentration of resources and of influence.

Free enterprise, like free competition, was a powerful stimulus to the growth of American industrial life and to the development of the efficiency with which we are familiar today. Both free enterprise and free competition have remained part of our economic ideals, and they continue to be strong verbal stimuli toward which the major portion of our population reacts favorably.

2. *Our Contemporary Economic Organization.* Our contemporary economic organization differs in important respects from the earlier system we have been discussing. We have replaced the typical small-scale enterprise of the past by huge concentrations of machinery adapted to the production of goods on the largest scale possible. Heavy investment of money in machinery, buildings, labor force, and many other items is necessary. In order to make a profit on our large investments of money we are forced toward the production of as many units of our product as possible, thereby reducing the capital cost on each unit. In turn, this kind of mass production demands mass consumption if it is to operate, with the result that modern markets are nation-wide and world-wide rather

than localized as they were in the past. Sales in such a mass market must be stimulated by elaborate advertising campaigns and other stimulative devices such as new models yearly.

The net result of this kind of organization from a purely economic viewpoint has, on the whole, been excellent. We are supplied with a wide variety of well-made and efficiently functioning goods at—in "normal" times—very reasonable prices. As we remarked earlier, those who hold to the production viewpoint of the economic system can regard its operation—again, in "normal" times—with satisfaction. Our problem here, however, goes beyond the economic system as such into the wider areas of social organization. We are concerned with the effect of our contemporary system on our economic ideals of free enterprise and of free competition.

The first of these effects is that free enterprise is hampered in its operation. It is becoming increasingly difficult for individuals without large sums of money to establish any new business or industrial ventures except small retail establishments. These sums of money must usually come through recognized financial channels—banks, the sale of stock, and the issuance of bonds. Through these money-raising devices, the judgment of many people other than the individual enterpriser becomes involved in the transaction. In addition, complicated questions of labor relations arise. Advertising is a necessity. In short, the establishment of a new enterprise is no longer a matter for a single individual or a few partners. It must be a co-operative venture involving some hundreds, and possibly some thousands, of people. The whole procedure becomes part of a complex, established, and more or less rigid series of relationships.

For that reason, among others, new ventures in manufacturing are often organized as branches of existing concerns which already have well-established credit, production, and sales systems; or by groups experienced in floating new concerns. There are, of course, a good many individual enterprises, especially in retail trade; but the bulk of our manufactured goods now comes from large-scale industry in which the older type of free enterprise is no longer operative.

Concentration of industry in large corporations also affects the area of free competition. The type of *monopolistic* competition which exists between a few large concerns in a given field of manufacture is not the traditional *free* competition which took place between many small enterprises. The reduced number of competitors now permits price-fixing agreements, concentration of influence, and other manipulations which may react against the public interest. Sales policies, quality of product, and fair-trade practices all become matters of agreement, often of covert but none the less effective agreement, between a few producers. Similarly wages, hours, and labor relations in general are fixed, not by the free interplay of demand and supply but by strategical "collective bargaining" between huge groupings representing management and labor.

Centralization of power in the hands of industrial and labor groups gives scope for the exercise of controls over, and influences on, the public far beyond the technical aspects of manufacture, namely through the press, radio, and education. The consumer is unable to evaluate the quality of product offered and the fairness of the price at which it is offered because he is confused by the maze of claims, counterclaims, and irrelevant statements which characterize much of modern advertising. Competition, then, becomes not competition based on quality and price but competition to exert influence through propagandistic devices. It is often the largest concentrations of influence, which are, in fact, the strongest forces operating against free competition, that most loudly demand "freedom" of various kinds.

The ideals of free enterprise and of free competition, then, remain significant factors in the American economic system. But contemporary economic practices have for some time been tending more and more in a direction which will not permit traditional free enterprise and free competition to operate. That fact is widely recognized. Attitudes toward the fact fall into three general areas. 1. One attitude suggests that we abandon our emphasis on the ideals of free enterprise and free competition and that we plan toward the development of some form of fully controlled economic system. Examples of this attitude include advocates of socialism, communism, the establishment of cartels, and the domination of the economic system by commercial, industrial, or labor interests exclusively. 2. Another attitude holds that we must retain an emphasis on the words *free enterprise* and *free competition*, without making any particular examination of the social realities involved in those words. This attitude is seldom crystallized and is almost never outspokenly presented in the bald terms used above, but it is implicit in a good many popular discussions of economic problems. 3. A third attitude recognizes the value of the ideals behind the words, and advocates a re-emphasis on those ideals and their application to current economic practices. This third proposal involves the critical examination of our own practices in the light of ideals, and a restatement of those ideals as applied to contemporary life. This third attitude promises the most constructive results. Some further discussion of these points falls under the topic of economic reorganization.

ECONOMIC REORGANIZATION

Some aspects of our economic system are in need of reorganization if the system is to function adequately in our social organization. One difficulty with the process of reorganization is that certain contemporary groups look on revision of our economic system as a species of magic which will automatically solve all our problems, while other groups believe that the current economic practices are sacred and should not be altered in any way. Both these viewpoints are defective.

Illustrative of the first viewpoint—that alterations in economic relationships are semimagical devices by which all of our social problems may be solved—are the followers of Karl Marx, who hold that a change in the ownership of the means of production, in the control of business and industry, and in the distribution of income will, in some simple fashion, bring about the rapid creation of an ideal society. The difficulty with that theory lies in the fact that the basic economic situation of a complex society remains much the same, whatever system controls the approach to that situation. The characteristics of impersonality of the economic system, of group rather than individual enterprise, and of complexity of relationships are present as a part of the social structure. What is required in economic reorganization is an analysis of the impact of such characteristics on group life, rather than the arbitrary imposition of a prearranged system.

Perhaps the basic defect of communism, and of other varieties of Marxism, from the sociological viewpoint is that it is completely unscientific, though it makes many pretensions to science. Essentially communism, as it is propounded in the United States, proposes to alter the economic system, not in accordance with observation and analysis, the fundamentals of science, but in accordance with a philosophical system elaborated by Karl Marx about a hundred years ago. Reference is made to his doctrines as a matter of faith. His explanation of history stresses the importance of the economic institution as the determiner of other cultural forms. It holds that capitalism is one step in the development of a final adjustment between man's subsistence needs and the resources of his environment. According to Marx, the specific contribution of the capitalistic system to man's economic development is the technological system, with its very efficient means of production, which characterizes capitalism. Its specific defect is that it does not recognize the alleged fact that the value of all goods arises from the labor which is expended in the production of those goods. Since capitalism does not recognize this theory, the capitalist, according to Marx, steals from labor the major portion of the values created in manufacture, allowing labor only enough in the way of wages to maintain itself in a fit state to perform its duties. As a result, all the evils of our times exist, especially the evil inherent in the struggle between economic classes. The Marxian solution, at least as currently interpreted by communists, is to establish a dictatorship of the proletariat, that is, of labor, and to abolish the capitalist as such. Marx further held that eventually this dictatorship of the proletariat would disappear, and we should have a *classless* state in which there would be no government because government would be unnecessary. This latter point is sometimes overlooked both by the critics of Marx and by his exponents.

Marx and others give convincing demonstrations of the truth of this theory by selecting from history those portions which can be adduced to support their viewpoint. Almost any theory can be "proved" in precisely that way. The approach has in it some of the appearances of the scientific method, but fundamentally it differs very markedly from the scientific method. It starts with certain propositions to be accepted on faith, and then, on the basis of those accepted propositions, it proceeds to erect an elaborate system. Science, on the other hand, starts with the observation of facts, and from that observation draws tentative conclusions, to be further tested and revised, until some coherent hypothesis is developed. This hypothesis, in turn, is subject to further testing and revision as the analysis of facts requires. As a result of the scientific method, we approach a clearer understanding of the existing relationships between facts. As a result of the Marxian and similar methods, the actual relationships are obscured by assumptions which prevent impartial analysis.

It is a familiar fact that communism, as practiced in Russia, has tried to make use of many of the capitalistic means of mass production which are common in America. It is also a fact that the Russian economy is facing somewhat the same general economic problems that the American capitalistic economy is facing. These facts should not be surprising, since the cultural environment of international relations with which the Russians interact is, from the economic viewpoint, much the same as ours. We should, therefore, expect similarity of results. The fact that Russian culture carries with it many defects found to a certain extent in our own culture, such as anti-intellectualism, political corruption, and intense nationalism, indicates that a transition to communism in America would result in no improvement of our situation and would very probably result in increasing our problems.

The opposite viewpoint—that contemporary practices in the industrial field are sacred and are not to be altered—occurs among extreme conservatives. Almost exactly the same criticism may be applied to this approach as that applied to the radical approach. Instead of accepting facts as facts and attempting to understand them through analysis, it obscures the existence of facts by insisting that established relationships are, and must remain, unchanging. As a matter of fact, there have been many changes in our practice of capitalism since its founding, say about 1800, but those changes have not resulted in the destruction of our capitalistic system. We have already noted the alterations in our application of the ideals of free enterprise and of free competition. Similar alterations have occurred in our concept of the right of private property. In the past it was assumed that the owner of a plot of land also owned the atmosphere to an unlimited distance above his land. An airplane flying over it was therefore trespassing. The continuance of such a doctrine would enormously hamper the operation of modern airlines; so we have changed the doctrine. The right of private property in land still exists, but it has been limited by the development of new techniques.

Other restrictions on the use of private property have been set up through zoning regulations in cities and through other statutory enactments. In spite of all these, we retain the institution of private property basically unharmed. A change in our attitude toward its unrestricted use has not destroyed the institution.

Changes have also taken place in other areas. The doctrine of *Caveat emptor*, that is, "Let the buyer beware," used to be widely accepted, the implication being that it was the responsibility of the buyer to see that the goods he bought were not defective. In contemporary practice it is not the buyer who must beware but the seller, if he is to escape prosecution. Laws relating to the sale of corporate stocks and of some types of bonds, those relating to pure foods and drugs, and those requiring accurate labeling of clothing to indicate the exact textile content are all examples of legislation to protect the consumer, an obvious shift from *caveat emptor*.

In the past only a limited participation was allowed women in many of our economic affairs. Not only were they not permitted to enter the professions and not welcomed in business, but they could not own or dispose of property. At present, however, they are engaging more and more widely in professional and business life.

These and other changes have taken place in the capitalistic system without destroying the essentials of capitalism, because we have retained certain basic beliefs in private property, in the freedom of the individual, and in civil liberties, even though we have altered the application of those beliefs in specific instances. It is useless to hold, as ultraconservatives do, that the pattern of capitalism existing today or at any other specific time is the only possible pattern.

What most sincere advocates both of change and of resistance to change are really seeking is not primarily an economic thing at all. Their goal is the expression in contemporary life of certain human ideals commonly held by some men in all ages, including the founders of this country. Such ideals as freedom, justice, and honesty are all important social goals. They are shared equally by Karl Marx—though not by all his followers—and by some of our most conservative thinkers.

For example, during one of our recent strikes a group of churchmen, social workers, and other professional people solicited funds by newspaper advertisement to buy food for the wives and children of strikers. Neither they nor the institutions which they represented could, by any stretch of the imagination, be identified with radicalism. They pointed out that, whatever might be the merits of the labor group or of the employing group involved in the strike, hunger should not be a weapon to force capitulation by either side. The issues, in their opinion, ought to be settled on the basis of justice and fairness. They contended that the values of human life transcended labor-management strife.

Such activity by disinterested groups may be, and was, interpreted as "taking sides" with labor against capital, since it is labor which goes hungry in the case of a strike rather than capital. Actually the situation represented not "taking sides" against the one group or the other, but "taking sides" in favor of an ideal—the ideal of justice and fair play. It represented the belief that justice does not result from the mere use of force or from the mere possession of superior weapons. We recognize that fact in the case of physical combat, and so we no longer decide the merits of a dispute by permitting the individuals concerned to fight it out in armed encounter, a custom which used to be fairly common. If, in the strike cited, hunger was a superior weapon or an instrument of force in the hands of one group, it became necessary to offset it so that justice could be determined on the basis of the merits of the case, not on the basis of a chance advantage.

This attitude may be extended from one specific situation to the general situation of economic conflict. We cherish ideals of freedom, justice, and honesty which do not change; but our mode of expressing them does change. A man riding a horse over his own broad acres may ride it as he pleases; a man driving an automobile on a crowded street may not drive it as he pleases. His freedom must be limited. Yet he is as free as any other person to drive his automobile on the highway within the limits of the law. That is the essential of democratic freedom: not that an individual is free to do as he pleases when he pleases, but that one individual has the same freedom as any other individual in given circumstances. Whatever restraints we find it necessary to establish apply alike to all individuals. As the circumstances change, specific freedoms also change, but they change for all of us.

It is the problem of our culture to examine our ideals and our economic practices in the light of current conditions of living, and to restate the ideals in terms which will apply to modern life. This does not mean giving up the ideals as social goals; it does mean giving up certain practices which, in the past, have expressed appropriate ideals but which no longer do so in our own times. There is evidence of a growing impatience with both labor and capital on the part of some segments of the public. We want goods and services from the economic system; let it adjust its internal difficulties and give us our goods and services. We are inclined, perhaps, to sympathize with that viewpoint; and yet it may have unfortunate results, since it may lead to an uncritical acceptance of radical proposals or to a harsh repression of progressive developments.

We have already suggested that the ultimate solution of economic problems lies in the realization that we are parts of an *inter*dependent system. Ideals must apply to all the parts of that system, not to any one segment of it alone. It is necessary to plan the reorganization of our economic system not from the viewpoint of any one class but from the viewpoint of the entire social organization.

SUMMARY: THE ECONOMIC SYSTEM

Economic systems originate in the necessity of providing for the satisfaction of basic human subsistence needs, and that remains one of their significant functions. In later developments the system includes many activities not directly necessary to satisfaction of basic subsistence needs, and develops many complex relationships with other social institutions, especially government.

In simpler societies the economic system functions to relate the individual to his society chiefly by teaching him the techniques accumulated by his culture. Its position is not a dominant one in such societies. In more advanced cultures division of labor and specialization of function bring about a situation of interdependence within the economic system. A majority of individuals can exercise their skills and thus obtain the means of subsistence only by functioning as a co-ordinated part of the system. They are thus related to the system, and through it to the society, perforce, since apart from it they could not survive. The economic system, under those conditions, tends to be the dominating system in the society.

The dominance of an economic system raises problems in relation to conflicting segments of the population, in relation to its coloring of popular attitudes, and in relation to population growth and development.

Contemporary economic problems with important social implications center about the purpose of the economic system, the control of the economic system, and the relationship between our traditional economic ideals and our contemporary economic practices.

The basic problem of economic reorganization lies in the area of reconciling our ideals and our practices.

READINGS

MacIver, R. M. *Society*. Farrar & Rinehart, Inc.. New York, 1937. Pages 298–314, "The Great Associations: Economic."

Dixon, R. A., and Eberhart, E. K. *Economics and Cultural Change*. McGraw-Hill Book Company, Inc., New York, 1938. A discussion of the relationships between economic systems and culture. Especially Chap. 1, "Economics and the Cultural Pattern," and Chap. 9, "The Industrial Revolution."

Lundberg, George A. *Foundations of Sociology*. The Macmillan Company, New York, 1939. Pages 386–400, "Economic Patterns."

The American Individual Enterprise System, by The Economic Principles Commission of the National Association of Manufacturers. Two Volumes. McGraw-Hill Book Company, Inc., New York, 1946. A conservative description of the typical American economic system and its practices.

Laidler, Harry W. *Social-Economic Movements*. Thomas Y. Crowell Company, New York, 1946. "An historical and comparative survey of socialism, communism, co-operation, utopianism, and other systems of reform and reconstruction."

THE RELIGIOUS INSTITUTION

RELIGION is one of the common traits of human culture, found almost universally in every human group. It is one aspect of our total human response to the drive for *security*, in this case security not only in this world but in the next, not only in our relationships to mankind but in relation to unseen beings or unseen forces. As such, it may exert a powerful influence on the social organization. We examine below some of the characteristics of religion and of the religious institution.

CHARACTERISTICS OF RELIGION

It is difficult to define religion for a number of reasons. In the first place, religion means many different things to different people, and it has meant many different things in different cultures, with the result that an inclusive definition becomes almost impossible. In addition some religions have elaborate modes of expressing themselves through carefully worked out rituals while others have very simple rituals. There is a tendency to identify religion itself with the ritual expressions of religion, so that individuals accustomed to ritual find it difficult to grasp the meanings of nonritualistic religions. Finally, religion is apt to be a personal and intimate experience often not clearly defined by the individual himself.

As we shall note later we may avoid some of these difficulties by defining not religion itself but the religious institution, in which we as sociologists are more directly interested than we are in religion itself. However, before we approach the discussion of the religious institution as such, it may be well to formulate two contrasting definitions of religion, without claiming that they are the only possible definitions.

DEFINITION OF RELIGION

The traditional definition of religion involves three points: (1) belief in a supernatural being or beings and in a supernatural world; (2) dependence on the supernatural for help, inspiration, and strength—cited by some students of religion as the chief characteristic of the religious attitude; and (3) behavior patterns which express this dependence in worship, and which include codes of conduct applicable to the daily life of the religious individual. Traditional Christianity, traditional Mohammedanism, and traditional Judaism can all be described in these terms, as can many other religions.

There are, however, contemporary religions which do not exhibit all these characteristics. The humanist group within the Unitarian Church in the United States, for example, does not require of its members a belief in God. Its emphasis is on morality in human relationships. In some other liberal branches of more orthodox denominations the articles of the Christian creed have been taken as metaphor rather than as strict statement of fact. Professor Albert Einstein has phrased his definition of religion in the following terms:

. . . a person who is religiously enlightened appears to me to be one who has, to the best of his ability, liberated himself from the fetters of his selfish desires and is preoccupied with thoughts, feelings, and aspirations to which he clings because of their superpersonal value. It seems to me that what is important is the force of this superpersonal content and the depth of the conviction concerning its overpowering meaningfulness, regardless of whether any attempt is made to unite this content with a Divine Being. . . . In this sense, religion is the age-old endeavor of mankind to become clearly and completely conscious of these values and goals and constantly to strengthen and extend their effects.[1]

This is a reverent statement as well as an earnest one, but it would not be accepted by orthodox religious people in so far as it makes belief in a Divine Being unnecessary to religion.

We have, then, these two contrasting viewpoints as to what re-

---

[1]*Science, Philosophy, and Religion* (a symposium published by the Conference on Science, Philosophy, and Religion in their Relation to the Democratic Way of Life, Inc., New York, 1941), Chap. XIII, "Science and Religion," by Albert Einstein. Quoted by special permission of the publishers.

ligion is—the one insistent on the characteristic of dependence on the supernatural, the other content with values of a superpersonal, though not necessarily supernatural, nature—with a good many variations between the two extremes. They illustrate the fact that religious disagreement may well be a matter of firm conviction and of honest belief, without also being characterized by bitterness and hatred as it sometimes is in the case of conflicts between religious demagogues and equally demagogic atheists. At what point the individual's own religious convictions lie is a matter for individual determination.

RELIGIOUS INSTITUTIONS

Leaving the definition of religion as such at that point, we now turn to the question of religious institutions. A religious institution is distinguished from the phenomenon of religion by the fact that religion is an internal manifestation, while a religious institution is a standardized, codified, formalized group reaction consisting of externally observable traits. In our distinction of a religious institution from other institutions we seek again for a specific function performed by no other institution, a function which is traceable even through many variations in details of structure and of practice. That function appears to lie in the formal distinction between sacred and profane, between right and wrong, between good and bad. We therefore suggest that the religious institution be defined as

> *The institution formally concerned with the determination*
> *of the sacred.*

The *sacred* is defined in a number of different ways in different cultures, but where there is some area of life set apart from ordinary affairs and devoted to uses considered especially significant and vitally concerned with the welfare of the group, that area corresponds to the sacred. Originally *sacred* meant "devoted," that is, devoted to the supernatural and hence untouchable by ordinary individuals and not usable for ordinary purposes. The meaning of the word has been extended somewhat, but this is still its basic connotation.

Even in the case of those who emphasize, as Einstein does, the human character of religion rather than its supernatural character, the sacred forms a part of its total structure. Einstein stresses a set of values which are *superpersonal*, that is, which are beyond the limited interests of any one person. The religious person is convinced of the "overpowering meaningfulness" of these values; religion is the attempt of mankind to become clearly and completely conscious of them and to strengthen their effects. The language used with reference to the value system described points to its being set apart from the individual, a goal toward which he may strive, something beyond the ordinary concerns of life—all characteristics of the sacred. Suppose that we assume that truth and honesty are two of these superpersonal values. Then we must assume also that an individual practising this kind of religion would not use truth and honesty as instruments of his own personal ambitions. He would not be truthful and honest because such traits would enhance his reputation and thereby bring him wealth or prestige; he would be truthful and honest because it was his duty to be so, even if his devotion to truth and honesty earned him hardships and suffering. The values are sacred, though not supernatural, because they are set apart as too important to be used as anything except ends in themselves.

Turgenev, the Russian writer, stresses somewhat the same idea. A friend wrote to him, "It seems to me that to put oneself in the second place is the whole significance of life." To this Turgenev replied, "It seems to me that to discover what to put before one's self, in first place, is the whole problem of life."[2] The placing of something apart from the self, before the self, is tantamount to placing that thing in the category of the sacred, even though no supernatural connotations are involved.

In the case of more conservative religions the importance of the sacred as the expression of God's will and purposes is plain. In simpler cultures both the deity and the sacred are apt to be defined in very narrow terms. God is the God of that culture only, not of any other culture; only the things held sacred in that particular culture are really sacred, those of other cultures are not; the purposes of God include that one grouping only, no other; and so on. A reading of the earlier portions of the Old Testament will illustrate this attitude among the Hebrews and also among other groupings with which they came into contact. In more complex cultures

[2] J. S. Bixler, *Religion for Free Minds*, Harper, New York, 1939.

the concept of the sacred also becomes more complex. God is the God of the whole world, not of one tribe only; ultimately all aspects of life become part of the sacred, since God's will rules all aspects of life and all belongs to Him.

Conversely, one indication of the decline in prestige of a religious institution is a loss of the concept of the sacred, a blurring of the distinctions between good and bad, right and wrong. Such a decline has often appeared even while the institution was officially recognized and while it practiced its ceremonial with pomp and regularity.

The religious institution in a culture, then, has for its function the determination of what is sacred, and of the proper relationships to the sacred. Often religious functions are performed by other institutions before the emergence of a religious institution as such. We may distinguish these religious functions of other institutions by their relationship to the determination of sacred and profane. To the extent that they perform such a function they are sharing in the religious function.

RELIGIOUS EXPRESSIONS

The external expression of religious emotion by the individual is called *worship*; its expression by, or through, an institution is called *ritual* or *ceremonial*. Ritual is, in fact, the codification and organization of formal ceremonies. In all religions with which we are acquainted the chief ritual is the retelling of the occurrences connected with the founding of the religion.[3] Thus in Catholic Christianity the Mass is the story of the Last Supper formalized. In the Hebrew religion the sacrifices made to God were accompanied by songs glorifying the goodness of Jehovah to his people. In modern Judaism the synagogue services include readings from the Law and the Prophets. Even in Protestant Christianity, with its emphasis on the sermon, the ritual portion of the service is connected with the teaching ministry of Jesus, since Protestant Christianity emphasizes the founding of the Church through teaching rather than through sacrament and sacrifice. Similar examples might be cited from other religions less familiar to us in the United States.

[3] A. Goldenweiser, *Anthropology*, pp. 268 ff. Crofts, New York, 1945.

RELIGION AND MAGIC

In most cultures, including our own, the growth of religion is paralleled by a development called *magic*. Religion and magic resemble each other in a number of ways, since both are concerned with certain aspects of the sacred. The chief difference between religion and magic lies in their *attitude* toward the supernatural powers. In the case of magic the attitude is one of control or of coercion. The possession of certain formulas or of certain objects, or the performance of certain prescribed actions under magical presuppositions is supposed to *force* the supernatural powers to do the will of the individual operating with the formulas. We are familiar with this attitude as expressed in myths, legends, and fairy tales.

In the case of religion, on the other hand, the attitude is one of *dependence* on the good will and graciousness of supernatural powers. Their favor is sought in prayer, the favorable exercise of their will is the subject of petition, the individual submits himself wholly to them. Reverence and humility characterize the religious approach, attitudes which are lacking in the magical approach.

The significance of this distinction in the present discussion is that some practitioners of religion fall into the habit of looking on their religion as a magical device. This is true not only of religions with elaborate rituals, but also of those with very simple rituals, or with no ritual at all. A belief or a doctrine, as well as a series of performances, may be made the basis of magic. Thus if we believe that the recitation of a creed or the acknowledgment of the truth of a certain doctrine automatically assures us of supernatural favor, we are indulging in a magical attitude. In many instances this shading over of religion into magic is unconscious; the individual concerned is not aware of the process. It is seldom approved by religious authorities, though they as well as their followers may be deceived by the essentially unconscious nature of the transition.

Overt protests against magical devices are fairly common on the part of religious individuals. Thus Mr. G. K. Chesterton, a thoughtful English Roman Catholic, asserts that it is a "strange and staggering heresy" to believe that human beings have some kind of inherent "right" to the good things of this world. He insists that the religious person looks on all that he has as the free gift of God, unrelated to the individual's merits.[4] Somewhat the same attitude

[4] G. K. Chesterton, *Autobiography*, Sheed & Ward, New York, 1936.

is expressed by conservative followers of Protestantism and Judaism. If we contrast it with the belief that ritual, as such, will assure us divine favor, or with the belief that the self-righteousness of the individual somehow puts the universe under obligation to treat him well, we shall have the distinction between religion and magic.

An expression of the same distinction, coming from the recent war, is this poem by Sergeant Hugh Brodie of the Royal Australian Air Force.[5]

A Sergeant's Prayer

Almighty and all-present Power,
Short is the prayer I make to Thee,
I do not ask in battle hour
For any shield to cover me.

The vast unalterable way,
From which the stars do not depart,
May not be turned aside to stay
The bullet flying to my heart.

I ask no help to strike my foe,
I seek no petty victory here,
The enemy I hate, I know,
To Thee is also dear.

But this I pray, be at my side
When death is drawing through the sky.
Almighty God, who also died,
Teach me the way that I should die.

The significant religious attitudes, as contrasted with magical attitudes, expressed here are (1) the acceptance of the will of God and dependence on his favor, without seeking special protection; (2) the realization that God's purposes, as expressed in the "vast unalterable way" of natural law, are more significant than individual goals or destiny; (3) the assertion that God's love is not con-

[5] *Time*, February 8, 1943. Quoted by special permission of the publishers of *Time*.

fined to one nation or to one race, but also includes "the enemy," an attitude not by any means common during war; and (4) the final request, not for escape from death but for courage in the faith which will enable the writer to accept death. One is, of course, at liberty to disagree with the theological implications of these attitudes, but they express clearly the specifically religious attitude as contrasted with magical attitudes.

Religious Patterns

In addition to ceremonial certain patterns characterize most religions. These patterns are of significance for social organization, since they influence not only the conduct of individuals but also the relationship between religion and other institutions.

1. *Morality*. Moral conduct is conduct which involves a choice between right and wrong actions. Usually the appraisal of the rightness or wrongness of behavior involves reference to a standard, or code, of morals, and usually such a code is developed in connection with religion. As we might expect, the details of moral codes vary considerably from one religion to another. Conduct which is approved by one religious group will often be disapproved by another. Polygamy, permitted in some religions but disapproved by Christianity, is a case in point. Usually the moral code is asserted to be a direct revelation of the will of God, as in the Ten Commandments, or an interpretation of his will, as in some of the dogmas of moral theology. We must emphasize the fact that moral codes differing from our own often permit types of conduct of which we thoroughly disapprove. They are, nonetheless, "moral" from the viewpoint of groupings which adhere to such codes.

The common orientation of the members of a society toward an accepted moral code introduces an element of order into a social organization. Regulation of conduct in accordance with the code, and under threat of sanctions for its violation, brings about a degree of predictability of conduct by virtue of which we may assume that groupings will, in general, react in given ways to given situations as long as the code retains its authoritative and accepted character. However, not every individual in a grouping subscribes realistically to the code, with the result that prediction of individual conduct becomes hazardous. But group reactions are more likely to proceed according to pattern.

One contemporary difficulty is that the moral code of the past has become less binding on significant segments of our population, and we have not as yet developed a new and accepted code. We therefore experience a certain amount of disorder in the area of moral conduct.

2. *Faith.* Most religions also demand the unquestioning acceptance of certain beliefs. The usual religious attitude is that, while those beliefs can be logically demonstrated, they are so self-evident that they do not require logical demonstration. They are to be accepted without demonstration and without argument. Such an acceptance is *faith* in the beliefs involved. This is such an important part of many religions that they are referred to as *the Faith*, as in the phrase, "The Faith once for all delivered to the Saints," common in Christianity, or the term *the faithful* used by Moslems to designate the adherents of Mohammedanism.

In our own times the issue of "faith" has been a sore point in religious controversy. To some scientists and to others committed to an objective approach to knowledge, religious insistence on faith often appears to be an attempt to avoid realism and to take refuge in fantasy. Scientists are apt to become extremely irritated with religious people because it is impossible to argue with those who hold certain matters of belief "on faith," and which they therefore accept without dissent or question. To the "faithful," on the other hand, the concern of scientists with objective demonstration of fact seems unimportant and irrelevant because the former hold that the wisdom of God is above the wisdom of this world and therefore not amenable to human analysis. When one of the early Church Fathers said, "I believe it because it is absurd," he was not intimating that absurdity is a virtue. He was suggesting that what seems absurd from a human viewpoint is not absurd to the believer, because God's ways are so far above the ways of this world that they naturally seem absurd to those bound to worldly processes of thought.

Religious faith may be a powerful incentive toward certain types of behavior. It is perhaps unfortunate that faith as such has been the object of such severe attacks by certain rationalists, because faith, as an individual characteristic, is not in itself objectionable. In fact, a good argument may be made for the point that without faith of some kind most people would not be able to live effectively, though the faith involved may not necessarily be religious faith. The unquestioning acceptance of certain beliefs characterizes most of us. The religious pattern that scientists and others had in mind when they attacked faith was usually not faith at all, but dogmatism, which is quite a different phenomenon.

3. *Dogmatism*. *Dogmatism* is the insistence that a particular form of, or expression of, faith is the only true belief, and that the whole of mankind must be forced to accept that form of belief. The term is also applied to an insistence on complete agreement with even the most minor aspects of a religion, in contrast to faith, which is a more generalized acceptance of the basic tenets of a religion.

Most religions exhibit the characteristic of dogmatism to a greater or lesser degree, with the result that there has been a good deal of conflict, not only within the area of a particular religion and between differing religions but also between the religious approach to life and some other approaches. When a particular religion is dominant in a culture, those who disagree with its dogmas are apt to suffer for it, as has often been the case in our own culture. A few centuries ago heretics, including scientists, were burned at the stake for announcing the results of their investigations in terms that contradicted accepted dogmas. At present schoolteachers, artists, writers, and other professional people are apt to suffer in some communities if they disagree with religious dogma, though they probably will not be burned at the stake.

One point must be made very clearly here. By no means all the persecutions based on dogmatism can be laid to religion. As we discovered in our discussion of the economic institution, one institution is inextricably related to the other institutions of a particular society. So in the case of religion; it has often been used as a political instrumentality, as a weapon to defend economic practices, and as a justification of educational and other systems. Attacks on individuals may allegedly be made on the grounds of religious belief or on the grounds of violation of the moral code. In many instances the religious allegations are a pretext only for the real grounds of persecution, grounds which it is not convenient to admit or which, if admitted, would not be as effective in gaining popular support as are the religious grounds.

In addition, it is not religious people only who are dogmatic. Dogmatism may just as readily be found in scientific, economic, and political beliefs as in religious beliefs. Dogmatism, in whatever area of life it appears, is a pattern which springs from an almost pathological need for security and for the reinforcement of security through the agreement of large numbers of people. As such, it is almost the opposite of religious faith, which also ministers to security, but which is stable enough so that it does not require externalized support from a mass of people.

4. *Denominationalism.* Denominationalism is the tendency of a religion to divide into sects, often on the basis of minor disagreements, and often with consequent bitterness and conflict. There are about 250 Christian denominations listed in the United States, plus several Jewish sects, and a number of other non-Christian bodies. Denominationalism is by no means limited to Christianity; it characterizes most major religions. The weakening effect of extreme denominationalism is perhaps obvious. Not so obvious is the fact that a limited denominationalism may be a source of strength to the religious institution, since it permits variation in religious expression by individuals of different temperaments and attitudes.

5. *Hierarchic Organization.* Most religions also exhibit a tendency toward internal stratification into a hierarchy. A specialized group exists which is set apart by some ceremony, as a result of which its members are supposed to have direct contact with the supernatural, and to operate as agents of the supernatural. They are the *clergy*, called variously priests, ministers, rabbis, adepts, or by some similar name. The other members of the religious group are the *laity*, the noninitiates who approach religious activity through the medium of the clergy.

The elaborateness of the hierarchic organization depends to some extent on the type of religion involved. There are two inclusive types of religion, and within one or the other of those types the major religions of the world fall. The first type is *sacramentarian* in nature. Sacramentarian religions hold that the essential of religion is the descent of the deity to man through ceremonies called sacraments, in Christianity at least. The Catholic Churches (Roman, Greek, and Anglican) are of the sacramentarian type. In those churches the ceremonies incident to the celebration of the Holy Communion have implicit in them the belief that deity descends to the altar on which the ceremony is being celebrated, and takes part in person. The ritual then becomes very elaborate and solemn, in order to provide a fitting framework for the descent of deity.

The second general type of religion may be referred to as the *fellowship* type. Its theory is that man rises to God through prayer, worship, and aspiration rather than that God descends to man through sacraments. In the fellowship type of religion God's spirit is assumed to be present to his worshipers without the necessity of elaborate ritual. The Holy Communion then becomes a memorial service stressing the fellowship of the believers. The officiating clergyman functions more as a leader of the congregation than as a priest mediating between the people and the deity.

Sacramentarian types of religion usually develop an elaborate hierarchic organization, with several grades of clergymen arranged in the order of their authority. Such an elaborate hierarchy is apt to assume a dominating place in the religious institution and to wield a great deal of influence. This influence springs naturally from the fact that the several grades of clergy provide access to the deity for the church members.

Fellowship types of religion usually have a much simpler hierarchy. There is apt to be only one grade of clergyman, though some may occupy positions of authority in an executive sense. The setting apart of the clergy in fellowship religions is usually performed by a group of fellow clergymen of equal rank with the newly admitted individual. Sometimes it is entirely a congregational matter, the ordination being imparted by the body of laymen with whom the minister is to serve. In general, though not invariably, the clergy of the fellowship type of religion do not exercise the dominating kind of authority over the laity that they do in sacramentarian religions.

RELIGION AND SOCIAL ORGANIZATION

There are a number of relationships between religion and social organization. One very important relationship lies in the fact that

Religion tends to validate the traditional way of life of a culture.

It is a matter of common observation as well as of sociological generalization that religion tends to be *conservative*. This conservatism expresses itself not only in the active support of traditional ways of living and ways of thinking, but also in the *validation* of those ways, that is, in giving meaning to, and justification for, the traditional way of life. Cultures, as we know, develop some relatively stable adjustments to the environment. The fact that the adjustments function adeqately in the life of the culture concerned is, in itself, the source of one type of *meaning* for them. Religion adds another type of meaning. The way in which things are traditionally done is the right way because it is sanctioned by God, because it accords with the accepted moral code, because it is found in sacred writings, or because it is supported by some more direct revelation of God's will. The culture which has developed those ways of living and of thinking is the best society as long as it does not depart from them.

And it remains the best society, even though it may suffer adversity. Thus the Hebrews looked on themselves as the "chosen people" and remained firm in that faith, even when the Hebrew state was demolished and the Hebrew people scattered. Israel, conquered and in dispersion, became the "suffering servant" of God who, through the very fact of his suffering, was to show God's will to the rest of the world. The same general idea pervades many other religions; their adherents are in intimate relationship with deity, and it becomes their mission to convert the unbeliever.

Obviously, in thus giving meaning to the traditional way of life and to the culture which follows that way of life, religion may be very influential in welding together the component parts of society. It therefore may perform a very significant function in social organization.

RELIGION AN OPIATE?

But the emphasis on traditionalism must not mislead us into the belief that religion always concurs in *current* culture patterns. Religion is sometimes accused of being an *opiate*, that is, a drug which deadens the sensitivity of individuals to existing injustice. It may, in fact, function as an opiate; but it may also function as a critic of current patterns of behavior, and in that way it may become a stimulus to social change. When religion applies its traditional values in a critical way to current practices, the results may be almost revolutionary.

At the present time, for example, the Federal Council of Churches of Christ in America is undertaking an investigation to discover to what extent current practices in the economic field and in some other areas of life conform to the Christian ethic.[6] The Christian ethic is regarded as basically the teachings of Jesus in the New Testament, that is, the traditional teachings of the Christian religion. Let us repeat that this evaluation of current practices in terms of a traditional ethic is really a part of the conservatism of the Church, even though it seems a very radical procedure to those who accept current ways of life uncritically.

The Federal Council is by no means the only religious body interested in social criticism. A number of papal encyclicals have stressed the fundamental importance of Christian justice, rather than economic laws, in economic relationships, defining justice in terms of the Scriptures and of the tradition of the Church. Catholic writers have applied the doctrines of the encyclicals to concrete problems in the United States. Their general attitude is the insistence on the necessity of economic reform in those areas of economic practice found not to conform to the principles of Catholic justice. Again we have radical proposals resulting from the application of traditional doctrines to current ways of life.

Aside from these more or less official approaches to social justice, individual clergymen have been interested in "social action" on the basis of Christian principles. They have at times walked picket lines with strikers, supported unions, set up canteens for strikers in church basements, and engaged in many similar activities. By no means all of the proposed programs have related exclusively to economic affairs. There are also programs for world peace, attacks on corrupt politics, and demands for reform in connection with the care we give the insane, the feeble-minded, and criminals.[7]

One point to be made here is that we have been discussing the role of traditional and long-established religions in promoting social change. We have not included the *modernistic* or *revised* forms of religion such as Unitarianism. It would not, perhaps, be surprising

[6]*Information Service*, Federal Council of Churches, Vol. XXV, No. 8, Part 2, "Christianity and the Economic Order."

[7]See *Life*, May 6, 1946, on conditions in mental hospitals.

if such revised religions showed more interest in contemporary life than in historical attitudes. Such an interest is rather unexpected in the case of traditional religions.

Another point to be made is that by no means all the religious groups of our day are in favor of the programs suggested by the Federal Council of Churches and by others. There are many people, some of them influential, who hold that social criticism is not part of the function of the Church. There are others whose chief aim is the justification of current practices, rather than their evaluation in terms of a traditional ethic, and who achieve such justification through forced interpretations of Scripture and in other devious ways. Our religious institution is not a unit in its social attitudes.

Religion, then, may perform a very important function for social organization by giving meaning to the traditional way of life of the aggregate. A second very important function of religion in social organization rests in its influence on the individual. Through its schools, through authoritative preaching, through denunciation of certain types of conduct and support of other types of conduct, and through persuasion religion may exert a powerful influence on the individual. In a stable society, with an authoritative moral code, the net result of this influence is to make the individual conform to accepted patterns, a desirable thing in that kind of social organization.

RELIGION IN COMPLEX SOCIETY

The relationships between religion and social organization in a complex society are somewhat different from those relationships in simpler societies. In general,

> As a society becomes more complex, the authority and prestige of religion tend to decline.

There are two reasons for this tendency. 1. In a complex society the population is *heterogeneous* in composition, which means that the backgrounds, interests, and behavior patterns of various segments of the population differ widely. This heterogeneity may arise from within the society through the interaction of different segments of the population with different segments of the environment, or it may result from contacts with other cultures and consequent borrowing of foreign ways of life. Different religions may be imported into the group which will compete with the "native" religion. New stimuli to revised ways of living and ways of thinking may appear as a result of culture contacts which tend to undermine the authority of religion in general. There are examples of both these phenomena in our own society.

2. A second reason for the decline of religious prestige in a complex society is found in the fact that substitutes for the religious pattern develop in such a society. These substitutes may not, in themselves, be religious at all, but they perform some of the functions of religion, such as setting life goals and values. In our own society the whole economic and industrial system functions for some individuals and for some groupings as a substitute for religion. The activities connected with economic life become ends in themselves. Individuals find a life meaning in their work or in making money. No religious or philosophical system is necessary in order to make life worth living or to give validation to the economic pattern.

The economic pattern is not the only substitute for religion in our own, and other, complex societies. Science, the intellectual life, the artistic life, and other interests may function in a similar way. To the extent that they live an individually satisfying life in terms of any of those activities, many people find it possible to dispense with religion. In less complex cultures science and the arts are either so rudimentary in development that they are not available as substitutes for religion, or they are controlled by the religious institution and made to serve religious ends.

Still other individuals find validation and goals of life in the mere process of consuming the products of their culture. They are fortunate, or unfortunate, enough to have all the money they want and they find the whole of life's significance in the spending of that money. In a simpler culture such a pattern would be limited to very few members of the grouping because the simpler economic techniques did not result in any great surplus of goods beyond the immediate needs of the aggregate, and almost incessant labor was necessary to provide even that amount of goods. In our own civilization, and in other advanced civilizations of the past, a considerable surplus of goods beyond bare necessities, an increase in the amount of leisure time available to an increasing proportion of the population, and efficient economic techniques have all operated to permit a relatively wide spread of the consuming and other pleasure patterns. As these become established, there is decreasing opportunity for the influence of religious validation and life goals.

All that we have been saying relates primarily to substitutes for religion in the individual's life. But the society may also find such substitutes adequate in that they perform for the social organization the functions, or some of the functions, that religion performs.

For example, we have suggested that religion functions in social organization by giving meaning to certain patterns of behavior which are characteristic of a given culture, and thus justifies the existence not only of those patterns but also of the culture of which they are a part. Substitutes may operate in precisely that way. Our industrial life is an extensive complex of interrelated activities, and the mere existence of this interrelationship in itself tends to bind the economic segments to each other and to the whole society. As we suggested in our discussion of the economic institution, interdependence may also bring about conflict between the segments. It is not an automatically unifying force. But neither is religion, especially when it is characterized by extreme denominationalism. The economic ties between segments of society are apt to be impersonal and the result of forced co-ordination. So also may the ties of religion be, especially when the religious institution is authoritative and hierarchic in nature. It remains to be seen whether an economy which functions as a substitute for religion will be an *adequate* substitute or not. Meanwhile, it is a fact that in our times it is functioning in that way, with the result that the authority and the prestige of religion have declined.

To a lesser degree than the economic system, science, the arts, and the intellectual life are also accepted by our group, or segments of it, as adequate substitutes for religion. One point of importance here is this: while all these patterns of behavior may be openly hostile to religion, their greatest effect springs not from such open hostility but from the mere development of ways of life that compete with religion. They were not developed intentionally as substitutes for religion; the process has been one of which we were largely unaware until recently. From a cultural standpoint we pay considerable formal deference to the religious institution. But actually we consider it an unimportant institution. We refer to others than the clergy for authoritative pronouncements, and we follow other than religious patterns in the great majority of our activities.

This whole situation we have been discussing is noted with concern both by individuals professionally connected with religion and by others. As an example of the "others," we may cite President Hutchins of the University of Chicago. He calls for an admission that "our faith that technology will take the place of justice has been naïve." He asks that we return to the belief that man is "a moral, rational and spiritual being" and that "every act of every man is a moral act, to be tested by moral, and not by economic criteria."[8] His concern is with the strengthening of the moral and religious outlook of man.

There are some current indications that such strengthening will perhaps come as the dangers of technology become more evident and we experience again the necessity for ethical control of conduct. The situation was foreseen by such fundamentally nonreligious thinkers as Mr. H. G. Wells, in his *Autobiography*, and Mr. Bertrand Russell. The latter stated in 1938 that there was little hope for the world unless power could be "tamed" and brought into the service of the whole human race. He pointed out that men used to sell themselves to the devil in order to acquire magical powers, whereas we now get those powers from science and ourselves become devils.[9]

One fact appears to be obvious. The "taming" of one great destructive power cannot be accomplished through the invention of an even greater destructive power without risk of the destruction of both—and all—powers. The only possible type of "taming" will come through some constructive approach. Religion, with its emphasis on ethical, internal, and voluntary controls has a great opportunity to function in this situation. In effect, what we face is a vast change in our environment, brought about by an increasing control of nature, which has culminated thus far in atomic fission. Along with this trend has gone a second, the progressive decrease of the isolation of one culture from other cultures. Rapid means of

[8]R. M. Hutchins, *Education for Freedom*, Louisiana State University Press. Quoted in *Time*, March 1, 1943.

[9]Bertrand Russell, *Power, A New Social Analysis*, pp. 33 ff. Norton, New York, 1938.

transportation and of communication have brought the nations of the world into closer contact. One social result of the decrease in isolation has been an increasing interdependence between cultures. The attitudes, the behavior, and the programs of nations distant from us in space now involve us and hence become of significance to us. All this means that factually our environment is much broader than it has been in the past. It is to this broader environment that religion must now adjust.

Finally, we may note a fourth way in which religion functions to relate the parts of a society to the whole society, that is, through its ritual and ceremonial. In general,

Religious ritual tends to make abstract ideas more concrete and hence more easily understood.

Ritual is essentially the "acting out" of certain details of religious belief. In Christianity, for example, the mission of Jesus, the atonement, and the sacrifice are repeatedly "told" in the Communion service, and along with the telling go actions which emphasize the high points of the story. Similarly, the formal witnessing of a marriage service stresses, in word and action, the meaning of marriage and the duties of the married pair. The ritual of the funeral service emphasizes the unimportance of the body and the significance of the soul. Baptism of an infant symbolizes his "second birth" as a member of the Christian community. Relatively few lay church members can explain clearly the theological doctrines on which all these ceremonies are based, but they share in the beliefs through the concrete ritual.

In Protestant Christianity, as we have indicated, preaching tends to become a ritualistic device. Customs, modes of expression, and subject matter all tend to become formalized. The purpose of most preaching is the explanation of a passage of Scripture, or the application of a Scriptural precept to daily-life situations common to the hearers. In other words, it is the attempt to make concrete certain ideas fundamental to the religion.

To the extent that basic ideas are made more easily apprehended, they function more effectively in relating the segments of a grouping to the whole grouping. In that sense they function more effectively in social organization. Aside from this "concretizing" influence the ritualistic performances incident to religion involve the common participation of individuals in a series of actions. This common participation extends beyond the particular congregation to include the membership of the whole denomination, and, in some cases, the membership of the whole Church. Obviously, common participation in ritualistic ceremonies may be a very significant binding force.

CURRENT PROBLEMS OF RELIGION

There are certain areas of relationship between the religious institution and the social organization in general which have become problems for religion. It will contribute to our understanding of the religious institution if we are familiar with some of those areas.

The Number of Church Members

Of first importance from the viewpoint of the religious institution itself is the problem of the number of adherents it holds in the total population. In simpler cultures the tendency is for the whole population to be included. In more complex cultures a smaller proportion displays an active interest in religion, as we might expect in view of the tendency of religious authority and prestige to decline and of the development of substitute ways of life.

In the United States about 47 per cent of the population were counted as church members in 1926, with 44 per cent similarly listed in 1936, and 52 per cent in 1945.[10] Since these figures are based on the total population of the country, and therefore include children who would not ordinarily be counted as members of a church, the percentage of the adult population listed as church members is probably somewhat larger. Even in that case, however, church membership is limited to only a segment of the population. It is further a fact that by no means do all the listed members of a denomination take an active part in religion, and therefore religion influences in a realistic way only a small part of our people.

The Federal Council of Churches has investigated the addition of new members to seven large Protestant denominations from 1850 to 1940. A graph resulting from the investigation shows considerable fluctuation from decade to decade, with a slowly declining

[10]Percentages quoted from *Statistical Abstract of the United States*.

average trend evident from about 1900 to 1940. It is interesting to note that according to this investigation there has been a marked decline in additions to church membership during each of the wars in which the United States has engaged, with some tendency to rise after the end of a war.

Other factors than war apparently influence accessions to church membership rolls. The "science controversy" of the 1880's and the long depression of the 1930's were both accompanied by a decline in new membership among the seven denominations listed.[11] If the graph is an accurate indication of trends, it undoubtedly means that, at least from the viewpoint of new members received, there has been a slow decline in the number of people interested in religious activity.

FINANCIAL SUPPORT

Perhaps a decrease in the vitality of the religious institution is also indicated by the amount of money contributed to religious purposes in proportion to the total expenditure of money by the United States population. Another Federal Council study indicates that in 1932 about 1.3 per cent of our total expenditures went to the Church; in 1936 the percentage was almost exactly 1.0; and in 1945 about 0.8 per cent.[12] These figures do not mean that the total amount of money given for religious purposes was less in 1945 than it was in 1932, since the total spending of the population varied in those two years. A low percentage of a large total expenditure may be higher than a high percentage of a small total expenditure. They refer to the *proportion* of the total expenditure which went for religious purposes.

The Federal Council suggests that one reason for the decline is that people tend to donate to "charity and welfare" instead of to the Church. This point is interesting as illustrative of the effect of substitute activities on religion, a matter we discussed earlier in the chapter.

DENOMINATIONALISM

We mentioned that there are about 250 denominations in the United States, according to the listing by the United States Bureau

[11]Graph reproduced in *Time*, January 26, 1942.
[12]Quoted in *Time*, May 20, 1946.

of the Census. Some of these are very small, and some are specialized aggregates within larger denominations, but all were distinct enough to have functioning organization and to report activities to the census. In some cases the basis of differentiation into sects is a matter of serious doctrine or practice; in others, it is a relatively minor matter. Whatever the reason may be, the functioning of religion in social organization is seriously hampered by division.

This fact, of course, is recognized by religious authorities. There is currently a great deal of stress on the desirability of "church unity," and there have been a number of examples of union between different sects. On the other hand, to some sincerely religious people it appears that unity has come, and can only come, from the surrender of vitally important doctrines, and that such surrender in itself indicates a declining vitality of religious conviction. It is also true that, in some instances, the creation of a new "united church" has led simply to another denomination, since there have been "continuing" members of the formally "united" denominations who have refused to enter the union and have maintained their own churches.

It is very probable that the future of church unity will lie in the direction of unification of fellowship churches into one group and of sacramentarian churches into another group.

THE "SCIENCE" CONTROVERSY

A third problem of contemporary religion lies in conflict with nonreligious, though not necessarily irreligious, systems of thought. Perhaps the most familiar example of this kind of conflict is the "science controversy." Some analysis of this controversy is necessary.

In so far as religion seeks to explain the origin of the world and in so far as it insists on the historical accuracy of occurrences such as miracles, it is certain to meet the criticism of people who offer other explanations of human origins and who deny the possibility of miraculous occurrences outside the realm of the laws of nature. The explanation of human origins in terms of natural law instead of in religious terms should be a matter of detached and objective search for facts. According to the canons of science, there should be no emotionalism or "evangelism" about the procedure. Actually, a good many scientists have not been content merely to publish their findings as tentative hypotheses. They have engaged in acrid debate with religious exponents in a number of instances. On the other hand, religious forces have responded to the attacks and have also initiated some attacks of their own. The resulting spectacle has not been exactly edifying.

One major difficulty here has been that the scientist and the proponent of religious views have often not understood the meanings involved in the controversy. For example, there are two basic differences in outlook between religion and science.

1. The findings of science in any field are the result of the application of the scientific method. If those findings are attacked solely on the grounds that they contradict traditional belief, that constitutes, for the scientist, an attack on his whole method and his whole reason for existence. Let us understand this point. Any informed person may validly attack the findings of a particular scientist on the grounds that those findings constitute an inept or an inaccurate use of the scientific method. That asserts only that the scientist in question is a poor scientist. He may object strenuously to that assertion, of course, but it will not arouse the body of scientists as a whole to defend him. But to attack the findings of a particular scientist is quite a different matter from attacking the scientific method as such. To say that that method, in itself and regardless of how carefully it is used, is a false method will certainly not meet with the approval of scientists as a body. Yet this is exactly what certain religious groups have insisted is the case. In denying completely the validity of the scientific method, they have opened a breach between religion and science. Admittedly also those scientists who have insisted that the scientific method is the only method by which we can arrive at truth in any field have done nothing to make the breach less obvious.

Another point should be made. Any informed person may attack a certain finding of science on the grounds that it is hypothetical and not completely demonstrated. It is one of the assumptions of science that most scientific knowledge is tentative and that continuing investigation may bring about drastic revisions of what may appear to be even the most firmly established hypotheses. Once more, this is simply to say that our scientific knowledge is incomplete, a fact which every scientist knows. It is far different from criticizing scientific findings because they do not accord with traditional beliefs. To attack them from that point of view is to attack the very core of the scientific approach to life.

Those who espouse the religious explanation of the origin of the universe have not always appreciated the meaning to the scientist of his method and approach. That meaning may be as deeply involved in the personality of scientists as religious meanings are involved in the personality of religious people. Little progress toward a better understanding between religion and science can be made until that fact is grasped.

2. A second important area of controversy between religion and science lies in their differing approach to facts. Science is primarily interested in the discovery of facts and of the interrelationships between facts. It has, until recently at any rate, been little concerned with the social or moral implications of those facts and relationships. This attitude has been characteristic not only in theoretical investigations, such as those concerned with the "evolutionary theory," but also in practical and technological developments. If a new industrial process is discovered through research, the tendency is to use that process with little regard for the dislocations resulting from its use, dislocations in the employment situation, in family life, or in any other area of social life. The fact, the process, is the important thing to the scientist and the technologist.

In contrast to this point of view, religion is by its very nature evaluative. The implications of facts are, for religion, usually as important as the facts themselves and often more important than the facts themselves. For example, the existence of God is a fact for religion. The implications of that fact lie in the area of its meaning for human life and human destiny. The implication is as important as the fact itself. The scientist often cannot understand this preoccupation with evaluation and with the implications of facts. He often sees no point in the statement "If we are to believe this fact, it will lead to unfortunate results." He is apt to reply, "The fact is the fact, and that is that."

Aside from this fact-versus-implication differential between science and religion, there is another aspect of their respective approaches to facts which causes misunderstanding. From the viewpoint of religion certain facts and their implications are at the very core of life. They cannot be discarded, changed, or modified except under very unusual circumstances, such as a new revelation, and even new revelations are not universally welcomed. The scientist, on the other hand, with his belief in the tentative nature both of his factual knowledge and of his hypotheses, can more readily change, discard, or otherwise modify his factual and theoretical structure. To illustrate, the word *atom*, according to its derivation from the Greek, means "something that cannot be cut or divided." Scientists, however, are now busy cutting up the atom which, for many years, was supposed to be the smallest particle of matter. The mere fact that they are now doing something that could not be done in the past, and that they have had to change a belief held by reputable scientists in the past, does not trouble them.

Now, as we intimated before, there is a great deal of dogmatism in science, accompanied by a tendency to cling to established theories. Not all scientists welcome change in their discipline. Our point, however, deals not with individual scientists but with the attitude which characterizes science itself. That attitude is more receptive to change in traditional beliefs than is the attitude of religion. It is also true that some segments of religion are more receptive to change than are other segments; but, on the whole, the membership of the liberal segments is smaller and perhaps less influential than that of the conservative segments.

Science and religion, then, look upon facts in very different ways. To the scientist religion is apt to appear dogmatic and reactionary; to the religious person, the scientists appear to "lack conviction" and to be degenerative of morality.

Reconciliation of the two attitudes will probably be difficult. A first step in such reconciliation must be the recognition not only of the fact that they exist but also of the deeper roots of the difference. They spring from the natural processes involved in religion and in science. It is not a case of all scientists being determined to destroy religion, nor is it a case of all theologians being hopeless ignoramuses. Both the religious and the scientific attitudes have a degree of validity, and the problem is to arrange a working agreement which will take account of such validity.

There is evidence that current scientific and cultural changes may exert an influence in the direction of agreement. For example, it is obvious that the implications of atomic fission are just as important as the fact of fission itself, and scientists cannot neglect those implications. On the other hand, theologians can hardly deny the fact of fission. The same thing is true of other developments. The facts exist, and no theologian unequipped with the tools of the scientific method can deny them. The social implications of science, and perhaps its moral implications, are equally obvious. Both facts and the implications of facts are of great significance.

We believe that this situation gives scope for a division of function between science and religion in which the two approaches will be of equal importance. Religion has as its function the evaluative, judicial approach to life; science has as its function the discovery of fact. Both together can function with equal validity. The "reconciliation of science and religion" will come about through common recognition of differing functions and of the validity of those functions.

SUMMARY: RELIGION IN SOCIAL ORGANIZATION

A religious institution has for its function the determination of the sacred, in whatever terms that may be defined. Traditional religions relate the sacred to supernatural forces; some recent religious attitudes relate it to concepts of values which may serve as life goals for the individual and his group, rather than to supernatural entities. Religion is contrasted with magic chiefly on the basis of the attitudes which characterize the two; magic coerces, while religion is dependent on the sacred. Typical religious patterns include morality, faith, dogmatism, denominationalism, and hierarchic organization.

Religion functions in social organization by validating the traditional way of life of the culture, but its prestige tends to decline in a complex society because substitute patterns perform this validating function.

Current problems of religion center in the development of such substitute patterns, with consequent effects on church membership, financial support, and the continuing controversy with science. That controversy may be settled by a recognition of the differing functions of the two, and a realization of the validity of both those functions.

READINGS

Science, Philosophy, and Religion. A symposium published by the Conference on Science, Philosophy, and Religion, New York, 1941. A collection of papers presented at the first meeting of the Conference. Especially pp. 21 ff., "Science, Religion, and Democracy"; pp. 209 ff., "Science and Religion"; pp. 215 ff., "Science and Democracy"; pp. 369 ff., "God and the World."

Sorokin, P. A. *Society, Culture, and Personality.* Harper & Brothers, New York, 1947. Pages 225–229, "Differentiation into Religious Groups."

Bates, M. Searle. *Religious Liberty: An Inquiry.* International Missionary Council, New York, 1945. A comprehensive discussion of religious liberty in many areas of the world.

Pendell, Elmer (Ed.). *Society under Analysis.* The Jacques Cattell Press, Lancaster, Pennsylvania, 1942. Chapter 16, "Religion and the Churches."

Panunzio, Constantine. *Major Social Institutions.* The Macmillan Company, New York, 1939. Chapter 18, "The Development of the Religious Institution"; Chap. 19, "The Contemporary Religious Institution."

CHAPTER XV

EDUCATION

THE EDUCATIONAL INSTITUTION is more directly a result of social pressures than it is of individual drives.[1] Every culture finds it necessary to condition and influence children toward acceptance of group patterns of living. There are two chief reasons for that pressure.

1. Young people must learn certain things about the environment in which they live and about cultural relationships to that environment in order to survive. To take an example from a simpler culture, children must know the dangers of their surroundings, the potential threats involved in animal life surrounding them, such things as the perils of the seasonal swelling of streams which may at other times be safe, and the evil that may result if the unseen world is approached in other than accepted ways. If they do not know these things, they face the danger of early death. The early death of a major portion of the children would obviously threaten the survival of their group.

In our own times the general pattern of teaching assumes much the same form, though the details differ considerably. We teach basic tools of understanding through the familiar "reading, writing, and arithmetic," instruments very useful in our own culture but which would be of limited meaning in a simpler "forest" society. We deal with matters of personal hygiene and of public health. We inculcate codes of behavior. So important do we consider schooling in all these areas that we enforce compulsory-education laws, our form of social pressure in favor of education.

2. Children and young people must also learn techniques which will enable them to assume a functioning position in the social

[1]Constantine Panunzio, *Major Social Institutions*, p. 242. Macmillan, New York, 1939.

structure. Referring again to simpler cultures, we note that they must learn the relatively simple economic and other techniques that will enable them to become self-sufficient. Today they also learn some kind of economic or professional skills, and in addition they are supposed to learn something of their function as citizens. Civics courses in elementary and secondary schools stress the general aspects of our government organization, the political duties of the citizen, and something of international relations. It is assumed that such instruction will permit young people to engage wisely in the common duties of a citizen in a democracy. Recently we have stressed preparation for economic life to a greater degree than that for citizenship, but in actuality the two are equally important.

Necessary as these two functions are, in an uncomplicated society it is possible often to have them performed in connection with some existing institution instead of developing them through a separate educational institution. Thus the economic institution may as part of its general pattern carry out instruction in economic techniques. The family may instruct children in the moral patterns of living and in the proper methods of approaching the unseen. It is when a population becomes larger in size and more complex in relationships that a separate educational institution appears. As we might expect, the educational institution in our own very complex society is very elaborate indeed.

EDUCATION AS A SOCIAL INSTITUTION

A sociologist approaches the study of education primarily as a part of a social organization. He is concerned chiefly with the relationships between the educational institution and other aspects of society, precisely the same kind of approach we noted in the case of the economic institution. An educator, as distinguished from a sociologist, investigates the internal relationships and organization of an educational institution—such matters as the construction of curricula, methods of teaching, certification of teachers, the ends and aims of education from a technical viewpoint. The sociologist is not concerned with most of those things. And, in the case of a common concern, the approach differs between educators and sociologists. Thus both are interested in the ends and aims of education: the sociologist as those ends and aims affect the social organization, the educator primarily, though not exclusively, as those ends and aims are part of a functioning educational system. We shall have occasion to refer again to this difference of emphasis between educator and sociologist.

DEFINITIONS

Sociological definitions of education commonly stress the fact that it is a *transmissive* pattern, in somewhat the following terms:

> *Education is the institution formally concerned*
> *with the transmission of culture patterns.*

Most cultures are convinced of the validity of their own ways of living and ways of thinking. They hold that their own patterns are necessary for psychosocial survival, as we said in Chapter VI. Granting that presupposition, the transmission of those ways of living and ways of thinking to the young becomes a prime necessity. It is sometimes said that the educational institution is conservative, the implication of that statement being that advances in science, philosophy, and in other fields of knowledge come from outside the educational institution rather than from within it. As we shall see presently, that statement is not wholly true. In so far as it is true, however, it indicates the essentially transmissive nature of education. It tends not to be *inventive*, a restriction placed on it by the community in which it functions.

Professional educators, again as distinguished from sociologists, are apt to be not too well pleased with the emphasis we have placed on the transmissive function of education. They point to the fact that education is by no means always a passive "follower" of culture patterns. They insist that it also functions as a "leader" by initiating new ideas and new approaches. For example, in the whole field of research the educational institution has developed a number of new techniques and theories, and in that sense it has very definitely influenced the course of cultural development. It is, of course, true that education does function as a leader in certain areas of life, and yet it is still dominated by cultural interests even in that function.

In general, it is true that

Education tends to function most actively in those areas of life which are of major interest to the culture of which it is a part.

In our own times, for example, technological and industrial processes are points of major interest. At present our educational institution stresses those areas of life very heavily in its curricula. Scientific research, instruction in technical subjects, and the whole laboratory approach are evidences of an increasingly technological society. In a similar manner, the growth of commercial departments in high schools and colleges is a response to the needs of the commercial aspects of our industrial society. During the 1930's, a period of business depression, social studies came to the fore, and emphasis on them has continued as our culture has appeared to be more and more threatened with disorganization. During the war the whole force of education was bent in the direction of war-related activities as war became the major interest of society.

But education did not in all cases, and especially at the college level, enthusiastically welcome these new additions to established curricula. There was, and still is to some extent, a marked resistance to their introduction and a marked tendency to insist on the sole validity for education of traditional classical and humanistic studies. As a result there has been a lag between the actual growth of commerce, industry, and science and the response of education. The tendency, then, is for education to function in areas of major interest to a culture. It very seldom leads in the development of new areas of interest, and in some cases it resists such development. Education is still primarily a transmissive institution, functioning for the grouping through the maintenance of cultural patterns considered to be of great importance for psychosocial survival.

No criticism of the educational institution of our times is intended in these statements. They are simply illustrative of a relationship between education and the culture in which it is functioning. It is a relationship important to an understanding of education because education is currently the subject of some popular interest. On the one hand, the hope is expressed that education will "save the world," that it is our only resource if we are to escape destruction, and that as education becomes more general the future progress of society is inevitable. This is much too facile an outlook to accord with the facts. Education is undoubtedly one resource for the future, but it operates in terms of a social organization and merely as one instrumentality in that social organization. It can function only to the extent that the other segments of culture permit it to, and in the way in which they permit. It does not lead the cultural forces which have been significant in producing our present ways of living. In fact, it has been dominated by other forces, partly economic, partly religious, partly reactionary, throughout most of its existence in our culture. That it can, in turn, influence those forces is true, but the process is slow and difficult, quite a different process from the automatic influence suggested by the optimistic proponents of education as the hope of the world.

On the other hand, there are some very bitter critics of education and of its alleged failure to be realistically functional. The same may be said with reference to this attitude; education functions only in terms of a given social organization. If it cannot automatically "save the world" apart from that social organization, neither is it to be blamed for all of the supposed faults of that social organization. It is one institution among many, and it can operate only in conjunction with other institutions.

THE CONTENT OF EDUCATION

Our discussion thus far indicates clearly that the specific content of education varies from culture to culture. It also varies within the same culture from time to time, as the orientation of cultural interest may shift. The general content, however, remains stable. As Mr. Graham Wallas has indicated,

. . . the social heritage which each generation of mankind hands down to its successors may be roughly divided into knowledge to be learnt and ideals or patterns of behavior . . . to be imitated.[2]

He further points out that the patterns of behavior may be either "external and muscular" or "internal and emotional." We are taught not only how to conduct outselves in given situations but

[2]Graham Wallas, *Social Judgment*, p. 29. Harcourt, New York, 1935.

also what attitudes, controls, and other emotional reactions are appropriate to given situations.

Education, then, transmits the basic "tool devices," the basic information, and the basic attitudes which are considered necessary for all individuals in a grouping to have. It also transmits techniques of a vocational nature to certain segments of a population, differentiating them on the basis of sex, intelligence, and economic and social status. The task of any society is to exploit the environment in which it lives and to assure some measure of peaceful relationships among its members. Education transmits material useful for both these tasks.

EDUCATION AND SOCIAL ORGANIZATION

Recalling our definition of social organization as the system by which the parts of a society are related to the whole society and to each other in a meaningful way, we may examine certain relationships between education and society which arise as the educational institution fulfills its part in the "relating" function.

EDUCATION IN COMPLEX CULTURES

Our first point is that

> *The complexity of an educational institution varies as the complexity of the culture of which it is part.*

This is an almost self-evident principle, but it is overlooked by some of the critics of education we mentioned earlier, who show a tendency to regret the passing of the "little red schoolhouse" and to deplore the appearance of large and crowded schools with all the apparatus of teacher-training which characterizes modern education. We have come so recently from a fairly simple rural culture that we have not adjusted to many of the facts of our complex culture.

In a simple culture in which there is little change, little economic specialization, and little contact with other cultures, the educational institution can also remain simple because it must take account of only few changes. In our own rural organization of a few generations ago the "native" culture tended to be dominant, change was slow, and economic techniques were relatively simple and uniform. Hence the educational institution could function adequately by inculcating a few "tool subjects," and by stressing a few widely accepted behavior patterns. These conditions no longer exist.

Complexity in our own culture is evidenced in a number of ways.

1. Specialization of economic activity and its resulting interdependence and class consciousness lead to segmentation of the society. Education, then, must itself specialize internally if it is to function meaningfully for the different segments. It is no longer possible to have one uniform educational system which will satisfy the needs of widely differing segments, especially in the higher branches of education. Attempts to meet this situation on the part of educators have led to the complex specialized educational institution with which we are familiar.

2. Complexity is further evidenced by growth of new patterns of institutional behavior. For example, the specialization of the economic institution has indirectly affected family life. Industry now makes clothes, launders clothes, bakes and cooks food, serves meals, and does many other things which used to be wholly within the province of the family. If to those functions we add commercial recreation, the fact that employment of women is common, and the emphasis on nonfamily values which characterizes our times, we understand the decline in the importance of family patterns which also characterizes our times. The significance of these facts for education is that the school can no longer assume that a certain amount of information will be given to children in their own homes and that certain behavior patterns will be taught in the home. The school must function in areas formerly covered by the home.

A further point is that the schools cannot assume that all children will *not* be taught at home to some extent and in some families, because family patterns differ. As a result, groups of children come to the classroom at different levels of knowledge, different levels of behavior, and with varying attitudes. To function in connection with these types of children demands specialization and complexity in the educational institution.

3. Our complex society has also developed means of mass influence and mass communication which compete with education for the conditioning of children. In self-defense, the school has had to

adopt some of those means of mass influence, such as motion pictures, radio broadcasts, and others. These may become very effective teaching devices, but they increase the complexity of the whole process of education.

4. Again, we have developed a fund of knowledge about human beings, and techniques for analyzing and classifying human beings into a number of types. These types express themselves in individual differences. Thus there are differences of mentality, of skills, of emotional balance and emotional needs, of general abilities, all of which we now recognize to a much greater extent and in a much more systematic way than was common in the past. As a result of such knowledge, we propose to treat educationally the different types in different ways. The feeble-minded person and the genius, for example, are not dismissed as "hopeless" or as "queer." Instead, specialized techniques with reference to these and other types are developed. This kind of development enables the educational institution more efficiently to perform its function in social organization, because it more effectively relates specialized individuals and aggregates to the total society. But again it increases the complexity of the institution.

5. Finally, the complexity of our contemporary society expresses itself partly through the heterogeneity of our population. In a nation composed largely of native stock, or in a nation which has had diverse groupings living together for such a long period that stable relationships have developed, there is less complexity than in a nation which is receiving new increments of different populations, as the United States has been until recently. The net result of this heterogeneity is increased differentiation in background, ways of living, and ways of thinking on the part of the school population. Our present schools have the task of making our culture meaningful, not only to English-speaking natives but to people of different languages and different customs. Special methods of instruction, special classes, and special attempts to integrate this heterogeneous population into a school system necessarily demand systems of some complexity.

Doubtless not all the complexity of our present educational system is the result of societal complexity. Some educational specialists, assuming an attitude common to specialists in many fields, tend to view their own specialty as of major importance to the culture.

They have therefore indulged, in some instances, in elaboration merely for the sake of elaboration.[3] But it is fair to say that the major portion of the elaboration has been a response to an increasing societal complexity.

THE CONTEMPORARY FUNCTION OF EDUCATION

We now approach the question of how education is to relate the various segments of society to the whole. There are two emphases of special significance in relation to that question.

1. *The Vocational Emphasis.* The first emphasis stresses the importance of vocational training, including in that term professional education for law, engineering, medicine, and so on. It is not too much to say that to many people the word *education* means training for a vocation.

The obvious necessity for most individuals to earn their own living is a strong point in favor of this view. It has been to some extent strengthened recently by the opportunity for veterans of the Second World War to attend college with government assistance. Training in special skills undoubtedly permits individuals to rise in the economic scale, a natural goal in our society. It is not surprising, therefore, that much of the education of veterans should be vocational, directly or indirectly.

One of the shortcomings of the vocational emphasis is the fact that individuals trained vocationally and not otherwise are uninformed about many aspects of contemporary life and are therefore apt to be somewhat naïve in their approach to contemporary problems.

2. *The General-Education Emphasis.* The second emphasis takes account of the necessity for broad information and the development of discriminative faculties in the citizen of today. Under the term "general education" it advocates a "core curriculum" which all students should follow before, or at some time in addition to, their vocational training. It stresses especially the impartation of facts about the history, problems, and current trends in our society, skill in language as a means of the accurate communication of ideas, and the development of the faculties of criticism and judgment.[4] The

[3] J. Barzun, *Teacher in America.* Little, Brown, Boston, 1945.
[4] *General Education in a Free Society.* Harvard University Press, Cambridge, 1945.

purpose of the program is to enable the individual to function as a citizen in an effective way because of his understanding of himself and of the society in which he lives.

Until the Second World War there was little patience with proposals for general education, although the need for it was recognized by some people. Even at present there is often little enthusiasm for the idea, since the emergencies directly connected with the war are obscured and the emergencies relating to peace either are not understood or are viewed as being of little significance. Perhaps that very fact is one of the strongest indicators of the necessity for a broader type of information and the development of critical faculties. Our emphasis on the economic life and its related activities has had the result of impressing most students with the importance of vocational training, almost to the complete exclusion of any other type of education.

In addition to this orientation of interest, another factor enters into the impatience with general education. A number of the adult members of our population are still going on the assumption either that our cultural environment and our societal relationships are actually simple or, if they are not, that they ought to be simple and in good time will become so. They hold to the view that the wisdom necessary to efficient functioning as citizens either is "instinctive" or is developed by the intimate processes of community and family living, as was the case in the rural society of the past. As previously indicated, our present family patterns are often not such as to develop responsibility and understanding in children; and the community itself has become so complex that understanding of it no longer comes from unconscious absorption of its ways of living and ways of thinking.

There are these two emphases, then, in answer to the question as to how education is to function in social organization. A moment's consideration will show that neither emphasis is exclusively correct. A combination of the two is indicated.

According to the theory of American democracy, an individual has always been related to his community in two ways: first as a "specialist," that is, as a businessman or a professional man, as a worker, or as a participant in the economic life of the community, and second as a citizen, or a voter, or an elector, or a functioning member of community government. Assuming that democracy is to continue as a functioning system we must also continue that double relationship in some sense, no matter how broad the community may actually come to be.

In simpler times the double relationship of citizen to community developed naturally, through processes of community interaction. In contemporary times, on the contrary, it must be developed by some agency because of the complexity of relationships involved. Education is one of the important institutions which can assist in this development. It must function both in the field of vocational education and in the field of general education, since the latter is the system which offers students the kind of general background necessary to citizenship functions.

General education becomes even more important, since there are trends in American life, and especially in American metropolitan life, which interrupt the relationship of citizen to community. One of these trends, long established, is the increasing power of political machines. The machine claims to be the essential of democracy, and to be completely responsive to the will of the people. Actually, it aims at centralized control of government through the passive acquiescence of the majority of the citizens in its activities. It does not encourage, to say the least, the exercise of critical and evaluative faculties on the part of the citizenry. To the extent that most citizens do not have such faculties in any case, the functioning of the machine is facilitated. To the extent that they do have such faculties but have no interest in applying them to community problems, the machine control of politics is easy. General education has as one of its aims both the development of critical abilities and the direction of interests toward contemporary affairs.

A second trend, more recent than the development of political machines and of quite a different kind, is the growth of specialists in government. The specialist has become necessary in many areas of government because of the complex problems involved in the control of a modern urban community. It is no longer true, if it ever was true, that every citizen is competent to perform every government function. Fire protection, police protection, sanitation services, maintenance of the physical structure of cities, inspection and regulation of food, transportation, and many other problems can be met in the modern community only by means of a specialized background and training. Even political machines have recognized this fact by mitigating their opposition to civil-service devices to assure permanency of careers in government.

The specialist in government meets problems of control, of planning, and of the interrelationship of function which can be solved only on the basis of a fair degree of knowledge of contemporary society and on the basis of an exercise of critical judgment by the controlling majority in a community. In the nature of the case, few citizens will be as well versed in a particular specialty as the official concerned. It is not more specialized knowledge that is necessary, but more judgment.

The program of general education also has as its aim the creation of precisely the faculties necessary to exercise wise control of the specialist. It urges the assumption of responsibility for community affairs by the student. It is a prime necessity in contemporary life.

But once again we must sound a warning that general education is not a magical device by virtue of which our problems will be solved. Nor is it a device which is enthusiastically welcomed either by a majority of students or by all the adult citizens of a community. Students look on the program, in some cases, as being composed of a "lot of useless stuff" because it is not directly related to their vocational interests. Indirectly, of course, it is related, since most vocations can be practiced only in a relatively orderly society, but that fact is not immediately obvious. Vested interests, political and otherwise, may give lip service to general education, but actually they are often opposed to it for the simple reason that they fear an informed citizenry. If the general-education program fails of its purpose, the cause of failure will not be exclusively with education as an institution. It will also rest in the other institutions of the community which have hampered the educational institution.

The contemporary function of education in social organization, then, includes not only such instruction as will permit the school population to assume a vocational position in the social structure but also some program of general education which will permit them to assume a functioning role as citizens.

CONTEMPORARY PROBLEMS OF EDUCATION

The problems of education which interest us here arise from the attempt of the educational institution to perform its function of relating many highly differentiated segments of contemporary society to the whole society. If education is to function adequately, it becomes necessary to include in its system most of, if not all, the individuals in our population, whatever segment they may typify. Some of the problems arising from that situation relate to the pressure of numbers of students on the school system, others to the philosophy of education, and still others to contemporary attitudes towards education. Let us consider these in order.

1. *Mass Education.* The problem inherent in our expanding school population, at all levels of instruction, is usually referred to as the problem of mass education. There has been, as we have noted, a tremendous expansion in the number of students with which the educational institution must deal. One estimate suggests that the enrollment in secondary schools is now seventy times what it was two generations ago, and that the enrollment in colleges is almost thirty times what it was two generations ago.[5] Naturally this increase has made necessary an increase in teaching staff, in supervisory staff, and in the physical plant and equipment of the educational system.

Important as the problem of numbers of students may be, even more important is the problem that arises from the fact that the increase in numbers of students has been accompanied by an increase in the different kinds of students with whom education must deal. As we suggested before, our differentiated population includes individuals different in abilities, skills, backgrounds, needs, and future plans. Doubtless other complex populations have also been highly differentiated in all these respects, but ours is one of the few in which the expectation is that all these types will find some place in a school system. Education in the past was usually the prerogative of members of the higher classes only. In our own past culture, it used to be open to members of all classes who could afford the leisure from earning a living and the expenses involved in tuition and other charges. But we now hold that education should be the prerogative of all, a position which implies that it should be free, or at least only nominally expensive. Only in certain localities have we actually established free education, but the trend is in that direction, with the result that all types of individuals must be served in some way by the educational institution.

[5]*General Education in a Free Society.* Harvard University Press, Cambridge, 1945.

Some students plan to finish high school and then go directly into a vocation. Others plan for college, others for business schools, others for trade schools. Yet they must all, however different their skills and their plans may be, function as citizens in their communities. More and more the high schools of the country have specialized their curricula to make provision for differing needs plus the common need of all citizens for basic citizenship instruction.

American colleges are now facing the same situation which a few years ago confronted the high schools. Students are attending college in increasing numbers, for different reasons, and with different plans. They are of differing levels of ability, of varied interests and backgrounds. The college, if it is to continue the process of relating all these individuals to the society in a meaningful way, must adjust to these differences. Some colleges are making genuine efforts to fulfill their function along the lines suggested. In others there is considerable opposition to the change on the part of those who wish to see the college remain as it was in the past. They hold that its purpose is intellectual stimulation and intellectual growth. And while they do not wish to see college education limited to any one caste in the community, they do insist that its primary purpose of intellectual growth be retained.

The problem of mass education then becomes a problem based not only on numbers or even on the differentiation in the student population. It becomes a problem of numbers and differentiation *plus* educational philosophy. There is a measure of disagreement in this area. One approach holds that we have tried to impose on a mass of students an educational system which still clings to a philosophy developed in connection with limited numbers of students. Since the relating of a mass of people to an organized society is a problem far different from the relating of a specialized segment of the population to an organized society, they hold that we must change our educational philosophy. The opposing group insists that the basic educational philosophy of human development must remain the same, and that specialized training schools must be established for those individuals whose interests lie outside the field of intellectual development. One critic goes so far as to insist that we have not spread education among the mass of the people; that we have tried to, but the result has been the destruction of "true" education rather than its spread among larger numbers of individuals. He suggests that courses in "beauty culture," in "how to be an air hostess," and similar offerings in some of our colleges are all useful courses but their intellectual content is such as to make them more suitable for some other kind of institution than a college. If they are admitted as college courses, they tend to "debase" the whole curriculum.

2. *Educational Philosophy.* This disagreement brings us to a discussion of the second contemporary problem of education mentioned earlier, the philosophy of education. We are using the term *philosophy* here in its popular meaning of "a more or less integrated system of ideals, goals, and programs." A philosophy in that sense is an important adjunct of any grouping, since it may influence very strongly the behavior of its members. It is a fact, however, that the goals and programs of most vital groups do change, as they adjust to changing cultural patterns. The ideals involved may remain stable; the specific expressions and applications of those ideals change. There appears to be no good reason why educational philosophy also should not change. Doubtless a professional educator, familiar with educational methods and techniques, can best indicate the directions of such change. We suggest here only the outlines of the changing relationships between the educational institution and the social organization which indicate the necessity of some kind of corresponding change in educational philosophy.

Since sociologists define education as a *transmissive* institution, the question arises what shall be transmitted and to whom it shall be transmitted. In turn, as soon as we attempt to answer that question, we enter the domain of educational philosophy, since we are dealing with the aims and purposes of the educational system.

As to what shall be transmitted, it is obviously necessary in a differentiated population to transmit somewhat different things to different segments, admitting that basic citizenship training should be available for all. Those individuals who do not have the capacities or the interests fitting them to engage in abstract intellectual investigations can hardly participate in an educational system based on intellectualism. They may, on the other hand, find their places in systems transmitting technical, trade, or other types of information. Obvious as such a statement may be, the implications of the proposal will meet with many objections. One major difficulty is that currently a good many people have made a fetish of the word *college*. Because a college education was once restricted to the "upper classes," they hold to the belief that it is a privilege to attend college, and they make every effort to become college students, not with the purpose of intellectual development but with the purpose of attaining the decorative appellation of "college graduate." To suggest that they enroll in some other type of institution because of their intellectual incapacity or their lack of interest in the traditional college curriculum is considered grossly insulting. As they insist on attending college, they inevitably cause a change in the purposes, standards, and other characteristics of the American college. This is a process which has been going on for a generation.

It is also the type of change which has taken place in secondary schools, according to reports of high-school officials. One educator charges, doubtless with exaggeration, that high schools exist mainly for the purpose of keeping hordes of students off the streets where they might get into trouble. He asserts that only a bare minority of students seriously work at their studies.

This modification of both high school and college is one aspect of the general social changes we have been undergoing. We have lengthened the period of childhood by requiring attendance at school to a more advanced age than formerly. We have intentionally made education available to the majority of our population. Labor organizations have developed which restrict the entry of young people into economic life. Our expressed standards of child care and of adolescent care are of a high order. But there is one point to be made about these changes: none of them is evil; all of them are good. The educational disorganization which has resulted, in part, from changes of that order came about unintentionally. We may suggest that it is disorganization of a temporary nature incident to the readjustment of our educational philosophy. As that philosophy comes to include more realistically the goal of adapting the educational system to the needs and capacities of individuals, reorganization will become possible.

Thus far, it is fair to say that the educational institution has responded to the needs of two groupings in the population: the subnormal and the average. Most school systems have special classes or special institutions for the subnormal individual. Most school systems have adapted curricula and standards to the capacities of the average student. Few systems have organized procedures whereby the above-average student may either proceed at a more rapid rate than his fellows or may, if he proceeds at the same rate, get more detailed and more thorough grounding in his subjects. Yet it is as important, perhaps more important, to utilize the capacities of the above-average as it is to utilize those of the average or subnormal student. This statement applies not only to elementary and secondary schools; it applies also to institutions of "higher learning."

One difficulty in the way of permitting the intellectually gifted to advance at a more rapid rate than other students lies in the fact that maturity of personality may be delayed until a late age. The immature student, permitted to advance intellectually, will emerge from the process with possible maladjustments. On the other hand, it is true that the ordinary teaching methods of the ordinary school, and possibly of the college, do relatively little to promote maturity of personality. Such areas of development as are inherent in the assumption of responsibility for the preparation of lessons, the encouragement of independent investigation, and originality of thought and approach are lacking in many of our schools and colleges. If the system were reorganized in such a way that the intellectually gifted were encouraged toward maturity of personality as well as toward intellectual development, maladjustment of the immature intellectual would be less likely to appear.

All that we have been saying implies the reorganization of the educational system in the direction of even greater complexity than it now exhibits, and it also implies a change in the application of our educational philosophy. Granted that the traditional high school and the traditional college have been modified by the influx of large numbers of students, it becomes necessary to supplement both with institutions of "higher learning" for the intellectually gifted. It is impossible to maintain all our secondary and college systems as purely intellectual systems because such a program would, if realistically carried out, exclude many students. Those who were excluded would presumably be left to a haphazard orientation to the social organization. It is part of the goal of contemporary education to include as many members of the population as possible, and that goal becomes valid from the sociological viewpoint because of the complexity and interdependence of the contemporary social organization. Additions to the existing educational system of the kind we have suggested are a necessity.

Steps in this direction have been taken. One program proposes the granting of a "first degree" at the end of two years of college work, which would be the terminal point for the great majority of students. Beyond the first two years, training would be highly specialized along scientific and intellectual lines. Other programs resemble this one in their emphasis on the necessity of "terminal courses" of one or two years' duration for the majority of college students, though they do not always advocate granting the traditional "first degree" at the end of that period. Still other programs propose to retain the four-year college curriculum but to compel students to undergo a period of general education during the first two of those four years, with more concentrated study during the final two years of their college career.

Whatever specific program is put into effect, it is encouraging to note that educators are concerned over the threatened educational disorganization and over the malfunctioning of our present system. A willingness to change educational philosophy and practices is becoming more common. The sociologist reiterates his emphasis that the change must be in the direction of relating the different segments of the population to the whole society in a meaningful way if education is to function adequately in the social organization.

3. *Attitudes toward Education*. In America education has been traditionally a major social value. From the earliest days of the settlement of the country, schools have been a primary concern and the schoolmaster has been an important individual in the community. The respect accorded to education and to the educated man was one of the characteristics of early American society.

There is some indication that our attitude toward education is in reality less favorable than it used to be, even though we still indulge in "speech reactions" which disguise our real feelings. Particularly it appears that we have lost something of the respect we used to have for education. The evidence for these statements comes from two directions.

First is the relative amount of money we spend for educational purposes. In a money economy, expenditures reflect something of the values we place on various objects and activities, though they do not by any means reflect the whole of our valuations. We do not spend as much money for education and for educators as we do for some other things which are obviously less important to social organization than is education. To cite only one example, the American Association for the Advancement of Science—a group not ordinarily given to emotional judgments or to moralistic pronouncements—in its *Bulletin* for November, 1946, points out that in 1940 the total cost of the salaries of all teachers in our elementary and secondary schools was about $1,314,000,000, a respectable sum. Yet during that same year the total Federal *tax* on liquors and tobacco was about $1,232,000,000. Note that this was not the total sum expended for those commodities; it was only the Federal tax collected. It is difficult to escape the conclusion that this spending pattern represents to some extent the relative valuation we place on education and on certain other commodities.

Other aspects of our expenditures for education are interesting. During 1942 we spent about $2,300,000,000 for public elementary and secondary schools in the United States.[6] This was a per capita cost of $17.25 for each person in the country. Of this total sum, $1,353,151,000 was spent for the salaries of teachers, principals, and supervisors. This represented an average salary of $1507 for each employee of the classes mentioned. In itself this is not a very large sum, but we must remember that it is an average, which means that some teachers received less than $1507 and some, more than that amount. Thus we find that certain states paid the following average annual salaries to teachers: $517, $750, $778, $787. The highest average salary noted is in New York State: $2618.[7] A few other states pay an average greater than $2000, but most of them fall below that level, some of them far below it. It is hardly to be expected that an impartial observer comparing these salaries with those of other occupations would conclude that we value education above other fields of activity.

Second, the matter is not entirely one of monetary expenditures. Our real estimate of the worth of education is shown by the further fact that we habitually accord an artificial position to the elementary and to the high-school teacher in many of our communities. We demand of them a type of restricted conduct and of subordination to outmoded community mores to which few of us would ourselves submit. The teacher is often the subject of exaggerated gossip. Most other women in the community may smoke, dance,

[6]*Statistical Abstract of the United States*, 1944–1945 issue, Table 242, p. 232.
[7]Ibid. Table 245, p. 235.

and even drink without exciting any particular apprehension. The teacher who does any of these things lays herself open to sharp reprimand and may be dismissed from her position. It is assumed that other girls in town will date a man or men, according to their good fortune. If the teacher dates, she is at once suspected of misconduct.

Now it is true that the above description of attitudes toward teachers is not typical of metropolitan communities, although remnants of discrimination against teachers may also be found there. It is, however, typical of attitudes in thousands of smaller communities throughout the United States. Such practices in relation to teachers may be evidence of a perfectly valid and desirable interest on the part of the citizen in the type of person who educates his children. Naturally, most people do not want children to be in intimate contact with undesirable people. If general community standards of conduct accorded more closely with the standards demanded of teachers, we might accept that explanation. In view of the fact that standards demanded of teachers differ from general community standards to such an extent that they may fairly be described as discriminatory, it appears that some other explanation is more likely to be true.

The American Association for the Advancement of Science, in the same issue of the *Bulletin* cited earlier, comes to the conclusion that the "schools are no longer one of the chief interests of the people of this country." It is somewhat surprising that our population should exhibit this lack of interest in education at the very time that we are planning to spend large sums for the development of research in science and in technology. The *Bulletin* further asks how so great a scientific structure can be erected on "so weak and crumbling a foundation as our poorly supported public school system."

To the sociologist, the explanation of our contradictory attitude toward education on the one hand and scientific research on the other hand lies in the fact that we have not, in America, viewed our educational system as an integrated unit. We have, of course, realized the fact that admission to higher branches of the system depends on the completion of work in the lower branches, but we have tended to assume that that was a purely formal relationship. We have overlooked the fact that the higher branches of the educational system assume not only that students will possess certificates indicating the completion of prescribed courses in the lower branches, but that, as a result of completing those courses, they will carry with them a foundation of knowledge on which to build further. The tendency has therefore been to view scientific and professional careers as entirely the concern of colleges and technical schools. Under those circumstances it is natural to assume that an elaborate structure of scientific research can be erected without reference to conditions in the elementary and secondary schools.

A second reason for the contradictory attitude noted may be found in the fact that we commonly assume that the "value" of an education lies in what it can do for the individual who is educated. It is supposed to help him to make more money, to secure a higher status in the community, to live more happily, and a number of other things. Education has produced this result for many individuals, of course, and there is every reason why it should continue to do so. Our point here is that if education is viewed so largely as a personal asset, it is natural that the support of education should be expected to come from those who have benefited, particularly in the case of higher education. The community has tended to establish and support only the minimum educational structure, leaving it to individuals to get as best they may their advanced training.

The fact of the matter is, as we have indicated, that education is as much a community instrumentality by which the orderly organization of society is furthered as it is an individual instrumentality by means of which individual goals are attained. The meanings which the educational instruction may have for the individual are perfectly valid meanings. The societal meanings of education differ from the individual meanings, but they also are valid. It is again a case of the balancing of meanings and, incidentally, of assets and liabilities. Our complex societal structure has brought us many assets not known in the simpler rural cultures, products of technology, leisure, and all the other adjuncts of civilization; but it has also brought with it the fact of interdependence, in itself a neutral fact, one which may be either asset or liability. It becomes a liability if the conditioning and training institutions of society are so weak that individuals on whom we depend are actually undependable, either because they lack skills or because they lack the emotional organization necessary to the performance of their functions.

One of the major conditioning and training institutions of society is education. If we permit it to crumble we face disorganization and conflict.

As increasing numbers of our population come to a realization of the fact that education is not an individual luxury but a necessary societal instrumentality, we may hope for a realistic change in popular attitudes towards it.

4. *Federal Aid to Education.* Traditionally in America the educational institution has been the responsibility of local jurisdictions. In some cases the locality involved corresponds to political subdivisions such as the city, town, and county. In many cases these subdivisions are further divided into school districts, the populations of which organize, finance, and otherwise manage their own school systems. This is an allocation of responsibility to minor population groups which is found in almost no other government activity.

In recent years the states have assumed a greater degree of control over local school systems by means of inspection, teacher certification, standardized curricula, and other supervisory functions. Some few states have carried this system so far that education is, to all intents and purposes, a state function. But in many other areas of the country the state authorities are limited to mild suggestions regarding school affairs, and those suggestions often are not welcomed.

Such being the case, it is not surprising that there has been a great deal of opposition to Federal supervision of education. In fact, Federal activities in education have largely been limited to research in educational techniques and practices of a general nature, except when Federal authorities have been specifically requested to make suggestions. Recently there has been made available to states, and through the states to localities, some financial aid which, if it were accepted, would enable many local jurisdictions to engage in significantly expanded educational programs. The difficulty is that these funds are available only to systems which meet certain standards set by Federal authorities. This setting of standards has been interpreted as "Federal control of education" and, together with fears of even greater "control," has come to be an area of disagreement and conflict among educators.

In addition to this generalized fear, there is the further specific fact that Federal standards forbid discrimination against minority groups in the educational system. In states with large numbers of Negroes this requirement naturally operates to prevent acceptance of Federal funds.

The whole question of Federal aid to education is one which professional educators must settle. We suggest, however, that if education is an important instrumentality of social organization, it seems plain that the Federal government, as the center of social organization, must assume responsibility for the school system. The obvious danger in such a procedure is that, conceivably, a dictatorial, centralized government might subvert the educational institution to its own purposes, a development we have witnessed in the case of some European "police states." On the other hand, such a development would probably come in education after a dictatorial government has been established and was in control of other areas of life. In any case, it is an eventuality that need not completely hinder Federal aid, as contrasted with control, in the educational field.

5. *Segmentation.* Finally, we note the problem of the segmentation of society, a process to which education has in part contributed. To the extent that the educational institution trains its students only in specialized vocations, it tends to assist the process by which our total population is broken up into separate groupings with little integration. The program of general education will, when it functions adequately, offset this tendency.

SUMMARY: EDUCATION IN SOCIAL ORGANIZATION

From the sociological viewpoint the educational institution is the system which transmits culture patterns from one generation to the next. It functions most actively in those areas of life which are of major interest to the culture of which it is a part. Traditionally it transmits not only knowledge to be learned but also ideals and behavior patterns to be imitated.

In general, the complexity of an educational institution varies as the complexity of the culture of which it is a part. In our own culture it is highly elaborated.

The function of education in contemporary culture is expressed in the two emphases—on vocational education and on general education—between which a reconciliation of viewpoints is necessary.

Contemporary problems of education include those arising from the phenomena incident to "mass education," readjustments of our educational philosophy, and attitudes toward education. As an increasing proportion of our population realizes that in our modern complex society education may function as a powerful agent of social organization, we may expect a more favorable attitude toward education to develop.

READINGS

PANUNZIO, CONSTANTINE. *Major Social Institutions.* The Macmillan Company, New York, 1939. Chapter 16, "The Educational Institution."

DONHAM, WALLACE B. *Education for Reasonable Living.* Harvard University Press, Cambridge, Massachusetts, 1944. The former Dean of the Harvard School of Business Administration develops the theme that the function of liberal education is to prepare men and women to make intelligent and purposeful adaptation to social change.

General Education in a Free Society, by a Committee of the Harvard Faculty, Harvard University Press, Cambridge, Massachusetts, 1944. A study of American education, with some emphasis on secondary education, and with proposals for its reorganization.

SARGENT, PORTER. *Between Two Wars: The Failure of Education, 1920–1940,* the author, Boston, 1945. A report of the findings, opinions, and recommendations of educators and scientists, with caustic comments by the author, who has had wide and intimate contact with education in the United States.

CHAPTER XVI

THE POLITICAL INSTITUTION

THE FIELD of government and of the state forms the specialized area
of societal life which is investigated by political science. Our concern here, as has been the case with other institutions, is not with
the internal functioning of government systems, but with the relationships between government and the social organization. As a
point of departure we propose to define several terms used in connection with the political institution.

POLITICAL TERMS

First of all we may define the political institution, the major
subject of our discussion, as follows:

> *The political institution is the institution formally concerned*
> *with the maintenance of order in society.*[1]

Order in this sense refers to the smooth and efficient interactional
functioning of individuals and of groups within a society. It is
not the same as organization, since organization implies an amount
of complexity not always found in connection with order.[2] Neither
is it the same as co-operation, for conflict may be orderly. Order
does not imply anything beyond the efficient interactional functioning of individuals, regardless of what the ends or purposes of
that functioning may be.

Maintenance of order is a necessity in any aggregate, but in
simpler associations that function is performed by a good many

[1] *Encyclopedia of the Social Sciences*, Vol. VII, pp. 8–15.
[2] H. P. Fairchild (Ed.), *Dictionary of Sociology*, p. 287. Philosophical Library,
New York, 1944.

groups and institutions as a by-product of their functions in connection with other areas of living. Religion very commonly has a share in the maintenance of order, as does the family institution when it is inclusive of large kinship groupings. It is only as the population aggregate increases and differentiation appears in the grouping that a separate political institution becomes necessary. Even after the appearance of such an institution, many groups continue to maintain order within their own structure by means of their own rules and regulations, referring to government only such matters as concern their relationships to other groups. A familiar example of this in our own times may be found in the relationship between management and labor. As far as internal structure is concerned, the two aggregates themselves provide for orderly procedures. But relationships between the two are regulated in terms of explicit statute law in the last analysis, though of course some of their relationships may be by mutual agreement without reference to statute law.

In our own times, as we might expect, government is an important aspect of social organization because of the high degree of social differentiation which we have developed. There is some evidence that it is becoming increasingly important, though the present trend may be a temporary phase of organization, to be replaced by more informal relationships as we learn to adjust the several segments of society to each other more effectively.

There are several terms commonly used with reference to the political institution which differ in meaning and connotation. Unfortunately there is some disagreement as to the exact definition of certain terms. The following meanings should be adequate if they are used consistently.

1. *The state* is a form of human association based on the allocation of powers of control, usually in accordance with a system of ideas such as those embodied in constitutions and bills of rights. It is important to emphasize the fact that the state is not the same thing as the community or society. The state is a creation of the community, or of society, with specific, limited functions and purposes.[3] Society is a form of human association, as the state is, but it is much more inclusive than is the state. In fact, the state is often

[3] R. M. MacIver, *Society: Its Structure and Changes*, p. 14. Long & Smith, New York, 1931.

forbidden to exercise its powers of control in certain areas of societal life—in religion, for example, and, in the United States, in many aspects of business affairs. The powers of the state may be restricted in some other areas of life, though their exercise may not be absolutely forbidden as in the case of religion. An example of elementary restrictions on the authority of the state may be found in our practices with reference to civil rights.

At some periods, both in the past and in more recent times, there have been attempts to make the state coextensive with the whole area of societal relationships, precisely as there have been attempts to make other specialized patterns—religion, for example—inclusive of the whole area. Such is the theory of contemporary totalitarian states, including Russia and other dictatorships. The difficulty with that kind of state, from the traditional American viewpoint, is that, while it may provide for the furtherance of interests common to the whole aggregate, it interferes seriously with the furtherance of interests which are primarily individual. Individual interests which differ in any degree from common interests tend, in fact, to disappear, because collectively controlled influences tend to shape all personality interests toward a common pattern. Rigid educational systems, guided propaganda material, and even recreational patterns may all be made to serve collective purposes. In case they do not operate effectively, the deviating individuals may be "liquidated" or confined in prisons. But the appeal to force becomes progressively less necessary when the conditioning influences operate effectively and individual dissent tends to disappear.

The state, then, is a specific form of human association to which specific authority is given in certain areas of life by the large collectivity we call society.

2. *Government* is the organized system of functions through which the authority of the state is applied to given situations and through which the other purposes of the state are carried out. In this sense, government is not a form of human association so much as an arrangement of functions in relation to each other and to the purposes of the state. Government does, of course, operate through human beings, but they are limited in their activity by the organized system of relationships in terms of which they must function. It is this activity which makes concrete the more or less abstract ideas contained in constitutions, bills of rights, and similar documents.

The specific organization of government may vary from time to time within a state, as cultural changes modify the patterns of behavior to which the activities of government apply. Such activities need not imply the desertion of the basic system of ideas on which the state is founded. Thus it has become necessary for the Federal government in the United States to assume a large measure of control over aviation and an increasing measure of control over certain aspects of industry and labor. This situation represents a change in the functioning of government, but as long as the change does not violate constitutional guarantees and other rights, it is not a change in the state as we have known it. Much more significant for our basic structure as a state are the evidences of gradual change in unofficial practice related to the guarantee of rights in connection with arrest, investigation by the police, and search and seizure. These practices are, let us repeat, not officially sanctioned. But in so far as they take place, they imply a desertion of the basic ideals on which our state has been founded, ideals relating to the rights of the citizen in conflict with his government.

Much more public objection has been made to changes in government function affecting business and industry than has been made to the gradual invasion of the rights of citizens. One reason for the differing emphasis is, of course, that many more people are involved in business and industry than are involved in situations likely to bring about an invasion of their civil rights. But another reason is that we are apt to confuse government, an organized instrumentality of the state, with the state itself, a form of human association based on the allocation of powers of control. Confusion of that kind often causes difficulties in the necessary readjustments of government functioning because the changes are interpreted as implying an alteration in the state rather than simply in the structure of administrative relationships. It also tends to cloud the issue in connection with insidious, but unauthorized, incursions on civil rights.

3. *Politics* is, in modern times, a term usually used with reference to the strategical practices by means of which certain special groups secure administrative positions in the government structure, through elections or by some other orderly procedure. When the groups concerned are of long standing, as they usually are, and when they are recognized as exponents of specific approaches to government

functioning, they are referred to as *political parties*. In America, and in some other countries, most political parties are concerned only with government; they do not propose to alter the fundamentals of the state. Democrats, Republicans, Socialists, and even Communists allege that they are devoted to "Americanism" as defined in the United State Constitution and the Bill of Rights. Their differences concern the methods by which government shall function in connection with our basic ideals.

The word *politics* often carries with it the inference of dishonest or "shady" practices, so much so that dishonest or dishonorable tactics in relationships other than government often bear the name *politics*. Thus when an individual secures promotion or other benefits in business, industry, education or religion through intrigue, he is said to be "playing politics." This connotation is a current addition to the basic meaning of the word which properly means simply the practical science of governing.

Politics in government is sometimes contrasted with civil service or merit systems. Civil service and merit systems are organized procedures which attempt, in general, to accomplish three ends in connection with government functioning. First, they try to secure individuals with specific abilities for given positions in the government service, usually by examinations intended to test the relative fitness of applicants; second, they try to systematize promotion procedures, evaluation of employees, and rate of pay within established job classifications in the government service; and, third, they try to prevent the operation of politics in government employee relationships, with special emphasis on the dismissal of employees from the service. The procedures involved in civil service and merit systems are much the same as those employed in private industrial relations, but there has been considerable misunderstanding of them and objection to them in government administration. In spite of objections, they are well established in most Federal bureaus and they are being extended to many state and municipal governments, naturally not without opposition from politicians and from those who view politics as the chief instrument for attaining positions in the government service.

4. *Bureaucracy* is currently a popular word in connection with the functioning of government, especially the Federal government. Essentially it refers simply to the type of administrative organization

by which the general functions of government are carried on through the operation of subdivisions called *bureaus*, to which are allocated specific functions. It is seldom used in that basic sense, however. Usually it refers to a rigid and routine officialism in the administration of government affairs which makes for stupidity, delay, and waste. As a term of reproach, very often unfairly applied, it should not concern us in this discussion of the nature of government, but, since our reactions may be colored by such "loaded" words we must pay some attention to it. The fact is that any large organization, government, business, or otherwise, shows a tendency to become unwieldy and cumbersome in its operation and to exhibit the bureaucratic characteristics of officialism, routine, and red tape. It is inaccurate to speak as though bureaucracy were confined to government organizations and absent from other types of organization. Undoubtedly bureaucracy is characteristic of present-day government, as it is of many nongovernment associations. It can be remedied by the employment of competent people and by the clarification of government administrative organization.

PATTERNS OF GOVERNMENT

Government is distinguished from other institutions by certain patterns which characterize it. The following are the important characteristic patterns.

1. *Force.* Government is the only contemporary institution which can legally use force in carrying out its functions. In most modern states the use of force is hedged about with many restrictions, the result being that much of government is actually noncompulsive in nature. But the possibility of using force remains in the background as one aspect of our relationship to government.

Other groups in our culture do use force, or the threat of force, to attain their ends. This need not be actual physical force, applied to injure the individual subjected to it in any physical way. It is often psychosocial, that is, it centers in threats to reputation, status, position, or security, a form of force which may be even more effective than the threat of physical force. The point is that in the case of those other groups the threat and the practice of force are illegal; while in the case of a government exercising, or threatening to exercise, force within prescribed areas and limits, the procedure is legal.

2. *Universal Application.* A second pattern characteristic of government lies in the fact that its procedures are applicable to everyone alike within its jurisdiction. This does not hold true of any other institution, unless it has some direct relationship to government. Religion in the United States is a purely voluntary matter, including only that segment of the population which chooses to follow religious patterns. Similarly, education is a voluntary matter beyond the area prescribed by government as compulsory. Business, recreation, and similar patterns are "free" except in so far as they are held to affect the public welfare and therefore become properly objects of interest to government. But government applies to all individuals alike.

Exceptions to that statement arising from the exercise of undue influence on government officials or from evasions of government regulations are illegal, and are held to be evidence of the malfunctioning of government. Hence, even though they exist, they do not contradict the principle of universal application.

There are, of course, regulations which apply to special categories of individuals rather than to the whole population. For example, doctors, lawyers, and other professional and semi-professional people are subject to special rules regulating their training, their licensing, and their mode of practicing their professions. Even in such instances, however, the regulations apply to all members of the given category alike, not to selected members only.

3. *Derivation of Authority.* Governments assert that they derive their right to exercise authority from some specialized grant which is either sacred or semisacred in nature. There are two general theories of the derivation of government authority.

First, according to the theory of the divine right of kings, the power to govern is vested by deity in an individual king, or in a king plus some kind of ruling class of nobility. In an exaggerated form this divine-right theory has been held to imply that "the king can do no wrong," no matter how hard he may try. In its more usual form it holds that king and nobility are specially gifted in matters of government and that they have divine sanction to perform the role of governors. There was undoubtedly some truth in that portion of the belief relating to special ability in governing when the majority of the population was ill-informed and when government was largely a matter of maintaining a corps of armed retainers to protect the ruling officials. The changing functions of government and the altered situation with respect to popular knowledge have made it currently an outmoded theory, though it is still held, in a diluted form, by some conservative people.

Rule by a limited class has been the commonest form of government. In simpler cultures the aged were assumed to be the proper segment of the population to exercise authority. Again, there was some logical ground for this belief when patterns of living changed very slowly, so that the experience of the aged prepared them to evaluate common situations in a way that the young could not; and when the exercise of authority involved chiefly the application of well-recognized and widely accepted standards. In some earlier democracies, whose verbal statements of ideals sound much like our own today, the right to rule was restricted to free citizens only. Slaves, who did much of the manual work and whose existence permitted a degree of leisure to free citizens, were either wholly without rights or else their rights were very much restricted. Our own culture in the past restricted the right to vote and to hold political office to individuals who owned property of a given value or who had a specified amount of money income. Even at present some jurisdictions in the United States require payment of a *poll tax* as a prerequisite to the voting privilege. This is the equivalent of restricting the franchise to that segment of the population which has an income sufficient to pay the tax. It has sometimes resulted in a situation whereby a minority as small as ten per cent of the potential voters actually vote, and hence that minority operates the government of the jurisdiction involved.

All these are examples of the restriction of authority and of the right to govern, directly or by representative, to a limited class of the population. They represent a weakened form of the divine-right theory, much removed from the overt statement that deity has given an individual king and his nobles the right to govern, but still implying that only a minority of the population has such a right. This diluted form of the divine-right theory is a phase of transition in belief to the second general type of theory relating to the derivation of the authority of government.

That second general theory rests in the belief that the authority

of government derives from the "consent of the governed," in varying ways and to varying extents. It holds that the population, as
a body, delegates to government the authority which it exercises.
The sanction for government operations comes not by gift from
deity to a special class, but from the willingness of a majority of the
"average citizens" in a population to submit to government. The
"will of the people" does, however, acquire a semisacred character
because it is assumed to be the expression of a force beyond the
capacities of any single individual or of any single class in the
population. This theory operates in connection with contemporary
democracies. We shall refer to it at greater length in our discussion
of the contemporary problems of government.

4. *Taxation.* A large portion of the cost of government is met by
the collection of taxes, payment of which is enforced by legal process. There have been many theories as to the fair apportionment of
tax burdens. The two most popular have been based on the benefits
received from government, according to which those who receive
most from the government should bear its costs, and the "ability to
pay" theory, according to which those who have the money to pay
taxes have to pay them. At present we combine the two theories,
but the fact is that the "ability to pay" theory is basic. Undoubtedly
the implication in tax apportionment is that those taxed have benefited from government operations and should therefore pay for
them. This belief is implicit in taxation by licenses, but in most
cases there is no attempt to adjust tax payments to benefits received.
If the citizen has the money or the property to pay taxes, he pays
them.

We can readily see that the exigencies of modern government
finance compel adherence to the "ability to pay" theory. Very
often those who receive most government benefits are not the financially well-to-do classes in the population. The large sums expended in government services can come only from those who have
a surplus of money beyond the needs of existence or the needs of
operating industry.

In any case, the tax structure of a state and the system of collecting taxes are further examples of the right of government to use
force, within the areas permitted by the state.

5. *Citizenship.* States establish, and governments administer,
procedures by which the special form of relationship to a state

known as *citizenship* may be acquired. Almost all states accord to persons born within their jurisdiction the rights of citizenship; and they also set up regulations by which at least some persons of alien birth may become citizens. Citizenship carries with it the privilege of participating in the rule of the state and also entails definite responsibilities to the state. Citizens are accorded the protection of their own government when they are traveling in, or doing business with, other jurisdictions.

In our own times we have tended to emphasize the rights and privileges inherent in citizenship rather than the responsibilities. One of the problems of government at present is to secure the intelligent participation of citizens in its processes, a problem which extends beyond the area of government into that of other institutions, as we noted in the case of education, which has as one of its functions the impartation of information and attitudes which will enable the average citizen to govern.

6. *Diplomatic Relations.* States also provide for formal relationships between their own governments and the governments of foreign powers, relationships which have become very complex and which are carried out according to strict regulations. These form the area of *diplomatic relations*, and have become increasingly important in present world organization. They are typical patterns of government because they hold a position different from the more informal relations which exist in business and other areas between groupings of citizens living in different jurisdictions.

GOVERNMENT IN SOCIAL ORGANIZATION

Government functions in social organization by providing a structure within which the activities of a society can be carried on. Component parts of that structure are laws, means of law enforcement and other protective devices, research organizations, and administrative units. All these function partly, of course, to protect the population against criminal activities, but much more significant is their function as a determiner of the legality of business and other civil affairs as contrasted with criminal affairs. Knowledge of what can and what cannot legally be done, both by the individual citizen himself and by others, is a prerequisite to many of the activities of daily life. We can proceed with a degree of assurance in the light of accepted definitions of *legal* and *illegal*, without which many of our relationships would be unstable. These facts are brought out when we travel in a country with a legal system different from that of our own.

To the extent that we live under an accepted system of relationships as determined by a government, we are obviously related to that government and to the culture of which it is a part. Government thus becomes a very important aspect of the social organization.

Aside from this **official** type of relationship, government also functions in maintaining the nexus of familiarity to which we referred in an earlier chapter as being an important aspect of culture. We may assume that people will drive their automobiles on the right side of the road; that railroads and other carriers will transport our goods according to agreement; that banks will, on the whole, be managed honestly; that many other occurrences will take place in accordance with an accepted code. Government is not the only agency which establishes such a nexus of familiarity; much of it comes from custom, for example. And yet one important aspect of government is that it legalizes custom and formally establishes certain habitual patterns as lawful. Even in the field of custom, therefore, government is not completely absent.

One result of familiarity with our own ways of living is that we, as individuals, are freed from the necessity of deciding the details of many transactions, and that therefore we can concentrate on our own specialized interests. Thus the owner of a business or an industry can devote his time to its operation instead of to the details of contract law, of a monetary system, or of the protection of his property, all of which are concerns of government.

One danger inherent in such a situation is that citizens may become so dependent on the complex of government relationships that they lose their individuality of initiative. Under such circumstances it is easy for the state, through the operation of government, to assume an increasing control over the major portion of societal life until it becomes totalitarian in nature. This may occur, not through the imposition of new controls against the will of citizens, but gradually, without awareness on the part of many citizens, and, in fact, with their co-operation when they are aware of it because each change appears to be minor in nature. This is a danger to which all complex states are open because

As societal relationships become more complex, the tendency is for government to expand its functions.

Differentiation of the population, the large numbers of individuals involved in social relationships, and the indirect nature of those relationships all give increasing scope for government activity.

A second danger is the possibility that minority interests in society—for example, business, religion, or a political party—may gain control of government functions and covertly subvert the government structure to their own minority purposes. In such a case it becomes difficult to dislodge the incumbents without threat of interrupting government services on which we have come to depend. Minority control of government thus becomes entrenched.

Government also functions in social organization, as we have suggested before, to apply concretely those basic ideals of the state which are considered important. In our own times we stress equality as an ideal; in some past periods class distinctions and class privileges were held to be more important than equality. In either case, some arrangements must be made to secure at least an approach to the concrete application of ideals in the area of actual human relationships. We must define *equality* in terms of human behavior and we must then erect structures to apply our definition. Or, in the case of the older view, we must allocate degrees of privilege and then establish agencies to make our allocation operative. It is government, in both instances, which functions in this respect.

In our own culture we have fallen far short of success in implementing the ideal of equality. Minorities of various kinds do not have equality of opportunity. Influences exerted by pressure groups lead to special attitudes and to the manipulation of legislative and other areas of government operation in favor of the groups concerned. Other situations of inequality exist. One important point must be made in connection with all of them. They are failures of the particular government concerned, not of the democratic state or of the ideal of equality. The remedy lies in greater emphasis on the democratic state and on the ideals of democracy rather than in the substitution of another kind of state or other ideals. This is an area in which it is necessary for the citizens as a whole to hold their government strictly to its responsibility to the state.

CONTEMPORARY PROBLEMS OF GOVERNMENT

The basic problem in the sociology of government is that of the distribution and the control of power. Government has the right to exercise authority in certain fields and to support its authority by the use of force. In democratic states the source of this power is the will of the people. And yet "the people" are amorphous and unorganized, while government is a compact and highly organized structure. There is every possibility that a given government may exceed the limits of its authority, that it may exercise power according to its own will rather than according to the will of the people. How is such power to be controlled and confined to the channels specified by the state?

It is from this basic problem that the specific problems we are to discuss below arise. Before proceeding to that discussion one may note that in our own state we have instituted a system of checks and balances between the executive, judicial, and legislative branches of our government. Other democratic states have taken similar steps. Since in these other democratic states power has escaped the control of checks and balances, and since in our own state political corruption, the manipulations of pressure groups, and public indifference have all tended to undermine the system of checks and balances, it would appear that the problem of the control of power remains unsolved. There are a number of suggestions as to how it might be solved, but the difficulties of putting those suggestions into practice are so great that they themselves become problematical.

Government Relationships

We have indicated that one of the functions of government is to provide a structure, or framework, within which activities of a society may be carried on. Certain groups insist that that is the *only* function of government, largely because they believe that the restriction of government to such a field is the only adequate way to control power. Other groups insist that it is *one* function, but by no means the only function, of government. They believe that the problem of the control of power can be solved in ways other than by the restriction of government functioning to a narrow field. Many of the current disagreements over government activity spring from this essential disagreement as to the relationships which government should bear to the other aspects of the social organization.

Those who subscribe to the "framework" theory of government assert that in general "the less government activity there is, the better." They believe that government should limit its functioning to the bare essentials necessary for the preservation of order and the maintenance of justice. Preservation of order implies not only the enforcement of criminal law and the prevention of rioting and other forms of disorderly conduct, but also the oversight of many activities in the interests of fair play. Fair-trade regulations enforced by government are held to be a proper field of activity by the state, since they apply to all business alike and their aim is to assure a common standard of honesty in trade relationships. Within the limits of fair-trade codes, individual and corporate enterprise, initiative, and competition are allowed to operate. It is the belief of the exponents of this view that the interaction of such factors as competition and free enterprise within the limits of minimum government control will result in the most efficient industrial system.

Similarly, exponents of the "framework" viewpoint believe that in such matters as those involved in the whole complex of relationships between management and labor the only function of government is to prevent oppressive practices which violate the law. Aside from the matter of such overt violations and their prevention, government has, according to this theory, no legitimate interest in the bargaining between labor and management.

We have been using illustrations of the "framework" theory taken largely from the economic field, but the restrictions suggested are by no means confined to economic relationships. The statement "that government which governs least governs best" is applied to all areas of societal life.

The theory we have been discussing is usually referred to as the laissez-faire theory, from the French phrase meaning "let [people] do, or make [what they please]." It is the doctrine that advocates giving the individual maximum freedom to follow his own interests with a minimum of regulation by the group. It is usually applied especially to economic relationships and to government regulation of economic relationships.[4] It is doubtful whether any group has ever advocated complete laissez faire in the sense of advocating no control of any kind. Those who claim to be laissez-faireists usually advocate also certain kinds of specialized legislation such as tariffs and other restrictions which would prevent people from literally "doing as they please." Laissez faire, then, is relative; it implies not the complete absence of government control but the restriction of government control in such a way that there shall be as little of it as possible.

In that sense very probably most of us are, or would like to be, advocates of the laissez-faire approach. There is no virtue in the exercise of control simply for the sake of control; and there is no particular assurance that controls will be wise and intelligent simply because they are instituted by a government agency. On the contrary, a social organization in which relationships were so controlled by common constructive motivations that no external controls were necessary would be close to an ideal state. Much as we might wish for such a state, however, it is doubtful if it will come to actuality in any measurable period of time.

The second school of thought in the matter of the relationships between government and other aspects of the social organization recognizes the values of the laissez-faire approach, but believes that modern conditions of life are such as to demand a greater degree of control by government than would be possible under the belief that "that government which governs least governs best." We may refer to this second school of thought as the direct-participation school, since its adherents believe that in certain areas of life it is necessary for government to take cognizance of situations not only as arbiter, or umpire, but as a participating force which makes its influence felt in any decisions that may be reached. Note that this is far from advocacy of government control simply for the sake of control. It is founded on the belief that the conditions of our interaction pattern are such as to require a change in the laissez-faire theory.

As an example of the direct-participation school of thought we may cite an illustration from the field of taxation, traditionally one of the important areas of government control. The advocates of

Fairchild, op. cit. "Laissez faire," p. 170.

laissez faire claim that the government is at liberty to levy taxes for purposes of revenue only, to meet necessary and legitimate expenses of government. The advocates of direct participation, on the other hand, believe that government may use its taxing power as an incentive, that is, as a means of influencing the actions of individuals or of groups. Thus the taxes on cigarettes are relatively high. They were first assessed not primarily for revenue but to raise the cost of cigarettes, for the purpose of preventing their sale, since they were assumed to be harmful. High taxes did not, of course, have the deterrent effect expected, since people continued increasingly to smoke cigarettes in spite of the cost. It is now apparent that cigarette taxes will produce an important revenue; and present taxes are undoubtedly designed primarily for revenue, though they were originally not so. Much the same situation exists in the case of taxes on liquors.

A more recent instance of "incentive" taxation may be found in certain of the excess-profits taxes and other corporation levies common during the past decade or so. Government authorities wished to encourage the disbursement of corporation income among the people, rather than permitting it to remain in the hands of the corporation as reserves. Unusually high taxes were placed on income so held as reserves instead of being disbursed to shareholders. One result was that the amount of disbursements was increased.

Criticism of such a government policy is twofold. (1) Are the ultimate purposes of government, in furtherance of which incentive taxation is applied, in themselves wise? (2) Regardless of the wisdom of the particular purposes involved, is it "right" for a government to use its taxing powers for incentive purposes? Laissez-faireists point out the possible dangers of such a course. It has been stated that the "power to tax involves the power to destroy." A tax which made a particular kind of activity unprofitable might have the net effect of destroying that activity. If it suited a government to prevent the operation of free education or of a free press, those institutions might be taxed out of existence, to say nothing of free enterprise in business and industry. That there is such an inherent danger in the operation of incentive taxation is undeniable.

Direct participationists, on the other hand, while they recognize the potential dangers of incentive taxation, also insist that we can guard against those dangers; and that in a complex society such as ours some pressure is necessary to secure the co-operation of special groups in programs for the general welfare of the people. They suggest that such pressure may well be exercised partly through incentive taxation. They ask what the condition of public education in the United States would be if there were no compulsory-education laws and no compulsory taxation for educational purposes. Doubtless many people would send their children to school and would pay the cost of operating schools. But to the direct participationists it seems obvious that some portion of the population would refuse to co-operate in an educational program without the exertion of some pressure. Public-education laws, then, become an incentive toward education. It is further suggested that there is little opposition to public education on a compulsory basis simply because the idea is an old one which we have gradually come to accept; while other forms of incentive taxation are new, and arouse opposition simply because they are new.

The controversy is not limited to the matter of taxation, however. Direct participationists also advocate government "interference" in labor-management disputes, in the control of wages and hours of work, in the control of prices, and in many other aspects of business and industry. They point out further that such government research bureaus as are maintained by the Department of Commerce and the Department of Agriculture are, in effect, government participation in business and in agriculture, not necessarily in the way of control but in the way of special aid and assistance.

Obviously, the controversy between the ideas of laissez faire and direct participation is by no means susceptible of easy or simple solution. In order to keep our picture of government as clear as possible, we should note that there is also a third school of thought regarding government and its functions, a school which is not common in America as yet, but which nevertheless has some advocates. This is the group which holds to the belief that "the more government there is, the better," a direct reversal of the laissez-faire approach. Very seldom are they as blunt in their statements as we have been in the last sentence, but the implications of communist and fascist government theories are, in effect, the exaltation of the state and of government to a position of supreme control. In many, if not in all, instances this theory is a completely cynical one, intended to benefit a minority interest, although it is presented as being necessary for the general welfare of the whole people. Totalitarianism as it exists in Russia, and as it existed in Germany is an example of this kind of approach.

Unfortunately, people who are opposed to what we have called the direct-participation school of government are apt to confuse that school with the totalitarian approach. Such an identification is not accurate, and it is unfair to the great majority of direct participationists. To say that the contemporary conditions of association require the intervention of government to a greater degree than did past conditions of association is not at all the same as saying that the intervention of government is in itself a desirable thing to be encouraged in every possible situation. The latter is totalitarian doctrine.

In attempting to evaluate the laissez-faire school in comparison with the direct-participation school, we ask a question couched in old-fashioned language, but one which strikes at the fundamental issue. The question is, "Where lies wisdom?" Wisdom implies not only a knowledge of facts relevant to the matters at issue, but also the ability to apply knowledge of facts to concrete situations; and it implies a certain personality-balance which will prevent distorted views of the matters at issue. If we contrast government activity and nongovernment activity, as the laissez-faireists do, where is wisdom? The answer at once becomes apparent: wisdom is neither exclusively with government nor is it exclusively with nongovernment; both have some share of it. Government certainly has the facilities to discover facts. Its research and informational divisions have almost unlimited opportunities to collect facts and to analyze them. Government also, in a democracy at least, represents the whole of the people. It therefore has a unique opportunity to avoid emotional unbalance and favoritism toward one party to an issue. It can evaluate a concrete situation, such as a particular strike in a given city, more dispassionately than can the labor or management groups directly involved.

On the other hand, the fact that government is removed from immediate relationship to a situation may lead its agents to oversimplify it. They may miss the realities of the relationships involved and view the situation as wholly a matter of information and research. Recent government policies have indicated that this attitude may seriously interfere with judgment, that is, with the application of factual knowledge to concrete situations. Certainly few people would argue that a stupid person automatically becomes wise when he is employed by the government!

Nongovernment participants in concrete situations often face the difficulties of not having all the facts which affect the situation, and of emotional bias because their own interests are directly concerned. Our own viewpoint often seems so nearly "right" that we cannot appreciate differing viewpoints. Again, the increase in class consciousness favors emotional bias in relation to our own class, with the consequence that there is an even greater need for an impartial arbiter of the issues involved. This is another example of conditions in a complex society which force us to alter our conduct from the patterns developed in connection with a simpler society.

The solution of the problems involved in conflicting views on the place of government in social organization will not come from mere advocacy of "more" government; nor will it come from complete opposition to government participation in the affairs of our daily lives. It will come only as a majority of our people can accept the fact that changes have taken place which have altered us from a simple to a complex society, and as we incorporate the fact of change into our thinking about government.

GOVERNMENT AND DEMOCRACY

We are committed to the faith that the best way to control the exercise of power by government and, at the same time, to bring about the most desirable type of social organization is the democratic way. Our own interest in the preservation of democracy requires that we consider what democracy is and what its implications for government and the social organization are.

It is commonly, and unthinkingly, said that democracy is "the will of the majority." That is a very questionable statement. The will of the majority is only a part of democracy. The majority may be wrong, or it may be unwise, or it may be prejudiced, or it may be ignorant. Democracy does not commit us to submission to a prejudiced or an ignorant majority of people simply because they are a majority. The mere fact that a majority "wills" that a thing be so, or that a certain course of action be followed, does not in the least guarantee that the thing will be so or that the course of action will be wise.

Much more important than the expressed will of a majority of people is *the basis on which that will is expressed*. If it is only the result of prejudice, of ignorance, or of the sheer force of numbers, it is evil, and no amount of rationalization will make it good. The founders of the American democracy made this fact very clear when they embodied a definite system of ideals in the Constitution, the Declaration of Independence, and the Bill of Rights. They had in mind certainly not the uncontrolled will of any majority of people. They conceived of the will of the majority as subject to the control of the basic system of ideals we have mentioned. An aggregate, majority or otherwise, is as much in need of self-control as is an individual. A group uncontrolled by democratic ideals is much more dangerous than an uncontrolled individual, simply because a group has more chance to exert arbitrary force than an individual has.

An expression of the basic doctrine of democracy in this respect appears in one of the state constitutions dating from about 1890: "Absolute, arbitrary power over the lives, liberty and property of freemen exists nowhere in a republic, *not even in the largest majority*."[5]

The last phrase, which we have italicized, indicates that the framers of the constitution in question felt it necessary to take cognizance of the growing belief that a majority, unwise though it might be and uncontrolled though it might be, was always right—a belief which had become common in the century between the writing of the United States Constitution and this particular state constitution. They felt it necessary to reaffirm the right of freemen to life, liberty, and property whenever that right was threatened, even by a majority.

Now a good many people will assent to propositions such as this; they will even assent enthusiastically. But the basis of their assent is more emotional than intellectual; they feel the force of the ideal without understanding it. Let us examine it further. The rights of "freemen" are protected from arbitrary action. But who are "freemen"? There is only one answer possible in our times. All men are freemen unless they have violated the criminal law and their violation has been proved by due process of law. Logically, then, Negroes, Japanese, Mexicans, and the members of all other minority groups are freemen. Logically also, no one, "not even the

[5]Constitution of Wyoming, Art. I, Sec. 7.

largest majority," has the right to exercise arbitrary power against their lives, liberty, or property. If the ideal is stated in this concrete way, the enthusiasm of a good many people for it will cool perceptibly. They will point out that many individuals in the minority groups we have mentioned are different from themselves; they are not as clean, or as well educated, or as honest as is the majority group. Such general statements are questionable, but even if we grant their truth the doctrine that they are not subject to arbitrary action still holds. The condition in which they are does not excuse discrimination; in fact, it should be an incentive to improve their status.

Democracy is a way of life, a way of establishing relationships with other people, based on a system of cherished ideals and beliefs. The practice of democracy in concrete situations may be very difficult. It is, however, the task of our society to meet that difficulty.

There is a further point. If we agree that the majority is not at liberty to exercise arbitrary power over a minority, the question arises, "What is a minority?" Again there is only one answer to that question. The ultimate and final minority is one person, the single individual. According to democratic theory no majority has the right to exercise absolute, arbitrary power over even one individual. Obviously, the majority *can* very easily oppress an individual, since it has the physical and psychosocial force to impose its will. But in a democratic state the majority is under obligation to exercise self-control and not to do what in many instances it could do. That is one aspect of equality. No single individual, and no minority group, is equal in force to the majority. The minority is "made equal" by the operation of self-imposed controls. A democratic government is under obligation to maintain that kind of equality both in so far as government may provide a framework and in so far as it may undertake direct participation in societal affairs.

Our discussion in the above paragraphs has been admittedly idealistic in the sense that we have been trying to state something of the system of ideals which underlies the democratic state. As we suggested earlier, these ideals are far from practical application in our own society. The point is that they must be preserved as goals, as ideals, even though at present they are not fully practiced. Their application in fact becomes an important social goal. It would be a mistake to drop the ideals simply because they are difficult of attainment.

There are a number of dangers in the democratic system as well as a number of advantages. Important among those dangers are the following.

1. The first danger is the belief that democracy is a system which will operate automatically. It is sometimes assumed that the mere fact that we have a democratic system of ideals and a government founded on those ideals in some way guarantees successful and happy living for individuals and an efficient and civilized organization for the society in which we live. This is not the case. "Eternal vigilance is the price of liberty." Democracy operates only to the extent that the average citizen makes it operate. It remains a potent force only as people live the democratic way of life. As we fail to do that, we find increasing problems arising in relation to the distribution of power.

2. Another danger is the belief that the ultimate in democracy is the granting of certain "rights" to citizens. This is a very popular emphasis at the present time. The democratic way of life is not simply the passive and placid enjoyment of a body of rights won for us in the first place by someone else and guaranteed to us by someone else. The enjoyment of rights is always conditioned by the exercise of responsibility implicit in the rights. The mark of a democratic society is not only to preserve its own rights, but also to accord to others those same rights. It is not only a matter of self-interest; it is also a matter of vital interest in others. As Professor Harold D. Laswell says, "Society is democratic in the degree that it practices mutual respect among men. Democracy is a commonwealth of mutual deference."[6] This is an emphasis uncommon in our own times, but it is vital to the existence of democracy.

Emphasis on rights to the exclusion of responsibilities is dangerous because it may lead to the concentration of power in the hands of government. Under the guise of giving new rights to citizens, a government may actually assume more and more responsibility until the point is reached at which citizens passively accept dictation by their government. The rise of tyrants has not always been the

[6]*Science, Philosophy, and Religion,* Chap. XIV, p. 238, Note 1.

result of forcible oppression. It has often been the result of gradual undermining of the functioning of the citizens under the guise of an extreme solicitude for their welfare.

3. A third danger inherent in the democratic system is the belief that political liberty can exist apart from other kinds of liberty. This also is a very common belief. It is held that political liberty can be maintained in an organization which does not also maintain religious liberty, the rights of minority groups, freedom of research and information, and similar patterns. Experience has indicated that liberty is one, not many; the loss of liberty in one field immediately threatens the loss of liberty in other fields. There are not four freedoms, or a dozen freedoms; there is only one, freedom undivided. We cannot permit the freedom of information, of education, of research, or of discussion to be limited without also limiting freedom in all fields. Some further discussion of this topic is necessary.

GOVERNMENT AND FREEDOM

Our third problem in relation to the distribution and control of power lies in the relationship between restraint and freedom and in the meaning of the word *freedom*. It is a difficult relationship to describe.

To a fair number of people freedom means the entire absence of restraint, so that an individual is at liberty to do as he pleases without regard to the results of his actions. This is a childish idea of freedom, and it remains childish even when it is held by adults. Freedom in that sense is impossible for any except an individual living in complete isolation. As soon as we enter into group relationships, we find ourselves affected by the actions, beliefs, and influences arising from the contacts we have with other people. Their reactions to our patterns of behavior and to the results of our patterns of behavior force themselves on our consideration.

To most of us freedom means the relative, not the complete, absence of restraint. We assume that there will be certain areas of relationship in which we shall have to restrain ourselves or be restrained by those about us. One difficulty with this concept of freedom lies in the definition of the areas of necessary restraint and in the determination of the degree of restraint permissible. Such definitions are largely matters of custom, changing with different cultural situations. In some instances, however, deliberate read-justments of areas of freedom are made, at times to the benefit of specialized groupings in the population. For example, business and industry call for "economic freedom," by which they usually mean a reduction in the amount of restraint on economic activity in their own sphere only. They advocate higher tariffs and other restraints on foreign goods at the same time that they insist most determinedly on freedom for the management of American industry. They object to "forcing" workers to join unions at the same time that they themselves are combining to control production and prices. Simi-larly, some religions ask for complete freedom for their own type of religion and demand strict control of deviating religions. The press is much interested in "freedom of the press" at the very time when it is exhibiting an increasing degree of monopolistic practices.

All this is simply to indicate that the definition of the areas in which we wish freedom varies with specialized interests as well as with custom and tradition. There is no concrete and generally accepted pronouncement on the matter.

We must note also a third definition of freedom, not a new defini-tion by any means, but one on which there is a new and increasing emphasis. According to this approach, "real" freedom is defined as freedom from responsibility, perhaps not directly in those terms but in terms which imply that belief. It leads to the somewhat paradoxical statement that the more control there is, the greater the freedom of the individual, in somewhat the following fashion. There are many areas of life in which decisions as to the proper course of conduct must be made by an individual. It is in many instances difficult to make wise decisions, and in all cases the makings of a decision involves effort. If a benevolent government establishes regulations in a large number of situations which define concretely the "proper" or "wise" course of procedure, an individual need not decide for himself what he should do under the given circumstances. He is told what to do. In other words, he is "free" of the necessity of making his own decisions, and he can use the freedom and the energy thus acquired to pursue his own interests.

For example, if regulations should be established requiring the wearing of a uniform, obviously we, as individuals, should not have to select the kind of clothes we wanted to wear, a selection involving decisions as to style, color, material, and so on. If regulations were

established allocating certain individuals to certain vocations, perhaps on the basis of aptitude and other tests, we should be free of
the troublesome business of deciding what to do to earn a living. If
recreation, education, or the radio were similarly controlled, we
should not be compelled to select for ourselves the patterns we
wished to follow in those areas. We should, again, be "free" from
the responsibility of making decisions.

Put in this blunt way, the concept of freedom we have been discussing doubtless seems complete nonsense. Yet, stated in more
suave and careful terms, it may appear to be very attractive. Thus
the president of an American college, returning to civilian life after
a period in the armed services, remarked that it was convenient to
have the Navy make decisions for the individual in "unimportant"
matters. Similarly, book clubs, news commentators, and other
propagandists can rather easily clothe their approach in the attractive terms of "a service rendered to the public," a service made desirable on the grounds that the public "does not have the time" to
make selections in the fields indicated. Since it is doubtful whether
the time of the majority of individuals in our own culture is completely consumed in work and sleep, the real meaning of the services
offered is that the time consumed in making decisions, time saved
under the system of preselection, can be devoted to other things.
In other words, individuals are "free" to spend their time in more
desirable ways than in the exercise of responsible choice.

The fallacy of this whole doctrine of "freedom from responsibility" is that there would be nothing particularly worth doing with
the freedom acquired through the kind of control which makes all
our decisions for us. Lacking the opportunity to make important
decisions, and lacking the opportunity to use constructively the time
"saved" because we did not have to make decisions, most of us
would quickly lose the status of adults and become as irresponsible
children. In fact, it is sometimes suggested by critics of this view of
freedom that that is the purpose of the whole approach—to make
the majority of the population into children who will do, eat, wear,
and believe what they are told.

If this should be the purpose or the result of "freedom from responsibility" it would obviously mean that the question of the allocation of power to government would disappear, since all power of
significance would automatically become the sole property of

government. The democratic state would disappear, and in its place would be erected a totalitarian state.

None of the concepts of freedom that we have outlined is without its own difficulties. The childish concept will not operate in a group; the "relative-restraint" theory demands that we define the areas and the amount of restraint necessary; and the "freedom-from-responsibility" approach requires a definition of "unimportant" areas of life in which decisions may be made for us, and also involves a possible concentration of power in the hands of government which will amount to totalitarianism. One of the tasks of contemporary society is to clarify its concept of freedom.

SUMMARY: GOVERNMENT IN SOCIAL ORGANIZATION

The political institution is the institution formally concerned with the maintenance of order in society. The state is a form of human association based on the allocation of powers of control to a government, which is the organized system of functions by means of which the authority of the state is applied to concrete situations.

Government is distinguished from other institutions by typical patterns associated with it, among them the legal use of force and the universal applicability of government activities, together with a system of sanctions on which the authority of government is based.

Government functions in social organization by providing a structure within which the activities of society are carried out.

Among the contemporary problems of government, based on the fundamental problem of the control and distribution of power, are disagreements as to whether government should function to provide a framework only for societal activities or whether it should engage more directly in such activities. A second significant problem is the clarification of the meaning of democracy and the application of the democratic patterns to concrete relationships. A third problem is the definition of "freedom" and the areas in which it may be applied in contemporary society.

READINGS

PANUNZIO, CONSTANTINE. *Major Social Institutions*. The Macmillan Company, New York, 1938. Chap. 21, "Government," and Chap. 22, "Persistent Problems of Government."

MACIVER, R. M. *The Web of Government*. The Macmillan Company, New York, 1947. An analysis of totalitarian, dictatorial, and democratic institutions of our times, with the aim of developing an intelligent philosophy of government. Especially Chap. I, "Man and Government"; Chap. V, "The Pyramid of Power"; Chap. VIII, "The Ways of Democracy."

PCUND, ROSCOE. *Social Control through Law*. Yale University Press, New Haven, 1942. A brief discussion of law as a means of social control in a politically organized society.

"Essential Human Rights," *The Annals of the American Academy of Political and Social Sciences*, Vol. 243, January, 1946. Discussions by a number of specialists, of the national and international significance of human rights and their protection.

CHAPTER XVII

SOCIAL ORGANIZATION AND DISORGANIZATION

WE HAVE DISCUSSED the function, relationships, and problems of five major institutions in social organization. There are other institutions in most advanced cultures, notably science, which are also significant for cultural processes; and in simpler cultures there may also be others than the ones we have discussed. We have limited our consideration to the five which are basic to all cultures. We propose now to summarize some of our findings regarding institutions in social organization, to consider briefly the topic of social disorganization, and then to take up the study of processes which affect social organization and disorganization.

INSTITUTIONS IN SOCIAL ORGANIZATION

Institutions are standardized group-reaction patterns. They develop in connection with situations which are common to all members of an aggregate and which are recurrent. They present to the individuals and the groups which make up the aggregate a number of established ways of meeting the common problems of life which are shared by most members of the aggregate. This "presentation" of established ways of living is an important part of culture, and therefore it is a significant portion of the basic interaction pattern of human association. It influences the development of individuals as well as the growth of group ways. We do not, as individuals, work out solutions to common problems; we accept the established solutions, and, by virtue of that acceptance, they exert strong influence on our personality growth. For most of us the institutional ways of behavior are so commonplace and so matter-of-fact that no other ways seem possible.

We are therefore "naturally" related to the culture of which our particular institutions are a part. The meaning of much of our conduct arises from the fact that it resembles that of our neighbors and that it is socially approved. We can observe this interplay of individual and social meanings in the willingness with which a good many people eagerly accept and follow changes in fads and fashions. They find satisfaction in wearing clothes which are "in the latest style," in possessing the latest models of automobiles, and in using the latest slang. Our participation in institutional patterns resembles this following of fad and fashion, with the very important difference that the institutions we have been discussing operate in much more significant areas of life than do fad and fashion.

Institutions, then, are important parts of social organization, the system which relates the segments of a society to each other and to the whole society in a meaningful way. That point may become clearer if we contrast our own way of life with the pioneer way of life common at a time not very far distant, especially in western America. The pioneer found no established pattern of institutions. As an individual, or as part of a small family group, he had to find the means of subsistence himself. There was no complex economic institution to offer him a job or to sell him food. He had to protect himself as best he could and to settle any disputes that might arise in any way that seemed feasible. There was no government institution to maintain order. He had to give his children such knowledge as he thought appropriate and necessary to their way of life. There was no educational institution to provide systematic instruction.

The mere fact, then, that we are used to a functioning social organization does not mean that it has always existed. Pioneer life either was unorganized or was organized very loosely and informally, not in connection with a functioning society. The study of the processes by which social organization arises in unorganized aggregates is itself an interesting study, but it belongs in a book especially devoted to social organization.

SOCIAL DISORGANIZATION

Disorganization in general is the progressive breaking down of a system of orderly relationships and functions. Confusion and malfunctioning follow the interruption of co-ordinated and integrated behavior.[1] *Social* disorganization is disorganization in some area, or areas, of human association. More formally,

[1]H. P. Fairchild (Ed.), *Dictionary of Sociology*, p. 95. Philosophical Library, New York, 1944.

*Social disorganization is the disarrangement and malfunctioning
of established group behavior patterns,
institutions, or controls.*[2]

Social disorganization is not an impersonal phenomenon; it involves people and their behavior. It is not a change in some remote system that exists apart from human beings in association, but rather a change that gradually takes place in the conduct of people. We see its evidences, not in abstract studies, but in the realistic behavior of people much like ourselves.

When the majority of people in a population conduct themselves according to accepted rules and patterns of behavior, we know, in a general way at least, what the purpose of their behavior is, and we can venture also to predict with some degree of accuracy what their major reactions will be. When accepted patterns lose their meaning and their power to influence the lives of people, human activity loses some of its obvious purpose, and it also becomes increasingly unpredictable.

In the latter case, the aggregate to which those people belong is tending in the direction of disorganization, although it may not become completely disorganized, that is, it may not cease entirely to function as an aggregate. Perhaps the most drastic example of social disorganization occurs in the case of nations which have been overrun by an enemy in war. Old relationships and accepted patterns of behavior disintegrate. Even when the conquering country tries to set up new relationships and new patterns, it cannot always stave off disorganization. The new relationships differ from the old; they are imposed by force; they do not have the meaning which comes from familiarity and from natural growth and development. Because they fail to influence the actual behavior of people, they fail also to become strong organizational forces. Human behavior remains unmotivated by common goals, and it remains largely unpredictable. Experiences incident to the Second World War illustrate this general situation.

Disorganization may also, of course, occur under other circumstances than the subjugation of a country in war. It occurs whenever there is a drastic lessening of the influences of established behavior patterns without a substitution of other and equally influ-

[2]Fairchild, op. cit. p. 280.

ential patterns. Our own society faces disorganization in a number of areas for precisely this reason, as was suggested in the discussion of several of our social institutions. For example, the whole process of conditioning children in such a way that they will adjust to societal patterns is not effective enough to prevent an increase in the rate of juvenile delinquency and other problems of childhood and adolescence. One of the major reasons why the conditioning process is ineffective lies not with institutions such as the family and education; it lies in the fact that we have no definite and universally accepted code of behavior to which children and adolescents should be conditioned, and in the further fact that specialists, such as child psychologists, child sociologists, and home economists, present conflicting theories of child development. The problem of conditioning children is not only a question of influencing them to conform to societal patterns; it is also a question of having definite, widely accepted, and clearly formulated patterns to which they may conform. We do not at present have such patterns to the degree that we had in our past culture.

The development of child psychology and other investigations of child behavior has undermined our traditional beliefs about childhood and about the relationship between parents and children. The "expert" in child care often advises procedures radically differing from the traditional patterns. But there is disagreement among experts. Especially is there disagreement between expert advice given at different periods. In 1933, for example, the latest theories held that children should be permitted to develop naturally, without any attention from parents beyond a bare minimum. This idea was presented not only in serious form by some child specialists but also in exaggerated and inaccurate form by newspapers and other organs of popular information, with the result that it attracted a great deal of attention. In 1943 almost exactly the reverse advice was given. It was then believed that children, including babies, needed the companionship of adults as they developed, so much so that in Bellevue Hospital, in New York, nurses and interns were assigned to "fondle and play with" babies who had to spend long periods in the hospital.[3]

Under such circumstances of changing "scientific" doctrine regarding the care of babies and children, interested and well-in-

[3]*New York Times Magazine*, April 12, 1942, p. 26.

tentioned parents, following the most recent pronouncements, were obviously misguided either in 1933 or in 1943. They could not adhere either to traditional or to current patterns of child care with any degree of certainty. The results were increased confusion as to parent-child relationships and as to child development. How much this specific situation has to do with current delinquency we do not know. The general state of confusion, however, is undoubtedly a contributing factor. It is not a question, in the instances we have cited, of deliberate neglect of children by parents, though of course in some instances that factor may be present. It is a question of responsible parents' being perplexed by differing codes of behavior, none of them of accepted and demonstrated validity.

As scientific understanding of family relationships increases and an objective standard of behavior in parent-child relationships becomes established, delinquency will tend to decrease. It is a passing phase of social disorganization. Our point in stressing it is to indicate the complexity of the relationships involved in the rise of delinquency. The breakdown of accepted codes of behavior means that there is no definite pattern to which children can be conditioned. Varying ideas as to the processes of child development and conditioning give rise to confusion. The behavior of parents in relation to children becomes uncertain. A phase of disorganization results.

As we might expect, examples of disorganization may be found in other institutions than the family; and they also are traceable to a decline in the authority of once-established codes of behavior. As we suggested in Chapter XV, there is a growing dissatisfaction with education, especially with high-school education. These complaints, taken as a whole, amount to the allegation that our high schools are malfunctioning and disorganized. To the extent that the allegation is true, the condition arises from the fact that the relationships between the high-school program, its purposes, and the needs of the contemporary population have become confused. There is no definite understanding as to what subjects shall be studied, what the standards of admission to a given course shall be, or what the standards of evaluating progress shall be. A recent news report carried the story of protests by parents in the case of one school system which passes and promotes all students, regardless of accomplishment.[4] Such a decline in established standards, without replace-

[4]*Time*, August 18, 1947, p. 62.

ment by other equally influential patterns, always results in disorganization.

So with conflicts in the economic field. The older system of relationships centered authority in management. In some cases this led to a paternalistic situation in which management exercised a benevolent oversight of its employees in the interests of their development and welfare. This was especially the case in some of the early New England textile mills. In other instances both paternalism and benevolence were conspicuously absent. Labor was treated as a factor of production and utilized as such with little regard for its human aspects. As a factor of production it was entirely under the domination of management. Undesirable as that system may appear to many of us now, it was a definite code of relationships which was widely accepted as the right, or at least the inevitable, system. Disorganization in labor-management relationships was much less of a threat than it is at present. With the breakdown of that system of relationships incident to the growing claims of labor to function as a co-operative and human aspect of the industrial enterprise, the threat of disorganization has become more apparent.

Again we may suggest that this threat of disorganization is a temporary phase of economic relationships. As a new and concrete pattern is established, organization will result. If, of course, no new pattern is established, the threat of disorganization will move in the direction of actual disorganization.

FACTORS IN SOCIAL DISORGANIZATION

We use the term *factors in* social disorganization instead of the term *causes of* social disorganization because we cannot trace any single set of causes which inevitably produce the condition we call social disorganization. It results from the interaction of a number of factors (some of which we shall discuss below), but it is not the result of any single, clear-cut situation. Popular, but mistaken, theories assign one single cause for disorganizational tendencies. To some people that cause is the decline of religion, to others it is the existence of capitalism and the profit motive, to still others it is the "degeneration" of our population resulting from immigration. All of these one-sided theories prove fallacious on investigation.

The same is true of social phenomena other than disorganization. One process does not directly and inevitably "cause" another process in any simple fashion. There is always a complex of factors out of which a given situation grows. That is only to say once again that all social phenomena develop from the basic interaction pattern of human association. Our task in the investigation of such phenomena is to trace the power of the several factors of that pattern in originating or influencing social trends.

There is always a degree of disorganization in every society. No aggregate has ever been perfectly organized in the sense of exhibiting no malfunctioning whatsoever. When an ideal society is described, in which there is no disorganization of any kind, it is referred to as a *utopia*, a word meaning "nowhere," the implication being obvious. Whether or not a given aggregate should be referred to as disorganized really depends on the relative amount of malfunctioning it exhibits. If that amount is such that the stability of the aggregate is gravely threatened, or so great that the stability has actually disappeared, we refer to it as disorganized. If, in spite of tendencies toward malfunctioning and confusion, it remains relatively stable, we do not consider it disorganized. Obviously, with the concept of disorganization itself so ill-defined and changing, it would be impossible to isolate fixed and well-defined causes. What we can do, however, is to describe the factors in social disorganization, that is, we can describe the situations which, in a majority of instances, accompany social disorganization. Thus

A breakdown of the accepted customs and ways of life common in a society tends toward disorganization.

This is in one sense simply summarizing what we have been saying in the last few pages. Our point is that when we observe a decline in the authority of customs, beliefs, and controls which were formerly of importance, we may expect social disorganization to follow unless the older customs are very rapidly replaced by newer and authoritative customs. One difficulty is that the replacement of older customs and controls by newer ones is almost never a rapid process. It takes time for the new to become systematized and to gain a sufficiently widespread acceptance to influence the behavior of any large portion of a population. In the meantime, behavior is under the dominance of individual or subgroup customs and authority, often unrelated to the larger society or only loosely so related. As a result the bonds between individuals or subgroups and the larger society are perceptibly weakened. Conduct becomes meaningful in terms of segment patterns rather than in terms of a common pattern. The society then approaches disorganization.

There is another important factor in social disorganization, especially significant in complex societies.

> *A discrepancy between the amount of interdependence*
> *in a culture and the amount of co-operation*
> *tends toward social disorganization.*

We have noted in our previous discussions that our society, and all complex societies, are characterized by an increasing amount of interdependence. Most individuals in such a culture are unable to maintain themselves except in so far as they can attach themselves to some system such as our economic system. They require the services of specialists in many areas of life. Not only is this true of individuals; it is also true of the groups to which individuals belong. Few families are self-sufficient; special-interest associations provide us with only a limited type of satisfaction; they cannot exist except in terms of a societal structure. Interdependence becomes a very important aspect of complex cultures.

Such interdependence and specialization may make for a very efficient and satisfying kind of social organization if there is also co-operation, if there is a mutual working together of the several segments involved. In the absence of co-operation we may have a great deal of conflict, with obvious results. But conflict is not the only problem involved. Even without open or concealed conflict the mere lack of active co-operation may tend in the direction of disorganization. The fact that some segments of the society on whom we depend do not perform their functions, or do not perform them well, or do not feel responsible to the society—all these, even without conflict, may lead to disorganization.

For example, political corruption is one of the vexing problems of our own times because it leads to malfunctioning on the part of the police, health services, inspection services, and many other areas of government. Bureaucracy, to which we referred in Chapter XVI, may have similar effects. Malfunctioning of the educational institution is important not only because the institution fails to benefit the individuals concerned but also because those individuals cannot, or do not, assume responsibilities after being "educated." The laborer who does a shoddy job not only fails as an individual but also fails the society which depends on his work. All these are examples of interdependence without co-operation. Their results are disorganizing and disintegrative of the social structure.

In our own culture there is considerable evidence that we have reached a point of very great dependence on other people without any sure way of bringing about the co-operation of those other people. The current wave of strikes is one example, though not the only example, that might be cited. A generation ago, in the case of a policemen's strike, a governor of Massachusetts asserted that no one had the right to strike against the "public welfare" at any time. In the case of a police strike, the threat to public welfare was obvious. But we may well ask whether many other activities are not as vital to the public welfare as that of the policeman. Railroad employees, dairy employees, coal miners, or building-maintenance employees become very significant in a pattern of activities which depends on them to the extent that we do currently.

Of course not all strikes are labor strikes. Producers, farmers, meat packers, clothing manufacturers, and builders of houses may all curtail production, as it is alleged many of them did during the period of government price control, with the result that goods were not forthcoming. This kind of activity follows the same general pattern as that involved in the more familiar labor strike.

It is sometimes suggested that we can secure co-operation on the part of people on whom we depend through legal means or through some other kind of pressure. The defect in this suggestion is that co-operation cannot be forced. It is essentially a matter of understanding and of enthusiasm. There are many ways to evade attempts at forced co-operation. It is also sometimes believed that the profit motive, that is, returns either in money or in some other kind of reward, will function to bring about at least enough co-operation to permit a workable functioning of social organization. The profit motive is undoubtedly an important motivation. Rewards, prestige, honors, and many other things not expressible in monetary terms are actually a type of "profit" arising from our activities, and they may act as powerful stimuli toward co-operation. They are, then, agencies on which we may count in increasing co-operation.

But they also have their shortcomings. Monetary returns are effective stimuli, but only within a limited area. They are the basis of what Professor Sorokin calls a "contractual group," the essential of which is an agreement to perform given functions for a stated return.[5] Such relationships are, of course, very common in our culture. One individual contracts with other individuals to build a house, to sell an automobile, or to provide some other kind of service at a stipulated price. Within the area of agreement the quality of performance may be very high, but aside from that area of agreement the typical contractual relationship tends to be ineffective because there is little or no responsibility on the part of the contracting parties outside the limited area. It is impossible for a society to be organized on a purely contractual basis because of that lack of general responsibility.

If, for example, we were to attempt to organize society on a contractual basis only, we should soon discover that the number of contracts necessary to include all areas of life would be infinite; that the process of bargaining inherent in contract renewals and modifications would be so complex as to make the system unworkable; and finally, that there are some relationships which are not amenable to contract, since they require a broad and general assumption of responsibility. For example, as Sorokin suggests, a mother cannot contract to care for her child a certain number of hours each day and then refuse to assume further responsibility for the child; she cannot agree that she will care for a sick child for, say, only a total of fourteen days each year, with the proviso that any further sickness is not her responsibility. Similarly, a citizen cannot contract to serve his government in war for a specified period of time or in limited ways only; he serves for such period and in such ways as may be necessary for the successful prosecution of the war.

One major difficulty with our present social organization is that we have attempted to rely on contractual relationships to an extent

[5] P. A. Sorokin, *Social and Cultural Dynamics*, Vol. II, pp. 30–35. American Book, New York, 1937.

beyond their power to function and in areas in which they are not effective. Extensive co-operation does not result from such a situation.

From the viewpoint of honors and prestige, rather than a purely monetary return, we face the difficulty that honors and prestige may result from non-co-operation as well as from co-operation. From the cultural standpoint we have failed to stress co-operation as a value. Our emphasis on extreme individualism often makes a non-co-operative attitude more praiseworthy than co-operation. In addition to that fact, honors and prestige are essentially similar to monetary returns, since they are rewards for the performance of specified duties.

We cannot assure co-operation, then, by force alone or by the stimulus of rewards alone, except in limited ways. Obviously, some other basis for an adequate system of relationships is necessary. We shall discuss this matter at greater length presently when we deal with co-operation as a social process. Our point here is that when there is a discrepancy between the amount of interdependence in an aggregate and the amount of co-operation, a tendency to social disorganization results.

A third important factor in social disorganization springs from the relative rates at which given social processes take place.

A lack of balance between integrative and disintegrative social processes influences tendencies toward social disorganization.

Most aggregates are characterized by two general types of processes: those which tend to draw the segments closer together, and those which tend to separate the segments. We refer to them as *integrative* and *disintegrative* social processes, respectively. As far as our knowledge goes, there has never been a society which did not include both integrative and disintegrative forces. It is also true that, since interaction is a changing and dynamic phenomenon, few cultures have been able to maintain an absolute balance beween the two kinds of forces. Trends toward disintegration are followed by strong integrative movements, at least in the case of those societies which have escaped complete destruction. Similarly, a period of close integration is followed by the growth of disintegrative factors. Readjustments become necessary in order to maintain stability, readjustments which may involve important changes in social organization.

As we suggested in Chapter X, social organization itself becomes a process as well as a structure, since it consists of a series of adjustments and readjustments in the direction of balancing disintegrative forces by integrative forces. If the disintegrative forces operate at a more rapid rate than integrative forces for any length of time, and if they include a larger segment of the population than do the integrative forces, disorganization becomes a major problem.

We now proceed to a discussion of some of the social processes important to social organization.

READINGS

SOROKIN, P. A. *The Crisis of Our Age.* E. P. Dutton & Co., Inc., New York, 1942. An attempt to analyze the problems of our times and to suggest a general remedy.

MANNHEIM, KARL. *Diagnosis of Our Time.* Oxford University Press, New York, 1944. "Our society is ill—what is the disease and what is the cure?"

TOYNBEE, ARNOLD. *A Study of History* (abridgment by D. C. Somervell). Oxford University Press, New York, 1947. Chapter XV, a discussion of the "breakdown" of civilization in terms of loss of command over the total environment in which we live.

PENDELL, ELMER (Ed.). *Society under Analysis.* The Jacques Cattell Press, Lancaster, Pennsylvania, 1942. Chapter 15, "Community."

PANUNZIO, CONSTANTINE. *Major Social Institutions.* The Macmillan Company, New York, 1938. Chapter 27, "Maladjustment."

CHAPTER XVIII

DISINTEGRATIVE SOCIAL PROCESSES

WE USED THE TERM *social process* during our previous discussion in such a general way that we did not trouble to define it. As we now approach a more concrete examination of selected social processes, it is desirable to formulate more definitely our ideas as to what a social process is.

THE MEANING OF PROCESS

A *process*, in general, is a series of related events leading to a specific result. Inherent in the concept is also the idea that the related series of events takes place more than once. If they occur only once they do not constitute a process. Social change is taking place about us all the time; out of the totality of that change we observe certain events between which we can establish relationships in time —they take place in close succession. We can also establish a relationship between the specified series of events and certain occurrences which result from the series. We call such related events processes.

Familiar examples of processes may be found in the field of physiology. The process of respiration consists in breathing in, holding the breath for a very short time, and then breathing out. This series of events is repeated, leading to specific results in body chemistry. So of the processes involved in the assimilation of food. Other processes in physical nature take place much more slowly. For example, the weathering of rocks and the erosion of soil require months or years for their completion. The thing that makes them processes rather than mere haphazard changes is the sequence of events which leads to the same results whenever it takes place.

Social Process

A *social* process is one kind of process. It is called social because it involves people, beliefs, customs, or some other aspect of human life in association. According to one definition, social processes are those social changes "in which we can observe a distinguishing pattern."[1] Note that it is the pattern, the series of *related* changes, which distinguishes a process from haphazard occurrences. When we speak of "disintegrative" or "integrative" social processes, we are referring to a series of related events which bring about, or which tend to bring about, the disintegration or the integration of a society. They need not be unusual, or revolutionary, or particularly striking events. Each event in the process may be, in itself, quite ordinary and commonplace. But when we observe the events in their totality, we can point to a definite result of their interaction. Again, this result may be quite commonplace and ordinary; or, it may be revolutionary, dangerous, or otherwise extraordinary. The total result of all the disintegrative processes, that is, the total disintegration of a society, is, of course, an extraordinary event. But that extraordinary event occurs as the result of many processes, each of which may be, in itself, not particularly striking. So of the results of integrative processes.

For example, every so often we elect a President of the United States. We do this by an orderly process, that is, by a series of prescribed steps, following each other in sequence. The results of this process are very important, but in the course of our national development they have come to be accepted as relatively ordinary and commonplace. We are aware of the steps in the process and we deliberately follow them in a certain order.

On the other hand, there are processes of which, from the cultural standpoint, we are not aware and the results of which we do not desire or even foresee. Naturally, these "hidden processes" have not been studied as thoroughly as have the obvious processes. In Part I several such trends were discussed. For example, migrants to our urban areas imitate urban patterns of living. One of those patterns consists of small family units rather than large. As migrants adopt this pattern, the rate of natural increase of our population declines. We do

[1] H. P. Fairchild (Ed.), *Dictionary of Sociology*, p. 289. Philosophical Library, New York, 1944.

not as yet know what the total result of this decline will be, but the process by which urbanism affects the reproduction rate is clearly defined. It is a process of which we have, until recently, been more or less unaware. We call it a process because the several events concerned are repeated not only in the case of individual migrants but also, historically, in all civilizations which have developed urbanism.

Social processes, then, may take place in accordance with a deliberate plan, or they may take place "naturally," without our planning for them and often without our being aware of them. In either case, their results for society may be very significant. The whole area of the operation of social processes is one which requires a great deal of investigation and clarification.

SPECIFIC SOCIAL PROCESSES

Of the many social processes taking place in our contemporary society, we select certain ones for discussion, partly because we do not know all the processes which are actually operative, and partly because only a few of those we do know have been analyzed. In the present chapter we discuss the disintegrative processes—competition, conflict, stratification, differentiation, and specialization. In the chapter following we deal with integrative processes—co-operation, accommodation, assimilation, social mobility, and interdependence. The one group of processes tends to balance the other group, as shown by the following chart.

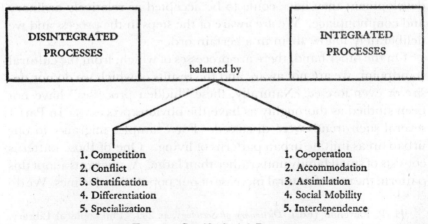

DISINTEGRATED PROCESSES		INTEGRATED PROCESSES
	balanced by	
1. Competition		1. Co-operation
2. Conflict		2. Accommodation
3. Stratification		3. Assimilation
4. Differentiation		4. Social Mobility
5. Specialization		5. Interdependence

FIG. 5 · *Specific Social Processes*

As we mentioned earlier, no society that we know of has ever maintained an absolute balance between integrative and disintegrative processes. Social organization is, in part, itself a process by which attempts at balance are made.

DISINTEGRATIVE SOCIAL PROCESSES

We proceed now to a discussion of certain very important disintegrative social processes.

COMPETITION AND CONFLICT

Competition and conflict are closely related social processes because both arise as the result of two facts. (1) Certain things are considered by a number of people to be valuable, desirable, useful, or otherwise worth having. We call these things goods, as in the term *economic goods*, that very use of the term indicating how desirable they are. (2) These desirable things do not exist naturally in unlimited quantities, so that effort, or effort plus skill, is necessary to secure them. If they did exist in unlimited quantities, as air and water did before our concentration in cities, we should still refer to them as goods, but we should call them *free* goods, thereby implying that they are available without the exercise of skill and effort. One of the characteristics of our present social organization is that there are few free goods left. Thus land may be very expensive in certain areas, and we pay for houses which are airy and light in preference to those which are crowded and dark.

The goods of life may be other than material possessions. They include such things as power, prestige, reputation, rewards, titles, and the satisfaction we get from being able to impress other people. To the extent that we consider all these things desirable, they function in the same way as material goods.

Bearing in mind these two facts, we may define competition as *the struggle for the use or possession of limited goods.*[2] The thing sought in the competitive process is the goods involved, a point we must bear in mind when we come to distinguish competition from conflict. Because the goods are limited, their use or possession by one group prevents their use or possession by another group. The

[2]Fairchild, op. cit. article "Competition."

"series of related events" involved in the process of competition, then, may be summarized as follows. Certain goods are limited in quantity; they become objects of desire by different groups or different individuals; a struggle for their possession or use ensues; and the result is that one group wins out over the other and actually possesses the goods, while thej other must forgo their possession. Competition is, of course, a familiar part of our business and industrial life as well as of many other areas of interaction.

Conflict, on the other hand, although it originates from the same two facts, differs in attitudes involved, methods used, and results obtained. It is defined as *the process by which two or more groups seek actively to thwart each other's purposes, to prevent satisfaction of each other's interests, even to the extent of injuring or destroying the other party concerned.*[3] The goal sought in conflict is not *primarily* the goods involved at all. It is the thwarting of the opponent's satisfaction. Possession of goods may be one aspect of the whole interactive pattern, but it is of secondary importance. Getting possession of the goods is, in a sense, a by-product of our desire to thwart. On the contrary, in the case of *competition*, the goods are primary and the thwarting is a by-product.

It is important to understand this idea if we are to grasp the significance of conflict. It is commonly said that "everybody loses in a war," and the same statement is sometimes applied to strikes. Wars and industrial conflicts very seldom "pay for themselves" in financial, territorial, or other benefits gained. It is the basic desire to thwart the opposing group which accounts for conflict, not the good which may be obtained by it.

The "series of related events" in the case of conflict, then, would be somewhat as follows. We observe certain groups possessing, or about to possess, limited goods; we object to that situation, usually for some such emotional reason as fear, jealousy of our prestige, or ignorance; we set out to thwart the other group; and a struggle ensues which may result in the death and destruction of one or both groups. War is, of course, the outstanding example of conflict on a large scale. Race riots and industrial strife are more localized examples. In the case of race riots, the conflict pattern is especially clear; the minority race involved usually is not strong enough actually to threaten the privileges and rights of the majority. In

[3]Fairchild, op. cit. article "Conflict."

spite of that fact, certain members of the majority race determine to "keep the minority in their place," that is, to thwart the minority in its plans for progress and betterment. Conflict of a serious nature results.

Attitudes toward competition differ from those toward conflict. In general, American thought favors competition and reacts against conflict. The same is true of much of world thought today, although there have been periods when the virtues of conflict have been extolled on the grounds that conflict "selects" the best type of individual for survival.[4] It is also true that in both Europe and America there is a tendency to move toward collective action instead of the individualized type of action characteristic of competition.

Our favorable attitude toward competition rests not so much on actual observation of its effects in contemporary social organization as it does on tradition. We have, as a society, been organized on the basis of competition for so long that we automatically accept it as a necessary part of our interaction pattern. This tradition, in turn, arises from the fact that competition did actually function in very important ways during most of our national history. For example, until relatively recent times the significant fact about economic goods was their real scarcity, a scarcity which arose from the fact that our economic techniques did not enable us to exploit the environment as efficiently as we now can. With all the effort that we might put forth, it was difficult to produce enough even for a low level of living for large segments of our population. Active competition was an efficient instrument to further the exploitation of the environment, since it stimulated individuals and groups toward the discovery of new processes.

Recall that the purpose of competition is to get possession of, or use of, scarce goods; it is not, as in the case of conflict, to prevent their use by others, and it does not have as one of its purposes the destruction of opponents, as conflict does. What we have, then, is a situation in which one grouping got possession of the goods, another did not. The dispossessed, not being destroyed or otherwise put out of the running, very often turned their efforts toward the development of substitute goods to replace those of which they had been deprived. The net result of all this was to increase the amount of economic goods, a result which was desirable under the

[4] W. H. Norton, "The Darwinian Citation of Mars," *Bios*, Vol. XIV, No. 1.

circumstances of scarcity. Consider an example from our own times. If aluminum is controlled in a semi-monopolistic way so that one company only can manufacture and use it, competitors develop stainless steel, magnesium, and other metals to be used in place of aluminum. Materials made from these other metals may become useful substitutes for aluminum. Obviously, in this example, the total of economic goods is increased since we are offered utensils not only of aluminum but also of stainless steel and other metals. In turn, metals are now meeting with the competition of plastics in many processes.

As we shall note presently, competition very often fails to function in this way in many areas of contemporary life. It did so function for the major portion of our national history, and its results were obvious. It has therefore become strongly entrenched in our traditions. We have called it a "disintegrative" social process because one of its results is to separate the population into segments. In past times this separation was not marked enough or serious enough to be dangerous to the social organization. Competition is, then, one of the milder disintegrative processes.

The difficulty in our own times is that competition is no longer a process which takes place between individuals or between small aggregates. It is competition between giant corporations, or between such large and impersonal aggregates as labor and capital, or between a majority and a minority. Tremendous power is concentrated in these groupings, a power which is directed not against other individuals but against other impersonal groupings. Most of us find it easier to destroy, or to accept the idea of destroying, an impersonal opponent than we do a personal opponent. Competition therefore passes easily over into the patterns of conflict, both because of the concentration of power and because of the impersonality of the process.

Conflict is much more disintegrative of the social group than is competition because the purpose of conflict is the thwarting of the opponent, and the attitude inherent in conflict is such that the actual destruction of the opponent may become a goal. His physical destruction is not necessary, although our history presents many instances in which conflict has led to the physical destruction of numbers of people. Usually, however, the "destruction" involves only the loss of power, prestige, social status, reputation, or some other attribute without which an opponent cannot function. For example, that portion of industry which is in conflict with labor does not seek the physical death and destruction of labor. It seeks only to destroy the influence of labor exerted through organization; and therefore it looks toward the destruction of unions. Pressure groups in any fields seldom try to kill those who oppose them, though they may in some cases. Instead, they try to prevent their opponents from exerting any influence, which is the equivalent of destroying their power and prestige.

Because of the danger inherent in a transition from competition to conflict under our present type of organization, we have, in America, controlled competition for the past fifty years or more through antitrust laws and similar devices. In one sense the phrase "control of competition" gives a wrong emphasis, since the purpose of control is not to inhibit competition as such, but to prevent the development of conflict from competition. In fact, the antitrust laws are concerned with maintaining competition by preventing monopolistic practices, on the assumption that such practices do not permit "free" competition. In some European countries systems have been adopted which do control competition as such by setting up "cartel" systems or other systems which allocate production and sales to specific producers in any one field of production. The European system differs from the American, then, in that important point: we have tried to maintain competitive conditions, whereas those Europeans who use the cartel system do not. It is important to bear this distinction in mind when we discuss attitudes toward competition.

Economists differ as to the desirability of trying to maintain a competitive system in modern industrial life. To the sociologist, competition appears to be desirable not only in industrial life but in other areas of interaction, provided it is controlled in such a way that conflict does not result, and provided that there are integrative forces which can balance the disintegration, mild though it may be, which arises from competition. Our point here is that competition may stimulate individuals or groups toward the development of new resources, both material and immaterial, whereas lack of competition may prevent such development. Take a familiar example from the field of education. Standards in many American colleges are so low, in the sense that little intellectual achievement is required, that the average student does not have to exert much effort in order to "stay in college." Because he does not have to exert much effort, his intellectual development is not stimulated. If standards were raised to the extent that only outstanding students could "possess the good" of a college education, others would be deprived of that good. A minority would not be able to meet the competition and would have to do without it; but many students would "compete," that is, they would work harder to develop their own intellectual resources and thus to meet the standard set. The net result would be an increase in good students. As far as our present evidence indicates, this result cannot be achieved by exhortation, or testing, or making classes more interesting, or in any other way than by setting a standard and permitting genuine competition within the terms of that standard.

We must also note, however, that the standard set is just as important as the fact of competition itself. There is no magic about competition as such which will in itself produce good results without reference to any standard at all. Our attempts to "regulate competition" lie largely in the area of setting standards within which it must take place, not only in the narrow terms of the example we have just cited, but in the broader terms of our general associational patterns. An important task of our present culture is to develop generally accepted standards within which competition can take place.

Competition and conflict, then, are disintegrative forces, or processes, because they tend to break a culture into segments. Our goal is to balance them by integrative forces to the extent that conflict will be minimized—though it is doubtful if it will ever disappear entirely—and competition take place in terms of accepted social standards.

STRATIFICATION

Stratification is the process by which society is divided into fairly identifiable and definite horizontal layers.[5] The word *horizontal* implies the placing of one class or segment of the population above other classes or segments usually on the basis of rights and privileges. It usually implies also that the responsibilities and the duties of the several classes differ. Thus in a highly stratified society it may

[5]Fairchild, op. cit., article "Stratification."

be assumed that education is the privilege of the higher classes and that government is the duty of the higher classes. Less important duties go with the less important privileges of the lower classes.

Note that the classes, or "layers," are only fairly definite and identifiable. This statement implies that in many cultures the differentiation into classes is by no means sharp, and also that in many cases there is considerable shifting of individuals from one class to another. On the other hand, of course, in some cultures class distinctions are very sharp and rigid, as in the case of Oriental societies organized on a caste system. Simply to say that an aggregate is stratified, then, means little. We must go beyond that general statement and indicate the degree of stratification, the rigidity of stratification, and the trends in stratification, if we are to analyze a society with any approach to accuracy.

In general, there are two contrasting bases for stratification, namely, hereditary rights and individual accomplishment, with some mixture of the two also common. Stratification based on hereditary rights is familiar in long-established and stable cultures That based on individual accomplishment is usually associated with newly developing or otherwise changing cultures.

In America conditions of association throughout most of our history have been such that individual accomplishment has been very important in our class structure. The degree of stratification, especially in small-town and rural areas, was relatively slight. For the most part, the higher classes associated with the lower classes in many activities. There is some evidence that, as our metropolitan culture develops, the degree of stratification may increase. Industry and business have become more complex, with the result that there has been a tendency toward stratification within the economic system itself. There are directors of corporations, major and minor executives, managers, white-collar workers, janitors, laborers, and many others. This internal stratification is reflected in the community status of the individuals concerned. The situation is not as yet having serious disintegrative effects.

Along with a relatively low degree of stratification in our past organization went a low rigidity in the class structure. In a few areas family background was, and has remained, important for membership in the "higher classes," but very largely it was, and is, a matter of wealth. Our aristocracy has been a financial aristocracy. Since wealth is shifting in nature, easily acquired and easily lost, the lines between classes have been blurred.

At present some class lines are coming to be more sharply drawn and rigidly maintained through the growth of "class consciousness," with the result that we may expect greater rigidity in some aspects of our class structure. Again this phenomenon may be traced largely to repercussions from the economic system. As we suggested in Chapter XIII, one of the characteristics of our industrial life has been a growing separation between the owners of tools, the *capitalists*, and the users of tools, *labor*. The subservience of the worker to his employer which used to be the expected thing is no longer evident. The desire to rise from the laboring class to a higher class is being replaced by (1) a growing pride in the status of labor and (2) a determination to increase the rights and privileges of the whole laboring class instead of an ambition to rise from that class. Labor leaders, who might through their skills and genuine abilities rise "above" labor to posts in industrial management, prefer to remain as influential members of the laboring class. The maintenance of class lines springs in this instance not from the pressure of externally imposed regulations outside the given class but from attitudes generated within the given class.

Class consciousness on the part of labor has its counterpart in class consciousness on the part of management; but this is not an unusual phenomenon, since the higher classes have usually been strongly aware of their "manifest destiny" to rule the aggregate, and have been strongly integrated as a class. It is more striking to find a "lower" class maintaining its own class lines from pride of position and of purpose. Stratification, then, has not been marked in America as a social process because of the conditions under which the majority of our population have lived. There is some evidence that it may be increasing both in degree and in rigidity.[6] What the results of such an increase will be depends to a large extent on the integrative processes which develop in the future.

DIFFERENTIATION

Differentiation as a social process is defined as *variation associated with interaction*.[7] This rather technical definition means simply that

[6] P. A. Sorokin, *Social Mobility*, pp. 133–163. Harper, New York, 1927.
[7] Fairchild, op. cit., article "Differentiation."

people tend to develop differences, in other words, to vary, as a result of the interactions they experience or as a result of the ways in which they experience interactions. This idea should be familiar enough to us, both from our own experience and from previous discussions in this book. Our general patterns of "living in association" produce different results for different people.

There are two mechanisms from the operation of which differentiation arises: (1) the interaction of "average" individuals with varying cultural and environmental patterns; and (2) the interaction of "unaverage" individuals with common cultural and environmental patterns. In the first case the individuals concerned are influenced by specialized circumstances to adopt beliefs, ways of thinking, or ways of living which differ from those of their associates. For example, the vocational interests of most of us arise not from inherent specialized skills and abilities but from interests stimulated by our specialized associations. The son of a professional man may react favorably toward the profession because of his association with his father. Another person may choose his vocation on the basis of values such as wealth and prestige which are highly regarded by his intimate group. Living in groups which value "service" or even asceticism more than wealth and prestige would provide a stimulus to choose vocations of that nature. We find at the present time, for example, that it is difficult to recruit members for nonlucrative occupations such as teaching and the ministry because the monetary returns do not accord with a standard of success set in terms of wealth. That standard, however, may be nullified by the experiences of individuals with their intimate groups which "filter" the general social standards. As a result some people do enter those vocations.

Vocations are also chosen in terms of inertia, that is, the individual concerned is not stimulated toward any particular work but follows the line of least resistance as dictated by his surroundings. Again, it is sometimes a matter of economic pressure. Whatever vocation is easily available becomes the choice because it will bring quick monetary returns. And so of many choices outside the vocational field; average individuals interacting with varying circumstances make different choices, not on the basis of any inherent differences in the individuals but on the basis of cultural and environmental circumstances. Differentiation results from this situation.

In the second type of mechanism producing differentiation the individuals concerned are "unaverage" in some way which affects their interactions. They may be better than average or worse than average. In this category come those persons who are gifted with special skills in music, art, writing, and other vocations, as well as those whose equipment is subnormal. Their interactions with common patterns of living tend to produce differentiation of behavior. This mechanism is perhaps more striking than the interaction of average individuals with varying cultural circumstances, but it is not as common.

Not only do individuals vary among themselves but groups also are differentiated one from the other. Again the two mechanisms operate: "average" groups interact with specialized cultural surroundings, and "unaverage" groups interact with specialized surroundings. Thus the urban aggregate is differentiated from the rural aggregate, residents of one urban area differ from those of another area, and customs common in a farming region differ from those common in livestock regions. On the other hand, as examples of "unaverage" aggregates we may cite minority groups such as our Negro population. They are differentiated partly by the fact of their racial characteristics but much more by the cultural environment characteristic of their status in our society. They are "unaverage" in the sense that they do not share the privileges of whites, and this fact seriously affects their interaction. A differentiation which may once have rested on the facts of race is now perpetuated on the basis of cultural facts. Other "underprivileged" groupings are in somewhat the same situation as far as their cultural environment goes.

As we have already suggested several times, contemporary American society exhibits a great deal of differentiation. Patterns of life differ between immigrant and native groupings, between residents of cities and those of rural areas, between religious denominations, between regions of the nation, between economic classes, and so on through a large number of categories. This differentiation has at times led to conflict, as in the case of race riots and industrial strife. At other times it has led to suppressed tensions, as in the case of anti-Semitism and religious bickering. At still other times it has led to a divergence of interests without overt conflict or tensions, but a divergence which has made unanimity of action very difficult. Even in the case of a crisis such as that inherent in the Second World War it was no easy task to secure voluntary co-operation in the multitude of activities necessary to the war effort. To as great a degree, divergence of interests hampers community projects of even so elementary a nature as plans for traffic control in large cities and programs for action against obvious political corruption. There are, of course, special interests actively opposing such reform programs, but a major factor preventing reform is the lack of interest displayed by a large portion of our people. Segmented interests take precedence over common interests. We have already noted the problems that differentiation raises for education as it attempts to deal with students of varying background and interests. The same problem exists for the whole of our culture in situations which require common action.

Social differentiation, with its conflict, latent tensions, and divergence of interests, is much more of a disintegrative force in our own times than is stratification or competition. It is difficult to balance by integrative forces because, especially as it creates divergence of interests, it has come to be so "natural" a part of our social organization that we are unaware of its disintegrative potentialities.

Specialization

Specialization is so closely related to differentiation that we may regard it as one kind of differentiation. It is defined as *division of labor* or *division of function*.[8] Obviously these are other terms for differentiation of labor or differentiation of function. Under conditions of specialization the several segments of a society or the several individuals in a group perform different functions. We are familiar with this situation in economic and industrial life, but the process is broader than that. It may appear in the family, in religious or educational activities, in government, or in any other form of association. In all those institutions, for example, we find specialized segments or individuals performing administrative functions, that is, functions associated with control and planning. Other segments perform operative functions, those associated with the carrying out of the purposes of the organization or institution. Others may be concerned primarily with research, criticism, and evaluation.

[8] Fairchild, op. cit. p. 305.

In addition to this broad type of specialization, there may be a great deal of detailed specialization connected with all the institutions we have mentioned. Again, we are most familiar with this kind of detail in industrial processes where operations are broken up into elaborate series of steps, each contributing a specific portion of the total operation. However, it is also characteristic of other areas of association. The specialist in government, education, and religion is an important individual in contemporary society.

Specialization in complex societies accompanies an increasing understanding and control of natural processes and an increasing elaboration of culture patterns in general. Significant also is a large population which not only gives scope for the activities of specialists, but also provides the resources of ability and talent necessary for the development of specialists. Population density alone is not sufficient for the development of the extreme specialization we have in our own times, since there are many examples of heavy population density without any great degree of specialization. It must be a population with capacities and understanding of ways of controlling and otherwise manipulating natural phenomena.

Specialization is particularly important in producing the segmentation of interests in a culture which we mentioned earlier, and, along with segmentation of interests, a narrowing of behavior. Especially in our metropolitan civilization persons of the same profession associate with one another in the same office buildings, the same scientific associations and the same recreation clubs. Much of their reading is confined to the area of their own special interests, with only summary contacts outside that area. Their attitudes and behavior are strongly shaped by their segmented interests. Much the same may be said of people in nonprofessional occupations.

Summary

Disintegrative social processes operate in various ways to segment a population. In past societies stratification was an important disintegrative process. In our own times stratification is less significant than are differentiation and specialization. Conflict, the ultimate segmenting process, may appear in connection with any of the other segmenting processes. In our own times it commonly appears as a result of uncontrolled competition and as a result of some aspects of differentiation.

READINGS

PANUNZIO, CONSTANTINE. *Major Social Institutions*. The Macmillan Company, New York, 1938. Chap. 25, "Change"; Chap. 26, "Struggle."

MACIVER, R. M. *Group Relations and Group Antagonisms*. Harper & Brothers, New York, 1944. Especially interesting in the area of religious conflict.

BERNARD, L. L. *War and Its Causes*. Henry Holt and Company, New York, 1944. A broad and thorough study of the nature and history of war and of its manifold causes.

SOROKIN, P. A. *Society, Culture, ana Personality*. Harper & Brothers, New York, 1947. Chap. 29, "Changes in Social Relationships"; Chap. 33, "The Cause and Factors of War and Revolution."

YOUNG, KIMBALL. *Sociology*. American Book Company, New York, 1942. Pp. 643–690, "Competition; Conflict"; pp. 787–844, "Specialization; Stratification and Class Structure."

CHAPTER XIX

INTEGRATIVE SOCIAL PROCESSES

THERE ARE a number of social processes which tend to bind the segments of a society more closely together, with respect both to each other and to the whole society. These are vital to the stability and continuance of a culture, since they counteract the disintegrative processes we have been discussing. The following are the important integrative processes.

CO-OPERATION

Co-operation is *the process by which individuals or groups combine their efforts, in a more or less organized way, for the attainment of common objectives.*[1] One of the characteristics of co-operative behavior is that the success of one member of the co-operative pattern contributes to the success of all the other members. It is obvious that this process is the opposite of competition. In competition the success of one party to the competitive relationship precludes the success of opposing parties. In co-operative endeavors the success of one promotes the success of all.

Co-operation is, by definition, only "more or less" organized. It has many informal aspects. Above all, it rests on a *voluntary* combination of efforts, on willing and often enthusiastic agreement. If individuals combine their efforts as a result of force or of some other kind of pressure exerted on them from outside, the situation is one of *co-ordination* rather than of co-operation. Co-ordination results largely from the operation of contractual relationships, discussed in Chapter XVII, or from compulsory relationships. It is therefore limited in area, though it may be of high intensity within that area. By contrast co-operation, springing as it does from favorable attitudes

[1]Adapted from H. P. Fairchild (Ed.), *Dictionary of Sociology*, article "Co-operation," p. 68. Philosophical Library, New York, 1944.

on the part of individuals concerned, is not limited to a specific contractual area. It is characterized by a "familistic" type of relationship, to use Professor Sorokin's terminology again. Familistic groups are based on positive attitudes and values which condition the totality of the outlook of individuals concerned in the association. Since the term *familistic* may seem to confine the relationships we are discussing to the family and family-related interactions, perhaps a better term would be *affectional* groupings. This term implies that the relationships in question are based on a strong emotion-feeling complex rather than on a contract or on force. Examples include the attitudes involved in patriotism, religion, marriage, and similar relationships. The affectional type of grouping is a very strong one, since it includes the major portion of the life activities of its members and since it is based on deep feeling.

Co-operation, then, is a relationship which is basically affectional in nature. It integrates the segments of an aggregate through adherence to, and enthusiasm for, a common goal. One point is especially important here. Co-operation integrates not only segments which are similar to each other but also segments which are unlike each other. We do not have to be identical in all respects in order to co-operate. We may differ in skills, in physical characteristics, in likes and dislikes, in language, in customs, and in many other ways, without impeding co-operation, because the shared attitudes toward a common goal make those differences relatively unimportant. Differentiation is not an obstacle to co-operation. In fact, it may be an asset, since different segments may make specialized contributions to the common goal. For example, in the operation of a university the work of administrators, teachers, laborers, police and fire officials, all kinds of specialists, is necessary for proper functioning. These classes differ from each other in the skills they bring to the institution, but it is precisely that difference which makes them function effectively. If they all were of identical skill and identical outlook, many of the university functions would not be carried out. The same may be said of business organization, factories, government administration, and most other complex aggregates in our culture.

A measure of co-operation, in fact, underlies many of our activities which, on the surface, seem to be antagonistic. Thus competition itself has many co-operative aspects, since it takes place within a framework of law and order which is observed through agreement between the competing parties. Even in conflict, it is assumed that there will be a degree of restraint practiced in accordance with international law and other stipulations. Breach of those stipulations is the basis for the trial of Nazi "war criminals" carried on in 1946 and 1947.

Co-operation is an especially important integrative process in a democracy, since democracy traditionally favors those "freedoms" which permit the growth of differentiation. The democratic attempt to integrate many different segments of society depends ultimately on the emotion-feeling complex characteristic of co-operation. Recent attempts to enforce co-ordination and to bring about a complete uniformity of behavior and of attitudes are departures from the democratic ideal. There is evidence that the democratic type of integration makes for a strong society in the sense of a co-operative society, even though it may lack the surface efficiency of co-ordinative systems. That type of efficiency may, in fact, lead to disastrous results, as we observed in connection with totalitarian states during the Second World War.

As we have suggested, in spite of the fact that co-operation is very important in a democracy, we have not, in our culture, strongly emphasized it in our "speech reactions." At the very times we have depended most on co-operation, we have glorified an extreme type of individualism together with the uncontrolled type of competition usually referred to as "cutthroat competition." As a matter of fact, the co-operative process is all-pervasive in our contemporary interaction patterns, so much so, perhaps, that we do not realize its significance. Whenever there is tacit or expressed voluntary agreement to observe rules, regulations, customs, or other accepted ways of behavior, we have a co-operative situation. This kind of tacit or expressed agreement controls numberless details of our daily lives.

One reason for our lack of emphasis on co-operation is a popularization of a misconception of Charles Darwin's use of the term "struggle for existence." He meant by that term the necessity for a continuous exertion of effort in order to survive. It has been mistakenly interpreted as meaning a state of continuous and all-embracing conflict. Darwin himself defined "struggle for existence" as follows:

I should premise that I use this term [struggle for existence] in a large and metaphorical sense, including dependence of one being on another, and including (which is more important) not only the life of the individual but success in leaving progeny.[2]

The "dependence of one being on another" and the aggregate purposes involved in "success in leaving progeny" both give scope for a great deal of co-operation. Darwin's theory in its true form has not secured wide popular acceptance, but overtones of his ideas have reached many portions of our population. It is unfortunate that they have also been inaccurate in this matter of equating the struggle for existence with conflict.

To emphasize co-operation, then, is to emphasize a significant process in our daily interactions which is no less significant because it is so common that we are not always aware of its operation.

ACCOMMODATION

Accommodation is *the process of altering social relationships in such a way as to reduce or to eliminate conflict and to promote mutual adjustments.*[3] In one sense, accommodation may be said to be an agreement to disagree. When one segment of an aggregate accommodates itself to other segments, there is no insistence on uniformity of behavior. Each segment retains certain behavior characteristics, at the same time modifying its actions in such a way as to avoid behavior which will promote disagreement and friction. A familiar example in our own culture may be found in the accommodation that exists between different religious denominations. Differences persist and conflict occasionally appears, but on the whole there is an agreement to disagree which enables the several denominations to exist in relative peace. This has not been the case in some other nations.

Accommodation may take place "naturally" over a period of time without involving a deliberate plan or intention to promote the process. Differentiated groups gradually work out a series of empirical, and more or less unstable, arrangements which reduce conflict and friction. On the other hand, we may engage in what has been called *creative accommodation*, essentially a planned search for, and development of, potential areas of agreement of an accom-

[2]C. Darwin, *The Origin of Species*, 6th London Edition, p. 59. Burt, New York.
[3]Fairchild, op. cit., article "Accommodation."

modative sort. Under those circumstances accommodation becomes a process of which we are consciously aware, and which we
attempt to further in significant ways. It differs from an ordinary
compromise because compromise implies the unwilling surrender of
cherished beliefs, privileges, or patterns of action. In a true accommodative situation the attempt is to retain cherished values characteristic of the several groups but to adjust behavior in such a way
as to minimize friction. Creative accommodation is becoming a
fairly common instrument of integration in our own culture. For
example, there is a growing interest in meetings of Catholics, Prot-
estants, and Jews to promote mutual understanding and tolerance.
The purpose of such meetings is not to convert the members of one
denomination to the beliefs of another denomination, but to bring
about an accommodative situation. Similar aims exist between
groups differing on other than religious grounds.

Accommodation obviously involves a certain amount of co-operation, since an agreement to disagree is implicit in the accommodative process. It differs from co-operation in that accommodation
involves a narrower area of interaction and does not emphasize the
common, or shared, goals characteristic of co-operation. Goals
remain to a large extent segmented. Accommodation is really an instrumentality by which *differentiated* goals may be more easily attained. Avoidance of conflict is valued because it will lessen potential interference with the differentiated goals and patterns of the
accommodating groups. For example, the relationships between
the Negro minority and the white majority in the United States are
accommodative in nature. On the part of the white majority this
arrangement is dictated by self-interest as much as by any altruistic
feeling for the Negro, and possibly more. The point is that we can
further our own interests more effectively if we are relatively free
from racial strife than if we are interrupted periodically by race
riots. This is even more true of the Negro minority; their very survival has depended on their acceptance of an accommodative situation which in many instances has been discriminatory against
them. They are not satisfied with it, but apart from it their condition would be even worse, since the majority wins out in race
conflict. Whatever avoids race conflict is an advantage both to the
majority and to the minority.

Accommodation, then, is a far different process from co-operation. It includes a limited area of interaction only, and it is apt to be unstable because it lacks the shared goals common in co-operation. It tends to break down under conditions of stress. Its terms must be readjusted to meet changing conditions. It is limited in time. These characteristics, among others, make accommodation *contractual* in nature, with all the limitations of contractualism. It is not a permanently integrating force.

In spite of all these defects, however, accommodation, and especially "creative" accommodation, is an important step in the direction of integration. It is not a final goal but a temporary instrument, to be replaced by co-operation when that becomes possible.

Assimilation

Assimilation, in the sense of social assimilation, is the process by which several distinct cultures, or several segments of one culture, are merged into a single, homogeneous unit.[4] In the process of assimilation the characteristics which mark a given segment as alien either disappear entirely or lose their social significance. For example, the Negro might be assimilated into white culture either through the operation of biological intermixture, which would modify his racial characteristics, or through processes of social change, which would make skin color and other racial characteristics unimportant. Persistence of racial traits would in that case be no bar to assimilation.

Our own nation has assimilated many diverse groupings in the sense that those groupings function as accepted members of our population in much the same way that "native" groupings function. Second- and third-generation members of immigrant stocks—Germans, Italians, or Poles, for example—retain some of their native customs and behavior patterns, but by and large they are indistinguishable from the majority of the population. It is important to note that assimilation does not always imply the complete disappearance of all differentiating traits. It is a social process rather than a biological one, by virtue of which different groups are admitted to a functioning status in a culture.

Assimilation, when it is permitted to operate, is one of the most powerful integrating processes because it affects the meaning of differences and the attitudes taken toward differences, thereby re-

[4]Fairchild, op. cit., article "Social Accommodation."

moving some of the chief sources of conflict arising from segmentation of a population. It would, for example, provide an ultimate
and final solution for the so-called "Negro problem." Strong prejudices exist, however, against its operation upon that problem and
other problems in the United States in which assimilation might
function. The source of much of this prejudice is a fear of the
different, which characterizes many people, and pride of ancestry, which also is common. As fear disappears and an appreciation of human values increases, assimilation may operate more
effectively.

SOCIAL MOBILITY

Social mobility is *the process by which people and cultural products
move from one position to another in the social structure.* There are two
well-recognized types of social mobility.

1. The first type is vertical social mobility, which involves movement from one class of the social structure to another by individuals
or by aggregates. For example, an individual starts life as an
"average" citizen from the viewpoint of his social status, but he
gradually acquires wealth, power, prestige, and titles which raise
his social status. He becomes a "leader" in his community and an
"outstanding" individual in his society. He develops relationships
with a higher class than that into which he was born. He has moved
vertically upward in the social scale. The reverse may also happen,
of course, as in the case of individuals of high status who lose their
wealth, or whose power and prestige are dissipated by revolution,
or whose position is altered by slow cultural change. They move
vertically downward in the social scale.[5]

Cultural products, like people, may move vertically upward or
downward in the social structure. This is true both of material and
of immaterial cultural products. For example, automobiles were
once the possession of the "higher" and wealthier classes exclusively,
a situation which is still to a degree true in some European countries. In America the automobile, along with many other kinds of
machines and household appliances, has descended through the
range of social classes until it is now distributed throughout the
social structure. The same is true of such immaterial cultural

[5]P. A. Sorokin, *Social Mobility*, especially Chap. VIII. Harper, New York, 1927.

products as ideas, beliefs, fads, fashions, and other codes, including the behavior patterns pertaining to them. Originating in the higher classes, they have moved downward, or are in the process of moving downward through all the classes in the social structure. Again, the reverse may take place, that is, patterns originating in "lower classes" may rise in the social scale to be accepted in the higher classes. A common example in our own times is the use of slang expressions, most of which travel upward from criminal and other "low class" individuals. The same is true of popular dances, popular music, and a fair amount of our popular literature. Circulation between classes takes place both from above down and from below upward.

2. The second type of social mobility is referred to as horizontal social mobility. That term describes movement in the social structure which does not involve a change in status or social position, though it does involve changes in social relationships. For example, individuals or aggregates may alter their political affiliations, their religious connections, or their recreational patterns without a change in status. In some instances horizontal social mobility is accompanied by geographical social mobility also, that is, by movement in geographical space. In many other cases geographical mobility either is entirely absent or is of very minor significance.

As in the case of vertical social mobility, horizontal mobility is possible not only for people but also for cultural products. Beliefs, customs, and ideas may spread from a limited grouping of people to wider groupings. In America this horizontal mobility of ideas and customs is very rapid. In some other cultures it has been very slow, with the result that there have been major differences in language and other culture patterns within a given population. For some years the inhabitants of northern Britain were almost wholly unable to understand the English dialect of the inhabitants of southern Britain. In Germany dialect changes were noticeable within the relatively short distance of forty miles from Berlin. The greater mobility of people and of culture patterns in the United States has tended to prevent this major type of regional differentiation, though there are, of course, minor differences between regions.

Cultures tend to develop "agencies of social mobility," through the operation of which the general process of circulation becomes systematized. The institution, or institutions, of major importance in a culture usually serve as channels by which individuals may rise in the social scale. In our own culture the economic system has served as a very important channel of vertical social mobility, since our class structure is largely based on the possession of wealth, and our cultural interest is very strongly oriented in an economic direction. The traditional pattern of success in America has been that of the poor boy who has "started at the bottom" of a business and has "worked up" to a superior position. The economic institution is still our commonest agency for social circulation.

In European culture five centuries ago the orientation of interest was largely in the direction of the religious institution. We are not surprised, then, to discover that religion was a very important channel of vertical circulation. People of various kinds of talent from the lower classes upon entering the Church could rise to positions of extreme influence in the religious hierarchy. This was not wholly a matter of religion, since the dominating position of the Church made it also an important political influence. Thus the famous Cardinal Wolsey, chancellor of England under Henry VIII, was the son of a butcher, a fact which irritated the "nobility," especially when they had to be subservient to him. The prestige and authority of religion has declined, but the Church still remains an agency of social mobility, particularly when it is organized according to a hierarchic pattern. Many of our contemporary church officials have come from the "lower classes," but they exert considerable influence because of their hierarchic position.

Other channels of vertical social circulation have varied with varying cultures. In imperialistic cultures the military and government services have been important; in others, the learned professions; and in still others artistic pursuits have been significant. Our point here is that the process of social mobility does not take place in a haphazard fashion. It is part of the totality of a given culture, and operates in connection with the areas of interest which characterize that culture.

The mobility of cultural products, material and immaterial, is furthered by the contemporary development of means of mass communication, mass information, and mass influence. Their spread is no longer the result of slow contacts between different classes in the population. It is planned, hastened, and otherwise facilitated at least to the extent that commercial interests may benefit from it. The result is, as we have suggested, that there are few isolated areas in the United States and few isolated individuals. Culture patterns resemble each other throughout the nation. This situation may or may not be desirable from the evaluative viewpoint, but from the viewpoint of social mobility and its effects there is no doubt of its efficiency.

Social mobility functions to integrate the segments of an aggregate in a number of ways. 1. Through its operation the composition of the several classes in society is more homogeneous than it was in those past cultures which restricted social mobility. The same type of individual, and in many cases actually the same individuals, make up the membership of higher as well as lower classes. Family relationships and previous status bind the population of the higher classes to those of the lower. There is, of course, a certain amount of exclusiveness and of pretense among the "newly rich" and other recent migrants to a higher status. But this is largely a surface affair. Resemblances between the members of our several social classes are stronger than differences.

The situation is quite different in contemporary societies, mostly Oriental, which are organized on caste lines, with relatively little social mobility permitted. Under those circumstances the population of a higher class differs abruptly from that of lower classes. A somewhat similar condition prevailed in Western culture some centuries ago when, for example, the upper classes of England spoke an entirely different language from that of the lower classes, and lived in an entirely different social world.

2. The dissemination of material goods throughout the several segments of our contemporary population is also integrative in effect. The possessions of the higher classes differ in degree from those of the middle classes but not markedly in kind. Clothing, furniture, automobiles, and similar possessions may be much more elaborate in the homes of the wealthy, but they are not of an entirely different construction, nor are they more efficient than those in the homes of the middle classes. Unfortunately there is still too large a portion of our people who do not have the possessions of the middle and higher classes. Consequently there is a residuum of people not wholly integrated into our social organization. But a much larger majority does share in the advances of civilization than

Interdependence, then, is in part based on the biological facts of childhood, adolescence, and old age. We are therefore accustomed to the situation and accept its extensions into areas not related to biological fact. Those extensions are many, resulting largely from increasing specialization in industrial and other fields. In turn, specialization arises from an increasing complexity of social and other relationships. For example, our contacts with other cultures and with other nations which have widely differing ways of life have increased markedly in the past hundred years. It is necessary to have a corps of specialists to assist our understanding of these other people and to formulate our relationships with them. Very often the individuals we choose as specialists are incompetent, or they are hampered by circumstances beyond their control, but that fact does not alter our need for specialists if we are to understand the problems of world relationships. That is only another way of saying that we are dependent on specialists in world relationships.

Similarly, our increasing understanding of nature has brought about the situation in which no one individual can comprehend in detail the whole of science or the whole of engineering. Again we are dependent on specialists, not only for the increase of knowledge but also for the application of knowledge to specific situations. Because specialization does produce goods and services in plenty and because it does produce an efficient industrial organization, we are favorably disposed toward it, accepting implicitly its accompanying condition of interdependence. It is only occasionally that the fact of interdependence is forcibly brought to our attention, and in such situations, as we suggested before, we blame individuals rather than the fact of interdependence.

But at this point the "necessity" aspect of interdependence intrudes. Even if we did not blame individuals, even if we should try to establish another type of social organization not so highly specialized and therefore not so characterized by interdependence, we should be met by almost insurmountable problems. For one thing, many of us would become functionless under any other than a specialized interdependent system. Our whole way of life has been developed so that our skills operate in connection with those of many other people. Our complicated system of exchange and of marketing would disappear, taking away the reason for existence of wholesalers, retailers, commission merchants, and many others.

Our standards of living include the assumption that goods and services will be cheap, efficient, and widely available. The fact is, then, that we are forced to cling to the specialized interdependent system we have developed, whether we want to or not, barring some kind of extreme revolution which would lead to the complete destruction of our whole social organization.

It is sometimes suggested that the fact of interdependence itself will lead to the destruction of our society. That is a mistaken viewpoint. Interdependence is a process of great significance in our times, but it is not inevitably freighted with doom. It is a situation which, if we understand it, we can use constructively as an instrument for social progress.

The way in which interdependence functions to integrate the segments of an aggregate is perhaps obvious from our discussion up to this point. First of all, it forces us into relationships with other segments than our own, even though we may not welcome such relationships. The fact is, to use the economic field as an example, that labor, capital, and consumer are so inextricably related that the one cannot function without the others. This situation is often glossed over by individual members of the one segment or the other who are seeking to further their own interests, but it remains a fact nontheless. Karl Marx's economic theories are inaccurate from the economic viewpoint, but they remain powerful political influences because they assert, among other things, that labor creates all value and that therefore labor is the only factor of production, a viewpoint that naturally appeals to labor. The same may be said of those theories that allocate to management a position of sole importance in production. In popularized form such beliefs ascribe a mystical quality to "captains of industry" which makes them not only intellectual giants but also models of benevolence and citizenship. These beliefs appeal not only to management but also to a goodly portion of our people, very probably because the concept is romantic and also because reliance on such leadership promises security to the common man. In reality, whether the fact is acceptable or not, labor, capital, and consumer are equally important in our economic system.

A second way in which interdependence integrates the segments of an aggregate is through the creation of favorable attitudes toward other segments on which we are dependent. It is true, of course, that antagonisms between segments also exist, but there is definitely the opposite and favorable viewpoint also.

SUMMARY

Integrative social processes are those which tend to draw the segments of society more closely together. Co-operation is one of the most significant of these processes because it underlies many of our daily activities and because it springs from strong emotion-feeling aspects of the co-operating individuals. Accommodation is a temporary form of integration, based on mutual agreement to disagree and to avoid areas of friction. It is contractual in nature and therefore limited. Assimilation is a powerful integrating force, but there are prejudices against its operation in important aspects of social relationships in the United States.

Social mobility and interdependence have been two of the most active integrative forces in our contemporary culture. It is important to remember that social mobility includes the movement of both people and cultural products.

READINGS

SOROKIN, P. A. *Social Mobility*. Harper & Brothers, New York, 1927. Chap. VII, "Social Mobility, Its Forms and Fluctuations."

YOUNG, KIMBALL. *Sociology*. American Book Company, 1942. Pp. 844–867, "Accommodation; Assimilation."

GILLIN, J. L. and GILLIN, J. P. *An Introduction to Sociology*. The Macmillan Company, New York, 1942. Pp. 655–705, "Processes of Association: Accommodation, Acculturation, and Assimilation."

LINTON, RALPH. *The Study of Man*. D. Appleton-Century Company, Inc., New York, 1936. Chap. XVI, "Participation in Culture."

CHAPTER XX

SOCIAL REORGANIZATION

Social reorganization is "the establishment of new systems of relationships or values in a social group or society, particularly after a period of disorganization or rapid social change."[1] The discussion of reorganization follows logically after our treatment of social processes, since both in disorganization and in reorganization the social processes involved are very important. Disorganization is the result of a breaking down of accepted modes of behavior, a situation in which the processes of differentiation, stratification, and specialization play a part. As we attempt to establish new modes of behavior to replace the old, we find that the processes of co-operation, accommodation, mobility, and interdependence are useful instrumentalities in furthering that effort. The process of reorganization is by no means a simple one. Some of its difficulties arise from the complex nature of the relationships between institutions and processes, a situation that requires further analysis.

THE AREA OF SOCIAL REORGANIZATION

One significant thing we have discovered in our attempt to discuss social institutions and social processes is that they exist and function as parts of a social whole—they cannot be discussed separately as unrelated phenomena. Thus in our treatment of the economic system we were forced to take cognizance of its political effects and of its relationship to the number and the kind of people in a population. Similarly, we discovered that education has to function with children many of whose basic attitudes have been set by their early experiences with their families and who therefore react to the educational system in terms of interactions occurring before

[1] H. P. Fairchild (Ed.), *Dictionary of Sociology*, p. 291. Philosophical Library, New York, 1944.

they entered school. In turn, both educational and economic systems affect the family institution by assuming functions which used to be carried on in the family, one result being that family patterns have lost some of the meanings they used to have, thus weakening our family system. Religion has been affected by the growth of substitute patterns which function for individuals, and to some extent for the aggregate, in ways similar to some of the traditional functions of religion. The whole field of government functioning has been vitally affected by changes in our economic, educational, and family institutions.

It is obvious, then, that institutions do not exist as separate and unrelated systems. Changes occurring in one are reflected in the status and functions of the others.

Much the same situation applies to the social processes we have been discussing. They are interrelated in very complex ways. Competition and differentiation both tend toward conflict, but they may also be met by integrative processes such as co-operation and accommodation. Specialization, which is disintegrative in tendency, gives opportunity for the functioning of interdependence, which is integrative in tendency. Social mobility of people and of cultural products operates to make stratification less segmenting in its effects than it would otherwise be. The operation of one process is interwoven with the operation of other processes.

We can go a step further and suggest that institutions and processes are also very closely related. As we saw in the case of social mobility, existing institutional patterns often function as agencies through which the process takes place. Institutions also aid or hinder the operation of other processes. For example, the economic system, as we have developed it, encourages the process of specialization to a marked degree and also facilitates the development of differentiation. Religion, on the other hand, has functioned to modify the process of social differentiation in those cases where it asserts that all men are children of one God and members of one Church. It may also modify the process of specialization by subordinating scientific and economic activity to its own patterns. Education has hastened the process of differentiation and of specialization by developing different curricula in response to specialized needs, curricula which have often been very narrow in scope because they were intensively concerned with one limited area of behavior. In recent times education has been engaged in an integrative attempt functioning through its "general education" programs. Similarly, government may aid or hinder the operation of processes of integration and disintegration.

What we have then, in reality, is not a collection of separate factors that we can designate as institutions and a collection of separate series of events which we can isolate as social processes. We separate and isolate them artifically for purposes of study, but in the actualities of human association they are bound so closely together that they are almost indistinguishable. If we consider our own lives as individuals, the picture may be somewhat clearer. We do not regard ourselves as participating in any such abstract things as social processes, nor do we habitually think of ourselves as functioning in accordance with institutional modes of conduct. Instead, we simply behave in ways which seem to us appropriate to particular situations, without analysis of the reasons for our behavior. The sources of our conduct patterns is undoubtedly in such cultural facts as institutions, customs, and social processes, but we are not consciously aware of that fact. To repeat, we behave as circumstances suggest that we should in view of our total background, habits, associates, and so on.

So it is in the case of the aggregates we study in sociology. The basic phenomenon we are investigating is human behavior in association. Sociological concepts such as institution and process are in part descriptions of certain modes of human behavior in association and in part instruments for the analysis of such behavior. Our primary interest is in the behavior itself.

The point here is that any plan for social reorganization must take account of the fact that human behavior in association is not logical in all its aspects in the sense of being adjusted to the attainment of given ends and the accomplishment of given purposes. If it were so, the investigation of our associational patterns would very probably be much simpler than it is. In fact, it is often impossible for our conduct to be completely logical, since we do not have clearly in mind what our purposes are. For example, what is the "general purpose" of our living together in association? We may give broad answers to that question, such as "the greatest good of the greatest number," but they are so broad that they are practically meaningless. Any more specific answers are apt to meet with disapproval by one segment of the population or another. Again, granted that we have in mind a specific purpose, often we do not know how to adjust the many factors in association to such purpose. There are too many other people with differentiated viewpoints involved in the situation; customs and beliefs are too firmly fixed to be altered readily; evaluations of different modes of behavior vary too widely. Thus one group will advocate a "scientific" program which will be repugnant to other groups convinced that the "real way to progress" is through "moral rearmament" or something of the sort. Human association, then, is not logical in all its aspects.

The following fact is important, however. While it is still true that an over-all pattern for social reorganization will meet with many difficulties, it is also true that in our culture we have learned how to co-ordinate widespread and complicated patterns of association much more efficiently than most past cultures. Industrial enterprise, for example, involves the concentration of raw materials from distant locations into a relatively compact area, the gathering together of labor and machinery in the same area, and systems for the dispersal and sale of products on a nationwide or a worldwide basis. All this requires far-flung planning. Similarly, many specialized services of government, such as the police and highway services, are equally involved and complicated; yet they are functioning with a degree of efficiency. Further plans for the operation of insurance and public-aid programs are proceeding along much the same lines. It is, then, by no means true that we are wholly inexperienced in the organization of projects involving many different kinds of people and processes of concentration and dispersal over wide areas. It is possible that an application of similar methods to general social reorganization may succeed to a greater degree than our ancestors would have supposed possible.

Methods of Social Reorganization

There are two contrasting viewpoints regarding the methods of social reorganization to be followed.

1. The first of those methods is familiar to us under the general term *laissez faire*, which advocates as little interference as possible with what are assumed to be the "natural" processes of adjustment and readjustment. As we have intimated several times in the course

of this book, laissez faire has been the most popular American approach to social problems. It has come to occupy the status of a strongly entrenched prejudice in some segments of our population, but in its origin and early development it was by no means simply prejudice. On the contrary, it was a coherent and logical system based on certain beliefs and assumptions.

Important among those beliefs was the doctrine that the "free" interaction of various patterns of behavior would lead to the survival of the pattern most appropriate to given circumstances and to the adoption of that pattern as the approved one. For example, suppose that an area of disorganization existed between labor and capital. According to the laissez-faire theory the thing to do would be to permit separate aggregates involved in the conflict to arrive at separate solutions. Thus in one enterprise the "reorganizational solution" might be complete dominance of labor by capital; in another it might be complete dominance of capital by labor; in a third, a system of organized bargaining; in a fourth, dominance of both labor and capital by consumers; and in a fifth, no permanent solution at all. These several "solutions" would continue in operation for a period of time, possibly an extended period of time, at the end of which the results of the "most appropriate" relationship would be so obviously the best that it would be adopted by the great majority of industrial concerns, the other systems falling into disuse. In that way the free interaction of different systems would lead to the "survival" and the adoption of the "best" system. Reorganization would have come about "naturally."

There are many other illustrations of the laissez-faire doctrine. For example, the manufacturer of inferior goods would, according to the theory, soon find it impossible to continue in business because, as buyers discovered the poor quality of his goods in comparison with those of other manufacturers, they would refuse to deal with him and there would be no sale for his product. Similarly, different systems of government would produce different results, good and bad. With the passage of time the quality of these results would become plain for all to see and the "most appropriate" system would survive, the others disappearing.

The basic laissez-faire belief in the value of "free" interactions rests on certain further assumptions. Important among these is the assumption that interaction will actually and in reality be free.

Thus in the case of the manufacturer of inferior goods cited above, it is assumed that there will be no combination of manufacturers to control the quality of product; that the buyers of a given product will have the knowledge and the opportunity realistically to compare different products, which implies only a restricted amount of advertising with the total absence of bombastic and misleading advertising; and that the products of different manufacturers will be equally available in various areas of the country. To the extent that these assumptions do not hold, laissez faire will not operate.

Similarly, in the case of free interaction between different systems of government, it is assumed that organized government propaganda, the isolation of populations from sources of information, the operation of secret police, and similar restricting influences will be absent. To the extent that they are present, laissez faire cannot operate effectively.

Our discussion thus far should indicate that the theory of laissez faire, as such, is by no means shallow. Given the assumed circumstances, its operation would in time produce an adjustment of group associational patterns to a given environment. We may even suggest that the adjustment would be a "strong" one, since it would develop from the processes of human behavior in a given environment rather than from the artificial imposition of a "plan" by a dominating minority group, and would therefore tend to be accepted as an authoritative cultural product. The difficulty in our own times is that the circumstances which the theory of laissez faire presupposes do not exist. Industrial combinations, flamboyant and irrelevant advertising, and instruments of mass influence and mass persuasion all combine to prevent "free" interaction of different behavior patterns.

Another belief which underlay the laissez-faire theory was that the operation of "natural" forces inevitably produced "progress." In other words, the theory of the good results of "free" interaction was extended from the relatively narrow area of one culture and of one restricted period of time to include the whole of human development. A by-product of Darwinism, this belief traced the gradual progress of mankind through a series of well-defined steps culminating in the European civilization of the later nineteenth century and presumably continuing beyond that time in much the same fashion as it had before. A "drive toward progress" appeared to be inherent in the very structure of the universe. Under such circumstances it was not only safe to permit the operation of free interaction, it was also the "right" thing to do.

In current thought the inevitability of progress is seriously questioned. Our understanding of evolution is such that we are impressed by its "neutral" character rather than by its progressive character. We note that many kinds of organisms which developed in the course of evolutionary change have disappeared from the earth. For those organisms, evolution meant destruction rather than continuance in a progressively "better" form. It is sometimes argued that, even granted that the above is true, the forms which have disappeared have been replaced by "better" forms, so that the total result of evolution is progressive, even though for specific forms it may not be. We have, however, no way of knowing whether or not our own culture will persist as one of the ultimate products of the evolutionary process. It may be one of the forms which will disintegrate and disappear as many past forms of culture have disintegrated and disappeared. Such a supposition would have been impossible for the influential post-Darwinian "classical" evolutionists.

This somewhat theoretical questioning of progress is reinforced by empirical observation. We note that war and other types of conflict are increasing.[2] We are distrustful of "over optimistic" plans to prevent war. In fact, we prophecy the onset of a third world war within a few years, on the basis of our experience since the year 1900. There is no proof that our expectations are accurate or that they will be borne out in fact. The point is that our whole world outlook differs from that of the classical advocates of laissez faire. We know of no "drive toward progress" inherent in the structure of the universe on which we may rely. Arguments for laissez faire are more counsel of desperation than assertions of faith.

A third proposition advanced in favor of laissez faire rested in the belief that our knowledge of human relationships was too limited to permit wise planning and intelligent control. This is a point of view which is still maintained to some extent, and which is still partially valid.

In the period from 1200 to 1500 A.D., roughly, control of all aspects of human relationships was the common practice, a control exercised chiefly by the Church. This system of organization was

[2]P. A. Sorokin, *Cultural and Social Dynamics*, Vol. III, Part Two.

logical in view of the common assumption that divine law had been revealed to the Church, that natural law was in accordance with divine law, and that human law had only to agree with those two superhuman systems in order to be morally right. Economic and political relationships were then simply matters to be arranged in accordance with human justice, which in turn rested on the unquestioned ideal of divine justice. Since 1500 there has been a marked decline in the world outlook which roots human and natural law in divine law, though the system is still maintained in Catholic countries.

What happened elsewhere than in Catholic countries was that a concept of natural law apart from any divine sanctions came to occupy a predominant place in explanations of the universe. At first the devotion to natural law in this sense was semimystical in character, partaking of the nature of a religion but without recognizing a higher law than that of nature. It was assumed that natural law produced an order in the universe similar to the order inherent in a well-constructed and efficiently functioning machine. The "happy life" consisted in discovering the principles of this order and living in accordance with them, both individually and collectively. The period differed from the preceding one in that natural law was not revealed; it had to be discovered by man through his own investigations. It resembled the preceding period in that, once the laws were discovered and human relationships were adjusted to them, social organization approached perfection and the world became a happy garden erected for man's betterment in which, as Pope said, "And spite of pride, in erring reason's spite, One truth is clear, Whatever is, is right." Naturally, a type of laissez faire would be the appropriate form of social action under such circumstances.

This period of mysticism was followed by an increased concern with natural law as a result of the operation of forces of nature, quite without regard to any religious implications. This was the era of the so-called "iron laws of nature" in which man was held to be an infinitesimal creature inhabiting an unimportant corner of the universe. Man's social organization and other relationships were assumed to be part of an inevitable complex of natural forces, but they were much less significant than the physical facts of the universe as unfolded in the "grand, but stern, drama of Nature."

In any case, man was under the dominion of the "iron laws of nature," and there was little he could do except adjust to them. The adjustment differed from that of Pope's happy garden, however. In Pope's thinking the laws of nature operated for the benefit of mankind; in the thinking of the "iron-laws-of-nature" school, natural law operated quite without reference to human benefit. It was a fact of the universe which we had to accept and which conditioned the whole of our life.

This viewpoint was advanced as a criticism of democracy, for example. In a famous passage Thomas Carlyle points out that if a ship has to get around Cape Horn certain procedures must be followed, regardless of the wishes of captain or crew. He suggests that the crew as a body may vote this or that or the other to their own satisfaction, but unless they follow the laws of navigation they will end on the rocks and not get around Cape Horn at all.[3] So of other plans for social reorganization: it was all very well to vote this or that, to advocate the other, and to demand what we would. The stern facts of nature remained unalterable, and only as we adjusted to them could we survive at all, much less "progress."

In turn, the "iron-laws-of-nature" outlook has been replaced by the modern scientific approach which regards its "laws" as more or less tentative expressions of the results of our investigations thus far, which may or may not be accurate. One test of accuracy is our ability to predict on the basis of our generalizations. Another test of accuracy is our ability to control natural occurrences. If we can predict and control, we believe that we understand. This seemingly innocent statement really has very important implications. It implies a shift in our whole outlook, a shift from a passive attitude toward nature and natural law to an active attitude. The "realm of nature" becomes not something to which we must inevitably adjust; it becomes something we can control and use for our own purposes. Admittedly, the element of adjustment is still present. We can use nature only by understanding it and by operating in accordance with its data. The point is that we use our understanding not only to bring our activities into agreement with natural law, the common viewpoint of the past, but to alter nature so that its circumstances are more suited to our purposes.

[3]Cited in *The Howling Mob*, by A Gentleman With a Duster. McBride, New York, 1927.

Illustrations of this procedure abound. Electricity is no longer a "curiosity of nature," but is a source of power we use in numberless ways; the "iron laws of gravity" are not things we take account of merely to keep us from falling down and injuring ourselves, but they become instrumentalities by which we fly airplanes; physiology is not simply an area in which we may add to our knowledge, but it is also an area in which we effect major changes through medical techniques. Human relationships, then, must also be an area in which the increase of knowledge is accompanied by greater ability to predict and by greater ability to control, unless we are to adopt the rather curious position that human relationships are entirely outside the realm of nature and are therefore not amenable either to scientific understanding or to intelligent control. As we suggested earlier, this view of human relationships is not uncommon. It is justified in so far as our knowledge is as yet limited. It can hardly be justified on the grounds that understanding and control are inherently impossible in that field.

Even if we agree that our knowledge is not yet sufficient to permit intelligent control and planning in human relationships, that agreement changes our attitude toward the whole situation. We no longer say that laissez faire is necessary because in the nature of the case no other procedure is possible, nor do we suggest that laissez faire is the only proper procedure in view of the presence of "iron laws of nature." We say only that we are still limited in our ability to control human relationships, which is quite a different viewpoint.

We have discussed the laissez-faire attitude somewhat at length because it is still to a large degree part of the popular philosophy of a large portion of our population. It is inaccurate to stigmatize the doctrine itself or the people who hold it as stupid and cantankerous. The doctrine itself has a long and honorable background. Changed attitudes toward it spring from the comprehensive changes which have taken place in science and the scientific outlook on the universe. But, in turn, those changes in scientific outlook are not yet fully organized with reference to human relationships and they have not as yet reached many strata of our culture. It is natural, under those circumstances, for many people to cling to the older outlook. It is also necessary, however, for us to examine the newer outlook.

2. That newer outlook is the second major viewpoint with reference to social reorganization mentioned some pages back. Essentially it is based on the belief that the phenomena of human relationships are "natural" phenomena to the extent that they can, in large part, be understood through the application of the scientific method, and that they can be controlled by the manipulation of our knowledge. It is sometimes said that the social scientist lags far behind the physical scientist in understanding his area of study and in the ability to use his findings for control purposes. In fact, that statement was very commonly made just after the Second World War, under the stimulus of the emotionalism incident to the discovery and the use of the atomic bomb. It was then pointed out that the physical scientist not only could fabricate an atomic bomb, and many other mechanical devices, but could also control their operation. The thing that could not be controlled was the use human beings would make of the bomb. The implication was that social scientists "did not know how to control" people and that social science "had better catch up to physical science" in respect to control.

All that sounds very plausible, but a good argument can be made against it. The statement that social scientists do not know *how* to control human relationships is inaccurate. The mere methods of such control are rather well known. For example, in totalitarian states the isolation of populations from world contacts, indoctrination through education, influence exerted by propaganda and other means of mass pressure, strongly emotional appeals, and the use of the several varieties of force, are all effective in controlling human conduct. To a lesser extent these same influences operate in our own culture. Advertising, for example, influences not only the sale of goods but also certain aspects of the public taste. The movies function in a similar way to set standards in some strata of our population, as do popular literature and the press. As Mr. Walter Lippmann pointed out some years ago, the major portion of our population does not react to its surroundings as they actually are but to those surroundings as they think they are. What they think they are is determined by the influence of whatever popular sources of "information" they consult. These sources include not only the newspapers, but also the increasing number of periodicals of a "commentary" nature and their counterparts on the radio.

In effect, all these means of influence introduce new factors into the basic interaction pattern of human association. Instead of permitting "free" interaction with all the factors of a cultural environment, those people who are interested in controlling human relationships restrict the interaction to specific and desired factors. Very often this does not involve the suppression of facts, but rather the "interpretation" of facts and extended "comment" on them, both of which give large scope for subtle, and very possibly unconscious, distortion of facts. The reaction of the average citizen is not to the facts themselves, but to the interpretation or commentary. The process is by no means entirely new. We are familiar with it in the form of political speeches, political platforms, and similar documents of the past. The older process, however, is being extended and amplified through the increased use of radio and the enlarged circulation of newspapers and periodicals.

There is no apparent reason to doubt that if this process were carried far enough an almost complete control of human relationships could be established. If all the influences impinging on an individual were carefully controlled and carefully manipulated, the controlling segment of a population could produce individuals whose reactions would be completely predictable. For example, a carefully controlled educational system, a completely subservient press and radio, censored motion pictures and other forms of recreation, repetition of desired ideas and patterns, plus stern repression of any "deviating tendencies," and public reward of conformity, would so restrict the interactions of a majority of a population that there would be little variation in reaction. One "advantage" of this kind of control would rest in the fact that force would become progressively less necessary because the whole pattern of uniform conduct would seem to the majority of individuals concerned perfectly normal, "right," and proper.

Yet very few of us in America would advocate the establishment of such a system. We know how to do it, but we do not propose to do it. The real problem, then, lies not in the lack of information on the part of the social sciences. It lies in the fact that we hesitate to apply such controls to people. Such hesitation springs largely from moral and ethical considerations. Human beings differ from machines, which the physical scientist controls, and our whole outlook on the problems of human control is affected by that difference.

It is not only the fact that other people resemble ourselves; it is also the fact that we regard them as values, or ends, in themselves. Manipulation of other people does not accord with the principles of democracy and the American conscience. When we lose respect for human beings, we are well on the way toward totalitarianism. Even when we assert that we control others "for their own good," the whole arrangment appears to be of doubtful validity.

The whole question of the ethical justification of controls is a complex one, and one that lies outside the domain of sociology. Incidentally, it is also one which does not occur to some of the rather naïve physical scientists who urge the social sciences to "catch up with physics." As we noted in an earlier chapter, co-operative social control of the group by itself is the only type which is justifiable in our traditional democratic theory. But that kind of control awaits an understanding by a majority of the population of its own processes of living, and it depends on the clear enunciation of democratic standards of association in terms of which co-operative control may be exercised. It will not be rapid, nor will it produce the kind of "efficient" results that control of mechanical devices does. Nonetheless, we believe that it is the kind of control to be sought.

The second attitude toward social reorganization, then, is based on the understanding of the processes of human association and on the use of those processes for co-operative control. It differs from laissez faire in major ways. It resembles the attitude of the modern scientist toward the universe which he studies, with the important difference that our valuation of human beings introduces a degree of restraint in relation to control not common in physical science.

Steps in Social Reorganization

Under the contemporary view of social reorganization as a positive process, in contrast with the laissez-faire view, there are a number of steps advocated to bring order into reorganizational activities. In many instances these steps represent an oversimplification of actualities, especially as far as neglect of the interrelationships of institutions and processes is concerned. In others the enthusiasm of the individuals concerned in the programs is apt to make them somewhat less cautious than the circumstances would warrant. The whole process of social reorganization is complex and requires careful investigation of certain areas of activity. Very often these investigations lie outside the domain of observational and scientific sociology. They involve social-work activities, philosophical speculations, and political planning. We shall examine them here as cultural phenomena; for they are behavior patterns which characterize our own culture, and some understanding of them as behavior patterns is necessary for an understanding of contemporary culture. We outline below the principal areas of investigation in relation to social reorganization.

1. *The Determination of Goals.* This is an area which is highly philosophical and ethical in nature, and it is also an area which is largely neglected in many programs for social reorganization. The necessity of having clearly in mind a definite goal or purpose as the ultimate aim of reorganization is perhaps obvious. For example, in the area of conflict do we propose to do away entirely with all conflict? Or do we want to reduce conflict to a minimum, admitting that there will be a residue of conflict? Or do we want to remove conflict in a restricted area of association—say, that involved in labor-capital relationships—rather than destroy conflict entirely? In the case of unemployment is our goal to provide employment for everyone? Or do we assume that there will always be an irreducible minimum of unemployed? Do we propose simply to provide "a job" as a source of income for everyone, or do we propose to adjust human abilities to certain kinds of work? Again, what do we want to do with criminals: isolate them for the protection of society, punish them, or develop them into usable citizens for the society?

Granting that we can state a goal in one or the other of these cases, to our own satisfaction at least, can we justify that goal? In other words, why do we want to pursue those ends? Enthusiastic as we ourselves may be about our program, others may take it coolly. Some justification of our proposals becomes necessary. Is the program based on the belief that the "best population" is that which is happy and healthy and contented because it has all it wants? But what shall we include in its *wants*? Should they consist of material goods only, or of immaterial values as well? Shall we admit differing definitions of *values* or shall we impose our own definition?

The number of questions that might be asked along these lines is almost limitless. Yet some of them must be asked, and answered, if an intelligent program of social reorganization is to be formed.

We discovered in our discussion of the economic system that disagreement as to the purpose of the system was one fruitful source of conflicting views regarding it. The same is true of projects relating to social reorganization. Without agreement on purpose—which must come at the very beginning of a program—the co-operative activity of a number of individuals is impossible.

It is sometimes intimated, in comparisons of the laissez-faire viewpoint with the contemporary viewpoint of social reorganization, that laissez faire is "too slow and cumbersome" in its operation to be useful in our times. Whether that intimation is correct or not, the fact is that "modern, scientific programs" for social reorganization will also be slow and cumbersome because of the necessity of preliminary determination of goals and their justification. Unfortunately, some enthusiasts labor under the misapprehension that the application of "modern science" to social problems will produce speedy and efficient remedies. This is not the case, chiefly because the interrelationships of institutions and processes in contemporary culture are such that we are confronted with many "unexpected consequences of social action" which may produce results quite different from those anticipated.[4] For example, an entirely benevolent attempt to raise the level of living of workers in a certain industry by forcing an increase in wages may make it cheaper for the employer to install new machinery and dispense with some of his workers. Those who are retained may benefit; those who are discharged will become part of the unemployed, temporarily if not permanently. The relationships between labor and management in that specific industry do not exist in social isolation; they exist as part of a total collection of processes and institutions, including the invention of new machinery. The same is true of the other relationships involved in social reorganization.

2. *Investigation of Resources.* Granted that some acceptable goal is stated in meaningful terms, the second step in most programs of social reorganization consists of an examination of the resources, actual and potential, which the society may use in moving toward the stated goal. These resources include human beings as well as accretions of wealth, knowledge, and ideals. Here again the complexity of interrelationships between processes and institutions is

---

[4] P. A. Sorokin, "Is Accurate Social Planning Possible?" *American Sociological Review*, February, 1936.

forced on our attention. Reorganization as a process is limited by
the amount of wealth produced by the economic system, by the
kind of human being resulting from the educational system and
other conditioning factors, by the efficiency and kind of government, and by the existence of special-interest groups whose goals
may conflict with the reorganizational goal. In America we have
vast accumulations of wealth, knowledge, and techniques, as well
as a population which is, by and large, physically superior to many
past populations and which is potentially the equal intellectually of
any population past or present. Obviously if, with our culture, we
were so technically poor and ignorant that we had to spend the
major portion of our time in acquiring the bare necessities of life, we
should have little time to give to social reorganization. Quite the
reverse, however, is true. One of the problems we now face is that
of how to occupy the leisure time of many of our people in some
constructive manner.

Our resources for social reorganization, then, both actual and
potential, are adequate even for ambitious plans. The difficulty is
that processes of differentiation and of specialization tend to impede
the co-operation necessary in carrying out social reorganization
projects.

3. *The Development of Reorganizational Techniques.* In view of the
existence of resources accompanied by differentiation and specialization, some techniques of reorganization become necessary. The
aim of such techniques is the actual use of resources for the goals
specified. Most plans provide for the use of established institutions
and systems such as education, propaganda, religion, and other
means of influence. The purpose here is to utilize all these for the
creation of a favorable public opinion and for the manipulation of
legislative and similar bodies. These techniques have been developed
to a high degree of efficiency in the case of "pressure groups," but
they have not as yet been applied to general reorganizational aims.

4. *The Setting of Immediate Plans.* The three preceding steps are
part of the long-time aspect of social reorganization. Such long-
time aspects are important, but without some immediate action
they may fail to gain public acceptance. These immediate steps
usually consist partly of publicity and partly of action directed at
some specific and, at least on the surface, simple problem which is
already of community interest.

SUMMARY

We have presented in general outline the procedures common to most projects of social reorganization, along with some of the difficulties inherent in the complex relationships between institutions and processes in our own times. We do not suggest that these difficulties are insurmountable, but we do emphasize the fact that the "scientific" approach to social problems will not be productive of immediate and magical results. Some of the difficulties and some of our accomplishments will be noted in Part III, which follows, and which deals with social problems and social policies.

READINGS

"Social Implications of Modern Science," *The Annals of the American Academy of Political and Social Sciences*, Vol. 249, January, 1947. Papers by specialists, dealing with the effect of modern science on technology, political institutions, social change, and the problems of values.

PANCOAST, OMAR. *Occupational Mobility*. Columbia University Press, New York, 1941. A plan for allocating our labor supply to obtain the optimum employment of human resources, involving widespread reorganizational activity. To be read critically.

HOFSTADTER, RICHARD. *Social Darwinism in American Thought, 1860–1915*. The University of Pennsylvania Press, Philadelphia, 1944. Traces the impact of evolutionism on social and ethical thought in America, with chapters on the dissenters from Darwinism.

SOROKIN, P. A. *Society, Culture, and Personality*. Harper & Brothers, New York, 1947. Chap. 34, "Life-Span, Mortality, and Resurrection of Social Groups."

PENDELL, ELMER (Ed.). *Society under Analysis*. The Jacques Cattell Press, Lancaster, Pennsylvania, 1942. Chap. 25, "Leadership."

PART THREE

SOCIAL PROBLEMS

AND SOCIAL POLICIES

INTRODUCTION

A PROBLEM is any situation which interferes with the orderly course
of life to the extent that it requires some activity directed toward its
modification. The significance of a given problem may vary from
individual to individual. Thus, a given set of circumstances which
interferes with the orderly course of one individual's life may interfere to only a slight extent, or not at all, with that of another individual. Correspondingly less pressure to modify the circumstances
will exist in the case of the second individual. For example, the fact
of being unemployed will seriously hamper a person of high standards and of a sensitive nature, not only because he is without funds
to maintain himself at his customary level but also because he feels
himself degraded in the eyes of his neighbors. To another individual
of different standards and of a more sturdy conscience, unemployment is much less of a problem. He willingly accepts public aid or
some other substitute form of income and enjoys his leisure. Similarly, the loss of a leg or some other crippling injury requires much
more drastic adjustment by an individual whose occupation re-

quires physical exertion than it does in the case of a writer or other primarily mental worker. To both, the injury would present problem aspects, but to the one it would be much more serious than to the other.

Problems, then, vary in significance between individuals, their seriousness being measured by the relative amount of pressure toward modification felt by the respective individuals. Of course it is impossible to set up a scale of seriousness and to measure off on such a scale the relative significance of various problems to different people. We are not proposing any such procedure. We are simply pointing out that there is considerable variation between individuals in the amount of pressure toward modification which does exist, whether the variation can be measured accurately or not. When modification takes place in such a way that the situation no longer interferes with the orderly course of life, the problem is said to be solved. Solution may come about in several ways.

1. One solution may be through the modification of the circumstances themselves. In the case of unemployment the obvious modification of the circumstances is for the individual concerned to get a job. In the case of a crippling injury the actual circumstances may not be modified, but artificial devices may operate to reduce the significance of the circumstances to a marked degree. Many problems cannot be solved in this relatively simple fashion.

2. Another possible solution is through a modification of attitudes toward the circumstances creating the problem. Again in the case of unemployment, attitudes may be so modified that the individual concerned no longer wants a job and no longer feels any stigma in connection with his unemployment. During the long depression of the 1930's discouragement, hopelessness, and loss of ambition affected a significant number of people. Unemployment came to be accepted as one of the facts of existence and, as such, acquired the character of an inevitable situation about which an orderly life was organized. The problem inherent in unemployment for the individuals who adopted this attitude was thereby "solved." Most of

us would hold that this was a bad solution, but it is a solution. Since most of us cannot realize the heavy pressure of discouraging factors on those who reached this solution, we are not equipped to judge realistically its goodness or badness.

3. A third solution may be reached through a modification of behavior such that the significance of the circumstances is altered. Thus some unemployed individuals enter college to complete specialized training of some kind which they believe will prepare them to secure a higher kind of work than they could without such training. This procedure does not immediately solve the problem of unemployment. It is an alteration of behavior in which the significance of unemployment is modified. One expects college students to be occupied full time with their college work; lack of a job is the "normal" thing.

Traditionally, a problem is considered purely personal or individual "so long as it is being dealt with within the person's usual resources of means, intelligence, and contacts."[1] It becomes a *social* problem under one or both of the two following conditions: (1) when the problem arises out of the conditions of interaction common in an aggregate or out of the cultural environment of an aggregate; and (2) when the problem can be solved only by the use of the collective resources of the aggregate.[2]

Under class 1 above are included many problems which appear in individuals but which are traceable to the cultural environment in which the individual lives rather than to any inherent individual deficiency. Crime, for example, is an individual behavior pattern, but its roots lie in cultural and social influences exerted on "normal" or "average" individuals. Criminals are not born with a constitutional equipment which predisposes them to a life of crime; they become criminals as a result of their interactions. Crime is a social problem. Congenital mongoloid idiocy, on the other hand, is not,

[1]H. P. Fairchild (Ed.), *Dictionary of Sociology*, p. 234. Philosophical Library, New York, 1944.

[2]Modified from Fairchild, op. cit. p. 289.

so far as we know now, traceable to cultural causes. Thus from the point of view of class 1 it is an individual rather than a social problem. Pathologies such as insanity, addiction to narcotics, and psychoneuroses occupy a middle ground, largely because our knowledge of them is still limited. Some students of those conditions believe that there is a degree of constitutional organic predisposition involved; others hold that cultural factors are the important causative elements.

The present tendency in sociology is to regard an increasing proportion of the problems of individual life as social problems, since current sociological views stress the influence of culture on the development of all individuals. Many problems formerly considered wholly individual and therefore outside the realm of sociology are now included in sociological discussions for that reason.

Under class 2 above are included problem situations which arise from defects of social structure and functioning quite apart from any one individual or any minority of individuals, and which can be solved only by collective effort. War is one example of such a problem, as are large-scale unemployment, political corruption, and mass ignorance. It is obvious that some problems appear in both classes. Crime, for example, may be included in both because it is culturally caused and because it arises from a defect of the social structure and requires a major collective effort for its solution.

As in the case of individual problems, social problems are situations which interfere with the orderly course of life to such an extent that some modification of them becomes necessary. Pressure toward modification varies in accordance with the standards of a particular aggregate. If those standards are largely rooted in the physical survival of the aggregate, problems will center in such matters as famine and its prevention, war and conflict, and the maintenance of a population balance. If the standards include not only physical survival but also psychosocial survival, pressure toward modification will arise in connection with problems related to the preservation of group integrity. Immigration, race mixture, and clash of cultures will become significant. Standards may extend beyond mere physical and group survival to a concern for individual values and development. In such a case, problems will grow out of inadequate educational facilities, inadequate care of children, and similar matters which are considered problems in our own culture.

This means that, just as with individual problems, social problems vary from aggregate to aggregate according to standards and other cultural patterns. Thus a high infant death rate is recognized as a problem in one culture, whereas in another it is not recognized as a problem. Even in our own culture a century ago it was assumed that large numbers of children would inevitably die. Under those circumstances there was no pressure to alter the situation and hence no problem existed. In recent years the infant-mortality rate has been greatly reduced, largely as a result of the application of medical knowledge after a change in our standards had caused it to be recognized as a social problem. So of slavery, a rigid caste system, child labor, the employment of women in industry, occupational diseases, and a host of other problems. From an absolute viewpoint these were always problems; from the sociological viewpoint they were not social problems until they were generally recognized as such and demands for their solution became widespread.

The sociologist, then, regards social problems as one of the products of interaction. Individuals who develop behavior patterns of a type which the aggregate regards as problems become proper subjects for sociological study because of the cultural influences which operate to produce the patterns in question. Situations beyond the power of any individual to cope with are also recognized as social problems when the aggregate feels a pressure to correct them. In the following pages we shall discuss in detail some of these problems, together with the policies adopted to meet them, as illustrative of the sociological approach.

CRIME AND THE CRIMINAL

AT THE OUTSET of our discussion of this important social problem it is necessary to agree on the meaning of certain words. First of all, crime itself is a violation of the criminal law, that is, it is a breach of the code of conduct specifically ordered and recognized by statute law.[1] The state, through its legislative assemblies, defines crimes and their penalties in detail. Conduct which does not fall within the terms of statute definition may be immoral, undesirable, detrimental to the social order, and a number of other things, but it is not criminal. The concept of crime varies from culture to culture and from time to time within any one culture. As a result, conduct which is criminal in a given culture or at a given time may not be criminal in another culture or at another time. Thus at a certain period in our own culture it was criminal to manufacture and sell alcoholic liquors; it is not a crime to do so now. A century ago, when the Federal income tax did not exist, there could be no such crime as the evasion of income taxes. Our point in thus narrowing the definition of crime is that we are dealing with a specific pattern; to extend or blur that pattern, for any reason, is to make the discussion less clear than it should be.

A criminal is a person who has committed a crime as defined by statute. A convict, on the other hand, is a person who has been convicted by a court of having committed a crime. This distinction is significant because most of our statistics relating to the kinds and characteristics of "criminals" really relate to the kinds and characteristics of convicts. Studies carried on in prisons, for example, all deal with convicts. Such studies suffer from the defect that they cannot include criminals who have never been convicted, and they

[1] H. P. Fairchild (Ed.), *Dictionary of Sociology*, p. 73. Philosophical Library, New York, 1944.

may therefore give a false picture of the criminal as such. Not long ago, for example, it was believed that most criminals were mentally deficient, and there are echoes of that belief still with us. One reason for the rise of that theory was that the mentally deficient criminals are more easily apprehended and convicted than those of normal or above-normal intelligence, with the result that inmates of penal institutions may well have been of subnormal mentality as a group, though certainly not invariably as individuals. We must be careful to distinguish between the information we have about convicts and that which we have about criminals.

A prison is a penal institution operated by a state government or the Federal government, and used only for adult offenders whose sentences exceed one year.[2] A jail, by contrast, is a place of detention operated by a local government, such as a county or a city, which cares for minor criminals whose sentence is usually less than one year, plus a miscellaneous collection of accused persons awaiting trial, "material witnesses," those suspected of having committed a crime, and transients of various kinds. It is a fact that an individual may spend some months in jail without having committed a crime and without being suspected or accused of committing a crime, since he may be detailed as a necessary witness in a protracted trial of some other person. Only convicts spend time in a prison, though it is true that persons wrongly convicted may be sentenced to prison, and therefore that noncriminals, in the exact meaning of the term, may have to serve time in prison. Varieties of prisons have been erected and developed for different types of convicts, ranging from prisons intended for the most dangerous types to those intended for convicts whose "reform" is more hopeful.

With these terms clearly differentiated, we may proceed to a discussion of crime and the criminal.

THE CAUSES OF CRIME

One of the areas in which there has been an important revision of our ideas is that of the causes of crime. The actual causes of crime, in the sense of the agencies or forces leading to violations of the law, have never been satisfactorily determined. Older views tended to oversimplify the actualities of the situation; modern

[2]Fairchild, op. cit. p. 232.

views recognize its complexity without fully analyzing all the factors that appear to be significant. A contrasting discussion of the older and the more recent approaches will clarify the trend.

Older Views of Crime Causation

The older view of the causes of crime was that crime is the result of human depravity, that is, that crime springs from the inherently evil nature of human beings. Some human beings, recognizing their tendency toward evil, "resist temptation" and refuse to indulge in criminal conduct. Other human beings, equally aware of their evil natures, deliberately and consciously choose to live a life of evil. They are the criminals with whom the law must deal. A criminal, then, was simply a bad man who surrendered to evil. It was not suggested that there were no social influences affecting the individual choice to be criminal or noncriminal. It was admitted that evil company, poverty, and malfunctioning in various areas of society might be strong incentives toward "evil courses." But it was further held that the individual's duty was to avoid evil company, to accept poverty as the will of God, and to overcome the malfunctioning of his culture. If he did not do his duty in these respects, it was tantamount to "choosing a life of crime."

If an individual became a criminal, it indicated either that he did not know what his duty was or that, knowing it, he deliberately chose not to do it. We have referred to this view as an "older" view of the causes of crime, but it is still the view very largely taken by many segments of modern society. For example, courts are apt to deal much more severely with an intelligent and privileged violator of the law, who is without political or other influence, than they are with an ignorant and underprivileged violator. Similarly, our system of juvenile courts is based on the theory that individuals below a given level of maturity do not know their duty or that they are unduly susceptible to malign influences. Court practices are in a stage of transition from the older view to some kind of different view of crime, but the older view still wields great influence.

Naturally, this older view of crime affected the treatment of crime and of criminals. Thus on the assumption that a criminal either did not know his duty or deliberately chose to disregard it, it became the business of society to teach him that "the way of the transgressor is hard." Very severe punishments were inflicted for what to us seem relatively minor crimes. The purpose of punishment was twofold: first, to "reform" the criminal, and second, to "protect society" against him, not only by changing his own way of life but by holding up to others a very stern example so that those others would be "deterred" from committing crimes. The theme of "protecting society" bulks very large in past criminological practice. In addition to these two overt purposes, there was implicit a remnant of theological doctrine in the severe punishments inflicted for minor crimes. That doctrine was that crime was also sin; that sin had to be expiated by suffering; hence the more the sinner suffered, the closer he was to forgiveness of his sin, with consequent benefits in the after life. Severe punishment was therefore justifiable, even if it did not reform the individual criminal in this life and even if it did not deter others from becoming criminal.

It is important to grasp the theological implications of punishment because it is still implicit in the attitudes of some segments of contemporary society toward crime. "Reformers" are fond of pointing out the fact that punishment does not, so far as our experience indicates, reform criminals and that it does not deter others from becoming criminals. They urge this viewpoint in an effort to get support for their plans to substitute some other kind of treatment for punishment, and they are occasionally irritated by what seems to them the "stupidity" of people who will not grasp their point. It is not a case of stupidity. Some proponents of severe punishment do understand the failure of punishment as a reforming and deterring agency, but they still believe that crime is sin and must be expiated by severe punishment in this life for the benefit of the next life. Punishment then becomes necessary, quite without regard to its alleged failure to reform criminals or to deter noncriminals.

All we have been saying applies largely to minor crimes under the older view. In the case of more serious crimes society did not try to teach the criminal his duty; it killed him by some approved means of execution. The assumption behind this process was twofold. (1) The criminal guilty of a serious crime had demonstrated his depravity to be such that he was unteachable and therefore a continuing menace to society. (2) The familiar doctrine of the deterrent effect of severe punishment on those who might be tempted to "evil courses" came into play.

The beliefs outlined above were applied in the case of children, at least those over the age of seven years, as well as in the case of adults. A reading of the records of the Old Bailey, the central criminal court of London, in the 1700's reveals case after case in which the whole trial is comprehended in six lines: a child is accused of stealing food, clothing, or other articles often valued at no more than twenty-five or fifty cents. Testimony follows, and the case closes with the two words, "Guilty, Death," and another child was hanged.

The stress on individual responsibility and on the necessity of severe punishment continued far beyond the 1700's, almost to our own generation. The excerpt below is from a letter written by Oscar Wilde to the *Daily Chronicle*, a London newspaper, on May 28, 1897. Wilde served a term in prison, and includes his own observations:

I learn with regret, through the columns of your paper, that the warder Martin, of Reading Prison, has been dismissed by the Prison Commissioners for having given some sweet biscuits to a little hungry child. I saw the three children myself on the Monday preceding my release. They had just been convicted, and were standing in a row in the central hall in their prison dress, carrying their sheets under their arms, previous to their being sent to the cells allotted them. . . . They were quite small children, the youngest—the one to whom the warder gave the biscuits—being a tiny chap for whom they had evidently been unable to find clothes small enough to fit. I had, of course, seen many children in prison during the two years in which I was myself confined. . . . The terror of a child in prison is quite limitless. . . . The child's face was like a white wedge of sheer terror. . . . The food that is given to it consists of a piece of usually badly-baked prison bread and a tin of water at half past seven. At twelve o'clock it gets dinner, composed of a tin of coarse Indian meal stirabout; and at half past five it gets a piece of dry bread and a tin of water for its supper. . . . In the case of the child to whom Warder Martin gave the biscuits, the child was crying with hunger on Tuesday morning, and utterly unable to eat the bread and water served to it for breakfast. Martin went out after the breakfast had been served, and bought the few sweet bicsuits for the child, rather than see it starving. It was a beautiful action on his part, and was so recognized by the child, who, utterly unconscious of the regulations of the prison board, told one of the senior warders how kind this junior warder had been to him. The result was, of course, a report and a dismissal.[3]

[3]Quoted by express permission of Random House, publishers of The Modern Library Series, from *De Profundis* by Oscar Wilde, and of the editor and proprietors of the London *News Chronicle*, owners of the copyright.

The circumstances described above differ to such a degree from modern theories of penology that it is perhaps necessary to clarify them for younger readers. The incident described took place in England in 1897, almost the beginning of our present century. The "warder," that is, prison guard, was dismissed not for cruelty, as occasionally happens today, but for kindness. The dismissal of the warder took place because he had violated a ruling of the Prison Commission, the official agency of government which controlled prison practice and procedure. Treatment of children, and other prisoners, in terms of almost unbelievable harshness resulted not from the carelessness or cruelty of prison personnel but from a deliberate policy set up by central authority. Harsh treatment was the rule, widely accepted as "right" in accordance with the theory we outlined a few pages back. The only unusual thing about the case to which Wilde referred was the kindness involved.

We have cited this instance at some length because unimaginative people occasionally advocate "stern and harsh" measures for the repression of crime, without quite realizing what such measures mean in actual practice. The history of prisons in America, to which we shall refer briefly later, shows many instances of perfectly well-intentioned practices based on the older theory of the causes of crime. Within the past ten years there have been exposures of deliberately cruel and inhuman punishments in the prisons of several of our most "enlightened" states.

RECENT VIEWS OF CRIME CAUSATION

We may now contrast the older theory of crime causation with more recent theories. It must be remembered that these more recent theories are by no means typical of all segments of our population. They are, in fact, held chiefly by sociological students of crime and by some prison authorities. But most sociologists of today would agree that we shall solve the problem of crime only as we apply the newer views of crime causation to the facts of crime in our own times. The first principle of which we take note holds that

> *Crime is a behavior pattern developed in the same way that any other behavior pattern is.*

A behavior pattern is simply a relatively uniform series of activities which result in observable regularity of conduct. It is conduct

in which we indulge under given circumstances as part of our individual "way of life."[4] Most of our lives are made up of a series of
behavior patterns. Thus we learn the patterns connected with a
vocation, those appropriate to certain social relationships, those
suitable to more intimate personal situations, and so on. The
mechanism by which behavior patterns develop is similar to that
by which culture develops in an aggregate. Whenever we, as individuals, repeatedly face certain situations, we develop individually
standardized ways of meeting those situations. Such standardized
ways are our behavior patterns.

Recall our illustration of the basic interaction pattern of man-in-
association in Chapter I. If we substitute an individual for the
group in that illustration, we shall have the mechanism of individual
interaction, thus:

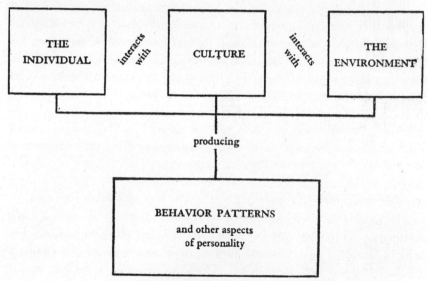

Fig. 6. *Development of Behavior Patterns*

As an individual interacts with his culture and, through his culture, with his environment, he develops standardized ways of reacting which come to characterize him as an individual. Behavior
patterns are a product of interaction, but, as in the case of culture
where an aggregate is concerned, those patterns also become part
of the individual personality, so that they in turn affect the inter-

[4]Fairchild, op. cit. p. 215.

action patterns. Let us choose a very simple example. If we develop a series of vocational patterns so that we become expert in a given professional or industrial field, the possession of that expert ability influences our whole interaction pattern. Thus we find it easier to earn money than we should without that specialized knowledge; we associate with others in the same occupation and share their attitudes and experiences; we view life in terms of our vocation; and we find important meanings in the exercise of our vocation and in the relationship between that vocation and others. When a well-known pianist and a well-known violinist heard a young prodigy on the violin, the violinist remarked, "It's getting hot and uncomfortable in here." The pianist replied, "Not for pianists!" In other words, the pianist was able to view with calmness the rise of a new musical genius who would be a serious competitor for established violinists. Our vocational and professional patterns condition our outlook on many occurrences. So of religious, educational, recreational, and other behavior patterns.

But we must remember that we were not born with these patterns. We developed them in the course of our interactions with culture and with the environment. We "learned" them through our experiences with life. When we say, then, that crime is a behavior pattern developed in much the same way that any behavior pattern is, we are simply saying that no person is "born" a criminal. He "learns" through the totality of his experiences to be a criminal. But that statement must not be misinterpreted. It is not so simple a process as imitating others around us, though imitation may be one aspect of the process. It is also the development of attitudes and patterns which may not be obviously related to crime at all, but which, under proper circumstances, will result in crime. Thus if we learn to value money in an exaggerated fashion, and if we are always in circumstances which provide us with plenty of money, we may never become criminal. If, on the other hand, we are in circumstances which deny us honest access to money we may well steal it, with the result that we become embezzlers. The attitude which views money as the greatest good in life is obviously not in itself criminal, and it may never lead to crime unless certain conditions exist.

Similarly, attitudes of extreme self-centeredness and disregard for the rights of others, a strong desire for power and prestige and intense hatred are all noncriminal in nature and they are all "learned" patterns. They may or may not result in crime. Thus Henry VIII of England exercised his will to power in a legal, if somewhat violent, manner as king of England. Given the same personality and different circumstances, he might well have become a rebel and a traitor to authority which restricted his will. He did, in fact, revolt against papal domination.

It would be naïve, then, to assume that criminals "learn" crime by a process of imitation or from mere instruction in the techniques of crime given them by older criminals. The process is much more complicated. They "learn" patterns, attitudes, and values which eventuate in a criminal way of life when individual and cultural circumstances are such that they cannot find satisfactions in socially approved ways. In this fact lies the justification for modern "crime prevention" programs which try to give "underprivileged" individuals opportunities for self-expression and for satisfactions of an approved rather than a disapproved kind. Such satisfactions can be found only in the culture segment in which an individual lives. If that culture segment is extremely limited in constructive potentialities, he will express himself destructively.

To a certain extent the above explanation has been deliberately simplified for use in this introductory textbook, but it is basically accurate. There is a further point, however. Once the attitudes, values, and patterns which characterize an individual have actually eventuated in a criminal behavior pattern through their interaction with his life circumstances, that pattern may become strongly entrenched in his personality.

> *The criminal behavior pattern, like other behavior patterns, tends to become integrated into the individual's life organization.*

Our lives do not consist of a series of isolated and unconnected behavior patterns. The patterns are related to each other, and these patterns-in-relationship form the "life organization" of an individual. Recall our discussion of social organization as the system by which the segments of a society are related to each other and to the whole society in a meaningful way. A society is "organized" when the arrangement of its segments contributes to the totality of its meaning and of its functioning. Likewise in the case of an individual: his personality is organized when its several divisions are related to each other and to his total functioning in life situations. Inasmuch as behavior patterns are one part, or division, of the total personality, they also are related in an organized manner to the total functioning of the individual. If they are not so related, to a greater or a less extent, the individual is unstable, neurotic, or insane, those terms describing varying degrees of personality *dis*organization.

Our individual lives, then, tend to become organized wholes, so that we do not live through isolated segments or portions of our personality, but with the whole personality. Whatever the situation we face, we bring to bear on that situation the whole of our knowledge, our attitudes, our faiths, our values, our special aptitudes, and our behavior patterns. We cannot choose a job, or a wife, except in terms of our total outlook; we cannot face the problem of sickness or of failure except in terms of our life organization; we cannot meet success—sometimes as difficult to meet as failure—except in terms of the organization of our past experiences. Obviously this situation would not exist if it were not for the integration among the several divisions of personality.

The statement that the criminal behavior pattern tends to become part of the life organization of an individual, then, implies that it tends to become deeply rooted in his personality. It is part of the whole complex which gives meaning to life. Let us point out here that that is saying much more than that crime may be a habit. A *habit* is simply a tendency to react automatically in certain ways, often without our being conscious of the reaction and often without regard to the circumstances of the moment. If, for example, we *habitually* whistle or burst into song or jingle change in our pockets, we do those things unconsciously and often on singularly inappropriate occasions. The point is that a habit is not a pattern of action called forth by the presence of given circumstances; it occurs under all circumstances. A behavior pattern, on the other hand, is a way of responding to specific circumstances. We assume an air of reverence in church, of dignity at funerals, and of jollity at weddings, all of which may be foreign to our average reactions. They are called forth by the fact that we have "learned" that they are appropriate to those specific situations.

So in the case of the criminal behavior pattern. It is a reaction which appears to the criminal appropriate to certain circumstances and which produces the kind of satisfaction, psychological as well as physiological, which he seeks. As such, it is more difficult to change than a mere habit would be.

The process of developing the criminal behavior pattern and the process of integrating that pattern into the human personality are, then, much the same as the processes of development and integration of other behavior patterns. We should not be surprised under such circumstances to discover that modern criminological theory holds that

Criminals, as a group and with individual exceptions,
tend to be physically and mentally average.

This is another way of saying that, from the viewpoint of health and of mental growth, criminals tend to be *normal*, a word which, in modern science, means much the same thing as *average*. Their *conduct* is, of course, not average, since the majority of people do not indulge in criminal conduct. Their mental and physical *equipment* does appear to be average. We must, however, proceed with some degree of caution in this area because, in spite of the many studies which have been made, there is considerable disagreement. As Professor Gillin points out, one group believes that prisoners are more often mentally defective than people of the same age and sex in the general population; others believe that prisoners are, as a group, mentally superior to the free population; and others restrict themselves to the view that a low I.Q., while it may be important in the case of some individual criminals, is of less importance in criminality as a social problem than it is in many other social problems.[5]

Earlier studies of "the criminal," as well as some recent ones, tended to show a very definite connection between low intelligence and criminal behavior. As a result the idea that criminals are in some way inferior intellectually to the general population has gained rather wide circulation. There are, however, two fallacies involved in many of those studies. The first is the fallacy already mentioned that "convicts" are the only "criminals," and the second is the mistaken belief that intelligence itself is a simple char-

[5] J. L. Gillin et al., *Social Problems*, Third Edition, p. 426. Appleton-Century, New York, 1943.

acteristic which can be simply determined and simply measured. We now believe that intelligence is a very complex phenomenon and that simple methods of measuring it are apt to be inaccurate.

We cannot, then, automatically assume that all criminals are deficient mentally; and we therefore cannot assume that programs for crime prevention can be related exclusively to the eradication of feeble-mindedness or to the raising of the general level of intelligence in the population.

In the matter of physical health there is evidence in individual cases that a physical defect may be such as to influence an individual toward crime under certain circumstances. For example, if the defect is such as to make ordinary jobs unavailable, and if there is no socially approved substitute way of earning a living provided, a criminal way of life may result. More significant than this rather simple process, however, is the more serious situation in which a physical defect may give rise to antagonisms, resentments, and feelings of insecurity and may therefore affect the emotional adjustment of individuals. In turn, emotional maladjustment may lead to behavior abnormalities of which crime may be one.

This idea brings us to a fourth principle in the modern view of crime, somewhat as follows:

> *There is evidence that emotional maladjustment*
> *is more common among criminals*
> *than among noncriminals.*

This principle has not been demonstrated. It is now the subject of study. The most we can say is that "there is evidence" that it is true, but not enough evidence to establish it absolutely.

In Chapter I we noted the fact that human beings are strongly impelled toward action by the operation of mechanisms we call drives. These drives are both physiological and psychological. Among the psychological impulses toward action are the drives for security, for recognition, for response, and for new experiences. If these impulses are consistently frustrated, the result is discomfort and pain which resembles the discomfort and pain arising from physiological drives. One type of emotional maladjustment springs from consistent frustration of the drives for security, response, and the other psychological impulses mentioned. The discomfort involved in such frustration may, for example, produce resentment and hatred which, in turn, may find expression in destructive behavior patterns. Crime is *one type* of such destructive behavior. To avoid confusion, let us emphasize here that crime is not the only type possible. Others include addiction to narcotics, alcoholism, neurosis, and suicide. We are not implying, then, that crime is the inevitable result of maladjustment; we are only suggesting that it is one possible type of behavior which may result from emotional maladjustment. Among convicts emotional maladjustment appears to be fairly common.

Let us recall the fact that when we are born we have very few innate behavior patterns. We consist in large part of potentialities— potentialities which can be developed in a number of ways. Vocalization may grow into the ability to speak English, Chinese, or some other language. Possibilities of co-ordination of muscular activity may similarly develop into many different kinds of skills. Likewise, potentialities inherent in the drive toward security, recognition, or response may be influenced by our cultural environment to develop into diverse patterns. If that cultural environment is such as to frustrate the growth of "normal" patterns, abnormal patterns, including crime as one possibility, will grow. If it is such as to pervert patterns of expression, that is, to provide and to place a value on abnormal patterns, crime may also result. This rather technical language may hide the familiar nature of the process we are describing. To illustrate: It is fair to describe the normal American attitude toward the police as one of rather amused tolerance in the sense that we obey their directions most of the time and rely on them in emergencies to protect us, but we do not have the exaggerated respect for police authority common in some other cultures. This normal American attitude leads to an adjustment to the existence of police authority that seldom brings about overt conflict between police and population, though it may do so occasionally, as in the case of strikes and race riots. A child developing in the average American community will quickly absorb the "normal" attitude toward the police. On the other hand, a child developing in a cultural environment which includes hatred of the police, resentment toward authority, and a favorable attitude toward conduct which is antagonistic to the police will absorb that attitude. He will find security in sharing the common values placed on the police and police authority; he will find recognition and response from his companions through behavior patterns which express these values; and he will find the satisfaction of new experiences in some kind of antisocial behavior. Note that this pattern of conduct is not a mere surface thing; it becomes deep-rooted because it provides major psychological satisfactions.

What has happened in the case we have cited is an example of the perversion of patterns of expression in the sense of providing abnormal patterns and placing great value on those abnormal patterns. The process is not, of course, confined to attitudes toward the police. It may include attitudes toward all authority, toward all accepted and socially approved patterns. We call it *emotional* maladjustment because it is not simply a matter of behavior. On the contrary, the behavior is rooted in the emotional satisfaction which comes as a result of the satisfaction of psychological drives.

Emotional maladjustment may arise in two ways, if we omit others which are not relevant to the present discussion. (1) It may originate in frustration of one or more of the major psychological drives. In this case, we assume an individual to be living in a "normal" environment, but one which for some reason does not permit him to find satisfaction for his drives. (2) It may come about through the expression of drives in abnormal ways. Here we assume an individual to be living in an "abnormal" environment, that is, one which encourages satisfaction of basic drives in socially disapproved ways. In either case emotional maladjustment results and crime is *one* of the possible expressions of such maladjustment Further study is necessary in order to analyze fully the force of these situations in crime. Examination of convicts indicates that it is a promising field of exploration.

We have contrasted at some length the older and the newer views of the causation of crime. The older view makes it a matter of the exercise of free individual choice. A criminal becomes such because he chooses to give way to his inherently depraved nature instead of resisting temptation and choosing the good life. The new view makes it a matter of learned behavior patterns. Individuals of average potentialities learn to find satisfactions in abnormal ways, and those patterns become integrated into their life organization. Neither the older nor the newer view can be absolutely demonstrated; but it is obvious that our acceptance of the one or the other will very importantly influence our programs for the treatment and prevention of crime. We now turn to an examination of those programs.

THE TREATMENT OF CRIME

One difficulty with a good many of our current programs for the treatment of crime is that they include a mixture of the older and the newer views as to the causes of crime. Specialists in criminology are largely committed to the newer view, and therefore erect their programs and determine their procedures in the light of that view. On the other hand, crime is a social problem which must be dealt with through agencies of society at large, and there are many segments of society at large which cling to the older view. The specialist feels that he is hampered by outmoded theories of crime; the average citizen feels that the views of specialists are foolish or "crackpot." As a result, a compromise has been reached, by virtue of which we as a society grant to the specialist limited facilities with which to operate, and the specialist placates conservative people by talking in terms of the older view. Under such circumstances an integrated program of crime treatment and crime prevention is hardly possible. We describe below certain areas in which disagreement is common.

PUNISHMENT

As we have already indicated, the older view of crime looks upon punishment as the chief instrument of crime prevention. In the newer view, punishment is of doubtful value.

> *Punishment, as such, has been of little effect in preventing crime or reforming criminals.*

This is one of the statements which is apt to seem most illogical and nonsensical to the average citizen. Yet an examination of the facts indicates its essential truth. The punishment of criminals is a procedure which must operate in terms of a total culture. It is not a device which exists apart from our attitudes, customs, and beliefs. If it were automatic, if, for example, punishment followed crime as inevitably as death follows touching a high-voltage electric wire, the situation might be other than it is. In fact, however, punishment is not automatic; it is conditioned by the whole social and cultural complex in which it operates.

One interesting experience of our culture with punishment results from the fact that apparently the average citizen is not willing to punish a fellow citizen severely unless there has been personal harm or injury to property of an extreme nature involved. We choose our juries from "unprejudiced" individuals, that is, from individuals who are, by definition, not personally concerned in the case they are to judge. Such bodies are largely unwilling to inflict severe punishments or to permit them to be inflicted. Thus when death was the penalty for many crimes in eighteenth-century England, juries refused to find the accused guilty of the crime with which he was charged. Instead, they would find him guilty of a lesser crime involving a lesser penalty. Much the same thing happened in our own times in connection with the Baumes law which made life imprisonment automatic on the fourth conviction of a felony involving use of a deadly weapon. Juries would not convict the accused, though they often did convict him of a less serious infringement of the law which would not carry an automatic sentence. Aside from these facts, juries have been notoriously influenced by oratory, the sex of the accused, local customs, and many other matters unconnected with the determination of the guilt of the accused. As a result punishment for crime has been by no means assured and automatic.

Now it is true that in the case of certain *individual* criminals punishment may be effective in preventing the commission of further crimes. It is also true that in the case of certain individuals who have not become criminal, punishment may be effective in preventing them from ever becoming criminals. But crime is not exclusively an individual phenomenon; it is also a collective problem. Considering criminals as a collective category, it appears that punishment is not an effective deterrent or reforming agent because it does not become a meaningful part of the whole interactive pattern of their lives.

There are several reasons why punishment is not meaningful. The first of those reasons we have already indicated. Punishment is not certain and automatic. It is more than a question of what attitude a jury will take. The facts also show that not every criminal is apprehended; that of those who are apprehended many are not convicted; and that of those who are convicted many are placed on probation, or fined, or otherwise dealt with in such a way that nothing which the criminal regards as serious punishment is inflicted on him. To many of us the mere fact of arrest and of appearance in court would be disgraceful, and therefore in itself a punishment. To many criminals, however, it does not appear so at all; in fact, it may enhance their reputation in the eyes of their associates.

We cannot say with accuracy what the chances of escaping punishment actually are. If we consider only relatively serious crimes, we find that there were in 1942 a total of 187,007 such offenses known to the police. This does not mean that there were actually only that many serious offenses committed; it means that that many were reported or discovered. How many more were committed and not reported or discovered, we do not know. Of the approximately 187,000 offenses known, only about 55,000 resulted in arrests. Of these, 15,000 were not prosecuted by the police, so that only about 40,000 were brought before a court. In turn, about 25,000 of these were found guilty of the offense with which they were charged and about 4000 were found guilty of a less serious offense. Adding these last two figures together, we find that about 29,000 people were punished in major or minor fashion for a total of 187,000 offenses known. As Professor Barnes remarks, this situation means that one person was found guilty for every six serious offenses committed.[6] Not even apprehension for committing a crime, much less punishment, is even approximately inevitable.

A second reason why punishment means little in the lives of some individuals is that they assume it as one of the risks of their "business," precisely as more honest men must assume certain risks in more honest business. As we have just seen, the risk of punishment is by no means an overwhelming one. It may be offset to some extent by membership in a criminal organization which can exert influence and has other resources at its command.

A third reason grows out of the emotional nature of crime, which comes to have so many deep meanings and carries with it so many psychological satisfactions that other meanings, such as those involved in the possibility of punishment, have little effect on the

[6]H. E. Barnes and N. K. Teeters, *New Horizons on Criminology*, pp. 262–263. Prentice-Hall, New York, 1945.

criminal. Again, for those of us who find our satisfactions in socially approved ways of life, prosecution and punishment for crime are terrible things because they destroy the fabric of our organized existence. Evidence of this may be found in those all too frequent instances in which individuals are wrongly convicted and undergo punishment for crimes they did not commit. Even after their innocence is established, after they are pardoned and reimbursed financially, the results of their experience remain with them. They are not in fact criminals, they have not established a criminal behavior pattern, none of the compensating satisfactions which exist for criminals are present. But for the criminal, in whose life social disapproval is an accepted fact and may even be a valuable asset from the viewpoint of his associates, the further disapproval attached to the idea of punishment is not a deterrent.

In all our discussion thus far we have condemned punishment as a societal device for handling its crime problem, not on the basis of any theoretical considerations but on the basis of the practical fact that it simply is not effective and that, since it must operate through, and in terms of, our culture, there is little reason to hope that it can be effective. In addition to these "practical" considerations, however, it is also true that, if the newer theory of crime causation is accurate, punishment cannot prevent crime, since it does not meet the psychological factors involved. A different approach becomes necessary, an approach based on modern developments.

Treatment Replaces Punishment

Treatment is "a process by which an individual is helped toward a greater use of his own capacities and resources."[7] In the usual meaning of the term, treatment is an individual matter. It may also be applied collectively, as when the members of a community co-operate to solve a community problem by the mobilization and development of community resources. It is applicable to the problem of crime in both its individual and group meanings.

Conservative individuals are apt to attack the treatment concept on the ground that it coddles prisoners and otherwise "lets them off easy." The assumption behind such attacks is apparently that treatment implies no activity on the part of the criminal in his own behalf and also that criminals will be "turned loose on society" to

[7]Fairchild, op. cit. p. 323.

constitute a menace. Let us at this point make it clear that the treament of criminals involves their separation from society just as imprisonment does. But in the case of treatment the purpose of the separation is not punishment, but rather to give facility to the process of analyzing and diagnosing the individual prisoner in such a way that we may discover (1) what the criminal way of life signifies to that individual; (2) why it has that significance for him; and (3) how he can use his individual resources, aided by the resources of society, to build up a socially approved way of life which will have as much significance for him as the criminal way of life does. Once these facts are discovered, it is the prisoner's problem, assisted by competent staff personnel, to build up for himself a new personality. This is by no means a simple and rapid process. Far from implying that the prisoner is "turned loose on society" in a short time, it implies rather that the term of detention incident to treatment would, in the case of some prisoners, be longer than the usual prison sentence imposed under our present system.

It is of course true that not all criminals would require incarceration in order to rebuild their lives. Precisely as under the present system, probation would permit criminals with hopeful prognoses to remain in the community during the period of readjustment. The point is that in the case of serious crimes, or of criminals with long-established patterns, imprisonment would be for as long a term as necessary to carry through the treatment processes. In some cases, as we have indicated, this would be for a longer period than the sentences at present imposed.

Treatment also has its social meanings, primarily centered in the prevention of crime. It is similar to individual treatment in that it involves the analysis of our culture in an attempt to discover (1) what cultural factors, if any, are contributing to the development of crime; (2) why they so contribute; and (3) what we may substitute for those cultural factors which will have the effect of lessening crime as a social phenomenon. This also is a long and involved process, and it suffers from the further difficulty that there may be wide disagreement as to the importance of certain cultural factors. For example, Professor Barnes mentions the "something for nothing" philosophy as characteristic of a large segment of the American people. Basically this philosophy makes getting something for nothing, or at least as much as possible for as little as

possible, an important life goal. It refers not only to amounts of
money paid for goods but also to the amount of genuine effort to be
expended in acquiring the goods of life.[8] The "something for
nothing" philosophy has long been characteristic of the criminal.
If it spreads among any significant proportion of our population
who are not criminal, it may act as a predisposing factor toward the
development of criminality. If it becomes sophisticated to get something for nothing, it follows that it is sophisticated to get something
dishonestly, and at least minor dishonesty becomes a general pattern
of conduct. It is not a great step from there to the point where
major dishonesty becomes a general pattern of conduct.

As Professor Barnes presents this argument it is very persuasive,
but there are many who question whether or not such a philosophy
actually is becoming more common, and there are others to whose
interest it is to deny that it is becoming common, whatever the facts
may be. Thus we have disagreement as to the significance of a given
cultural factor. The same holds true of other cultural situations.
For example, does the presentation of "crime" stories on the radio
influence children towards delinquency? For a number of years
that question either was avoided or was answered in the negative.
On September 13, 1947, the radio stations affiliated with the National Broadcasting Company voted unanimously to refuse to
broadcase "crime or mystery shows" before 9.30 P.M. News reports
state that "the network's action was designed to minimize the likelihood of such programs being heard by children."[9] The policy was
formulated as a result of widespread criticism of radio crime programs by parent-teacher groups, women's clubs, and the American
Bar Association. The company declared in announcing the new
policy that "the vivid, living portrayal of such dramas on the air has
an impact on the juvenile, adolescent, or impressionable mentality
that cannot be underestimated." A measure of agreement as to
the significance of this cultural factor is thus introduced, but there
is still disagreement as to the effects of the movies, crime literature,
and similar influences. It is obviously necessary to study in some
detail the relationship between culture patterns and criminality before an intelligent program of social treatment of crime can be
inaugurated.

[8]H. E. Barnes, *Society in Transition*, pp. 681 ff. Prentice-Hall, New York, 1939.
[9]*New York Times*, September 14, 1947, p. 1.

A further difficulty in the social treatment of crime lies in the fact that, even after relationships have been demonstrated, we are somewhat at a loss to know just what to do about the situation, since financial and other vested interests often object to modification of their patterns in the interest of the public welfare.

The full details both of individual treatment of the criminal and the social treatment of crime belong in a specialized book on criminology. We have outlined in general the approach current among criminologists, and some specific details will be noted in the following discussion.

CHAPTER XXII

SOCIETAL RESOURCES AGAINST CRIME

SOCIETY's present agencies for meeting the crime problem include (1) the police, whose duties are to prevent crime by maintaining a police patrol and to discover, through a criminal investigation department or detective bureau, the perpetrators of crime and to hold them for trial; (2) a system of lower and higher courts, with judges, prosecutors, probation officers, and other officials; and (3) a system of prisons in which to confine persons found guilty of crime and sentenced in accordance with established statutes. These three complicated systems must function together in an efficient manner if the interests of society are to be protected. Failure in any one of them affects the whole relationship.

THE POLICE

The police are the most directly concerned with immediate crime problems of all these agencies. They are therefore the target for public criticism whenever there is an outbreak of crime, or when inefficiency is charged against our system of crime prevention. The police are not invariably brilliant, efficient, or honest, but the fact remains that a great deal of the criticism directed against them is unfair and irrelevant. The function of the police is limited to the apprehension of criminals and to the presentation of evidence against them in court. They may, of course, fail in both these functions. On the other hand, they may do their work with skill and efficiency, only to have the criminal they have apprehended released by the prosecuting officer of the court, by action of the judge or jury, or through some other procedure in the system beyond their control. In such a situation, the police may not be at fault, but they usually bear the blame in the eyes of the public.

In addition to that fact, the police operate in terms of the cultural patterns, customs, and ultimately the wishes of the community. A community lax in its interest, easy in its interpretation of what constitutes a violation of the law, and willing to wink at political corruption can hardly expect to have an honest and efficient police force. It is also, of course, true that the most alert community cannot entirely prevent inefficiency. But in general any community gets the kind of police service that it insists on having.

Actually the police face very difficult situations in modern society. Crime has been organized to the extent that only minor and occasional crimes are committed by lone individuals. In the racketeering type of crime, with all its ramifications, the criminal organization is often as efficient as the police organization, and it is not hampered either by legal rules or personal scruples. It may also be broader than any specific police organization—except the Federal police, whose jurisdiction does not include most of the ordinary types of crime—so that in certain crimes it may bring "specialists" from locations distant from the place of crime commission and therefore unknown to the local police. If such "specialists" come to a particular city, commit a crime, and then return to their own home cities, it is obviously very difficult to trace them. Criminal organizations are also able to make contact with influential politicians and other authoritative persons in a community. All this means not only difficulty for the police in actually discovering the criminals involved, but also that they cannot in many cases make their arrest and prosecution "stick" because of elaborate alibis, expert defense, and pressures of various kinds exerted on the court.

Apart from organized crime of the racketeering type, even the lone criminal presents difficulties. Modern means of transportation offer easy means of escape; the impersonality of city life, with its anonymity, enables individuals to live unknown to their neighbors and to conceal themselves by adopting new names and occupations with relative ease; the huge amount of crime, serious and otherwise, which takes place daily in cities tends to become too much of a task for a police force limited in numbers.

Most police forces suffer from a lack of personnel, a lack of money, and a lack of public support in their efforts. At best the work of a police officer is not very attractive. When it is made even less attractive by low pay, "influence," and the discouragements of slow and inefficient court procedure, it is not surprising that relatively few people of enterprise and intelligence have been ready to undertake police service.

It is true that recently public authorities have been willing to spend more money for equipment to be used in the "scientific" detection of crime, such as fingerprint systems, means of communication through radio and teletype, and facilities for chemical and physical analyses. All these devices are useful and necessary to modern police work, but they are not the sort of "black magic" which detective fiction makes them out to be. They are, in fact, most useful only in connection with known criminals, whose fingerprints are on file, or with obvious suspects directly related to a given case. In the case of chance or occasional criminals, or in the case of strangers imported by an organization to commit a crime, scientific methods are handicapped because they can only suggest that the crime was committed by a person whose fingerprints are of a specific type, who was wearing a particular kind of clothing, perhaps whose hair structure and physical characteristics were of a certain type. They cannot point to a given person unless his characteristics are already on record and available to the particular police force involved. Furthermore, intelligent and experienced criminals take care not to leave a record of their characteristics.

The development of a central Criminal Identification Bureau in the Federal Bureau of Investigation at Washington has been a very significant step in the direction of making scientific crime detection much more effective, precisely because scientific methods depend on the existence of a comprehensive file of criminal characteristics. The existence of the Federal Bureau of Investigation itself has had other good results and presumably will have more in the future, unless it is perverted to political ends. Its efficiency, freedom from "influence," and its practice of employing an unusually high type of personnel have all tended to impress the public with the importance of police work and with the possibilities of expert service in that field. As this impression "carries over" to state and local police, we may expect improvements there.

In the face of all the difficulties incident to modern police work, some departments have virtually given up the attempt to function efficiently. They surrender to pressures exerted on them and perform such tasks as come easily to hand without demonstrating much of a progressive outlook. One disturbing factor is the lawlessness of the police themselves, especially in the matter of the so-called "third degree." The third degree consists of a system of procedures for the methodical torture of suspected persons, some physical and some psychological, the purpose of which is to extort "confessions" from the victims. Police ingenuity in the development of third-degree methods has been almost diabolical. To cite only two examples: In one instance a man of unusual physical endurance could not be beaten into confession. He was therefore tied securely in the chair of a dentist located near the police station, and the dentist proceeded to drill into the pulp chamber of one of his teeth with an old and very dull drill, which he turned from side to side as he approached the nerve. Confession followed as it would, doubtless, in the case of most of us, whether we were guilty or not.[1]

The second illustration introduces us to an electrically wired carpet covering the entire floor of a cell. When the current is turned on, sparks fly and the prisoner leaps in the air, screaming in agony. The procedure is not fatal, it is very painful, and it leaves no marks —all of which recommend it to police desiring a spectacular instrument of torture.[2] Of course, these more elaborate methods are ignored by some departments in favor of the good old-fashioned way of beating the subject with a club or a hose.

The following are the principal objections to the third degree.

1. It is illegal, and police using it are therefore themselves violating the law. In addition to that fact, confessions extorted by third-degree methods are subject to rejection by the court if the use of force is proved. Such rejection, however, is becoming less' of a probability as courts apparently take a lighter view of the matter than they did formerly. Occasionally a judge of a higher court will protest against third-degree methods, but the evidence is that most judges, particularly of police courts, evade the issue by accepting the police explanation that the obviously bruised prisoner "fell when getting out of the patrol wagon," or "fell downstairs at headquarters." Such collusion in lawlessness speaks for itself.

2. The third degree is applied indiscriminately to all kinds of people and to all kinds of suspects, except those known to have

[1]H. E. Barnes, *Society in Transition*, p. 738. Prentice-Hall, New York, 1939.

[2]H. E. Barnes and N. K. Teeters, *New Horizons on Criminology*, p. 275. Prentice-Hall, New York, 1945.

influence with politicians or with criminal organizations. Status in the community other than that kind of status, previous good reputation, or innocence of the crime being investigated is no protection against brutality.

3. The third degree is a device which frees the police from the necessity of doing police work in the scientific sense of the term, and hence it prevents the development of an efficient force. It is easier to "pick up" likely or unlikely suspects and to force confession than it is to indulge in the labor of criminal investigation.

Serious as this criticism of the police and courts is, we must point out again that they operate in terms of community customs and in accordance with community wishes. The public is not interested in the third degree, and the many attempts to expose it in the hope that it might be eradicated have failed, largely because of lack of public interest. The public accepts the police explanation that the third degree is "necessary" for efficient police work; that it is applied only to "known criminals," which, as we have said, is not the case; and that the police do not use the third degree anyway. Unfortunately, a certain variety of "hard-boiled" detective fiction has helped to spread the belief that the police are at liberty to mistreat anyone, suspect or not, in any way and at any time.

The police, then, as the first agency of society involved in the "treatment" of crime do not present a very encouraging picture. They face problems of admitted complexity and of serious difficulty. They are hampered by a lack of public support, financial and otherwise, and by a lack of trained personnel. In the face of this situation there has been a tendency to surrender to "influence," and to adopt lawless methods of procedure. Both the surrender and the lawless methods are justified by specious arguments, which are apparently coming to be more and more acceptable to the public.

THE COURTS

In the Anglo-Saxon theory of crime control, the public has always been given an important function, a contrast with some other systems of justice which have relied more on specialists of various kinds. Our court system furnishes an illustration of this fact.

The lowest court, which has the authority to dispose of minor infractions of the law and before which major criminals usually must appear to be held for a higher court, is manned by one or more justices of the peace or police magistrates who are not necessarily lawyers or even trained in the law. They must, of course, be familiar enough with the statutes to carry out their duties, but their primary function is, as designated members of the public, to examine cases from a "common sense" viewpoint.

In the case of major violations the suspected person's case is heard by a *grand jury*, again a group of citizens, also not trained in the law, whose function is to hear the evidence against the alleged criminal. If that evidence indicates to them that there is a probability that he may be guilty, the grand jury *indicts* him and he is held for trial by a higher court. If the grand jury is not convinced by the evidence, a *no bill* is returned, and the suspect is freed.

Persons indicted by the grand jury are tried formally in a higher court. In some jurisdictions they may, if they wish, ask that the trial be held before a judge only, but the usual practice is to have a *petit jury* composed of ordinary citizens hear the evidence for and against the accused and determine his guilt or innocence. Sometimes the jury may also recommend a sentence, but the actual sentencing of those found guilty, together with the maintenance of court procedure and practices during the trial, is usually the prerogative of the judge.

Obviously, the public has the direct opportunity to control the prosecution of criminals at three points: (1) in the justices' or magistrates' courts; (2) in the processes of grand-jury hearings; and (3) in its determination of guilt or innocence as petit jury. This whole system of public control of the courts is cumbersome and may fail at any one of these three points. For that reason suggestions have been made that we abolish the grand-jury system and curtail the functions of the petit jury. Those suggestions appear to be most unwise, since, if they were followed, the courts would be turned over wholly to specialists. Specialists may or may not be efficient; and they are apt to regard their own specialty as the only important area of life. It has not yet been demonstrated that any group of specialists can be left to practice their own specialty without some means of public control.

It is especially important to maintain public supervision of the police and the courts in view of the tendency we noted earlier to engage in lawless practices. For example, it is a tradition of Anglo-Saxon law that a suspect is innocent until he is proved guilty.

Obviously a policeman—who is a specialist—using third-degree methods considers his suspect guilty before trial or proof. It is difficult to conceive of a normal individual beating a man whom he considered innocent. But it is the duty of the policeman to consider him innocent. The public is apt, unfortunately, to regard the idea that a suspect is innocent until he is proved guilty as an outmoded ideal if, in fact, they have ever heard of the theory at all. Public control of criminal processes, therefore, is not as effective as it might be. But the very fact of public apathy or ignorance, as the case may be, is an argument for strengthening public interest in the matter, rather than for turning the whole process over to specialized agencies. Totalitarian governments in Germany and Russia have shown us the dangers of discarding public control of the administration of justice.

The suggestion that the grand-jury system be discarded is particularly dangerous, since by tradition the grand jury, once summoned, does not have to confine itself or its investigations to material presented to it by the prosecuting attorney. It may investigate any public matter it wishes, including the conduct of judges, courts, and other government agencies and officials. Such a grand jury, which goes beyond the area presented to it for investigation, is usually referred to as a "runaway" grand jury. Naturally, officials who for any reason fear investigation would be in favor of abolishing the grand jury and its functions. True, not all such suggestions come from those who fear the grand jury. Some come from people who are honestly attempting to increase the efficiency of the courts. But uncontrolled efficiency may in itself be harmful.

Only part of the malfunctioning of our courts may be laid to the jury system. Granted that juries are often unduly influenced by "weepers" and other dramatic experts in the legal profession, the solution of that problem lies in the reform of court procedure, not in the abolition of the jury system. That there is room for reform in our courts few people doubt, but reform is as necessary in the domain of legal specialists as it is in that of the public.

PRISONS

The third of the societal agencies for dealing with crime consists of our system of prisons and reformatories. Our present prisons are the result of a long history of changing theories resulting in a trial-

and-error development. At first prisons were intended primarily to be jails, that is, places where suspects could be held in safekeeping until the time of their court hearings, and where convicts could be confined for a short time until their sentences, usually death or transportation to a foreign colony, could be carried out. There was no thought of confining individuals for long periods of time purely as a punishment device, except in the case of debtors, and there the proceedings were not criminal. Our own county jails and "police lockups" now perform the function that all prisons did two centuries ago.

One of the earliest uses of prisons as *penitentiaries*, that is, for purposes of discipline and reform, originated with Pope Clement XI when he built a prison for delinquent boys in 1704.[1] Independently of this development, England established a series of workhouses for beggars and minor lawbreakers in which they were confined, punished, and made to work. Our system of prisons springs from these two sources.

In America the Quakers in Pennsylvania were active in prison reform in the early days of their settlement there. They developed the system of "solitude," or "separate confinement," of prisoners. According to this procedure, prisoners were given no opportunity of seeing or talking with one another. Even the exercise yards were fenced in such a way that each prisoner had his own private area, and a system of partitions in chapel, plus the watchfulness of guards, made communication difficult even there. The theory was that solitary meditation on life would reform the individual, and that the work he was given to do in his own cell would develop his skills.

The "separate" system was widely criticized as producing insanity and brooding, as being too expensive to operate, and as failing in its purpose, which was to reform prisoners. The rival system of prison structure was developed at Auburn, New York, in 1816 and the years immediately following. There prisoners worked together in shops during the day, and were confined in separate cells at night. They were supposed to be silent at all times. Even when they were together in the shops, no communication was permitted. The assertion was made that the "Auburn system" had all of the advantages of the "separate" system and none of its disadvantages.

[1] Barnes and Teeters, op. cit. pp. 475 f.

However that may be, American prison architecture has followed the Auburn system, and the "separate" system has been abandoned except for short periods and for the "worst" prisoners.

In many contemporary prisons, the inmates are allowed more freedom to talk with each other than in the older prisons; their work is adapted more or less to their abilities; there are programs of education and of vocational training; attempts at classification are made so that the more promising prisoners are separated by groups from the less promising; and in some prisons there is even a measure of self-government allowed inmates. Similarly, modern prison personnel is classified according to function and training. *Security officers* perform the traditional function of prison guards; *house officers* perform counseling functions; social workers, educators, and vocational instructors perform educational and rehabilitative functions; parole officers supervise prisoners who have been released before the expiration of their sentence. The modern prison, then, is a much different place from either the Quaker or the original Auburn prison. Moreover, specialized prisons receive certain kinds of inmates. Reformatories house younger prisoners for whom there is a chance to reform; prison farms care for prisoners who do not require close confinement and who can do farm work; juvenile institutions accept offenders not old enough to be classified as criminals.

Improved as they may be, however, most prisons fail very largely in their "reforming" functions. They are more successful in their detention functions, though, of course, escapes are by no means unknown. The chief shortcomings of American prisons, from the viewpoint of the therapeutic treatment of criminals, are as follows.

1. They are mostly old buildings, some of them more than a century old, with few of the modern sanitary, health, or educational facilities necessary to constructive living in groups. Because they are old and were not built to accommodate a large number of criminals, they are almost all seriously overcrowded. Overcrowding results in difficulties which prevent adequate classification of prisoners, so that new and old inmates are often jumbled together haphazardly. Young offenders are instructed in the ways of crime by older offenders, sex perversions are common, and often the penitentiary is actually a school of crime and vice.

2. The personnel of many prisons is of an unnecessarily low type. Conditions of work, scale of pay, and the ever-present influence of politics all combine to make prison work in most institutions decidedly unattractive. Exceptions to the statement are found chiefly in Federal prisons under the jurisdiction of the Federal Department of Justice, and in the prisons of a few states.

3. Most prisons are burdened with a set of almost completely senseless rules and regulations relating to almost every aspect of an inmate's life. Obviously some rules are necessary, but the fact is that in most prisons rules have been multiplied apparently with the purpose of making the prisoner's existence more burdensome, and possibly with the purpose of making it easy for guards to report any prisoner for violation of regulations, since no one can avoid some infraction of one or more of the multitude of rules.[4]

4. Horrible and grotesque punishments are meted out for violations of rules. Most of these punishments serve little purpose except to arouse intense resentment among the inmates and to terrify some inmates so that they are driven mad. As recently as 1941 in the prisons of one state the convict to be punished was made to lie on the floor nude and was beaten with a leather strap more than two inches wide and about two feet long attached to a wooden handle which the beater grasped with both hands. He evidently did not hesitate to use his strength, and we may gather that the punishment was painful from the fact that one prisoner cut off his leg, another broke his leg, and a third cut off his foot in order to escape it. These men insisted that they were too weak to do the work assigned them and that, if they did not do the work, they would get the "bat" as the above punishment was called. The state legislature, after an investigation, abolished the use of the "bat."[5]

Other common punishments in some prisons include the following. 1. In "cuffing up," a prisoner is handcuffed to the top bar of his cell in such a way that his toes just touch the ground. He supports himself by his toes until they will not bear his weight; then he hangs by his wrists until the pain of the cuffs becomes unbearable; then his toes must support him for a while, and so on.

2. In warm areas of the country the "sweat box" is used, a small wooden movable closet with almost no ventilation, too small for its

[4]Frank Tannenbaum, *Crime and the Community*, Ginn, Boston, 1938.
[5]Barnes and Teeters, op. cit. pp. 588 ff.

inmate to sit down. It is moved from time to time so that it can be kept in the hottest sun. An extended period spent in the "sweat box" will seriously injure most prisoners and has killed some. In one of our progressive Northern states guards, not finding the natural heat of the sun sufficient, locked a number of prisoners in a closed cell, the water was turned off, and in midsummer the steam heat was turned on. They were left there overnight, with the result that in the morning some were dead and others were saved only by great effort on the part of doctors. The whole incident made a three-days stir in the newspapers and was then forgotten.

3. Various kinds of "water cure" are used, including some not mentionable in polite society. Cold baths, playing a strong hose on the nude body, alternating dashes of hot and cold water, and drip systems, by which drops of water fall on a prisoner's head at regular intervals, are some of the simpler methods of torture. Sometimes the prisoner undergoing the water cure is blindfolded. In that case he does not know from what direction the stream of water will come next, a situation that adds to the pain.

It is difficult to see how these punishments, and many more which might be cited, could be devised and inflicted by people who are not pathological. It is even more difficult to follow the mental processes of those who insist that this kind of treatment may be counted on to "reform" prisoners. Convicts subjected to it will hardly leave prison with a kindly attitude toward society or filled with a determination to "go straight and be honest citizens."

4. In many prisons much of the actual "keeping prisoners under control" is delegated unofficially and covertly to "kangaroo courts," that is, gatherings of prisoners presided over by "leaders" among the convicts who arrange for punishment of those who violate the prisoners' code of conduct. Naturally the severest punishments are often meted out for "snitching" to guards and for other types of co-operation with the prison administration. As a result there is a tendency for the majority of newcomers to fall into the inmates' way of life, rather than to attempt any genuine reform.

5. Many prisons lack any realistic resources for the rehabilitation of their inmates. In general, it is only the Federal prisons and the prisons of a few states which make any genuine attempt to develop strength in the individual prisoners and to prepare them for readjustment in the community after sentence.

These are the major abuses of many prisons in the United States. They are sufficient to account for the fact that our prisons have failed to perform their function of the rehabilitation and reform of prisoners. Again we must make it clear that the roots of this situation lie not by any means wholly within the prisons themselves or with the prison administrations. Prisons are part of a societal system for dealing with crime; they operate in terms of the culture of which they are a part. Ultimately it is the population which shares in that culture which determines the kind of prisons we have.

SUGGESTED REFORMS IN CRIME CONTROL

Current suggestions for reform in our system of crime control are mostly related to the newer view of crime causation and to the belief that treatment should be substituted for punishment. Most important, perhaps, of the tenets of reform programs is the belief that criminals can be rehabilitated only as they are dealt with on an individual basis. This is the equivalent of saying that analysis of the individual personality involved in the commission of a particular crime is a prerequisite to understanding the genesis of the crime. It is also the equivalent of saying that any specific crime, such as murder or theft, represents not a common pattern of behavior identical in the case of all individuals, but an individual pattern which varies from one person to another. Implied in this statement is the further belief that no "blanket" statutory sentence imposed on everyone who commits a certain crime can be just or useful for the treatment of criminals. To a certain extent this viewpoint has been recognized in statutory law. For example, there are provisions in many instances for maximum and minimum sentences to be imposed at the discretion of the judge, according to the circumstances of a particular case. Provision is also made for probationary treatment instead of prison sentences in the case of certain types of crime and certain types of individuals. The modern programs for reform of our criminal procedure would extend this rudimentary application of "individualization" to a much greater degree than is now possible under the statutes of most states.

Thus under the conditions proposed a criminal who was apprehended would undergo intensive examination by physicians, psychiatrists, and other specialists; his environmental background would be investigated by social workers; and, in conference, an analysis of all the factors entering into the commission of the crime would be presented. On the basis of this analysis a program of treatment adapted to his individual situation would be set up. The presumption is that the judge would impose a "sentence" in accordance with the treatment program, although some criminologists advocate removal of the sentencing power from the hands of the judge entirely and vesting it in a board of trained therapeutists.

Only a glance at this outline of proposals is needed to indicate the fact that it is not likely to be adopted with any degree of rapidity or enthusiasm in the near future. It differs very greatly indeed from the traditional view of the treatment of crime. Its application would involve the loss of prestige by the judiciary, the legal profession, and other court attachés, all of them influential in most communities and able to block any proposals for change. It involves also a readjustment of our traditional ideas of justice which have assumed that "equality" of justice meant "identity of treatment under similar circumstances." It demands that we give opportunity for the application of highly technical knowledge in a field which has traditionally been assumed to be an area of "human rights" rather than of science. Acceptance of all these new ideas will be very gradual.

Proponents of reform have therefore worked toward changes of a specific nature in the several agencies connected with crime control, instead of attempting to apply a general program. We note below some of those specific changes.

THE POLICE

Changes in police organization and functioning have been largely in the direction of an increase of specialized services. For example, large departments, in addition to the long-established and traditional bureaus of traffic, of special types of crime, and of missing persons, now have bureaus of crime prevention, of juvenile affairs, and of domestic problems. Smaller police forces, whose size will not permit the organization of separate bureaus, are coming more and more to assign individual officers to special activities involved in crime prevention and in the handling of juveniles. Policewomen function especially in connection with female delinquents. This whole procedure is a repudiation of the older view that "blanket" practice applied to all offenders was the standard. Implicit in it is a recognition of the importance of individualization in treatment of offenders, along with some perception of the responsibilities of the police beyond the area of the apprehension and punishment of law-violators. There is evidence of a genuine interest by some police officials in the newer program.

There was always, of course, some individualization on the part of the police in cases which presented strong sentimental or other emotional aspects. The point here is that in some progressive departments individualization is now being applied with some degree of logic as a definite treatment procedure.

Our discussion of current police practice a few pages back will indicate the fact that by no means all police officials have been converted to new modes and new practices. There is still a great deal of the older view of crime remaining. We may suggest, however, that the changes which have already taken place are hopeful signs.

THE COURTS

One of the most significant developments in court procedure within the past generation has been the development of *probation* systems. Probation is, essentially, an attempt to rehabilitate a convicted person without sentencing him to prison or other place of confinement. The assumption is that he will be able to reach a satisfactory adjustment to normal community living through the development of his own strengths without the necessity of the restricted type of environment which a prison affords. The procedure is somewhat as follows. When a finding of guilt is made, the judge, in conference with social workers who have analyzed as many of the factors involved in the particular crime as possible, evaluates the probabilities of response to normal community life by the defendant. If, in the opinion of the judge, circumstances such as a long previous criminal record, a "vicious" crime, or un-co-operative attitudes on the part of the defendant indicate small hope of adjustment without confinement, a sentence to a prison follows. If, on the other hand, the previous record of the defendant, his own attitudes and those of his family and associates, and his emotional balance and other potentialities all indicate that confinement is not necessary, the judge may order that the defendant resume his place in the community under the *supervision* of a probation officer. Supervision implies counseling, advising, and befriending the probationer.

Since the probation officer is a court official, and since it is usually provided that he may "surrender to the court" for a new sentence—often a prison sentence—a probationer who does not co-operate, an element of force and authority is present in the whole relationship. If this is wisely used by the probation officer, it may be an asset; if it is abused, it renders the whole attempt meaningless.

Experience indicates that if probation is to be successful it must operate in terms of a total pattern of which the following are important elements. (1) Probation must mean something to the probationer other than a chance to escape confinement in prison. It must mean an opportunity actually to change his behavior patterns, which in turn implies a genuine desire to reform. (2) The probationer must have the assistance of intelligent, interested, and trained probation officers, since, with the best will in the world, he often does not know concretely what steps to take to help himself, and since it is often difficult for him to escape his former associates. (3) The community must assist in the process by accepting the probationer's status as a genuine one. He must, for example, have some kind of job, he must be able to establish new associations, and he must not be stigmatized as a lawbreaker and isolated from normal community patterns. If he is subjected to suspicion and to the contempt of self-righteous people, he will almost certainly not be able to develop his own character resources.

We now have a system of probation in almost all the state and Federal courts of the country. Unfortunately, in many instances it is a complete failure in the sense that it does not rehabilitate probationers, though of course there are also some examples of conspicuous success. The fact that it is so largely a failure has led to suggestions that it be abolished. As in the case of similar suggestions in relation to the grand jury, movements to abolish probation systems are most unwise. They indicate a complete lack of understanding of the reasons for the failure. The chief reason, realistically stated, is that in our cultural system we believed that probation would work automatically and in a magical fashion. Hence we have not provided the necessary adjuncts to probation mentioned above. We have not provided intelligent and trained probation officers in sufficient quantity; we have not provided a genuine stimulus for the probationer to make his period of probation mean something; and, as a community, we have not been willing to assist in the process of probation. Above all, we have permitted probation to become a routine matter, with the result that only scant and cursory attention is paid to the potentialities of a defendant for self-development, and little specific planning is involved. In some jurisdictions probation has been made a "right" to which every defendant is entitled, sometimes referred to as the "right to another chance." If probationary status is viewed as a right rather than as a responsibility of the defendant it is not likely to be taken seriously in a good many cases.

This whole situation is one example of the confusion between the older and the newer views of crime. A good argument may be made for the view that we have never tried probation as a means of combating crime; we have tried a system which we call probation, but which lacks many of the essentials of a real probationary procedure.

Defective as the system may be, however, it is an indication of a gradual change in the outlook of our courts, usually the most conservative institutions in a community. Individualization is possible to a greater extent than under former codes of practice. Statutes defining crimes and assigning punishment for given infractions of the law are less definite than they used to be. Alternative sentences, including probation as one possibility, are allowed at the discretion of the judge. Implicit in all this is the assumption that crime is not a single pattern with a single cause, but a varied pattern which may result from the interaction of many different causes. This assumption is, of course, part of the newer view of crime. As it becomes more generally accepted, not only by courts but also by the community, we may expect a more intelligent approach to the control of crime and the treatment of the criminal.

PRISONS

The court procedure we have been discussing is in the nature of a substitute for prisons. It is, however, apparent that we shall have to have institutions for the confinement of certain prisoners during their period of treatment, and perhaps for the permanent confinement of a minority of criminals. It is also apparent that our prisons as they are now established will not serve that purpose. Changes both in the type of prison and in the concept of the purpose of prisons are necessary.

We now have three kinds of prisons, referred to as "maximum, medium, and minimum security," and distinguished according to

the degree of restraint they employ. Most of our state penitentiaries are "maximum security" institutions since they were originally intended primarily to assure the confinement of their inmates.
Many state farms and some reformatories are, from the viewpoint
of structure, "medium security" institutions, with primary emphasis
on the rehabilitation of their inmates and only secondary emphasis
on confinement. A few "minimum security" institutions exist in
which the intention is to accept as inmates only those prisoners who
are thought to be susceptible to rehabilitating influences without the
necessity of close confinement. Careful classification of inmates is a
necessity if minimum-security institutions are to function, and there
is little doubt that the conspicuous failures of one or two of them
have resulted from indiscriminate transfers of unsuitable prisoners
to them from other institutions.

We shall probably have to have maximum-security prisons for
a minority of convicts for a good many years to come. One intelligent suggestion with reference to that situation is that maximum-
security prisons be concentrated in a few areas of the nation to
which surrounding states could send prisoners needing that kind of
confinement. Very probably such institutions should be under the
control of the Federal government. The care of really dangerous
criminals is a profession for skilled and intelligent people, and such
persons are more frequently found in the Federal service than in
state services. In addition to this fact, the construction and maintenance of maximum-security prisons is expensive. States with
limited funds tend to construct one type of prison only, to the detri-
ment of any program of classification and individualization in connection with criminals. The type which is suitable for dangerous
criminals is not suitable for young offenders and less dangerous
criminals. If maximum-security prisons were Federally controlled
and operated, state funds could be devoted to other crime-control
programs.

In the case of other than really dangerous criminals, systems of
parole may be made to function. Most states now have such systems, in which the assumption is that certain prisoners have developed sufficiently under conditions of confinement to enable them to
live in the community without further incarceration. All the requisites mentioned earlier as being necessary for a probation system are
also necessary for a parole system. They are also lacking in most

parole situations, with the result that parole also often fails. Not only does prison confinement not give a stimulus toward socially approved conduct, but the community takes an even less sympathetic attitude toward the parolee than it does toward the probationer. He is looked on as a "jailbird" from whom anything, except good, can be expected. His family and friends mistrust him, openly or otherwise. Recommendations for parole come in part from prison officials, and many factors enter into that recommendation other than the most important one of whether the prisoner in question is actually ready for community living. Final granting of parole rests with a board which is often politically controlled and often wholly untrained for its functions. In some states a prisoner automatically becomes eligible for parole after a given portion of his sentence has expired. Eligibility for parole does not actually mean that he has a "right" to parole; it means only that he has the right to be considered for parole. The common interpretation of the phrase among prisoners and others, however, equates eligibility for parole with the right to parole. As a result, parole in some instances becomes a routine and a meaningless thing.

Parole as a system of releasing certain prisoners from confinement before the expiration of their sentence is an integral part of any "treatment" system, as contrasted with "punishment" systems, since the assumption in treatment systems is that the capacities of individuals for self-adjustment vary. Much of a failure as parole may be under present circumstances, it would be a mistake to reject the system as such. Once again it should be recalled that we have not tried parole in the genuine sense of a crime-control device; we have tried something which we call parole, but which is far different from the realistic program necessary for postinstitutional treatment.

CRIME–PREVENTION PROJECTS

The societal resources we have discussed thus far deal very largely with the treatment of individual convicts after they have committed crimes. Supplementing that kind of program are various projects for the prevention of crime which are intended to help individuals from becoming criminal and thereby to lessen the necessity for treatment facilities. Under present circumstances crime-prevention projects are limited in their application in the same way that treatment projects are limited. Both operate in terms of a culture which includes strong patterns unfavorable to newer beliefs about crime. Few people believe that programs to prevent crime will be widely effective or rapid in their application. They are merely the beginnings of an approach, which may, in time, have very fruitful results.

In the nature of the case, most crime-prevention projects concentrate on young offenders or potential offenders, since the recruit to the ranks of crime comes from youth. One of the striking facts about our contemporary crime picture is that an increasing proportion of our serious crimes is being committed by boys and girls in their early twenties and often considerably younger. Under the newer view of the causes of crime, this situation indicates that our general interaction pattern is such that delinquency is a natural product of cultural factors. We cannot ascribe it in any causative sense either to the "moral degeneracy" of youth or to the deliberate perversion of youth by people interested in increasing delinquency. The pattern of delinquency follows naturally from alterations in certain of the factors with which youth interacts.

This being the assumption, some type of "social treatment," mentioned in Chapter XXI, becomes logical. But all the difficulties in the way of social treatment also arise. For example, what cultural factors are operative in producing delinquency? There is little specific agreement as to the answer to that question. In general we can say that family and religious controls have broken down; that our focus of interest as a culture has been oriented away from the value systems of the past, and those values have not as yet been replaced by new and constructive integrating values; and that the life goals of a portion of our young people simply include more antisocial and wholly individualistic patterns than they used to. True as all these statements may be, they are only generalized beliefs, not specifically demonstrated facts.

There has always, of course, been some delinquency, some of it serious, but most of it minor "malicious mischief" committed by children and by young adolescents. In the normal course of events most postadolescents abandoned their destructive patterns and adopted the socially approved mores of their group. The fact at present appears to be that an increasing number of postadolescents are finding it impossible to abandon destructive patterns and to assume an average adult role in their communities.

There are two significant points to be made here. 1. We do not know with any degree of accuracy what the *rate* of delinquency is, nor do we know whether that *rate* is increasing, or, if so, how much it is increasing. Published statistics usually deal with only a limited number of courts. Even granted that there is an increased rate of delinquency in connection with those courts, we do not know the cause of the increase. It may reflect an actual growth of delinquency as a behavior pattern; or it may reflect increased activity on the part of juvenile authorities incident to our current interest in delinquents. Such increased activity would result in the court appearance of children who, in the past, would have been "treated" without becoming a court "statistic." In any case, the 200,000 children who appear in court represent only a portion of the delinquents. They correspond to the *convicts* among adult criminals whom we distinguished from *criminals*, that is, from offenders who were either not apprehended or not convicted of crime. Many delinquents, especially those who come from influential families, never reach court; many others are never apprehended. Court statistics, then, reflect only a part of the total picture.

2. News reports of delinquency and periodical articles on the subject may distort facts, and should not, therefore, be taken as representing actual situations. Usually it is only the more spectacular acts of delinquents that are reported, or acts which are otherwise of local interest. To generalize these into "typical" descriptions of the total delinquency situation is to falsify the realities of the problem.

Confronted by this lack of factual knowledge and by cultural predispositions against careful and factual analysis of crime problems, the advocates of crime-prevention programs have, as we intimated, confined themselves to limited and specific areas of activity. Important among those are

1. Enlistment of the aid of school authorities in the diagnosis of problem children and potential delinquents;

2. Establishment of child-guidance clinics through which home situations and parent-child relationships are improved, along with diagnosis of specific factors predisposing toward delinquency in individual cases;

3. development of juvenile courts with adequate staffs and intelligent practices to treat young offenders;

4. increased use of foster-home care for delinquents, which avoids the many difficulties arising in connection with "reform schools";

5. information and education projects relating to the newer views of the causes of delinquency;

6. settlement houses, recreational facilities, and other developmental agencies established in "underprivileged" neighborhoods;

7. attempts to control the influence of radio, press, and movies in so far as they are assumed to have any influence on delinquency patterns;

8. programs for the strengthening of family association;

9. mental-hygiene projects to offset the development of destructive attitudes in the general population;

10. community organization projects in which the co-operation of major segments of the community is sought with the purpose of developing a continuing attack on crime problems in given communities.

It is difficult, if not impossible, to evaluate the relative success of these prevention programs thus far. The most that we can say is that there is no evidence that they have completely failed, and we can suggest that they are worthy of public support.

READINGS

GLUECK, SHELDON and ELEANOR. *After-Conduct of Discharged Offenders*. Macmillan Company, London, 1945. A summary and interpretation of several well-known studies published by the authors in the United States.

MERRILL, MAUD A. *Problems of Child Delinquency*. Houghton Mifflin Company, Boston, 1947. A relatively brief and very careful study of delinquency.

VON HENTIG, HANS. *Crime: Causes and Conditions*. McGraw-Hill Book Company, Inc., 1947. A specialized approach dealing particularly with the causes of crime and the sociological analysis of factors influencing crime.

BATES, SANFORD. *Prisons and Beyond*. The Macmillan Company, New York, 1936. A careful discussion of our present prison system, with suggestions for future improvement.

HEALEY, WILLIAM, and BRONNER, AUGUSTA. *New Light on Delinquency and Its Treatment*. Yale University Press, New Haven, 1936. A discussion of delinquency, its causes, and its treatment from the psychiatric viewpoint.

OTHER SOCIAL PATHOLOGIES

CRIME, the subject of the two preceding chapters, is one example of a *social pathology*, but it has for so long a time been discussed separately that it has acquired the status of a special and distinct problem. Under the heading of "social pathologies" we usually consider problems other than crime which center in individuals but which are social both from the viewpoint of their origin and genesis and from the viewpoint of their potential results for an aggregate. They are distinguished from such social problems as cyclical unemployment, war, and conflict, because the latter do not center in individuals but result from major social processes. There is a great deal of contemporary interest in social pathologies, so we devote considerable space to their discussion.

THE CONCEPT OF PATHOLOGY

The word *pathological* means, in common usage "diseased"; and *pathology* is the study of diseased conditions. The terms are common in medical discussions, but their application to social conditions is more recent.

THE MEANING OF SOCIAL PATHOLOGY

If we define *social pathology* as the study of diseased conditions in a society or other aggregate, we must develop some criterion by which we can recognize such a diseased condition, and we must also indicate how it is social, since the study of strictly individual pathologies is the field of medicine and psychiatry. We suggest the following criterion: a condition is diseased, and therefore pathological, if it is such that its spread throughout a society would lead to the ultimate destruction of the society. For example, is

461

alcoholism a proper subject of study for the social pathologist? According to our criterion it would be, because if it spread throughout the population making up a society it would prevent the functioning of an increasing proportion of that population, and hence would lead ultimately to the destruction of the aggregate. Is a declining birth rate a pathological condition? The question in that form is unanswerable; it depends on the circumstances under which the decline is taking place. If we can predict the potential destruction of the aggregate as a result of such decline, we are justified in saying that the condition is pathological. Is the wearing of beards pathological? Very probably not, because there is no evidence that it affects the functioning of individuals in an aggregate, and hence it would hardly lead to the destruction of the aggregate if it became common.

This criterion whereby we can distinguish "social" pathologies sounds simple, but there are a number of problems connected with its practical application which make the actual situation much more complex. For example, a great deal of judgment is involved in the prediction of the future results of any condition, we lack the facts on which to make such judgment in a good many cases, and there is danger of confusion in meanings between concepts such as "pathological" and "normal and abnormal" conditions, all of which hamper our understanding of actual situations.

JUDGMENT

How can we know that a given condition, if it spreads through a major portion of a population, will ultimately destroy the aggregate? The only answer to that question, under present circumstances, is that we cannot always know. The history of human association indicates that groupings have often persisted in behavior patterns that were ultimately destructive. Examining the course of their development and decline after they have been destroyed, we can say with some degree of assurance that certain patterns actually contributed to their destruction. But during the flourishing period of their existence few people correctly evaluated those patterns. We have already mentioned the matter of a declining birth rate. In our own culture there is little agreement as to whether it is pathological or not. Some students of the matter hold that it is; others say that it is actually beneficial, since it will permit us to balance our social organization to a given population; and still others believe that the birth rate makes little difference either way.

Much the same may be said with reference to urbanism. At the beginning of this century there was general optimism about the results which might be expected from the growth of a city civilization. At present some writers view urbanism as an important contributing factor in many of our current pathologies. Similarly, toward the end of the last century science was hailed as the hope of the world; but at present the results of our scientific activity are viewed with a distinctly critical eye by some students of society. So of our industrial system; there is no agreement as to whether its ultimate results will be constructive and integrative or degenerative and disintegrative.

All these examples indicate that judgments as to whether a particular condition is pathological or not vary widely. Until more facts are available and reliable predictive processes are developed, they will continue to vary. We shall limit our discussion here to those pathologies about which there is a measure of agreement.

CONCEPTS OF NORMAL AND ABNORMAL

It is important to understand the relationship between the meaning of *pathological* and that of *abnormal*, because there is a tendency to consider only that conduct pathological which is also agreed to be abnormal. If we hold to that point of view, we exclude from consideration some conditions which may be pathological, and therefore we have only a partial view of fact.

There have been two ways of deciding what is "normal" conduct, both applied currently.

1. One of those ways is to set a definitive standard of conduct and to say that any deviation from that standard is "abnormal." We follow that procedure, for example, when we adhere to religious or ethical systems, or when we accept more or less uncritically the customs of our own aggregate as a standard from which deviation is not allowable. In times past the setting of an arbitrary standard such as these was the commonest way of distinguishing between normal and abnormal conduct. In our own times traditional moral standards are not as authoritative as they once were, and the current emphasis is not on philosophical or ethical approaches to conduct. As a result, standards are in a state of flux.

2. A second way of deciding whether a given pattern is normal or not is to hold that the normal is simply the thing that most people do under given circumstances. Thus, it is "normal" to eat three meals a day because most people do; it is abnormal to have only one arm because most people have two arms; "normal" intelligence is intelligence which enables an individual to do what most people of his age and social status can do. Judgment of normality then becomes very largely a matter of statistics. We count the number of people who behave in a given way; if they are a majority, then that behavior is normal. Of course, in the actual use of this concept more refined statistical devices may be employed, but the importance of the mere number of people who follow a certain pattern is evident. In effect, the normal becomes the same as the *average*.

One advantage of this way of determining the normal is its simplicity and its relative accuracy. One disadvantage is that it lacks stability; it changes with the passing years. Thus a hundred years ago it was normal to have large families; today it is not. A few years ago it was abnormal for women to smoke in public; today it is normal. We have no way of knowing what will be normal a few years from now. This disadvantage has not been important enough to prevent the common use of mathematically determined judgments of normal and abnormal.

Partly because of this lack of stability in the meaning of "normal" and "abnormal," and partly because we want to avoid confusion between abnormal and pathological patterns, we suggest that we omit entirely the use of the words "normal" and "abnormal." They mean very little, actually, in relation to social pathology. A given condition may be both pathological and abnormal, as in the case of drug addiction. It is abnormal because it is "unaverage," and it is pathological because it is potentially destructive of an aggregate. A condition may also be pathological and normal, as in the case of childless families, or small families, which is at least coming to be normal, but which is asserted by some people to be pathological. Finally, the condition may be abnormal but not pathological, as in the case of men wearing beards. The significant term for us here and in this connection is *pathological* rather than *abnormal*.

Generally recognized social pathologies include drug addiction, alcoholism, insanity, prostitution and vice, and some emotional disorders.

APPROACH TO PATHOLOGIES

Our study of crime will furnish us with the groundwork of an approach to pathologies, since it is basically the same as our approach to crime.

CAUSES

A pathological condition is the result of an interaction between an individual and the factors of his total environment. As in the case of crime, we may say that

> *A pathology is a behavior pattern developed in the same way*
> *as any other behavior pattern.*

Recall the fact that a *behavior pattern* is "observed regularity of conduct" developing from our continued reaction to certain environmental situations. Suppose, for example, that the environment makes demands on an individual which he is not equipped to meet. This obviously presents a problem to him, in the sense of our definition of a condition which exerts pressure for modification. Most of us meet that problem in one of two ways: either we change the environment so that the demands are no longer present; or we develop our own personality resources in such a way that we can meet the demands adequately. For example, an individual who finds himself employed in a position which is beyond his skill either changes positions or develops his skills. An individual subjected to marital tensions gets a divorce, deserts, or otherwise removes the tension from his environment; or he develops his own resources of understanding and patience so that the demands incident to tension can be met. A change of environment, or the development of new resources, is the usual, or "average," way of solving this particular problem.

But there are some cases in which that solution is not possible. Suppose, for example, that an individual cannot change his environment and either does not have any resources to develop or does not know how to develop them. In that case he continually faces situations which demand of him things beyond his capacity. He must remain in his position subject to nervous strain; he must endure marital tensions without relief. In that case his logical and rational faculties may desert him to a greater or less extent, and unconscious and irrational faculties take over the solution of the problem. It is important to grasp that point. The problem is not left unsolved; it is solved in terms other than those of the real facts of existence. For example, a "functional disorder" may develop, that is, a disease which affects the physiological processes of the body but which has no apparent physiological basis: it is "emotionally" and unconsciously caused. If, for example, an individual develops a painfully swollen leg, he cannot be expected to leave his bed and work. He has solved the problem of employment which makes demands on him beyond his skill. The question naturally arises as to why this circuitous course is followed. Why does not this particular individual simply give up his job and get another one, if he cannot develop his own skills? The answer to that question is very complex, leading us into the realm of the diagnosis of pathologies, which is beyond the scope of this book. We can, however, say that in general the reason why he adopts a circuitous course to solve his problem is fear, a fear that arose in some way from his previous experience. He may fear that if he gives up one job he may not find another, he may fear that he will disappoint his mother who expects great things of him, he may fear the derision of his associates, he may fear any number of things. His fears may be quite illogical and quite unrealistic in the sense that they are not founded in fact. They may also be largely unconscious, so that he is not aware that they exist. But, whether logical or not, they are potent influences in his life.

The development of functional disease is not the only solution for these "unsolvable" problems. In more serious cases the individual concerned may develop delusions. He may come to believe, quite honestly and sincerely, that he is Napoleon or Hitler or God. His problem is then solved; Napoleon or Hitler or God cannot be expected to appear daily at some kind of office and perform the duties of a particular position, hence the individual who believes that he is one of these beings does not have to do so either. Or, in the case of marital tension, Hitler was not married, Napoleon was certainly not married to this particular woman who gives our patient such a bad time of it, and God is above the fleshly concerns of marriage. In other words, the marriage which causes so much trouble does not exist, and our troubled individual is free of it. Unfortunately, in freeing himself of this particular problem he has also denied himself access to reality. He must give up the ordinary associations and pleasures of real life, since the individual he fantasies himself to be would not engage in such associations and pleasures. The very fact that this "flight into unreality" involves so much sacrifice indicates how strong was the pressure to solve the original problem. Its solution is "worth" losing all else.

Now again the question arises as to why a more direct and realistic solution was not sought. And again the answer is that the past interactions of the individual concerned have created in him attitudes of fear and anxiety which make direct solution impossible. He fears public censure, the opinion of his associates, the disappointment he will inflict on those who trust him. Fortunately, this circuitous solution is not the "average" solution. It is the occasional solution of a distorted personality. But the roots of that distortion are in the past experiences of the individual concerned, and hence the whole development is a social pattern. And it is also true that if this kind of pattern spread through the population of an aggregate, the aggregate would risk destruction; hence it is a pathological pattern according to our definition. What we have, then, is a "social pathology."

We must emphasize again that these two solutions—through functional disease and through insanity—are not the only possible solutions. Many other patterns such as alcoholism, narcotics addiction, prostitution, suicide, and murder may operate. Nor, of course, are employment and marital situations the only environmental surroundings which may have this effect. Almost any kind of situation may be unendurable for certain individuals.

The "causes" of social pathologies are many; the basic pattern from which they spring is the interaction of a personality with certain environmental factors. The same factors which Individual A will solve without difficulty in a direct fashion will drive Individual B to some circuitous solution. The difference lies in the personalities involved.

FUNCTION

The pathological individual, according to the terms of our analysis above, is not a mysterious or wholly perverted creature beyond our understanding. His pathology is a behavior pattern much like other behavior patterns in its origin and genesis. Just as in the case of crime, the *results* of the pathological pattern are different from the results of nonpathological patterns. In the case of pathologies we are led progressively away from contact with reality. In the case of nonpathologies we are able to approach reality directly and use it constructively.

Implicit in our discussion above is also an estimate of the function of pathologies. In general terms, they function to solve problems which the personality cannot solve in a logical and realistic way. The solution is a poor one and involves many sacrifices, but it appears to the individual concerned the only solution possible. Because it functions in so important a manner, it has intense meanings for the individual involved, with the result that he makes strong efforts to retain it, even when attempts at treatment are made. In general terms,

> *Pathological behavior patterns become significant parts of the individual life organization.*

If treatment is to have permanent results, therefore, not only must the pathological pattern be removed, but some adequate and more realistic substitute must replace it.

TREATMENT

The treatment of pathologies involves analysis to discover the origin and the meaning of a given pathology in the life of an individual, and its replacement by new patterns. Such treatment should, of course, be undertaken only by a trained physician who has specialized in psychiatry. Amateurs, faith healers, and other varieties of well-intentioned but incompetent individuals are to be avoided. Unfortunately, the belief that the kind of pathology we have been discussing is somehow disgraceful is very common. One result of this belief is a hesitancy on the part of a good many people to admit its existence and to consult psychiatrists. They willingly call on a physician for help in the case of a physical disease, but they try to conceal the existence of mental or emotional difficulties. The one type of disease is no more "disgraceful" than the other, and treatment is as necessary in the one case as in the other. It is also true that in the present state of medical knowledge the treatment of mental and emotional ills is more successful than the treatment of some physical diseases, cancer for example.

TYPES OF PATHOLOGIES

There are a number of pathologies with which we should be generally familiar and which may be briefly mentioned in an introductory book of this kind, even though a detailed study of them must be deferred to a more specialized book.

PSYCHOSIS

Psychosis is the modern term applied to what used to be called insanity. It is defined as "a relatively severe mental disease, involving a loss of or disorder in mental processes."[1] The originator of this definition himself notes that, so defined, the term is vague and indefinite, having little descriptive value. Most other definitions are equally vague. Perhaps Dr. Karl Menninger's description of psychosis is the clearest. He makes the following statement:

That one virtually destroys himself if he so far abandons loyalty to reality as to yield to impulses contrary to natural laws or social standards is perhaps obvious. If such a departure is so extreme, if the impulses are so powerful as to escape all inhibition and express themselves in a chaotic, disorganized fashion without regard to any reality, we have what is designated medically as *psychosis* and, legally, as *insanity*.[2]

The basis of a psychosis is a loss of effective contact with reality in the ordinary affairs of everyday living. If an individual's behavior patterns demonstrate in exaggerated fashion that he is out of touch with reality, he is said to be psychotic, or insane.

NEUROSIS

Neurosis is even less concisely defined than is psychosis. It is often said to be a functional disorder of the nervous system, with no demonstrable organic disease. In other words, the nervous system does not function adequately, though there is no evidence that it is actually diseased. Such a definition is too broad to be of much value.

[1] H. P. Fairchild (Ed.), *Dictionary of Sociology*, p. 240. Philosophical Library, New York, 1944.
[2] Karl Menninger, *Man against Himself*, p. 212. Harcourt, New York, 1938. Quoted by special permission of the publisher.

Dr. Karen Horney lists the following as the characteristics of a neurosis. (1) Neurotics differ from average individuals in their reactions. (2) They show a certain "rigidity" of reaction, in other words a lack of the flexibility which characterizes average people and which enables the average person to react appropriately to different situations. A neurotic is always suspicious, or always undecided, or always resentful, whereas a nonneurotic will exhibit these reactions only under more or less appropriate circumstances. (3) They show a discrepancy between potentialities and accomplishments. For no observable external reason, the neurotic individual cannot make use of his abilities, cannot adjust adequately, cannot make use of his resources. This situation is habitual, not confined, as in the case of normal individuals, to occasional incidents. (4) Fears and anxieties beyond those common to our culture combine in the neurotic with an inability to use culturally provided defenses against fears, such as customs, religions, or other adjustive devices. (5) Conflicting tendencies are present in the life organization, of which the neurotic individual is not consciously aware, but against which he does build up unconscious defenses. Dr. Horney summarizes by saying that a neurosis is a psychic disturbance brought about by fears and the defenses erected against fears, and by attempts to find compromise solutions for conflicting tendencies.[3]

Dr. Menninger also stresses the compromise function of neurosis:

The explanation for this, according to our psychiatric conception, lies in the very nature and purpose of the neurosis, namely, that it is a compromise device intended to save the personality from . . . direct and serious consequences of the demands of the instincts and of the conscience. The . . . discriminating intelligence has the task of adjusting these demands and if it finds itself failing, it makes the best bargain possible. . . . The result may be silly and it may be serious but it represents the best that the ego of the neurotic can do. The psychotic patient, on the other hand, ceases to attempt any such bargaining and hence one sees the extreme and bizarre self-mutilations common to them. . . . The normal person is normal because he can make so much better a bargain than the neurotic.[4]

Both these descriptions of neurosis stress the importance of conflict, a conflict within the individual arising from the operation of basic

[3]Karen Horney, *The Neurotic Personality of Our Time*, Norton, New York, 1937. Summarized from Chapter I. By special permission of the publishers.

[4]Karl Menninger, op. cit. pp. 13–87, 187.

drives on the one hand and the culturally created conscience on the other. Demands for modification of behavior in accordance with social codes conflict with the natural tendencies of the individual. If this were the whole situation, however, it would be relatively simple. It is complicated by the fact that neurotics are apt to have an extremely sensitive conscience which may convert the most innocent actions into morally reprehensible behavior. As a result conflict is increased often to the point at which integrated action is almost impossible.

These descriptions of neurosis indicate the lack of absolute clarity in the definition of the term, but they also enable us in a general way to understand what neurosis is. The neurotic is a person who cannot combine his own capacities with the resources of the environment as effectively as the normal, or "average," person can, and yet who is not at a disadvantage in comparison with the average person from the viewpoint of his actual abilities.

PSYCHOPATHIC PERSONALITY

Psychopathic personality is a term from older psychological usage, but it is not very commonly used at present. The person formerly referred to as a psychopathic personality is now usually regarded as one variety of neurotic. Psychopathic personalities are neurotics who are chronic failures at whatever they undertake to do. If they are criminals, they commit stupid crimes and are easily caught; if they are law-abiding, they nonetheless manage to do a poor job of whatever they attempt. Their conduct simply is not appropriate to any situation they meet.

The background of the psychopathic personality is that of the neurotic described in the last section. His conduct is also a bargain or compromise. In psychoanalytic theory, the genesis of his behavior is traced to an unconscious feeling of guilt, arising from an oversensitive conscience, and a consequent unconscious desire to punish himself. The compromise in this case is with some more serious form of self-punishment. Thus the psychopath escapes suicide and the dangers of alcoholism or narcotism by courting failure through inappropriate and improper conduct. His public failures bring down on him the scorn and sometimes the wrath of his associates, a punishment in itself.

SELF-DESTRUCTION

Again we borrow a term from Dr. Karl Menninger, who includes under the concept "chronic self-destruction" all the multitude of devices by which individuals destroy themselves, or attempt to destroy themselves, slowly and over a period of years. It is a form of suicide, but a gradual suicide. Of these many means of self-destruction we shall mention only three, because they are of special importance as social pathologies: alcoholism, drug addiction, and vicious practices such as prostitution.

1. *Alcoholism.* Alcoholism is not the same as occasional drinking, nor is it the same as drunkenness. Many people drink, and some get drunk periodically, without becoming alcoholics. Indeed, we may say that some alcoholics are never observed in a state of drunkenness. Alcoholism, accurately defined, is the phenomenon of self-destruction through irresistible addiction to repeated and excessive drinking of alcohol, but it usually does not lead to the boisterousness of conduct commonly associated with the word *drunk.* More often it leads to a condition resembling a continuous coma, in which the alcoholic individual's reactions are deadened, though there may be outbursts of fear and paroxysms of the body.

Alcoholism as a pathological behavior pattern arises from the interaction of an individual personality with a given environment. In some cases, the personality involved may be defective. For example, there may be unconscious inner fears and anxieties present which are quieted by alcohol. Because the fears are unconscious, the alcoholic does not realize their presence. He only finds that alcohol deadens them and therefore he indulges in it as a "flight from himself." This is a rather common explanation of alcoholic behavior; but if we stop there we miss the point that a "flight from" the self is an attempt to put the self out of existence, that is, it is an unconscious attempt at self-destruction.

The environment may also be such as to contribute to the development of alcoholism, regardless of personality defects as such. More usually it is the environment which helps to create a disorganized personality which, in turn, finds alcohol a medium of escape from the self. The early surroundings of the alcoholic have not been such as to give him a feeling of security, of freedom from fear and anxiety. Instead he becomes characterized by conflicting tendencies. His later environment has not provided him with means to offset the tendencies developed in childhood—means such as self-understanding, psychiatric aid, or religion—or he has not been able to utilize those means. The environment further contributes to the condition by providing alcoholic liquors as one means of flight, even as a socially approved means of flight.

Not every person in an environment which provides alcohol as a possible instrument of self-destruction will actually become an alcoholic. Similarly, not every person who suffers from fears, anxieties, and conflicts becomes an alcoholic. The condition results from an interaction between a given personality, a particular environment, and chance factors. Typical of such chance factors is the moral judgment of drinking which an individual happens to develop. If his purpose is unconscious self-destruction and if he has developed a belief that drinking is immoral, then drinking serves his purpose because it is morally bad and its use brings moral destruction. If he believes drinking to be unimportant from the moral viewpoint, he will tend to choose some other, more evil practice because that will the better serve his unconscious purpose of self-destruction.

The treatment of alcoholism follows the procedures we suggested in general terms as appropriate to dealing with pathologies. It is necessary to analyze the alcoholic, to discover the meaning for him of his alcoholism, the reasons it has this meaning, and the function of alcoholism as a pattern in his individual case. The pathological pattern must then be replaced by a socially approved pattern, and the goal of self-destruction must be replaced by a constructive goal. We must emphasize the fact that surface treatments are useless. We cannot "scare" an alcoholic out of his habits by showing him the "dreadful consequences" of his behavior, for the simple reason that he is already "scared" enough. Fear and anxiety are at the basis of his difficulty. We cannot "appeal to his better nature" by asking him to consider his family, his friends, or his career because he has already considered all those things. His consideration of them has resulted in an increase of the feelings of guilt which are already tormenting him and from which he flees in drink. Other and much deeper methods of treatment are necessary.

2. *Drug Addiction.* The background of drug addiction is much the same as that of alcoholism. The use of drugs is, however, "worse" than alcohol because it is socially disapproved. But what

makes them "worse" to the normal individual makes them more efficient instruments of self-punishment and self-destruction to the pathological individual.

In the case both of alcoholism and of drug addiction, the self-destruction involved need not be physical self-destruction; that is, it need not result in death. In fact, death may be avoided because it would end the process of punishment which the pathological individual desires. Instead of physical death, the alcoholic and drug addicts seek "flight from the self," as we suggested earlier; they seek destruction of the personality rather than of the physical body only. Destruction of the self, or personality, demands the breaking down of social relationships which have been established, along with the degeneration of intellectual faculties and emotional balance. For these purposes, and especially for the purpose of breaking established social relationships and of losing established social status, the use of drugs is especially effective because of its socially disapproved character.

To some students the explanations we have given of these behavior patterns will seem very involved and most improbable. It is necessary to recall in that connection the fact that we are dealing with "abnormal" individuals whose patterns are apt to be circuitous and not readily understandable in terms of either our accepted logic or our average emotional reactions.

3. *Prostitution.* Most prostitutes appear to be neurotic types, which is a far different thing from saying that they are mentally deficient, or feeble-minded. Undoubtedly some of them enter a life of prostitution under the stress of some strong emotional upheaval incident to such socially disorganizing events as war. Undoubtedly also others become prostitutes largely through the influence of imitation. In certain environments it is difficult for many girls to escape the obvious fact that prostitution is one way of life. Some others are enticed into prostitution, though seldom forced, by the agents of organized vice rings which gather recruits by various methods. The fact remains, however, that not all girls in a given environment or a given social class succumb to any of these influences. Once again, it is a certain type of personality, the neurotic type, interacting with the particular environmental factors which produces the prostitute.

It is also true that some girls become prostitutes, or become sexually promiscuous, under conditions which none of the above circumstances will adequately explain. For example, some individuals of relatively high social and intellectual status take up a life either of promiscuity or of prostitution. In such cases the operation of an urge toward self-punishment, or self-destruction in the sense we mentioned above, appears to be obvious. Their conduct results in a lowering of their status and a "smashing" of established social relationships. The extreme unpleasantness associated with some forms of promiscuity, damage to reputation, progressive degeneration, all function as punishment devices. It is significant also that in cases such as these there is often little attempt at concealment. Questionable conduct either is a matter of open and unconcealed fact or is revealed in more devious ways which appeal to the pathological personality. The relationship of this pattern of nonconcealment to self-punishment is obvious.

4. *Suicide*. Suicide, the "acute" form of self-destruction involving physical death as well as the disintegration of social relationships, also results from the interaction of a specific personality with a given environment. It is one of the most involved psychopathological phenomena that we know. No simple analysis and explanation of it is possible. We must, therefore, in this introductory text content ourselves with the statement that both personality defects and environmental factors are important. Again it is usually a matter of the environment making demands on an individual beyond his capacity to meet them, and thereby creating a problem which he cannot, with his personality equipment, solve in an average way. For a variety of reasons the pathological solutions implicit in neurotic, psychotic, and other psychopathic devices are not available to the individual concerned. Suicide results in those cases which do not promptly receive some kind of psychiatric assistance.

Perhaps more significant for our purposes here than a discussion of suicide from the causative point of view is the opportunity we have to dispel some of the illusions prevalent about it. First, suicide is not inherited, nor is there any evidence that a "tendency toward suicide" is inherited. People commonly ask whether, if they marry, their children will commit suicide because a grandfather or some other relative did. Often this interest in children conceals a genuine worry about the possibility of suicide in the questioner himself, a worry which he does not like to put into words. The answer to their question is simply that their children will not commit suicide simply because their grandfather did; and that the belief in the heritability of suicide is a useless and cruel superstition. It is, however, true that a tendency to suicide may be observed to "run in families." What this fact means is that the whole interaction pattern of members of the same family is very similar. The fact that suicide has been common, with resultant worry for those remaining, may be a significant factor in that interaction pattern, leading to the development of a neurotic personality to which suicide is a much more real possibility than it is to an average personality. But that is not inheritance in any true meaning of the word; it is interactional in origin, and may be guarded against by control of the environment and by hygienic measures directed toward the development of a healthy personality.

Second, while the act of suicide is usually sudden, the determination to commit suicide does not come suddenly. The potentiality of suicide is developed slowly through a long series of interactions; and there are usually, though not always, warnings that an individual is tending to "break under stress." For most of us, as observers, those warnings are not sufficiently detailed to enable us to predict suicide, but they do indicate a personality disturbance and should lead to psychiatric consultation.

Third, it is not true that "a person who talks about committing suicide will never do it," a superstition which has gained some currency. Sometimes suicides do not talk about their intentions, sometimes they do. We cannot rest on the assumption that the person who talks about suicide is safe from it.

Fourth, there is nothing romantic, or noble, or self-sacrificing about suicide, any more than there is something romantic or noble or self-sacrificing about contracting a physical disease such as cancer or tuberculosis. Suicide is a pathology of the personality just as those diseases are pathologies of the physical organism. In fact, there is a great deal of evidence that one of the factors in the total picture of suicide is an intense hatred directed against the self and against other persons, hardly a noble or romantic emotion.

PREVALENCE OF PATHOLOGIES

Because we often lack a clear diagnosis of many neuroses and of many of the patterns of self-destruction, we do not know accurately how prevalent they are. Even in the case of psychoses, concealment incident to the common attitude that they are disgraceful often interferes with the accurate gathering of statistics. What we can say here will therefore be only partially accurate.

GENERAL PATHOLOGIES

We know that more people are seeking treatment for pathological conditions than sought such treatment in the past. But we do not know whether this fact means that there is an increase in the prevalence of pathologies, or whether it means that current methods of diagnosis and of treatment are more efficient at revealing the existence of pathologies than were the methods common in the past. At the end of 1941, before any effects of the war could interfere with "average" conditions, there were about 370 mental patients actually in hospitals for each 100,000 of the population of the United States. In 1926 there were only 217 mental patients actually in hospitals for each 100,000 of the population. This is, of course, a marked increase in somewhat less than twenty years. But it is also true that during the same period there was an increase in the number of mental hospitals for the insane.[5] Patients who could not find hospital care in 1926, and who therefore were cared for in their own homes, could, by 1941, find accommodation in mental hospitals.

Very probably both factors are important in accounting for the increase of pathologies. There is probably an increase in the actual incidence of pathologies, and there is also an improvement in the means of diagnosis and care. We do not know the true facts with any degree of accuracy.

PSYCHOSES

Psychotic patients account for most of the admissions to mental hospitals, though some without psychoses are also admitted. The following figures refer to the year 1942, again a year before any major effects of the war would be reflected in statistics:[6]

[5]J. Gillin, *Social Pathology*, Third Edition, pp. 136–137. Appleton-Century, New York, 1945.

[6]*Statistical Abstract of the United States*, 1944–1945, p. 91.

Patients in mental hospitals at beginning of year 490,448

First admissions during 1942

    With psychosis 98,424
    Without psychosis 14,703
    Total 114,102

Leaving hospitals during 1942

    With psychosis
        Discharged, improved 30,932
        Discharged, recovered 16,047
        Discharged, unimproved or condition not reported . . . 5,696

    Total 52,675

Deaths in hospitals 33,807

Obviously, on the basis of even these limited figures, we are justified in concluding that psychosis is affecting a significant number of people. There were about half a million people in mental hospitals in 1942, but the actual number affected by psychosis was greater than half a million because the population of mental hospitals is a "circulating one," that is, some are newly admitted, others discharged during each year.

It is of interest to note the age groups in the population which are affected by psychosis, as far as statistics relating to admission to mental hospitals reflect age distribution.

First Admissions to State Hospitals for Mental Disease, with Psychosis			
AGE	TOTAL	MALE	FEMALE
Under 15 years	400	218	182
15–19 years	3042	1803	1239
20–24 years	5760	3327	2433
25–29 years	6272	3344	2928
30–34 years	7166	3775	3391

    [Total under 35 years of age] 22,640
    35–59 years 29,408
    Over 60 years 23,599

Again these figures are for the year 1942. They indicate the fact that psychosis is not exclusively the problem of any one age group.

There are significant admissions to mental hospitals from youth, middle age, and old age.[7]

SUICIDE

Using figures for the year 1940 in order to avoid complications that may have been introduced into the total pattern by the Second World War, we find that in that year there was a total of 18,907 suicides in the United States.[8] The figure in that form is perhaps not impressive, but it may be expressed in another form: 18,907 suicides in one year is about 2 per hour for a twenty-four hour day, or about one suicide each half hour. These figures may help to indicate somewhat more vividly the prevalence of suicide.

Again it is interesting to note the age distribution of suicide in 1940.[8]

AGE	NUMBER OF SUICIDES
Under 15	49
15–19	434
20–24	1028
25–29	1350
30–34	1532
Total under 35	4393
35–59	9838
Over 60	4649

Suicide, according to these figures, tends to be a pattern of the middle-age groupings, but it is also present in youth and in old-age groupings. Again we must make the point that these figures refer only to suicides which have been determined to be such and officially reported as such. There may be a greater number than is here indicated, though the discrepancy may not be as great in the case of other pathologies, since concealment of suicide is somewhat more difficult.

Regarding those other pathologies we do not have accurate statistics, though there are many estimates. Those estimates indicate only that the pathologies are widespread in our population, and that they are by no means confined to any one age category.

[7]Ibid. pp. 91, 93.

[8]United States Bureau of the Census, Vital Statistics, Special Reports, Vol. 14, No. 2.

Youth, middle age, and old age are all represented. It may be well to indicate, however, that the statements of popular writers and speakers who represent that there are huge increases in pathological behavior should be received with caution. It is very doubtful whether they have accurate general statistics which are not also available to other people; and it is probable that they are generalizing from a limited sample of the population with which they may have direct contact. This procedure is always dangerous from the viewpoint of accuracy.

SOCIETAL RESOURCES AGAINST PATHOLOGIES

Societal resources against pathologies fall into two main categories.

TREATMENT RESOURCES

The first significant element in the treatment resources available to society is the trained personnel which we have developed over the past years. Included in this personnel are psychiatrists, psychiatric social workers, psychiatric nurses, and clinical psychologists. Preparation for all these professions is long and relatively expensive. In the case of all except the practicing psychiatrists, financial returns are not markedly greater than those from other professions which require less training. The conditions of work, often involving residence at an institution and always involving contact with pathological individuals, are not attractive except to certain rather unusual types of individuals. Schools and other educational agencies equipped to give psychiatric training are not plentiful.

For all these reasons there is a shortage of skilled personnel in the psychiatric field, with consequent lack of adequate treatment facilities in many parts of the nation. Programs directed toward the relief of this shortage deserve public support.

The second significant element in our treatment resources consists of our hospitals and other institutions for the insane. Since psychosis is a disease, hospitalization is often a prime necessity for its treatment. By and large our hospital system is also inadequate. Many of the buildings are old, many are overcrowded, and many were constructed originally with detention rather than treatment as the primary purpose. It is also true that disproportionate sums are often spent for decorative architectural embellishments in the more public portions of our institutions, while the more intimate and more practical portions are left undeveloped. The fact is that, precisely as in the case of prisons, those who deal with the mentally ill are trying to treat them under conditions which make the task an almost impossible one.

Under such circumstances it should not be surprising that tales of brutality, of neglect, and of inefficiency are more or less constantly being told about our mental institutions, some of them doubtless exaggerated, but many of them with a foundation of truth. It is important to recall the fact here that mental hospitals operate in terms of our total culture; they are, in the last analysis, what we want them to be, or what we permit them to be. Public indignation at sensational exposures, and the visiting of that indignation on scapegoats among institutional personnel, are a little beside the point. The fact is that large portions of our people regard hospitals for the mentally ill, as they regard prisons, chiefly as places in which pathological individuals may be isolated from society, rather than as places in which treatment is possible. Until there is public enlightenment in this area, our societal resources for the treatment of pathologies will remain inadequate.

PREVENTIVE RESOURCES

Preventive resources in the field of mental and emotional illness have been organized under the term *mental hygiene*, a movement which originated in America during the early years of the present century. Its original program was directed very largely toward the improvement of conditions in mental hospitals, and one of its major objectives continues to be public enlightenment about those conditions and about the necessity for improvement. It has extended its activities in recent years far beyond institutional care for the insane, to include informational and therapeutic work in connection with the promotion of mental health and the prevention of mental and emotional unbalance in the general population. Important in this work is the dissemination of information relating to the facts about mental and emotional disturbances, in an attempt to transfer them from the domain of ignorance and superstition to that of popular understanding. Equally significant is the mental-hygiene emphasis on the development of constructive relationships and behavior patterns. It is not, in other words, simply a collection of warnings about what to avoid; it is also a positive statement of methods by which individuals may develop their own strengths.

All these objectives are carried out through the National Committee for Mental Hygiene, a centralized body, and state committees which reach into most local communities. Especially effective have been approaches to juvenile delinquency and other areas of work with children. One very important method of applying mental-hygiene principles has been through social work. Since social work has also been important in other ways as one of our preventive resources against pathologies, we devote the next chapter to its functioning.

READINGS

MENNINGER, KARL A. *The Human Mind.* Afred A. Knopf, Inc., New York, 1945. A discussion by a psychiatrist of personality organization and disorganization: especially Chap. I, dealing with modern conceptions of mind and health; Chap. III, dealing with symptoms; and Chap. V, dealing with treatment.

MENNINGER, KARL A. *Man against Himself.* Harcourt, Brace and Company, New York, 1938. Pathological personality as it affects human behavior. Especially pp. 144–160, "Neurotic Invalidism," and pp. 160–185, "Alcoholic Addiction."

HORNEY, KAREN. *The Neurotic Personality of Our Time,* W. W. Norton & Company, Inc., New York, 1937. Especially Chap. I, "Cultural and Psychological Implications of Neuroses," and Chap. XV, "Culture and Neurosis."

BROWN, L. GUY. *Social Pathology.* F. S. Crofts & Co., New York, 1942. A textbook in social pathology.

CHAPTER XXIV

CONTEMPORARY SOCIAL WORK

CONTEMPORARY social work is a collection of processes which have as their goal the development of satisfactory relationships between an individual and his total environment, including the people and the cultural patterns which surround him. Actually, our definition stated in these terms would include education, religion, and a number of other institutions usually excluded from the concept of social work proper. We give the definition as it stands in order to emphasize the broad purpose of social work and to stress the fact that its activities go far beyond "charity," or "giving relief," or any such limited area. It involves work with individuals, work with groups, work in hospitals; its funds come partly from taxes, partly from private donors; it is managed in some cases by government officials, in others by the officers of private philanthropic agencies, in others by members of religious groups; it engages in numerous technical and specialized activities. Obviously, social work is one of the major enterprises of our culture.

In practice, we include in the term *social work* only those agencies which work with individuals having *difficulty* in establishing satisfactory relationships with their surroundings. Social work usually deals only with individuals who do not have access to professional services of a private nature, either because these professional services are not commercially available in their community or because they do not have the extra funds to pay for commercial services. This narrowing of the term excludes the ordinary processes of schooling, many of our religious activities, much of the functioning of the family, and the other aspects of social organization which are important in developing constructive relationships between the individual and his total surroundings. Even with such exclusions, however, social work remains a significant institution in our times.

483

FACTORS IN THE DEVELOPMENT OF SOCIAL WORK

Attitudes toward social work are by no means favorable in all segments of our population. Objections are frequently voiced against it on the grounds that it "coddles" people, that it is leading to degeneracy since it enables the "unfit" to survive, that it is a wild scheme concocted by "crackpots," and for a number of other curious reasons. Many of these objections arise from a misunderstanding of social-work origins and of its objectives. The fact is that social work, like every other cultural pattern, is an outgrowth of the general interaction between our society and its total environment.

Thus Professor Fink notes that changes in social work are a product of the fundamental economic conditions and trends within the social order and of their accompanying social philosophies.[1] In other words, social work is a reaction, a collective behavior pattern, in the face of certain conditions and on the basis of certain beliefs. We attempt to state below the significant conditions and beliefs in our own times which have affected the growth of social work.

CONDITIONS

The first condition which has affected social work in our own times is the fact that there are large numbers of people who have difficulty in establishing satisfactory relationships with their total surroundings. Recurring depressions have seriously affected the economic stability of a good many people. Even in prosperous times there are some people, perhaps a million of them, who cannot get and keep a job. As we noted in the preceding chapter, there are many neurotics, psychotics, alcoholics, and other pathological individuals in our population, all of whom by definition experience difficulty in establishing satisfactory relationships. Other social problems are inherent in the increase of delinquency, divorce, and marital tensions. The very fact that these problem situations exist and that they involve large numbers of people is one of the conditions which have influenced the growth of modern social work.

A second important condition is centered in our increasing ability to diagnose maladjustments. Undoubtedly there were many maladjusted individuals in the past who were not "social problems"

[1] A. E. Fink, *The Field of Social Work*, p. 19. Holt, New York, 1942.

simply because they were not recognized as such. Along with their recognition has gone an increasing sense of collective responsibility for their care.

A third condition lies in the changes in our social organization which prevent adequate care being given to "problem" individuals by relatives or friends. In our rural past, families were large and the conditions of farm life provided tasks that could be performed by many different kinds of people. Thus aged parents could be cared for in a large farmhouse and often could be of considerable help. The mother of the family found very useful the help of "old maid" aunts and other relatives. Children were an asset in the sense that they could lighten the burdens of the many ordinary tasks about house and farm. It was natural, then, for relatives to receive into their own families the children of sick or dead relatives. Kinship feelings were strong, and it was considered a duty to help even distantly related "problem" individuals.

A comparison of that mode of life with our modern city existence will indicate the differences. Houses, flats, apartments are all small. There is insufficient room even for "normal" relatives, much less "problem" relatives. Income depends on a pay check, usually on one check to a family, and problem relatives do not help to make the pay check go farther. Families break up as the children grow up and marry and establish their own small, self-contained homes, often at a distance from the parental home. The sense of kinship is weakened. As a result of these and other trends, there are many individuals who live lives of social isolation from which problem reactions may develop. It is part of the function of social work to deal with such reactions.

A fourth condition also results from changes in family organization. The family as an institution does not function as effectively in training and conditioning children as it did in the past. This is especially true of those families in which there are tension situations, but it is also relatively true in the case of stable families. Children are subjected to strong influences, commercial in nature, which the weakened family structure cannot combat. As a result problems of child care and of parent-child relationships arise which social-work agencies try to meet.

A final condition affecting social work results from the increasing complexity of our society and of the social relationships which individuals must establish. It is more difficult for individuals to adjust today than it was when our social organization was simpler. They must now find some integrating meaning in an environment consisting of many divergent ways of life, beliefs, customs, and attitudes, together with different kinds of people. It is no longer a matter of establishing relationships with a relatively stable and homogeneous culture. As a result individuals who might find no difficulty in adjusting to the circumstances of our past society are not able, without help, to meet those of the present. Social work is equipped to provide such help.

BELIEFS

All these conditions would not in themselves necessarily require social work. They have all, in varying degrees, existed in some past civilizations without producing anything comparable to modern social-work methods. Cultural attitudes and beliefs are just as significant as the conditions of social interaction. A number of current beliefs are significant.

First, our humanistic view of life, with its accompanying technical and scientific developments, has led to the common supposition that the solution of problems of human relationships is an important field for study and analysis. The application of science to human problems has become a significant field of interest, just as the application of those methods to industry and commerce became significant many years ago. This interest has provided not only a technique for helping people out of trouble, to use a traditional phrase, but also a motive for helping them out of trouble. We know how to do it and we find satisfaction in doing it. Such satisfaction tends to replace the religious motive that was common when social work began.

Second, the whole series of beliefs relating to the "rights of man" and to humanitarianism which stemmed from eighteenth-century Europe and America has continued to color our approach to social problems. The democratic doctrine as to the inherent worth of human beings, its insistence that social class and caste are not valid bases for the allocation of special privileges, its belief that education and other products of civilization should be common to all men— all these have had a distinct influence on the development of social work.

In recent years a third belief has been of growing significance; the belief that security, adjustment, and effective living are essentially collective products and that therefore the community as a whole has a responsibility toward those of its members who find difficulty in attaining them. This differs from the older idea that certain privileged individuals in the community (so-called "Lady Bountifuls") were under obligation to care for those less fortunate than themselves. We now believe that the obligation lies on the community as a whole. Hence we organize groups to act as "agencies" of the community, some of them publicly supported by tax funds and functioning as part of government, some supported by donations to "community chests" and other financial drives, but both tapping the resources of the community as a whole. The term *social agencies* applied to social-work organizations stresses their function as agents of the whole community in meeting social problems.

Finally, the belief has been growing that, since we no longer live under conditions of an "economy of scarcity," there is no inherent reason why problem individuals should be and remain underprivileged. The social worker holds to the belief that the spread of purchasing power to his clients will not only benefit those clients but also indirectly stimulate the economic system.

From the interaction of a number of conditions and a number of beliefs we have the growth and development of modern social work. It is not an artificial device foisted on our culture by any one group; it is a natural outgrowth of cultural developments.

THE PHILOSOPHY OF SOCIAL WORK

Social workers have crystallized their beliefs and attitudes into a *philosophy*, that is, a systematic statement of their ideals, goals, and purposes. Different social workers would doubtless express this philosophy in different ways, but the following general summary accurately expresses their basic approach.

1. Human beings, and the human personality, are ultimate values; they are the most significant facts of existence. This is a belief not limited to social work as such; it is shared by a number of other professions, including education, religion, and some aspects of law and medicine. Social workers were among the first to emphasize it because it acted as a dynamic in their own profession.

2. A society is "good" when it promotes the development of personality, "bad" when it inhibits such development. This is, of course, an evaluative statement to which we are at liberty to object. It does, however, represent the belief of social workers.

3. The chief instrument of personality development is participation in group living and in group experiences. Essentially this statement means that individuals develop as they have constructive contacts with group patterns, either direct contacts resulting from association or indirect contacts resulting from reading and other forms of indirect experience.

4. Any characteristic of an individual, or any social situation, which inhibits or prevents such participation is a problem situation or characteristic and is therefore of concern to social workers. For example, blindness, crippling, emotional instability, poor health, are all conditions in the individual which inhibit participation. Hence individuals so afflicted require the assistance of a social worker unless they are financially established to the extent that they can pay for professional services relevant to their condition. On the other hand, a child living in a family group characterized by drunken or immoral or feeble-minded parents, people living in slums, and people living in poverty are all examples of social situations which inhibit participation, regardless of whether any defect may exist in the individual. The social worker views such situations as problems.

5. The field of social work includes both the treatment of individuals whose capacity for social participation is less than average and programs directed toward the correction of social situations that inhibit participation. In America the attention of most social workers is occupied by individual treatment, but recently there has been a growing interest in social legislation and other aspects of social reform.

6. Social work is a profession, partly a science and partly an art. It is a profession because it requires formal training, involves the application of a definite technique, and is guided by a code of professional ethics. But in the application of that technique, and in its requirements of insight and understanding, it is an art.

This outline of attitudes and ideals is in the nature of a faith. It is not susceptible of logical proof in a good many of its propositions. But as a faith or philosophy it is important to the social worker and to the citizen who is trying to understand social work in his own community.

THE FIELD OF SOCIAL WORK

Social work has developed a number of specialized areas of service. They are not separate and unrelated; in fact, they often overlap considerably because an individual under treatment lives in a complex of relationships which bind him to other people and to situations other than his own. A social agency working in the children's field, for instance, has to take into account the child's family relationships. Similarly, an agency working primarily in the field of family welfare will find itself involved in problems related to children. Specialized areas of social work are more in the nature of differences of emphasis than completely different activities. We shall discuss the principal emphases below.

Family-Welfare Work

Family-welfare work is the oldest of the social-work specialties and it is also probably the commonest type of social work. As the name implies, it consists of all those activities which are primarily related to the establishment and maintenance of satisfactory family relationships. There are several areas of family-welfare work.

1. It provides *relief*, either in money or otherwise, for those families in which poverty is a problem. In cases of emergency of a temporary nature, the provision of relief may be the only contact an agency has with the client involved; but when the poverty is chronic, that is, of long standing, modern agencies never stop at the mere provision of relief. They combine relief with an analysis of the reasons for the continuing poverty and with some attempt to treat the causes of the condition. It is accurate to say that the emphasis of privately supported social agencies has swung away from relief aspects of social work to therapeutic measures and nonrelief problems. Public agencies are, for a variety of reasons, hampered in their attempts at therapeutic approaches, and still find it necessary to concentrate to a large extent on relief-giving.

2. It provides many kinds of special services for family members, some of them involving relief, others not. Examples of such services

are consultation regarding a "problem" member of a family and recommendation of treatment measures, such as referral to a psychiatrist or other specialist; working with a family in which the father or mother is chronically sick, in prison, or dead; or provision of glasses, special clothing, or other articles for family members. The point about many of these cases is that the family is often able to maintain itself as far as the ordinary needs of life are concerned, but it requires assistance in the special circumstances. This is particularly true of "broken" families in which the prime requisite is counsel and advice.

3. It provides what has come to be called "family counseling," a specialized term which usually refers to advising with the members of a family in relation to such problems as marital discord, parent-child relationships, contemplated divorce, and similar matters. This is a fairly new and recently developed social-work project. Very often the families concerned are not "charity cases" in any sense of the word. They have funds but they need advice, and the family welfare agency serves them largely because in many communities there is no one else with comparable experience to perform the service. Sometimes specialists in family counseling operate through family-welfare agencies by preference, since it is better to have a connection with an established institution than to start entirely anew.

4. Information services provided by the family agency are another fairly recent development. It is acquainted with the resources of the community which may be used to meet given problems. When there is no specialized informational agency in the social-work field, the family agency usually carries out informational functions.

Family-welfare services, then, are broad in scope and important to many people in addition to relief clients. The trend recently has been more and more toward support of family agencies from public funds. By and large, most public-welfare projects are essentially family-welfare agencies.

CHILDREN'S SERVICES

Three specialized social-work agencies deal with children.

1. Preventive agencies are usually incorporated under the title of "Society for the Prevention of Cruelty to Children," or "Humane

Societies," or some similar name. They function to investigate cases of neglect and of mistreatment which come to their attention, to work with the families in which such conditions exist, and, if no remedy appears possible, to plan for the removal of the children from their homes through court action. This last step is undertaken only in "hopeless cases" and only after other plans have failed. In the past most of the preventive agencies were privately sponsored, though recently the police and some other public bureaus have undertaken preventive work.

2. Children's aid societies, whose primary field is assistance with the care of children who are not neglected or mistreated but whose families are handicapped by poverty, illness, or some other circumstance. Many such children are helped in their own homes; others are placed in foster homes or in institutions, with the co-operation of the parents. The aim of children's aid societies is to maintain the children in their own homes if that is at all possible. Most of the children's agencies have been privately operated, but the child-welfare services of the Federal and state governments are increasingly active in the field.

3. Child-guidance clinics, a recent development, provide services for children with behavior difficulties of a more or less serious nature such as delinquency, temper outbursts, inability to get along with other children, serious school problems, and so on. These clinics are not established primarily for feeble-minded children or for those of subnormal mentality, since experience thus far has indicated that such children do not respond well to clinic methods. The most hopeful cases, from the clinic point of view, are those of average or better mentality.

Child-guidance clinics are staffed by psychiatrists, clinical psychologists, and social workers. Their aim is to analyze the difficulties of a child in the light of his whole family situation and social relationships, and in co-operation with the parents to enable both child and parent to achieve a more satisfactory adjustment. They are coming to be one of the most important and effective social agencies.

We have classed one type of children's agency as "preventive" in accordance with the usual nomenclature, but in reality all of them are preventive in a broad sense, since the net effect of their work with children is to help produce well-adjusted adults in later life by correcting difficulties which appear in childhood and in adolescence. They help to correct personality defects in childhood, thus decreasing the number of potential adult alcoholics, neurotics, and other pathological individuals.

Social Work in the Courts

In both juvenile and adult courts specialized social workers are employed under the title of *probation officers*. The function of the probation officer is twofold.

1. He gives to the judge a social history of the individual found guilty of committing a crime, with the purpose of providing a comprehensive view of all the factors that led to the crime pattern and also of such factors in the total situation as may be useful in rehabilitating the criminal concerned. It should be made clear at this point that social workers have no function in court procedure as far as the determination of the guilt or innocence of the accused is concerned. That is the function of the jury, the lawyers, and the judge. If, of course, an individual is found not guilty of the crime with which he was charged, probation officers do not function at all.

But after a determination of guilt, when the question of an appropriate sentence arises, the investigations of the probation officer are useful. In some cases prison may be a necessity; in others the convicted person may be placed under the supervision of the probation officer for a stated period; in still others no formal sentence may be given, the case being merely "continued" or "placed on file," with the assumption that the guilty person can reconstruct his life without formal supervision. Without some knowledge of the social history of a defendant—which is a very different thing from a legal knowledge of the circumstances of his case—the judge cannot wisely decide between these various possible dispositions.

2. The probation officer supervises and counsels those individuals whom the court "places on probation." The purpose of such counseling is to help them make the best use of their opportunities for rehabilitation and to assist them to discover resources within themselves which will permit them to establish constructive and satisfactory relationships with their surroundings. At the end of the specified period of probation, the probation officer may recommend to the court the discharge of the probationer from further super-

vision; or he may at any time "surrender him to the court" for some other sentence if the probation appears to be a failure.

Many courts also use the service of other kinds of social workers, though they may not be employed directly by the court. Child-guidance clinics, children's aid societies, and family-welfare agencies are all resources for constructive treatment of adult and juvenile offenders.

INSTITUTIONAL SERVICES

Social workers also operate in connection with medical hospitals, mental hospitals, prisons, and other institutions. Visiting teachers in connection with school systems are, in effect, social workers. The essential duty of the social worker in all these institutions is to work with individuals and with the families of individuals so that better relationships may be established. This involves counseling with the inmates of the institution during their stay there, and with families when there is a plan for the discharge of the inmate. Some "follow-up" in community living after discharge is also undertaken.

Modern hospitals, school systems, and prisons employ large staffs of social workers and evidence an increasing reliance on them as part of the total picture of treatment.

GROUP WORK

Group social work has the same aim as any other type of social work; it is directed to the development of resources in an individual, by means of which he will be able to establish more satisfactory relationships with his environment. Its method, however, differs. Group social work attempts to attain its end by the use of direct participation in group activities; other forms of social work rely more on individual therapy, as we shall note presently. It is important to stress this fact, since there is some popular misunderstanding of group-work methods and aims. The aim is to rehabilitate or otherwise benefit individuals; the group is only a method.

Group social work has been long established in some areas of the country. Typical of such projects are the "settlement houses" which are organized in "underprivileged" neighborhoods and which provide athletic, artistic, musical, dramatic, and other instructional facilities. Very often they operate in connection with colleges which provide a number of volunteer leaders in all these activities. The kind of direct participation provided by group work is of great value to many individuals.

These five areas include the bulk of contemporary social-work activity. All of them are preventive, as we have already remarked, since they function to prevent the development of problems in some cases, and all of them are also therapeutic, since they also treat individuals.

THE METHOD OF SOCIAL WORK

The basic method of social work is called *case work*. It is defined as the process of helping individuals by developing their resources and thereby assisting in the establishment of more satisfactory relationships with their surroundings. Social workers emphasize the fact that case work is not doing something for a person; it is doing something in co-operation with a person. In the last analysis each person, except those who are seriously defective, must solve his own life problems. They cannot be solved for him. The most valuable thing that can be done for him is to help him to realize the capacities, potential as well as actual, which he has but may not be aware of for the solution of his own problems.

The next most valuable thing that can be done for him, perhaps, is to help him to realize the community resources which are available for his use. Educational services, library services, churches, and other cultural opportunities, all these things exist, but many people in every community are not aware of their existence or do not know definitely how to use them.

The third most valuable thing that can be done for an individual is to help him to accept his own limitations. This statement may be somewhat surprising in view of our previous emphasis on the development of individual resources, but the fact is that limitations are just as significant in working out a life adjustment as are resources. We must come to a realistic balance in terms of both.

The function of case work is to remove the *artificial* limitations which exist because of an individual's unawareness of his own capacities, because of his failure to use community resources, or because of such external surroundings as slums, poor working conditions, and unfortunate human relationships. Relieved of these limitations, the individual can more effectively make his own adjustments. But he must also accept his *natural* limitations as one of the factors in his total situation. Compensations may be developed to offset some of those natural limitations, but unless their existence is recognized this development will not take place. For example, a crippled condition is a fact which may be approached in a number of ways. At one extreme the crippled person may develop strong attitudes of resentment which will color 'his life organization and life approach. At the other extreme behavior adjustments may be of such a nature that the fact of a crippling affliction is of minor importance. Between these two extremes a number of adjustments may be made.

Much the same is true of such natural limitations as lack of potentialities for the development of certain types of abilities. Not every person can be successful in every walk of life which may attract him, but most people can, if they realize their own capacities and limitations, live satisfying and constructive lives in some field of endeavor. By contrast, an individual who refuses to recognize his own limitations may spend a long and unhappy existence in attempting to be what he is not and to do things for which he is not fitted. Case work deals with such a person by helping him to face the facts of his own personality and the realities of his own potentialities.

An example of the case-work approach may clarify these statements. Suppose that a social worker has contact with the family of an unemployed man which is in need of relief. Just what procedure she would follow in a given case will vary with her own experience and the circumstances of the case, but in general the pattern would be somewhat as follows.

1. Very probably the first thing to be done is to give the family relief, either in money or in the form of groceries, clothing, medical care, or whatever else is necessary. In the minds of a good many people that is all there is to social work. As a matter of fact there is much more to the process. Merely to continue relief-giving would not be a very constructive process.

2. As a second step the case worker will probably visit the family, interview the various members, and collect as much information as possible. She will probably be met with suspicion, since her clients

may assume that she wants the information to prove that they are not in need and that they should therefore not be given further relief. Actually, she wants the information for quite other reasons. She is trying to analyze the situation in which the family finds itself. She will ask herself why this man is unemployed. Much of her planning will rest on the answer to that question, an answer not usually obtainable in one interview, but requiring a good deal of further investigation and contacts with people inside and outside the immediate family.

For example, if it is a period of widespread seasonal or cyclical unemployment, the case worker may find that the cause of unemployment in this particular case is primarily unrelated to the individual on relief. He may be simply one of some millions whose jobs have disappeared in the disastrous slump in industry. If that is the case, plans of the social worker are limited by the general circumstances. She may be able to do nothing more than continue relief; or she may be able to put the family in contact with neighborhood projects which will give them opportunity for self-development and constructive use of their enforced leisure while they continue on relief. Again, she may be able to help them to jobs which will provide temporary income.

On the other hand, there are many cases of unemployed individuals which occur in "average" times, when there is no marked industrial recession. In that case there may be a number of reasons why a particular individual is unemployed. It may be that he was employed at work which did not suit his abilities, though in another kind of job he would do very well. It may be that he had the latent ability to do his job, but had not developed that ability. It may be that his employer was the kind of person with whom not many people could work in harmony. It may be because of the pressure of worry over debts, family matters, legal complications, or some other situations not directly connected with employment. It may be that the actual pressures are not heavy but that the unemployed person is a neurotic type, on whom the impact of even minor worries would have significant effects.

If a case worker can discover what the cause of a given problem is—in this instance, what the cause of the unemployment is—she can plan for a solution which will be permanent or which at least will be of more value than short-time rule-of-thumb solutions.

3. The third step in the case worker's procedure would probably be concerned with the diagnosis of the total situation she is dealing with. Assuming that in step 2 she has gathered information, step 3 involves the correlating of that information in such a way that the worker can suggest what the significance of the several factors may be. It is seldom possible to trace any social situation to one factor, or to one cause, only. Numerous causes operate in a complex of relationships. The case worker tries to evaluate the relative importance of several factors. If she is successful, it is said that she has *diagnosed* the situation.

Diagnosis is not a simple procedure, nor is it infallible. There are many imponderables present which cannot be adequately weighed. It requires training, experience, and insight both into personality and into the operation of social processes.

4. On the basis of the diagnosis made, a plan of treatment is set up with the co-operation of the clients and also of any community agencies which may assist. Recall the fact that treatment through social case work is not doing something for an individual but doing something in co-operation with him. He develops his own capacities under the guidance and counsel of other people, but ultimately through his own efforts at self-understanding and at self-development. He learns, for instance, to manage a neurotic personality (if that is a factor in his case) through psychiatric treatment. He meets financial and legal problems with the assistance of a Legal Aid Bureau or some other specialized service. He accepts the fact of his child's illness, if that is a factor in the total situation, and he is assisted to provide treatment for the child rather than to worry about or to rationalize the situation.

All these are part of the total case-work process. If it is a successful process—and, again, we must realize that it is not infallible—the constructive adjustment of the individual to his environment is of a lasting nature. Apart from such complete analysis, diagnosis, and treatment, adjustments are only temporary. An unemployed individual left permanently on relief may degenerate; an unemployed individual for whom a job is found without analysis of the reasons for the original unemployment will soon be unemployed again; and the person who is simply helped out of one legal difficulty will be in further legal difficulties in a short time.

It is sometimes said that a case worker's job is to make herself unnecessary. In a very real sense that is true. The case worker tries to develop the inner strengths and the self-reliance of her clients to the point where they no longer need case work. One of the problems of modern social work is to find individuals with the training and the personality to do effective case work. It requires a sympathetic understanding of people, an insight into the meanings of situations for various kinds of people, and the ability to formulate plans within a framework of individual and environmental capacities and limitations.

READINGS

FINK, A. E. *The Field of Social Work.* Henry Holt and Company, New York, 1942. A standard textbook for the beginning course in social work.

CLARKE, HELEN I. *Principles and Practice of Social Work.* D. Appleton-Century Company, Inc., New York, 1947. Designed "to introduce students . . . to a birds' eye view of this field." Especially Chap. I "What Is Social Work?" and Chap. IX, "Social Action—Social Reform."

LOWRY, FERN (Ed.). *Readings in Social Case Work, 1920–1938.* Columbia University Press, New York, 1939. A collection of reprints for the case-work practitioner. Especially pp. 38 ff., "Philosophical Trends in Modern Social Work," and pp. 54 ff., "Social Work and the Social Order."

KINNEMAN, JOHN A. *The Community.* F. S. Crofts & Co., New York, 1947. A textbook in community organization. Especially Chap. 12, "Community Solidarity," and Chap. 13, "Welfare."

CHAPTER XXV

SOCIAL POLICY AND SOCIAL PLANNING

OUR DISCUSSION of social problems thus far has dealt largely with those problems which center in the individual and which we observe chiefly in the behavior and reactions of individuals. We have called them *social* problems because they are socially caused, that is, because their causative factors lie in the interactive patterns between individuals and their total surroundings. There is a second variety of social problem which arises from, and is evident in, malfunctioning of social processes and maladjustments of group relationships, such problems as cyclical unemployment, war, race conflict, and the maldistribution of economic goods. For the sake of clarity we may refer to this second kind of problem as a *societal* problem as distinguished from a social problem. The societal problems incident to this maladjustment and malfunctioning have serious effects on the individual, but they are far beyond the power of any one individual to control. They require co-operative effort exerted under the specific conditions if they are to be solved.

In one sense the treatment of crime and other social pathologies that we discussed in the last four chapters may also help toward a solution of societal problems. As the number of criminals, for instance, decreases, or as the number of neurotic and other pathological individuals lessens, societal malfunctioning and maladjustments are affected to the extent that individual pathologies contribute to them. In a similar manner, the development of realistic educational systems, of a realistic religion and moral system, and of other elements of social organization may help to eradicate societal malfunctioning and maladjustments. But the effect of all these on societal problems is somewhat in the nature of a by-product. Under current conditions both the treatment of social pathologies and the development of functioning institutions in social organization are

499

directed largely toward individuals. Their effects on societal problems are secondary.

We approach now the question of mobilizing societal resources specifically against societal problems, with the primary purpose of correcting malfunctioning and maladjustment in the major social processes. Involved in this discussion are the important and controversial concepts of social policy and social planning. There is a large measure of disagreement in this area, disagreement not only as to specific programs but also as to the very possibility of social planning and the development of social policies. Some serious students of society hold that our knowledge of social processes, and our ability to predict their outcome and otherwise to control them, are so slight that comprehensive planning and policy-making is impossible. This is somewhat different from the usual laissez-faire approach that we discussed earlier in this book. According to traditional laissez faire, it is "wrong" to attempt any interference with "natural" processes. According to those sociologists who are skeptical of our ability to control processes, there is nothing particularly wrong about the attempt; the fact simply is that we cannot control them. There is often a suggestion that it would doubtless be an excellent thing if we could establish workable social policies. The limitations of our own knowledge prevent it, not an ethical imperative lying somewhere in the "natural order."

At the opposite extreme from this skeptical school lies the group of enthusiasts who, generally oversimplifying the total situation with which they are dealing, assume that the control of social processes and the establishment of social policies are simple matters of applying techniques which we have already established. If, for example, it is easy to sell more hats by advertising, it should also, in their view, be easy to sell a social policy by much the same procedure. Quite obviously, such suggestions overlook the difference between the simple relationships involved in the sale of goods and the complex relationships involved in dealing with matters in which the force of custom and of other cultural factors is very powerful and in which huge numbers of people play a part.

From the emotional standpoint, most of us are unwilling to admit that we cannot control social processes. We believe also that somewhere there should be the wisdom necessary to establish wise social policies. Our feelings in relation to the matter do not affect the facts. But we do not know what the facts are unless we attempt some analysis of the whole situation. We approach the outline of such an analysis in the following pages.

THE MEANING OF SOCIAL POLICY

A *policy* in the ordinary meaning of the word is "a settled or definite course or method adopted and followed" in relation to a given situation. The definition does not imply that policies are unalterable; they may, and do, vary as the circumstances of the situations to which they are applied change, or as knowledge, ideals, and beliefs change. A *social policy* is defined as "a consistent attitude toward the direction of social control, either in respect of its goals or of its methods,"[1] Again we must emphasize the fact that consistency does not mean complete unalterability. In fact, a social policy, as thus defined, is a very general statement of goals and of the general methods by which those goals may be attained. By contrast, a *program* is at once more limited and more detailed than a policy. It is applicable to a well-defined area of interaction, and includes definite steps to be followed in approaching that area of relationships.

A social policy with respect to education, for example, would consist of general ideals and goals, expressed in such statements as "Education should be available to all," or "Education should be made an instrument of social progress." It would also include general statements of methods, such as "Education must be used in a democratic rather than a totalitarian way" or "Education must be made available to all through tax-supported schools and colleges." On the other hand, a social program with respect to education would present definite plans by which the policy could be put into effect, as well as detailed methods to be followed in a direct fashion. We might propose to make education free to all by following such and such procedures; education must be made an instrument of social progress, through such and such concrete groups, to begin operations at once.

This distinction between a social policy and a social program is of some importance, because criticisms of social programs are sometimes made to apply to social policies and to the feasibility of the

[1]H. P. Fairchild (Ed.), *Dictionary of Sociology*, p. 288. Philosophical Library, New York, 1944.

establishment of social policy as such. To say, for example, that the social policy we outlined in connection with the treatment of crime is impossible of fulfillment is a much more serious criticism of our approach to the problem of crime than to say that the social program we suggested in relation to crime is ineffective. In the first case we imply that the whole statement of goals and ideals is faulty; in the second we suggest only that the specific methods proposed are of doubtful effectiveness. Some valid criticisms of given social programs become invalid when they are applied to social policies.

THE MEANING OF SOCIAL PLANNING

Social planning is defined as "an interactional process—investigation, discussion, agreement—of projecting order upon human relationships."[2] It is essentially the establishment of a social program rather than of a social policy, since it involves agreement principally as to what conditions can actually be established in certain human relationships.[2] It deals not with a statement of goals, or ideals, or any other judgment as to what "ought to be," but only with what may be, what the possibilities of action are under given circumstances. The implication in the case of social planning is that, whatever "natural "order there may be in human relationships, there are many situations in which we cannot rest content with that natural order. Instead we must introduce an order of a different kind, an order which arises from deliberate human activity and which reflects human direction.

There are a number of areas in which social planning has been effective in our own culture. The field of public health is one such area of considerable significance. The steps taken to control epidemics through compulsory vaccination, through sanitary measures, through education and other informational devices, have all been major instruments of social planning. They have not been wholly effective in the sense that they have prevented completely the incidence of epidemic diseases, but they have introduced an element of human order into the situation, with the result that epidemics do not occur with great frequency nor do they affect as many people as they did some centuries ago. The results of epidemics are also different from those which occur under the "natural order." Presumably, under conditions of natural order, the result of a smallpox

[2]Ibid.

epidemic would be to remove from the population those individuals who were not resistant to the disease or whose general state of health was not sufficient to protect them from it. This result would come about quite without regard to any other characteristics, such as intelligence, skills, or morality, which such individuals might have. In this specific example, it is difficult to follow the reasoning of those critics of social planning who object to the projection of human order on the "natural" course of events. There is no evidence that the natural elimination from the population of individuals not resistant to smallpox would be of major benefit to society.

Much the same may be said of the great reduction in the infant death rate which has taken place over the past few generations, and of the reduction in the incidence of blindness in newborn babies which has resulted from the enforced use of mild antiseptics at birth. It is surely being somewhat arbitrary to hold that our population has been weakened by either of these trends, or that it would be strengthened by a lack of planning in those areas.

In spite of these obviously successful applications of social planning in the area of public health, there remains a large measure of objection to its application in other fields, especially the economic field. One basis of this kind of objection is the fact that social planning is supposed by a fair number of people either to be the same thing as socialism or to be heavily tinged with socialism. This has been a very unfortunate confusion. Socialism is an economic doctrine, an economic program, and is therefore *one example* of *one kind* of social planning. But there is much social planning which is wholly unconnected with socialism in any accurate meaning of the term. To condemn all social planning on the grounds that it is socialistic is much the same thing as to condemn all music because we happen not to like the tone of an oboe. There is much music in which oboes are not involved; there is much social planning in which socialism is not involved.

Social planning does admittedly require a great deal of co-operation and of co-operative endeavor. This fact accounts for some objections to it, since the reaction of some portion of our population to co-operative endeavor is largely negative. As we noted in Chapter XIX, many people do not realize the prevalence of co-operation in our own times. Not only is it implicit in much of our social order, but it is standardized practice in the planning of business and industrial developments, in programs of education, and in many other areas of life. This fact is particularly evident in the case of large corporations, owned by thousands of stockholders and managed by specialized officials, involving the establishment of functioning relationships with labor and with other groupings.

A third reason for some of the popular objections to social planning lies in the fact that recent projects in planning have been applied in the economic and industrial fields, especially in connection with the depression of the 1930's and with the Second World War. Both those times were periods of strong emotional upset and insecurity on the part of many people. In addition to that fact, social planning in both those areas encountered strong opposition from vested interests and from the traditional mores of American culture. That opposition has "carried over" and is exerted against all suggestions advocating social planning.

In addition to all those cultural reasons for opposition, there is the fact that the administration of certain aspects of the social planning of the 1930's was often fumbling, a good many mistakes were made, and many curious situations arose in connection with it. The reasons for such mistakes were undoubtedly many and various. The difficulties lay perhaps partly in the persons who administered the plans, partly in lack of adequate investigation and agreement on programs, and partly in the fact that planning on the scale contemplated was a new device. It is important to remember that the social planning of the 1930's was begun after three years of a serious depression. It was not a system prepared in advance to meet given contingencies, but a development hastily set up under the pressure of the very contingencies it was supposed to meet. The results resembled the behavior of an individual placed in an emergency situation which demands new and unfamiliar adjustments. Most individuals, under such circumstances, react at first by random and un-co-ordinated movements which only later become organized and integrated into a systematic plan. The same was true of the collective reaction during the early 1930's. The industrial emergency was replaced by the international emergency of the Second World War before much of the "depression" planning could be organized and integrated. It is important for us to realize that, although there are many suggestions emanating from reputable economists for meeting future depression conditions, and although there is a large measure of agreement as to the fundamental steps necessary in any such planning, we are still refusing to erect any constructive program in advance of actual emergency conditions.

Some of the criticism directed at the relatively few projects in social planning we have had in the United States, then, is justified on the grounds that planning has not functioned effectively in times of industrial emergency. But much of that kind of criticism can be met by reference to planning in the field of public health which has operated effectively. Perhaps the most adequate summary statement with reference to social planning as a cultural device is that we do not know whether or not it is possible or useful because we have not attempted planning on a large enough scale or under non-emergency conditions, and thus have no basis for judgment. It merits further study and application.

INSTRUMENTS OF SOCIAL PLANNING

Perhaps a further shortcoming in the social planning of the past few years has been the fact that we have used only a limited number of instruments for planning, and have often neglected to build up a background of understanding among our population which would enable most people to participate intelligently in plans. There have been four chief instrumentalities of planning in the United States.

1. *Laws.* It is a familiar fact that we in America place a great deal of reliance on statute law and the penalties imposed in statute law as devices to regulate human conduct. As we said in our discussion of the political institution, laws are necessary to the maintenance of order; but they do not automatically produce order, nor are they applicable in all areas of social interaction. To the extent that they are effective in social planning, laws involve a great deal of agreement and voluntary co-operation on the part of a majority of the population. Laws which meet strong public opposition, whatever the reason, are effective in regulating the externals of conduct only, which, in effect, means that we conform only when we are under direct observation or when we are afraid of the penalties attached to nonconformity. It is obvious that such limited conformity will have little result for much of our conduct and for many people.

Once again, however, it should be remarked that we do not know with any degree of accuracy how effective statute law might be in planning, since many of our statutes either have been hastily drawn without full consideration of all the factors involved in the situations with which] they were [intended to deal, or have been drawn by ill-advised enthusiasts for a particular viewpoint. It is also true that the most carefully drawn and carefully worded statute may be defective when its practical application is attempted. Laws drawn up on the basis of a complete statistical and socio-psychological analysis of a given situation and impartially applied to that situation might have very different results from those common in the past.

Law, then, is not by any means a useless instrument of social planning, but it is to be used under different circumstances from those common in the past.

2. *Government.* Much of the over-all planning of the past few years has been initiated, sponsored, and carried out by agencies of government. It has, of course, involved the statute law at many points, but it has also been a broader application of government functioning than mere statute law. Bureaus of research, of information and statistics, of consultation and advice have all been important. In fact, so important have they been that social planning has come to be the equivalent of government planning in the minds of a fair number of people.

Government in a complex society such as ours may function as an important instrument of planning, but it has certain defects and it is not all-inclusive. For example, it is difficult to maintain a consistent policy under conditions in which almost all the policy-making officers of government and some of the administrative officers of government change as changing political parties come to power. It is even more difficult to maintain a consistent program under those circumstances. As we have indicated, consistency may be maintained along with adaptability which will permit making changes to adjust to varying circumstances, but the point about changes of a political nature in government is that they are arbitrary rather than adaptive in nature. Party affiliation or party services, or both, are considerations more important in the appointment of executive personnel than actual accomplishment. To a large extent this statement remains true even under civil-service systems, precisely because those systems usually do not include important policy-making officials.

Other defects of government as a planning agency lie in our

general opposition to authoritarian projects, financial limitations in the matter of personnel, and the influence of politics. On the other hand, government has advantages in large-scale projects because of its inclusive nature and its vast resources for research. It may function in important ways within its limitations.

3. *Education.* Education is a third device we have used only to a limited [extent. We have informed children, among other things, about the geography of the world and of the nation, and about our system of government and the duties of citizens. The difficulty is that we have not always been able to be realistically critical and evaluative in these fields, especially in the matter of local civic affairs and in the matter of economic reorganization. In our culture we have also assumed responsibility only for primary and secondary schooling. Important as these schools are, their students are not of a sufficient degree of maturity to appreciate and to understand many of the problems of human relationships. Training beyond the secondary school and into the college and adult-education area has been of less community concern that it might be.

Education is perhaps the most valuable instrument for social planning of a long-time nature, if we can make it realistic education.

4. *Mass Influence.* We have relied to a very great extent, both in government planning and in privately sponsored plans, on means of mass influence such as the radio, newspapers, periodicals, and the movies. There seems little doubt that they all have important effects on mass reactions and that therefore they are useful instruments of social planning. Unfortunately, we have tended to use them in limited ways only. Thus, we have built up, through the instrumentality of the radio and the press, a tremendous force of "crowd opinion" which can vitally affect the course of social life. Crowd opinion is not the same as public opinion, although the two are sometimes confused. Crowd opinion is a reaction based to a great extent on ignorance, artificially induced prejudices and values, and emotional appeal. Public opinion is not a reaction primarily, it is the basis for a reaction; its components are information, judgment, and some degree of thought. When we have a crowd-opinion situation, we have a reaction which is immediate, unconsidered, and unstable. It is that kind of thing we have built up through our instrumentalities of mass influence.

As a result, certain aspects of our contemporary interactions omit entirely the intellectual processes, and the exercise of judgment, which have been assumed to come between stimulus and response in human behavior. The purpose of mass influence, as currently used, is very largely to produce instantaneous and automatic reactions such as those incident to willing acceptance of a highly advertised product, to casting votes for a candidate on the basis of hasty and surface evaluations, and to acceptance of popular beliefs and fads. This kind of reaction is estimated by various "public-opinion polls," and doubtless estimated with a degree of accuracy. It is fair to suggest, however, that such polls do not test opinion, because opinion does not exist in many instances. An opinion proceeds from a broad knowledge of the facts concerned, from judgment exercised on those facts, and from ability to make judgments. All these are excluded from the operation of instruments of mass influence as we have used those instruments.

That is not to say, however, that they could not be used in other ways. They could be used to spread accurate information, to give vivid illustrations of contemporary life, and to stimulate the formation of opinion. There are examples of such uses, very limited but nonetheless present, in certain radio programs, certain motion pictures, and certain newspapers and periodicals. That such newspapers, movies, and radio programs are far from the most popular products of mass influence is beside the point here. We should not expect them to be popular in view of the counterinfluence exerted by the purveyors of crowd opinion and by the widespread dissemination of mass reaction patterns. The point is that our means of mass influence could be used in ways other than those in which they are used, and that they could, under those circumstances, be useful instruments in social planning.

THE FUTURE

The future of social policy and social planning rests on three broad developments.

1. The first is the development of "life goals" on which policies may be based and which will be accepted by large portions of our population. At present, segmentation of life goals between age groups, sex groups, occupational categories, and other divisions of our population is as common as segmentation in other aspects of life. Utilitarian and materialistic goals include large numbers of

people and may therefore play an important part in the development of social policies, but they are at present vague and without formal acceptance by our culture. In our "speech reactions" we place idealistic above utilitarian and materialistic goals in our value system; in our behavior reactions we often do the reverse.

We are not implying that materialistic goals should be those of our culture, or that we should behave in a materialistic way. All we are suggesting is that some inclusive life goals are necessary for the determination of social policies. It is not a part of traditional sociology to erect such goals; and it will perhaps be difficult for any discipline, such as philosophy, ethics, or religion, to develop them in a useful manner. In any case, without them social policy will continue to be fumbling.

2. Research in human behavior is necessary in order to contribute to a further understanding of society if we are to have social planning which is effective. As we have said several times, the knowledge we have about human behavior and social relationships is considerable; we are by no means ignorant in the field. But there are still areas of relative lack of understanding.

This kind of research will be in two directions: first, in the direction of stating clearly the reasons for the current developments in our culture, a definite analysis of how we reached our present stage of relationships; and second, in the direction of predicting from present situations what future behavior will be under given conditions. It is only as we have further knowledge in these two fields that we can approach the question of co-operative control of trends which will utilize social planning as a significant device. There will always be unpredictable variables in the conditions under which our co-operative control will operate, with the result that no social planning will be absolutely and undoubtedly effective. But it will be possible to reduce the number of those variables.

3. Evaluation of the various instruments available for social planning is the third basis for its development. It was indicated above that we used only a limited number of instruments in our attempts at planning, and we used most of them in a limited way. One of the first steps in such evaluation is an attempt to determine what instruments actually influence the mass of people, to what extent they exert that influence, and what the results of their influence thus far have been. Studies of this nature have been going on

for some time, so that we are beginning to build up a fund of fact about them. There is still much more to be done, however.

A second important step will be the attempt to discover how effectively these instruments of mass influence may be used in deliberate social planning of an intelligent type. Whatever results we may discover from our analysis of their actual operation now, the fact remains that the movies, the radio, and the newspaper very largely present their influence under the guise of entertainment or of some other recreational pattern. The influences they exert on crowd opinion in the determination of tastes, fashions, and fads are mostly by-products. The intention is to entertain; the influence on behavior incident to that intention is secondary. Is it possible to use those same instruments with the primary intention of informing public opinion? We do not know as yet.

The assumption is, however, that whatever influence we can exert through the means of mass influence and with the purpose of deliberate social planning should be co-operative—that is, it should not be a by-product of alleged recreation. We assume that the population will be adult in the sense of being willing to exercise the responsibilities of judgment. We can hardly contemplate a situation in which the majority of the people would be so childish that they would have to have a "sugar coating" of some kind to make duty and responsibility palatable. If those assumptions are accepted, the methods by which we use means of mass influence, including education, will have to be altered.

A third important step in the evaluation of instruments of mass influence will lie in the direction of developing new instruments. Again this is not a suggestion that our present instruments must be discarded. It is simply a suggestion that new instruments will be developed, and that they in turn must be "placed" in any system of co-operative social control or social planning.

On the whole, then, we hold the belief that social planning is possible, even though it has not operated effectively in the past, and even though it may not be made to operate effectively for some generations to come. We return to the statement made in the first chapter of this book regarding the purpose of sociology. That purpose is primarily the understanding of society, and secondarily the co-operative control of society. As those purposes are attained, social planning will assume greater importance.

READINGS

LANDIS, PAUL H. *Social Policies in the Making*. D. C. Heath and Company, Boston, 1947. A "dynamic view of social problems" by a well-known writer in the field of sociology.

PHELPS, HAROLD A. *Contemporary Social Problems* (Third Edition). Prentice-Hall, Inc., New York, 1947. Especially Part IV, "An Approach to Social Planning."

GILLIN, J. L., DITTMER, CLARENCE G., COLBERT, ROY J., and KASTLER, NORMAN. *Social Problems* (Third Edition). D. Appleton-Century Company, New York, 1943. Especially Chap. 19, "Factors Affecting Social Adjustment" and Chap. 20, "Proposed Ways Out."

BARNES, H. E., and REUID, O. M. *The American Way of Life*. Prentice-Hall, Inc., New York, 1942. Part IX, "Programs of Economic and Social Reconstruction."

516   BASIC SOCIOLOGICAL PRINCIPLES

Divine right of kings, 331
Divorce:
  attitudes toward, 232
  causes, 233
  in complex society, 230
  in primitive society, 217
  rate of, 220, 231
  system of, 230
Dogmatism, 283
Domestic-relations courts, 241
Dower rights, 212
Drives:
  basic human, 207
  physiological and psychological, 7,
    430
Drug addiction, 473

Economic institution:
  as channel of social mobility, 388, 396
  contemporary problems, 254–267
    control of economic system, 257
    ideals and practices, 262
    purpose of economic system, 255
  defined, 128, 244–246
    collecting economies, 244
    complex-transformative economies,
      245
    mixed economies, 245
    simple-transformative economies,
      245
  interdependence in, 393
  place of, in social organization, 246
  results of economic dominance, 249–
    254
    coloring of attitudes, 251
    growth of class consciousness, 249
    population influences, 252
Economic laws, erroneous conception
    of, 64
Economic system, 243–273
  need of reorganization, 267–272
    conservative approach, 269
    radical approach, 267
  summary, 272
Economics, relation of, to sociology, 42
Education:
  artifacts and mentifacts in, 88
  as channel of social mobility, 396
  contemporary function of, 309–312
    general-education emphasis, 309
    vocational emphasis, 309
  contemporary problems, 312–323
    attitudes toward education, 318
    educational philosophy, 315
    Federal aid, 322
    mass education, 313

    segmentation, 323
    defined, 114
    as group function, 84
    institutional basis of, 129, 301
    as instrument of social planning, 507
    lack of integration, 200
    in social organization, 323
    as social institution, 302–306
      content of, 305
      definitions, 303
    social organization and, 306
Einstein, Albert, 275
Emotional maladjustment, 430
Emotion-feeling situations, 62
Emotions, 62
Employers' groups, 69, 137, 250
Encyclicals, papal, 287
Endogamy, 223
Enterprise, free, 264, 265, 266
Environment:
  contemporary, 101–110
    adaptation to, 103
    problems of adaptation, 109
  cultural, 101
  heredity versus, 187
  influence of, 91–101
    on personality, 181
    social change, 96
    social control, 98
    social differentiation, 92
  kinds of, 87–89
    cultural, 88
    physical, 87
    social, 88
  meaning of, 87
  physical, decreasing influence of, 101
  race, culture, and 169, 174
  role of, in pattern of human associa-
    tion, 9
  segmentation, 89
  sociological significance of, 203
  urban, 132
Epidemics, 502
Ethnocentrism, 97
Evolution, 104, 401
Exchange process, 79
Exogamy, 223
Experience and planned association, 75
Experimental method, 24

Facts, place of, in scientific method, 36
Faith, religious, 282
Familistic relationship, 381
Family:
  cultural lag in problems of, 122
  defined, 211

Social mobility, 386
Social pathologies:
  approach to, 465–468
    causes, 465
    function, 467
    treatment, 468
  concept of, 461–464
    judgment, 462
    normal and abnormal conduct, 463
  defined, 461
  prevalence of, 477–480
    general pathologies, 477
    psychoses, 477
    suicide, 479
  resources against, 480–482
    preventive, 481
    treatment, 480
  types of, 469–476
    neurosis, 469
    psychopathic personality, 471
    psychosis, 469
    self-destruction, 472. *See also*
      Crime
Social planning:
  divergent views of, 500
  future of, 508
  instruments of, 505–508
    education, 507
    government, 506
    laws, 505
    mass influence, 507
  meaning of, 502
  objections to, 503
Social policy:
  establishment, 500
  future of, 508
  meaning, 501
Social problems distinguished from so-
    cietal, 499. *See also* Crime, Social
    pathologies
Social processes:
  control of, 500
  defined, 365
  disintegrative, 362–363, 367–378
    competition and conflict, 367
    differentiation, 374
    specialization, 377
    stratification, 372
    summary, 378
  integrative, 362–363, 380–394
    accommodation, 383
    assimilation, 385
    co-operation, 180
    interdependence, 391
    social mobility, 386
    summary, 394

  meaning of *process*, 364
  relation of, to institutions, 396
  specific, 366
Social program distinguished from so-
    cial policy, 501
Social reorganization. *See* Reorganiza-
    tion, social
Social work:
  defined, 483
  factors in development of, 484–487
    beliefs, 486
    conditions, 484
  field of, 489–494
    children's services, 490
    courts, 492
    family welfare, 489
    groups, 493
    institutions, 493
  method of, 494
  philosophy of, 487
  relation of, to sociology, 45
Socialism:
  as social planning, 503
  sociology confused with, 41
Societal problems distinguished from
    social, 499
Society:
  form of collectivity, 69
  understanding of, as purpose of so-
    ciology, 15. *See also* Organization,
    social
Sociology:
  as man-in-relationship-to-men, 12
  attitudes of, summarized, 202
  basic pattern, 3–12
    culture, 11
    environment, 9
    man, 7
    summary, 12
  defined, 3
  purpose, 14–19
    co-operative control, 17
    understanding of associational life,
      15
  relation of, to other sciences, 40–67
    antagonism of physical scientists, 40
    anthropology, 46
    confusion with socialism and com-
      munism, 41
    economics and political science, 42
    history, 44
    misconception of human nature, 41
    psychology, 53
    social work, 45
    summary, 66
  results of, 19

524   BASIC SOCIOLOGICAL PRINCIPLES

scientific approach, 24–39
    classification of observed facts, 28
    controlled observation, 24
    hypothesis, 29
    limitations, 36
    prediction, 33
    principles, 30, 34
Socius, 6
"Something for nothing" philosophy, 437
Sophistication, 115, 135
Sorokin, P. A., 361, 381
Specialization, 392
    in complex cultures, 359
    as disintegrative social process, 377
    economic, growth of, 79
    industrial, as factor in social differen-
        tiation, 95
Spencer, Herbert, 390
State, defined, 326
Sterilization, 121
Sterility, threat to biological survival, 118
Stimulus-response pattern, 53
Stockholder, role of, in corporation, 260
Stratification as disintegrative social
    process, 372
Struggle for existence, 382
Subsistence, 246
Suicide, 475, 479
Supply and demand, law of, 64
Survival:
    biological, 117
    as criterion in evolution of culture,
        124
    process of, 47
    psychosocial, 119
Survival of the fittest, 103, 104
Sweat box, 449

Taxation:
    incentive, 340
    as pattern of government, 333
Technologist, conflict of, with financier,
    259, 262
Technology:
    as integrative cultural force, 144
    role of, in economic institution, 244
Third degree, 443
Totalitarianism, 99, 327, 335, 382, 405,
    416
Totemism, 223
Traditionalism, religious, 286
Turgenev, Ivan, 277

Unemployment, 408
Unitarian Church, 275
Unitarianism, 287

United States:
    co-ordinative control in, 100
    population of, 147–156
        age composition, 153
        growth of, 147
        net reproduction rate, 148
        sex composition, 150
    racial and cultural conflicts, 141
    sectional differences, 140
United States Congress, 72
University of Iowa, projection test, 27
Upper classes as goal in social process,
    390
Urbanism:
    environment, 132
    as factor in current pathologies, 463
    net reproduction rate and, 149
    typical attitudes, 133–139
        conspicuous consumption, 136
        lack of self-sufficiency, 134
        respect for human abilities, 134
        sophistication, 135
Utopia, 358

Veblen, Thorstein, 136
Vocational patterns, 426
Vocational training, 309
Vocations as factor in social differen-
    tiation, 93

Wallas, Graham, 305
War:
    social disorganization in, 354
    sociological and historical approach
        to, 44
Wasps, 51
Water cure, 450
Wells, H. G., 291
Wiggam, A. E., 157
Wilde, Oscar, 423
Will of the people, 333
Wolsey, Cardinal, 388
Women:
    increasing freedom of, 270
    position of, as factor in mate choice, 229
World problems:
    interaction and, 139–145
        conditions promoting conflict, 142
        conditions promoting co-operation,
            143
        conflict, 139
    sociology in solution of, 21
Worship, religious, 278
Writing in transmission of culture, 114

Zimmerman, C. C., 220, 236

Date Due

SOCIAL SCIENCE SERIES
EDITED BY R. M. MacIver
COLUMBIA UNIVERSITY

▼

Crime and the Community. By FRANK TANNENBAUM
Social Causation. By R. M. MacIver
The Sociology of the Family. By M. C. ELMER
An Approach to Social Problems. By ABBOTT P. HERMAN
Basic Sociological Principles. By M. E. JONES

▼

Other volumes in preparation